Legal Executions in
Illinois, Indiana, Iowa,
Kentucky and Missouri

Also by Daniel Allen Hearn
and from McFarland

Legal Executions in Georgia: A Comprehensive Registry, 1866–1964 (2016)

Legal Executions in North Carolina and South Carolina: A Comprehensive Registry, 1866–1962 (2015)

Legal Executions in Delaware, the District of Columbia, Maryland, Virginia and West Virginia: A Comprehensive Registry, 1866–1962 (2015)

Legal Executions in New England: A Comprehensive Reference, 1623–1960 (2008 [1999 hardback])

Legal Executions in Illinois, Indiana, Iowa, Kentucky and Missouri

A Comprehensive Registry, 1866–1965

Daniel Allen Hearn

McFarland & Company, Inc., Publishers
Jefferson, North Carolina

ISBN (print) 978-0-7864-9870-3
ISBN (ebook) 978-1-4766-2001-5

Library of Congress cataloguing data are available

British Library cataloguing data are available

Cover image: Missouri execution, 1896 (Library of Congress)

Printed in the United States of America

McFarland & Company, Inc., Publishers
Box 611, Jefferson, North Carolina 28640
www.mcfarlandpub.com

The Angel of Death has never been unemployed.

Table of Contents

Preface

This volume is the latest in an ongoing series from McFarland that presents a chronological resume of capital punishment in the United States of America prior to the temporary suspension of that practice in 1972. Its purpose is to set the historical record straight and to provide a reliable reference for those seeking information on this subject case by case. No attempt is made to play politics. The author does have an opinion on the overall topic but trusts in the ability of his readers to discern for themselves whatever conclusions—if any—the accumulated facts indicate. Other publishers have previously gone to press with written efforts to expound on this matter in the jurisdictional regions covered by this book. Their quality varied. I read them all. I found most to be sloppy and poorly researched. This volume is intended to present the unvarnished data.

I have chosen to concentrate on the century after the Civil War. The primary reason for this is the insurmountable problem of lost and missing records from the earlier period. Still, appendices are provided for each state in order to give the serious scholar at least an idea of what research has so far turned up in the years prior to 1866. I hope to assimilate the earlier material in a future volume. Meanwhile, I leave legislative and constitutional histories of capital punishment to others.

My immediate motive is to provide the essential facts of each case that resulted in an actual execution so that those desiring to do so may study them further. Once one is embarked on research in this field, there is little foreknowledge (my experience has shown) of where it might lead. There are numerous legal, personal and public ramifications. This is confirmed by the feedback that I have received from other volumes in this series. Indeed, if there is one thing that the study of crime and punishment has taught me, it is that there will always be a risk of learning more than one would like to know. Some readers have voiced surprise at finding there to have been precedent where they had thought there was none. People doing genealogical research have even told me that they've found these books to be revealing in their searches for controversial ancestors—an unintended consequence of true crime research that I myself had not foreseen.

Acknowledgments concerning the information-gathering process that I used are few because I bore most of the burden myself. I worked on my own time and entirely at my own expense. State and county officials with whom I corresponded were almost unanimously good about answering inquiries. So were local historians, librarians and archivists. One debt of gratitude that I owe in particular is to Ms. Harriet Frazier of Kansas City, Missouri, a retired law professor and ever-cordial fellow author in this specialized area of study. She and I have traded information on occasion and benefited mutually thereby. Our political views may not always be in accord but there are few who equal Harriet's expertise and attention to detail. Her previously published inventory of Missouri executions formed the basis for the list of Missouri executions before 1866 in the book.

Illinois

1866

Gabriel Forsee (white, age 23). *Murder.* The crime was committed on 7/13/1865 in Monroe County. Executed for the deliberate killing of 36-year-old Elizabeth A. Darwin (white), she having had her throat cut. Motive: revenge. The woman had previously testified against Forsee in a court matter. He was hanged at Waterloo on June 2, 1866. Source: *History of Randolph, Monroe and Perry Counties, Illinois* (Phila., PA: J. L. McDonough, 1883), 158. See also: 1860 U.S. Census (Randolph Co., IL), which notes both parties.

James Poke Lemon (white, age 21) and **Brighton Van Aradell**, alias "Barney van Arsdell," alias "Van Ausdell" (white, age 20). *Murder.* Their crime was committed on 3/7/1865 in Sangamon County. Handgun slaying of John Saunders (white, age not recorded). Motive: armed robbery. Both of these killers were hanged at Springfield on July 20, 1866. Source: *Chicago Tribune*, 7/21/66 (1:5). *Madison County (IL) Courier*, 7/26/66 (1:1). *Daily Missouri Democrat* (St. Louis), 6/7/66 (1:2) & 7/21/66 (1:4).

George P. Chase (white, age abt. 27). *Murder.* The crime was committed on 4/24/1864 in Will County. Prison-guard killer. Executed for the slaying of Joseph P. Clark (white, age not recorded), the deputy warden of Joliet Prison. Clark was fatally struck on the head with a rock. Motive: jailhouse grudge. The killer was hanged at Joliet on July 27, 1866. Source: *Chicago Tribune*, 7/28/66 (4:1). *New York Herald*, 7/28/66 (2:6).

John Kennedy (white, age 39). *Murder.* The crime was committed on 11/20/1864 in Cook County. Accomplice in the handgun slaying of Patrick "Taylor" Maloney, age 60+ (white). Motive: murder for hire. Venue changed from Cook County to Lake County. Kennedy was hanged at Waukegan on July 27, 1866. Two other men named Jerry Corbett (white, age 25) and Walter Fleming (white, age 34) were executed at Chicago on December 15, 1865, for complicity in the same crime. Source: *Chicago Tribune*, 11/22/64 (4:4), 12/15/65 (4:2), 12/18/65 (4:3) & 7/28/66 (3:1).

1867

John Guedel (white, age 39). Murder. The crime was committed on 10/2/1864 in Madison County. Shotgun slaying of Adam Zimmerman (white, age not recorded), the victim's head having also been dashed in with the butt of that weapon. Motive: robbery. Venue changed from Madison County to St. Clair County. Guedel was hanged at Belleville on April 26, 1867. Source: *New York Herald*, 4/30/67 (8:1). *Daily Missouri Democrat* (St. Louis), 4/27/67 (4:4). Appeal: 43 IL 226–231.

1869

John W. Moore (white, age 22). *Murder.* The crime was committed on 7/5/1868 in Bond County. Executed for the killing of 18-year-old Louisa McAdams (white), she having been slashed to death with a jackknife. Motive: attempted sexual assault. The assassin was hanged at Greenville on October 22, 1869. Source: *New York Herald*, 10/26/69 (5:3). See also: 1860 U.S. Census (Bond Co., IL), which notes Moore.

William C. Bell (white, age 37). *Murder.* The crime was committed on 11/21/1868 in Madison County. Shotgun slaying of Herman Wendell (white, age not recorded) and illegal burial of his body in a pig pen. Motive: because the killer coveted the victim's wife. Bell was hanged for this at Edwardsville on November 12, 1869. Source: *Alton (IL) Daily Telegraph*, 11/27/68 (4:3) & 11/28/68 (4:3). *The Intelligencer* (Edwardsville, IL), 11/18/69 (4:1). *New York Herald*, 11/16/69 (5:1).

1870

Joseph Meyers (white, age 33). *Murder.* The crime was committed on 4/12/1868 in Shelby County. Rifle slaying of 64-year-old Plassibo Calhoun (white). Motive: gangland killing. The killer was hanged at Shelbyville on July 29, 1870. Source: *New York Times*, 8/1/70 (5:2). See also: 1860 U.S. Census (Shelby Co., IL), which notes the murdered man as "Plasabow Calhoun," and 1870 U.S. Census (Shelby Co., IL), which notes the assassin as "Joseph Myers."

1871

Bartholomew Barnes (white, age 18). *Murder.* The crime was committed on 2/27/1871 in Calhoun County. Fatal kicking and stomping (beyond recognition) of 43-year-old John Gresham (white). Motive: heated argument. Venue changed from Calhoun County to Pike County. Barnes was hanged at Pittsfield on December 29, 1871. Source: *Quincy (IL) Daily Herald*, 12/30/71 (4:2). *New York Herald*, 1/2/72 (3:6). See also: 1860 U.S. Census (Pike Co., IL), which notes Gresham.

1873

Henry McNulta (white, age 34). *Murder.* The crime was committed on 9/22/1872 in Peoria County. Uxoricide. Fatal beating of 36-year-old Eliza McNulta (white). Motive: alcoholic brutality. This wife-killer was hanged at Peoria on February 7, 1873. Source: *Chicago Times*, 2/8/73 (2:1).

George Driver (white, age 45). *Murder.* The crime was committed on 11/29/1872 in Cook County. Handgun slaying of 32-year-old Ann Driver (white), his ex-wife. Motive: heated argument. He was hanged at Chicago on March 14, 1873. Source: *Chicago Times*, 3/15/73 (2:3). *Chicago Tribune*, 3/15/73 (5:1). See also: 1841 National Census of Scotland, which notes the killer as a boy in the Orkney Islands.

John Marion Osborne (white, age 26). *Murder.* The crime was committed on 8/5/1872 in Knox County. Executed for the murder of 23-year-old Adelia Clark Mathews (white), who was bludgeoned with a brick and had her throat cut. Motive: sexual assault.

The killer was hanged at Knoxville on March 14, 1873. Source: *Chicago Times*, 3/15/73 (2:7). *Chicago Tribune*, 3/15/73 (5:1). *The World* (New York) 3/15/73 (8:1). See also: 1870 U.S. Census (Knox Co., IL), which notes both parties.

Joseph O'Neal (white, age 26). *Murder.* The crime was committed on 9/26/1872 in Whiteside County. Mutilation murder of 19-year-old Hiram Rexford (white). Motive: rivalry for a female. Venue changed from Whiteside County to Carroll County. O'Neal was hanged at Mount Carroll on May 16, 1873. Source: *Chicago Times*, 5/17/73 (1:3). *Chicago Tribune*, 5/17/73 (1:4). See also: 1870 U.S. Census (Allegan Co., MI), which notes Rexford.

William Clark Campbell (black, age 25). *Murder.* The crime was committed on 4/24/1873 in Alexander County. Executed for the murder of Thomas Doyle (white, age not recorded), who was struck down from behind with a "round stick of cordwood." Motive: disgruntled employee. The killer was hanged at Cairo on August 29, 1873. Source: *Cairo (IL) Bulletin*, 4/26/73 (4:4), 4/27/73 (4:3) & 8/30/73 (2:1).

Andrew J. Perteet (black, age 57). *Murder.* The crime was committed on 9/16/1871 in Cook County. Uxoricide. Executed for the murder of 44-year-old Martha Perteet (black), she having been slashed to death with a razor. Motive: marital estrangement. Venue changed from Cook County to Will County. The killer was hanged at Joliet on December 19, 1873. Source: *Chicago Times*, 12/20/73 (4:1). *Chicago Tribune*, 12/20/73 (1:5).

1874

Christopher Rafferty (white, age 23). *Murder.* The crime was committed on 8/5/1872 in Cook County. Police killer. Handgun slaying of about 40-year-old Patrick O'Meara (white). Motive: resisting arrest. Venue changed from Cook County to Lake County. Rafferty was hanged at Waukegan on February 27, 1874. Source: *Chicago Times*, 2/28/74 (3:1). *Chicago Tribune*, 2/28/74 (1:7).

1875

Nathan Burgess (white, age 27). *Murder.* The crime was committed on 10/29/1874 in Fayette County. Shotgun slaying of about 40-year-old Joseph Robbins (white). Motive: robbery and personal malice. Venue changed from Fayette County to Effingham County. Burgess was hanged at Effingham on June 18, 1875. Source: *Chicago Times*, 6/19/75 (3:1). *Chicago Tribune*, 6/19/75 (1:4). *Steubenville (OH) Daily Herald & News*, 11/10/74 (1:4).

John M. Casey (white, age 37). *Murder.* The crime was committed on 8/25/1874 in Edgar County. Uxoricide. Executed for the murder of about 40-year-old Rebecca Park Casey (white), she having been slashed to death with a razor. Motive: alcoholic tantrum. This violator of his marriage vows (among other things) was hanged at Paris on June 18, 1875. Source: *Chicago Times*, 6/19/75 (3:2). See also: 1840 U.S. Census (Tazewell Co., IL), which notes the Park family.

1876

Marshall J. Crain (white, age 26). *Murder.* The crime was committed on

7/31/1875 in Williamson County. Executed for the shotgun slaying of 58-year-old William Spence (white). Motive: blood feud or clan rivalry. Crain is confirmed to have also murdered George W. Sisney (white, age 44) by the same means and for the same reason at Carbondale IL on 7/28/1875. He was hanged at Marion on January 21, 1876. Source: *Decatur (IL) Republican*, 8/12/75 (6:2), 9/23/75 (4:3) & 10/28/75 (5:4). *Chicago Times*, 1/22/76 (4:4). *Chicago Tribune*, 1/22/76 (1:6). See also: 1870 U.S. Census (Jackson Co., IL), which notes Spence, and 1870 U.S. Census (Williamson Co., IL), which notes Sisney.

Henry Jacobi, alias "Henry Jacobs" (white, age 50). *Murder.* The crime was committed on 5/26/1875 in Will County. Uxoricide. Strangulation and illegal burial of 44-year-old Othilda Hohnhaussen Jacobi (white). Motive: impending divorce. The killer was hanged at Joliet on January 21, 1876. Source: *Chicago Times*, 1/22/76 (4:1).

William Lee (white, age 28). *Murder.* The crime was committed on 11/6/1875 in Henderson County. Executed for the murder of about 19-year-old Jessie McCarty, alias "Whiskey Jess" (white), who was beaten, kicked and stomped beyond recognition. Her body was dumped in the Mississippi River. Motive: wrathful pimp. This killer was hanged at Oquawka on June 16, 1876. Source: *Burlington (IA) Daily Hawk-Eye*, 11/30/75 (8:2). *Chicago Times*, 6/17/76 (5:4). *Chicago Tribune*, 6/17/76 (5:1).

William Harrison Johnson (white, age 35). *Murder.* The crime was committed on 12/17/1875 in Edgar County. Handgun slaying of 17-year-old Jacob Redmon (white), his stepson. Motive: domestic cruelty. Johnson was hanged at Paris on June 23, 1876. Source: *Chicago Times*, 6/24/76 (10:1).

1878

Charles Burns (white, age 26). *Murder.* The crime was committed on 10/20/1877 in Edgar County. Handgun slaying of 34-year-old Elijah Birdwell (white), the victim having been shot point-blank in the groin. Motive: gangland retribution. The killer was hanged at Paris on June 21, 1878. Source: *Chicago Times*, 6/22/78 (3:3). See also: 1870 U.S. Census (Harrison Co., IN), which notes Birdwell.

Jeremiah Connelly (white, age 18) and **George Sherry** (white, age 22). *Murder.* Their crime was committed on 1/19/1878 in Cook County. Fatal stabbing of 51-year-old Hugh McConville (white). Motive: hooliganism. Both of these killers were hanged at Chicago on June 21, 1878. Source: *Chicago Times*, 6/22/78 (3:1). *Chicago Tribune*, 6/22/78 (1:5). See also: 1870 U.S. Census (Cook Co., IL), which notes the murdered man.

Harrison Burklow (white, age 45). *Murder.* The crime was committed on 7/5/1877 in Johnson County. Handgun slaying of David Waggoner (white, age not recorded). Motive: drunken bravado. Burklow was hanged at Vienna on July 5, 1878. Source: *Chicago Times*, 7/6/78 (3:2). *Chicago Tribune*, 7/6/78 (5:1).

1879

Charles Glass (black, age 36). *Murder.* The crime was committed on 3/23/1879 in Alexander County. Ax murder of 19-year-old Carter Newman (black), the victim having been attacked in his sleep. Motive: rivalry for a female. This killer was hanged at Cairo on September 16, 1879. Source: *Cairo (IL) Daily Bulletin*, 3/25/79 (4:3), 9/16/79 (4:4) & 9/17/79 (4:2). See also: 1870 U.S. Census (Pulaski Co., IL), which notes Newman.

1880

Johannes DeBoer (white, age 18). *Murder.* The crime was committed on 10/19/1879 in Woodford County. Fatal beating of 17-year-old Ella Martin (white). Motive: sexual assault. Venue changed from Woodford County to Livingston County. DeBoer was hanged at Pontiac on March 17, 1880. Source: *Chicago Times*, 3/18/80 (2:4). *Chicago Tribune*, 3/18/80 (5:1). See also: 1870 U.S. Census (Woodford Co., IL), which notes the victim as "Ellen" Martin.

1881

Frederick Koester (white, age 29). *Murder.* The crime was committed on 8/21/1879 in Iroquois County. Uxoricide. Executed for the murder of pregnant 21-year-old Minnie Burmeister Koester (white), she having first been wounded by a shotgun blast and then finished off with an ax. Motive: connubial tension. Venue changed from Iroquois County to Vermilion County. The killer was hanged at Danville on January 21, 1881. Source: *Chicago Times*, 1/22/81 (6:1). *Chicago Tribune*, 1/22/81 (6:1).

Clement Gallion (white, age 21). *Murder.* The crime was committed on 12/10/1880 in Henry County. Executed for the murders of 47-year-old Thomas Dilley and 36-year-old Carrie Dilley (whites, a married couple), who were attacked while asleep in their bed. The man was shot in the right eye with a handgun at point-blank range. The woman was battered to death with a wooden shovel handle. Motive: burglary. The killer was hanged at Cambridge on September 16, 1881. Source: *Chicago Times*, 12/13/80 (2:1) & 9/17/81 (5:2). *Chicago Tribune*, 9/17/81 (15:3). See also: 1880 U.S. Census (Henry Co., IL), which notes Mr. & Mrs. Dilley.

1882

William Heilwagon (white, age 53). *Murder.* The crime was committed on 9/5/1881 in Rock Island County. Executed for the murder of 24-year-old Dora Kleinau Heilwagon (white, his daughter-in-law), she having been bludgeoned with a rock that had been made into a slingshot. Motive: supposed anger at the victim for unguarded remarks. William Heilwagon was hanged at Rock Island on March 24, 1882. This case merits further study to determine whether it was a miscarriage of justice. Otto Heilwagon (the estranged husband of the murdered woman and son of the executed man) reportedly admitted on his deathbed (in 1888) that it was he who had committed the homicide. Fabricated stories of this kind have long been a ploy of anti-death penalty crusaders, so caution is demanded. Source: *Chicago Times*, 3/25/82 (4:1). *Chicago Tribune*, 3/25/82 (16:1). *Master Detective*, 11/46. See also: 1880 U.S. Census (Adams Co., IL), which notes the executed man. See also: Passenger manifest of the German immigrant ship *Goschen*, which arrived at the Port of New Orleans on 6/7/1860 bearing Dora Kleinau (age 3) and parents Emanuel & Elisa Kleinau, who stated their destination as Hampton, IL (Film M-259, Reel 49, List 182, National Archives).

Thomas Coyne, alias "Patsy Devine" (white, age abt. 44). *Murder.* The crime was committed on 8/4/1879 in McLean County. Handgun slaying of 48-year-old Aaron Goodfellow (white). Motive: mugging. Venue changed from McLean County to DeWitt County. The killer was hanged at Clinton on May 12, 1882. This man was reportedly a fugitive from Chester, PA, where he was said to have murdered another man named Bernard Winger (white, age abt. 34) circa 1867 by braining him with a rock. Motive: personal grudge. Source: *Chicago Tribune*, 5/13/82 (16:1). *Clinton (IL) Public and Central Transcript*, 5/12/82 (1:1). See also: 1870 U.S. Census (McLean Co., IL), which notes Aaron Goodfellow, 1860 U.S. Census (Chester Co., PA), which notes Bernard Winger, and 1880 U.S. Census (Madison Co., IL), which notes the killer as "Thomas Devine."

James Vaughn (white, age 31). *Murder.* The crime was committed on 8/4/1881 in Perry County. Police killer. Fatal stabbing of 39-year-old William Watts (white). Motive: obnoxious drunk; resisting arrest. Vaughn was hanged for what he did at Pinckneyville on June 16, 1882. Source: *Chicago Times*, 6/17/82 (3:5). *Chicago Tribune*, 6/17/82 (3:7). See also: 1880 U.S. Census (Perry Co., IL), which notes Watts.

Samuel Redden, alias "Redding" (black, age not recorded). *Murder.* The crime was committed on 1/22/1878 in Pulaski County. Handgun slaying of Adolphus Zimmerman (white, age not recorded). Motive: robbery. Venue changed from Pulaski County to Massac County. Redden was hanged at Metropolis on September 15, 1882. Source: *Chicago Times*, 9/16/82 (3:1). *Chicago Tribune*, 9/16/82 (6:7).

James Ristengbrock, alias "James Tracy" (white, age abt. 30). *Murder.* The crime was committed on 2/3/1882 in Cook County. Police killer. Handgun slaying of 40-year-old John Huebner (white). Motive: burglary gone awry. This miscreant was hanged at Chicago on September 15, 1882. Source: *Chicago Times*, 9/16/82 (5:1). *Chicago Tribune*, 9/16/82 (16:1). See also: 1880 U.S. Census (Chicago, IL), which notes the slain policeman.

1883

Philip B. Mathews (white, age 20). *Murder.* The crime was committed on 5/28/1882 in St. Clair County. Handgun slaying of 21-year-old Annie Geyer (white). Motive: scorned lover. Mathews was hanged at Belleville on January 12, 1883. Source: *Chicago Times*, 1/13/83 (2:8). *Chicago Tribune*, 1/13/83 (12:3).

George W. Traughber (white, age 20). *Murder.* The crime was committed on 10/28/1881 in Christian County. Handgun slaying of 38-year-old Joseph McKinney (white). Motive: highway robbery. Traughber was hanged at Taylorville on January 26, 1883. Source: *Chicago Times*, 1/27/83 (2:5). See also: 1880 U.S. Census (Christian Co., IL), which notes both parties.

Sylvester McKinson (white, age 24). *Murder.* The crime was committed on 8/26/1882 in Henry County. Executed for the murder of 27-year-old Maggie A. Copeland (white), she having been bludgeoned with a piece of scantling wood and then finished off by shots fired from a handgun. Motive: robbery and mendacity. The killer was hanged at Cambridge on May 11, 1883. Source: *Chicago Times*, 5/12/83 (3:1). *Chicago Tribune*, 5/12/83 (12:1). See also: 1880 U.S. Census (Stark Co., IL), which notes the homicide victim.

1884

Christian Reibling (white, age 32). *Murder.* The crime was committed on 12/25/1883 in Whiteside County. Handgun slaying of 19-year-old Albert Lucia (white). Motive: obnoxious drunk. The killer was hanged at Morrison on May 16, 1884. Source: *Chicago Times*, 5/17/84 (5:1). *Chicago Tribune*, 5/17/84 (3:4).

William Brown (black, age 39). *Murder.* The crime was committed on 2/26/1884 in St. Clair County. Ax murder, dismemberment, partial cremation and illegal burial of a peddler, age 60+, known only as "Lavigne." Motive: robbery. The murdered man was also described as "an old Jew" and "a Russian exile," which probably meant a refugee from the pogroms. His killer was hanged at Belleville on May 30, 1884. Source: *Chicago Times*, 5/31/84 (6:3). *Chicago Tribune*, 5/31/84 (10:7). *Daily Gazette* (Ft. Wayne, IN), 5/31/84 (2:4).

Isaac Jacobson (white, age 54). *Murder.* The crime was committed on 4/29/1884 in Cook County. Handgun slaying of 52-year-old George Bedell (white). Motive: disgruntled employee; wage dispute. Jacobson was hanged at Chicago on September 19, 1884. Source: *Chicago Tribune*, 9/20/84 (10:1). *Daily State Journal* (Lincoln, NB), 5/2/84 (7:3). See also: 1880 U.S. Census (Chicago, IL), which notes Bedell.

1885

William Felix Henry (black, age 22). *Murder.* The crime was committed on 3/27/1883 in Madison County. Shotgun slayings of Henry DuPage and Albert Ross (blacks, ages not recorded). Motive: gang feud. The killer was hanged at Edwardsville on January 16, 1885. Source: *Chicago Tribune*, 1/17/85 (3:4). *Chicago Times*, 1/17/85 (3:1). *Alton (IL) Daily Telegraph*, 1/16/85 (3:3) & 1/17/85 (3:4).

Thomas J. Chapman (white, age 23). *Murder.* The crime was committed on 8/17/1884 in Coles County. Handgun slaying of 43-year-old Nicholas Hubbard (white). Motive: robbery and treachery. Chapman was hanged at Charleston IL on January 23, 1885. Source: *Chicago Times*, 1/24/85 (6:1). *Chicago Tribune*, 1/24/85 (6:6).

Charles Houlden (white, age 46). *Murder.* The crime was committed on 3/22/1884 in Menard County. Uxoricide. Executed for the murder of 46-year-old Rebeckey Hinds Houlden (white), she having been struck down with an ax and her neck sawed through with a serrated knife. Motive: because she had refused to sign away her late husband's property. Her current husband (and killer) was hanged at Petersburg IL on May 15, 1885. Source: *Chicago Times*, 5/16/85 (4:7). *Chicago Tribune*, 5/16/85 (13:3). See also: 1880 U.S. Census (Menard Co., IL), which notes the executed man as Charles "Holden" and the murdered woman as "Rebeckey Hinds."

Giovanni Azzaro (white, age 30), **Augustino Gilardo** (white, age 22) and **Ignacio Sylvestri** (white, age

22). *Murder.* Their crime was committed on 4/29/1885 in Cook County. Strangulation of 20-year-old Filippo Caruso (white), whose body was then stuffed into a trunk and shipped by rail to a distant city. Motive: robbery and deceitfulness. The three killers were hanged at Chicago on November 14, 1885. Source: *Chicago Tribune,* 11/15/85 (3:6). *Saturday Herald* (Decatur, IL), 5/9/85 (7:5). *Daily Northwestern* (Oshkosh, WI), 11/14/85 (1:1).

1886

Noah Merriman (black, age 29). *Murder.* The crime was committed on 4/10/1885 in St. Clair County. Uxoricide. Handgun slaying of Mamie Grant Merriman (black, age not recorded), she having been shot in the back. Recidivist killer. Merriman (as a teenager in Monroe Co., IL), had fatally shot his uncle William Merriman (black, age not recorded) in "a trifling dispute." He served a prison term for manslaughter. He was hanged at Belleville on January 15, 1886. Source: *Belleville (IL) Weekly Advocate,* 4/17/85 (8:2) & 1/15/86 (8:1). *Chicago Times,* 1/16/86 (2:5). *Chicago Tribune,* 1/16/86 (6:3). See also: 1880 U.S. Census (Jefferson Co., MO), which notes the killer as "Noah Merryman."

Franz Mulkowski (white, age 41). *Murder.* The crime was committed on 8/22/1885 in Cook County. Executed for the murder of pregnant, 24-year-old Agnes Kledzeick (white), she having been battered to death with a heavy chisel. Motive: robbery and gross perfidy. Recidivist killer. A Polish immigrant, Mulkowski had spent the years 1861–1883 in prison for a homicide committed in his homeland. He had originally been sentenced to death in that case but somehow wrangled a commutation. He was hanged at Chicago on March 26, 1886. Source: *Chicago Times,* 8/23/85 (6:1), 8/26/85 (8:1) & 3/27/86 (8:1).

James Dacey (white, age 39). *Murder.* The crime was committed on 5/13/1884 in Cook County. Handgun slaying of 37-year-old Michael Gaynor (white), a Chicago alderman. Motive: dirty politics. Venue changed from Cook County to McHenry County. The assassin was hanged at Woodstock IL on July 16, 1886. Source: *Chicago Times,* 7/17/86 (2:6). *Chicago Tribune,* 7/17/86 (3:1). See also: 1880 U.S. Census (Chicago, IL), which notes the murdered man.

William S. Wilson (white, age 45). *Murder.* The crime was committed on 1/7/1886 in Union County. Uxoricide. Handgun slaying of pregnant 43-year-old Margaret Lambert Wilson (white). Motive: temper tantrum. Wilson had neglected his wife and children to a point where they were destitute. Neighbors (out of pity) bonded together on the above date for the purpose of cutting firewood in sufficient quantity to get the expectant mother and her little ones through the rest of that winter. Stung and embarrassed by this, Wilson berated his wife for allowing the neighbors to act. He chased the heavily pregnant woman out of their cabin and shot her down in the mud and slush. The sight of her near-term unborn baby vainly kicking against the interior wall of her abdomen appalled witnesses, who could do nothing to save it. Details such as these illustrate the brutality that often characterizes these all-too-common wife-killing cases. William Wilson was hanged at Jonesboro on November 12, 1886. Source: *Jonesboro (IL) Gazette,* 11/13/86 (1:1).

Chicago Times, 11/13/86 (3:3). *Chicago Tribune*, 11/13/86 (15:2). See also: 1860 U.S. Census (Johnson Co., IL), which notes Mrs. Wilson by her maiden name.

1887

George Engel (white, age 47), **Adolph Fischer** (white, age 26), **Albert Parsons** (white, age 38) and **August Spies** (white, age 31). *Murder.* Their crime was committed on 5/4/1886 in Cook County. Alleged police killers. They were specific- ally executed for the bombing death of 34-year-old Mathias J. Degan (white), a Chicago police officer. Motive: inciting a riot, or so it was charged. Seven other policemen were fatally injured in the same incident, some by shrapnel and some by gunfire. The exact identity of the bomber was never ascertained. It is also possible that most of the gunshot victims died due to so-called "friendly fire" by other policemen who began shooting when the bomb exploded in their midst. The seven additional fatalities were John J. Barrett (white, age 34) and George Miller (white, age 28) who died from shrapnel on 5/6/1886; Timothy Flavin (white, age 35) who died from a gunshot wound on 5/8/1886; Michael Sheehan (white, age 29) who died from a gunshot on 5/9/1886; Thomas Redden (white, age 50) likewise on 5/17/1886; Nils Hansen (white, age 37) who died of a shrapnel wound on 6/14/1886; and Timothy Sullivan (white, age 49) who succumbed to complications of a gunshot wound two years later on 6/13/1888.

1888

Zephyr Davis (black, age 23). *Murder.* The crime was committed on 2/27/1888 in Cook County. Child killer. Executed for the hatchet slaying of 15-year-old Maggie Gaughan (white) during the course of an attempted sexual assault. He was hanged at Chicago on May 12, 1888. Source: *Chicago Tribune*, 5/13/88 (10:1). *Logansport (IN) Journal*, 5/13/88 (4:3).

George W. Milligan, alias "Milliken" (white, age 23). *Murder.* The crime was committed on 3/5/1888 in Gallatin County. Uxoricide. Executed for the shotgun slaying of his wife, name and age no longer recorded. Motive: adultery on his part. Local records of this case were lost in a flood and no newspaper account has been found that is any more specific. Milligan was hanged at Shawneetown on November 23, 1888. Source: *Paducah (KY) Daily News*, 3/7/88 (3:4) & 11/26/88 (3:5).

1890

James Maxwell (white, age abt. 40). *Murder.* The crime was committed on 6/25/1890 in Grundy County. Executed for the murder of 48-year-old Charles E. Decker (white), who was bludgeoned with a whiffletree. Motive: burglary. The killer was hanged at Morris IL on October 17, 1890. Source: *Morris (IL) Herald*, 7/4/90 (5:1), 7/11/90 (5:1) & 7/18/90 (5:1). *Chicago Tribune*, 10/18/90 (9:7).

1891

William H. Crawford (white, age 25). *Murder.* The crime was committed on 8/26/1890 in Macon County. Executed for the murder of 25-year-old Lina Culver Mathias (white), she having been decoyed from her home and her throat cut. Motive: unreciprocated love. The killer was hanged at Decatur on March 14, 1891. Source: *Morning Review* (Decatur, IL), 8/28/90 (4:4) & 3/15/91 (1:1).

Charles Ford (white, age 21). *Murder.* The crime was committed on 6/23/1890 in La Salle County. Executed for the murder of about 60-year-old David Moore (white), who was beaten to death with a railroad coupling pin. Motive: badger game. The killer was hanged at Ottawa IL on May 9, 1891. Source: *Atlanta (GA) Constitution,* 6/30/90 (1:4). *Ottawa (IL) Republican,* 12/5/90 (3:4) & 5/14/91 (2:2). *Chicago Tribune,* 5/10/91 (5:3).

1892

Patrick Boyle (white, age abt. 28). *Murder.* The crime was committed on 8/12/1891 in Madison County. Handgun slaying of 26-year-old John Muench (white), the victim having been shot in the back. Motive: robbery and dirty dealing. This killer was hanged at Edwardsville on January 23, 1892. Source: *Alton (IL) Evening Telegraph,* 1/23/92 (5:3). *Edwardsville (IL) Intelligencer,* 1/23/92 (1:1).

Thomas Davis (black, age 21) and **Henry Dickerson** (black, age 26). *Murder.* The crime was committed on 12/27/1891 in Washington County. Executed for the murder of 23-year-old Marcus Deitsch (white), whose head was knocked in and his throat cut. Motive: highway robbery. The killers were hanged at Nashville IL on May 14, 1892. Source: *Nashville (IL) Journal,* 1/1/92 (3:2) & 5/13/92 (3:1). *Daily Review* (Decatur, IL), 5/15/92 (7:3). See also: 1880 U.S. Census (Richview, IL), which notes the miscreants.

1893

William J. Jamison (black, age abt. 40). *Murder.* The crime was committed on 4/19/1892 in Adams County. Handgun slaying of 32-year-old Charles N. Aron (white). Motive: medical quackery turned violent. The killer was hanged at Quincy on August 18, 1893. Source: *Chicago Times,* 8/19/93 (9:7). *Chicago Tribune,* 4/20/92 (1:6) & 8/19/93 (9:6). See also: 1880 U.S. Census (Adams Co., IL), which notes the murdered man as Charles N. "Aaron" and his race as Caucasian. Some news reports erroneously stated that both parties were negro.

Harvey Pate (white, age 21) and **Frank Stiers** (white, age 19). *Murder.* Their crime was committed on 8/25/1893 in Vermilion County. Handgun slaying of 43-year-old Henry J. Helmick (white). Motive: highway robbery. These young killers were hanged at Danville on December 8, 1893. Source: *Chicago Times,* 12/9/93 (8:2). *Daily Northwestern* (Oshkosh, WI), 12/8/93 (1:6). See also: 1880 U.S. Census (Vermilion Co., IL), which notes Mr. Helmick.

1894

Ernest LaCore (white, age 23). *Murder.* The crime was committed on 8/6/1893 in Will County. Child killer. Executed for the murder of 13-year-old Ella Byron (white), whose neck was broken when her attacker wrestled her to the ground. Motive: sexual assault. LaCore was hanged at Joliet on January 19, 1894. Source: *Sterling (IL) Standard*, 12/28/93 (7:4). *Chicago Tribune*, 1/20/94 (14:3).

George Painter (white, age 35). *Murder.* The crime was committed on 5/17/1891 in Cook County. Executed for the murder of 28-year-old Alice Martin (white), she having been clubbed to death. Motive: lovers' quarrel. The killer was hanged at Chicago on January 26, 1894. Source: *Fort Wayne (IN) Sentinel*, 5/18/91 (1:2). *Chicago Tribune*, 1/27/94 (9:1). *Intimate Detective*, 5/40.

John Hart (white, age 34). *Murder.* The crime was committed on 9/5/1893 in Winnebago County. Sororicide. Executed for the murders of 26-year-old Mary Hart and 23-year-old Nellie Hart (whites), his sisters. The elder victim was shot four times with a handgun. The younger victim was forced to swallow corrosive poison (Paris Green) before being hit on the head with a hammer and shot once with the same handgun. Motive: to gain control of their late father's estate. John Hart was hanged at Rockford on March 16, 1894. Source: *Logansport (IN) Daily Register*, 9/7/93 (1:1) & 3/17/94 (1:7).

Thomas Higgins (white, age 23). *Murder.* The crime was committed on 9/3/1893 in Cook County. Handgun slaying of 42-year-old Peter McCooey (white). Motive: burglary. This offender was hanged at Chicago on March 23, 1894. Source: *Chicago Tribune*, 3/24/94 (9:7). *Stevens Point (WI) Journal*, 3/31/94 (6:6). See also: 1893 Cook Co. death cert. no. 12862.

Patrick Eugene Prendergast (white, age 23). *Murder.* The crime was committed on 10/28/1893 in Cook County. Handgun slaying of 68-year-old Carter Harrison (white, the mayor of Chicago), who was shot five times. Motive: disgruntled campaign worker. This assassin was hanged at Chicago on July 13, 1894. Source: *Chicago Tribune*, 7/14/94 (9:1). See also: 1893 Cook Co. death cert. no. 7736.

George Michael Centrell (white, age 24). *Murder.* The crime was committed on 8/7/1894 in St. Clair County. Handgun slaying of 46-year-old Frederick Kahn (white), the victim having been shot in the back and his head cracked open with a hammer. Motive: adultery. The killer was hanged at Belleville on November 30, 1894. Source: *Belleville (IL) Weekly Advocate*, 8/10/94 (7:1) & 12/7/94 (8:1). See also: 1880 U.S. Census (St. Clair Co., IL), which notes Mr. Kahn.

1895

Douglas Henderson (white, age 22) and **Frank Jeffrey** (white, age 27). *Murder.* Their crime was committed on 12/20/1894 in Jackson County. Handgun slaying of 45-year-old James Towle (white). Motive: mugging. These killers were hanged at Murphysboro on May 31, 1895. Source: *Fort Wayne (IN) News*, 12/24/94 (10:5). *Southern Illinois Herald* (Carbondale), 12/29/94 (3:2). *Chicago Tribune*, 6/1/95 (5:3).

Henry Lyons (white, age 34). *Murder.* The crime was committed on 2/9/1895 in Cook County. Fatal pistol-whipping of 36-year-old Albert B. Mason (white). Motive: mugging. This predator was hanged at Chicago on October 11, 1895. Source: *Chicago Tribune*, 10/12/95 (14:1). See also: 1895 Cook Co. death cert. no. 12027.

Charles N. Smith (white, age 38). *Murder.* The crime was committed on 9/28/1895 in Macon County. Filicide, etc. Handgun slayings of 5-year-old Louise Smith and 17-year-old Edna Buchert (whites), his daughter and daughter-in-law respectively. Motive: drunkard in denial. Smith was hanged at Decatur on November 29, 1895. Source: *Chicago Tribune*, 11/30/95 (6:3). *Chicago Times-Herald*, 11/30/95 (2:4). See also: 1860 U.S. Census (Madison Co., IN), which notes the killer as a minor.

1896

Henry Foster (black, age 23). *Murder.* The crime was committed on 10/4/1895 in Cook County. Handgun slaying of 51-year-old George W. Wells (white). Motive: street brawl or thwarted mugging. The gallows permanently removed Henry Foster from society on January 24, 1896. Source: *Chicago Tribune*, 1/25/96 (14:3). See also: 1896 Cook Co. death cert. no. 5053.

Albert Wallace (white, age 39). *Murder.* The crime was committed on 2/19/1895 in Tazewell County. Sororicide. Shotgun slaying of 23-year-old Belle Wallace Bowlby (white). Motive: disputed inheritance. This sibling-killer was hanged at Pekin IL on March 14, 1896. Source: *Daily Republican* (Decatur, IL), 3/14/96 (1:1). *Chicago Tribune*, 3/15/96 (13:6). See also: 1870 U.S. Census (Tazewell Co., IL), which notes Wallace as a minor, and 1880 U.S. Census (Tazewell Co., IL), which notes Belle Bowlby by her maiden name.

Alfred C. Fields (black, age 26). *Murder.* The crime was committed on 2/20/1896 in Cook County. Executed for the murder of 27-year-old Ellen Randolph (black), she having been battered to death with a clothes iron and a metallic lemon squeezer. Motive: landlady-tenant dispute. Alfred Fields was hanged at Chicago on May 15, 1896. Source: *Chicago Tribune*, 5/16/96 (9:7).

John D. Jones (white, age 44). *Murder.* The crime was committed on 8/30/1895 in Union County. Executed for the murder of Susan Mendenhall (white, age not recorded), who was beaten and kicked to death. Motive: dispute over wages. Venue changed from Union County to Jackson County. Recidivist killer. Jones had reportedly spent six years in prison for killing a man named "Champion" in Union County circa 1883. He was hanged at Murphysboro on May 20, 1896. Source: *Edwardsville (IL) Intelligencer*, 9/3/95 (2:5), 3/20/96 (5:5) & 5/22/96 (4:3). *Evening Bulletin* (Decatur, IL), 9/2/95 (2:3). See also: 1880 U.S. Census (Union Co., IL), which notes Jones.

Joseph Windrath (white, age 27). *Murder.* The crime was committed on 6/23/1895 in Cook County. Handgun slaying of 34-year-old Carey B. Burch (white). Motive: robbery. This killer was hanged at Chicago on June 5, 1896. Source: *Chicago Tribune*, 6/6/96 (5:3). See also: 1895 Cook Co. death cert. no. 2020 and 1896 Cook Co. death cert. no. 20915.

Julius Mannow (white, age 29). *Murder.* The crime was committed on 6/23/1895 in Cook County. Accomplice in the handgun slaying of 34-year-old Carey B. Burch (white). Motive: robbery. Mannow walked to the gallows at Chicago on October 30, 1896. Source: *Saturday Evening Telegraph* (Alton, IL), 10/31/96 (1:5). See also: Joseph Windrath (executed 6/5/96).

Benjamin Boehmer, alias "Fred Behme" (white, age 49). *Murder.* The crime was committed on 4/5/1896 in Hamilton County. Uxoricide and filicide. Executed for the Easter Sunday killings of 40-year-old Mary Boehmer and 3-year-old Thomas Boehmer (whites), his wife and son respectively. Motive: religious quarrel. The killer was a Methodist convert from Roman Catholicism. His wife, however, remained steadfast in the Romish faith. Rankled by this, Boehmer forbade that the couple's children (seven in number) be baptized by a Catholic priest. Mary Boehmer disobeyed her husband and had their youngest child (Thomas) baptized in secret. Learning of this, Benjamin Boehmer went berserk. He beat the woman's head in with a mallet and hanged the baptized toddler from a barn rafter. He himself was hanged at the hands of the law at McLeansboro on December 4, 1896. Source: *McLeansboro (IL) Times*, 4/10/96 (4:2) & 12/4/96 (4:3).

1897

Daniel McCarthy (white, age 27). *Murder.* The crime was committed on 5/12/1896 in Cook County. Uxoricide. Handgun slaying of Adeline McCarthy (white, age not recorded). Motive: alcoholic brutality. This wife-killer was hanged at Chicago on February 19, 1897. Source: *Chicago Tribune*, 2/20/97 (14:7). *Cedar Rapids (IA) Evening Gazette*, 5/13/96 (2:2).

Frederick Wilhelm Hoelman (white, age 38). *Murder.* The crime was committed on 12/2/1896 in Ford County. Suspected serial killer. Executed for the murder of Weibke Geddes (white, the wife of Frederick Geddes, age not recorded), who was severely beaten, raped and hanged by means of twine strung over the top of her bedroom door. Motive: sexual assault. Prime suspect in three other identical murders: Carrie Lenz (the wife of Albert Lenz, white, age not recorded) near Danforth IL on 11/26/1896; Augusta Seifkin (white, age 60+) near Melvin IL on 6/13/1896; and Catherine Mohr (white, age 73) near Ripon, WI, on 9/22/1896. A further report that Hoelman had also murdered "an old woman" at Ombrau, Germany, is too vague to be accredited. He was hanged at Paxton IL on May 14, 1897. Source: *Paxton (IL) Record*, 6/18/96 (1:4), 12/3/96 (3:3) & 5/14/97 (3:3). *Chicago Tribune*, 5/15/97 (7:5). *Daily Republican* (Decatur, IL), 5/14/97 (1:5). *Sterling (IL) Evening Gazette*, 9/23/96 (3:5). *Stevens Point (WI) Daily Journal*, 10/10/96 (3:7). *Intimate Detective*, 7/41.

John Lattimore (black, age 25). *Murder.* The crime was committed on 11/29/1896 in Cook County. Executed for the murder of Louis Maravic (white, age not recorded), who was bludgeoned with a rock. Motive: mugging. This inner-city predator was hanged at Chicago on May 28, 1897. Source: *Chicago Tribune*, 5/29/97 (7:5). *Saturday Evening Telegraph* (Alton, IL), 5/29/97 (1:5). See also: 1897 Cook Co. death cert. no. 10969.

William Thomas Powers (black, age 23). *Murder.* The crime was committed on 12/29/1896 in Cook County. Executed for the murder of 25-year-old John J. Murphy (white), the victim having been battered to death with an iron stove poker as he lay asleep in his bed. Motive: robbery and ingratitude. The killer was hanged at Chicago on

May 28, 1897. Source: *Chicago Tribune*, 5/29/97 (7:5). *Reno (NV) Evening Gazette*, 5/28/97 (1:2). See also: 1896 Cook Co. death cert. no. 13701.

Scalicia Santo Nikoli, alias "James French" (white, age 32). *Murder.* The crime was committed on 7/19/1896 in Winnebago County. Uxoricide. Handgun slaying of 28-year-old Catherine French (white), she having been shot seven times. Motive: marital estrangement. This wife-killer was hanged at Rockford on June 11, 1897. Source: *Rockford (IL) Daily Register-Gazette*, 7/20/96 (3:3) & 7/21/96 (7:7). *Chicago Tribune*, 7/20/96 (4:1) & 6/12/97 (7:5).

1898

James Mingle (white, age 41). *Murder.* The crime was committed on 7/27/1897 in Sangamon County. Baby killer. Executed for the hatchet murder of 18-month old Dollie Briscoe (white, his illegitimate daughter) and severe wounding by the same means of 18-year-old Mary Briscoe (white), the mother thereof. Motive: atavistic machismo. This brute was hanged at Springfield on February 11, 1898. Source: *Chicago Tribune*, 2/12/98 (6:6). See also: 1898 Sangamon Co. death cert. no. 8983.

Christopher Merry (white, age 26). *Murder.* The crime was committed on 11/19/1897 in Cook County. Uxoricide. Beating and strangulation of 22-year-old Paulina Merry (white). Motive: sheer brutality. Merry's own mother said that he was a bully and a sadist who regularly mistreated her as well. He was hanged at Chicago on April 22, 1898. Source: *Chicago Tribune*, 4/23/98 (14:1). See also: 1897 Cook Co. death cert. no. 12606 and 1898 Cook Co. death cert. no. 12258.

John Druggan (white, age 21). *Murder.* The crime was committed on 1/11/1898 in Cook County. Handgun slaying of 38-year-old Robert F. Gudgeon (white). Motive: armed robbery. Druggan was hanged at Chicago on October 14, 1898. Source: *Chicago Tribune*, 10/15/98 (10:3). See also: 1898 Cook Co. death cert. no. 6142.

George H. Jacks (white, age 37). *Murder.* The crime was committed on 2/26/1898 in Cook County. Executed for the murder of 68-year-old Andrew F. McGhee (white), the victim having been knocked in the head. Motive: robbery. Jacks was hanged at Chicago on October 14, 1898. Source: *Chicago Tribune*, 10/15/98 (10:3). *Fort Wayne (IN) Morning Journal*, 10/15/98 (4:4). *Saturday Evening Telegraph* (Alton, IL), 10/15/98 (1:5). See also: 1898 Cook Co. death cert. nos. 13196 and 9063.

Richard Collier (white, age 33). *Murder.* The crime was committed on 9/3/1898 in Champaign County. Handgun slaying of Charles Freebryant (white, age not recorded). Motive: dishonor among thieves. The shooter in this case was hanged at Urbana on December 16, 1898. Source: *Chicago Tribune*, 12/17/98 (2:7). *Decatur (IL) Evening Republican*, 11/3/98 (8:4). See also: 1880 U.S. Census (Clark Co., IL), which notes Collier as a teenager.

Carter Martin (white, age 28). *Murder.* The crime was committed on 10/3/1898 in Coles County. Handgun slaying of 37-year-old Albert Buser (white), who was shot three times in the back. Motive: highway robbery. Carter Martin was hanged at Charleston IL on December 16, 1898. Source: *Daily*

Republican (Decatur, IL), 12/15/98 (1:3). *Newark (OH) Daily Advocate*, 12/17/98 (2:3). See also: 1880 U.S. Census (McLean Co., IL), which notes Buser, and 1880 U.S. Census (Coles Co., IL), which notes Martin as a child.

1899

Robert Howard (black, age 32). *Murder.* The crime was committed on 11/9/1898 in Cook County. Accessory to the fatal stabbing of 36-year-old Frank C. Metcalf (white), the actual killer not having been caught. Motive: mugging. Robert Howard was hanged at Chicago on February 17, 1899. Source: *Boston Globe*, 11/11/98 (7:5). *Chicago Tribune*, 2/18/99 (10:1). See also: 1898 Cook Co. death cert. no. 12521 and 1899 Cook Co. death cert. no. 7569.

August Becker (white, age 33). *Murder.* The crime was committed on 1/27/1899 in Cook County. Uxoricide. Ax murder of 28-year-old Rachel Sutterlin Becker (white), she having been chopped into pieces and her body parts parboiled to more effectively reduce them to sludge. Motive: so the killer could be free to marry the victim's sister. August Becker was hanged at Chicago on November 10, 1899. Source: *Daily Northwestern* (Oshkosh, WI), 7/7/99 (8:1). *Chicago Tribune*, 11/11/99 (9:6). See also: 1899 Cook Co. death cert. no. 1711.

Michael Rollinger (white, age 38). *Murder.* The crime was committed on 12/16/1898 in Cook County. Uxoricide. Strangulation and partial cremation of 37-year-old Theresa Rollinger (white). Motive: so he could be free to pursue another woman. This fickle husband was hanged at Chicago on November 17, 1899. Source: *Daily Northwestern* (Oshkosh, WI), 12/22/98 (1:5). *Chicago Tribune*, 11/18/99 (9:4). See also: 1898 Cook Co. death cert. no. 16878 and 1899 Cook Co. death cert. no. 16756.

William Martin (black, age not recorded). *Murder.* The crime was committed on 10/8/1899 in Alexander County. Handgun slaying of Joseph Landrum (black, age not recorded), who was shot once in the head and then finished off by two more shots in the back. Motive: rivalry for a female. The killer in this case was hanged at Cairo IL on December 29, 1899. Source: *Evening Citizen* (Cairo, IL), 10/9/99 (3:2) & 12/29/99 (3:1).

1900

Riley Powell (black, age 20). *Murder.* The crime was committed on 10/11/1899 in Alexander County. Police killer. Handgun slaying of 27-year-old Elmo Frie (white). Motive: saloon brawl. This pistol packer swung to his death (legally) at Cairo IL on April 20, 1900. Source: *Evening Citizen* (Cairo, IL), 10/11/99 (2:1) & 4/20/00 (3:1). See also: 1880 U.S. Census (Wake Co., NC), which notes Powell as a minor.

John Owens (white, age abt. 35). *Murder.* The crime was committed on 9/22/1900 in Edgar County. Handgun slaying of 21-year-old James F. Hogue (white). Motive: attempted mugging. Owens dropped through the trap of a gallows for what he did at Paris IL on December 21, 1900. Source: *Paris (IL) Daily Beacon*, 9/24/00 (1:5), 9/27/00 (1:5) & 12/21/00 (1:3).

1901

George Dolinski (white, age 35). *Murder.* The crime was committed on 10/28/1900 in Cook County. Mutilation murder of 26-year-old Anton Lizl (white), who had been shot with a handgun; his face was slashed to ribbons, his throat was cut from ear to ear and one eye was gouged out. Motive: because the killer coveted the victim's wife. Dolinski was hanged at Chicago on October 11, 1901. Source: *Daily Gazette* (Janesville, WI), 10/29/00 (6:2). *Chicago Tribune*, 10/12/01 (4:6). See also: 1900 U.S. Census (Chicago, IL), which notes Lizl, and 1901 Cook Co. death cert. no. 3910.

1902

Joseph Ellsworth Hinkle (white, age 29). *Murder.* The crime was committed on 9/18/1901 in Peoria County. Uxoricide. Executed for the murder of 31-year-old Artie Hinkle (white), she having been slashed to death with a knife. Motive: because she had refused to prostitute herself at his behest. This miscreant was hanged at Peoria on February 28, 1902. Source: *Fort Wayne (IN) News*, 9/19/01 (1:1). *Decatur (IL) Daily Review*, 2/28/02 (1:2). See also: 1900 U.S. Census (Tazewell Co., IL), which notes this couple.

Lewis G. Toombs (white, age 42). *Murder.* The crime was committed on 12/30/1901 in Cook County. Strangulation of 23-year-old Carrie Larsen (white) and illegal disposal of her body in the Chicago River. Motive: probably because she had spurned his advances. Lewis Toombs was hanged at Chicago on August 8, 1902. Source: *Chicago Tribune*, 8/9/02 (7:5). *Master Detective*, 1/41. See also: 1901 Cook Co. death cert. no. 11278 and 1902 Cook Co. death cert. no. 15205.

1903

Jeremiah Graves (white, age 21) and **Calvin Price** (white, age 21). *Murder.* Their crime was committed on 3/16/1903 in Franklin County. Handgun slaying of 49-year-old Nellie Reichelderfer (white), whose body was then heaved into a hog pen where it was partially devoured by swine. Motive: home invasion. Venue changed from Franklin County to Williamson County. These killers were hanged at Marion IL on July 10, 1903. Source: *Decatur (IL) Herald*, 3/19/03 (1:2). *Carbondale (IL) Free Press*, 7/15/03 (1:4). *Master Detective*, 11/41 & 3/55. See also: 1900 U.S. Census (Franklin Co., IL), which notes the murdered woman.

Michaelangelo Filipse (white, age abt. 40). *Murder.* The crime was committed on 2/21/1903 in Kane County. Ax murder of Nicola Tomasso (white, age not recorded). Motive: robbery. This killer was hanged at Geneva IL on November 20, 1903. Source: *The Twice-A-Week Republican* (Geneva, IL), 2/25/03 (1:7), 10/21/03 (1:4) & 11/21/03 (1:7).

John McCrea (black, age 39). *Murder.* The crime was committed on 6/23/1903 in Peoria County. Police killer. Handgun slaying of 37-year-old William F. Murphy (white). Motive: resisting arrest. McCrea was hanged at Peoria on December 11, 1903. Source: *Peoria (IL) Star*, 6/24/03 (12:1), 6/25/03 (16:1) & 12/11/03 (20:2).

1904

Louis Pesant (white, age 23). *Murder.* The crime was committed on 9/18/1903 in Cook County. Executed for the murder of 49-year-old Mary Spilka (white), she having been beaten and kicked to death. Motive: grand larceny. Louis Pesant was hanged at Chicago on April 15, 1904. Source: *Chicago Tribune*, 4/16/04 (15:3). See also: 1903 Cook Co. death cert. no. 16582 and 1904 Cook Co. death cert. no. 13719.

Gustave Marx (white, age 19), **Peter Neidermeier** (white, age 23) and **Harry van Dine** (white, age 21). *Murder.* Their crime was committed on 8/30/1903 in Cook County. Spree killers and police killers. Executed for the handgun slayings of 38-year-old James B. Johnson and 19-year-old Francis Stewart (whites). Motive: armed robbery. Marx and his accomplices are also confirmed to have murdered six other people during a 4-month crime spree as follows: Otto Bauder (white, age 19) at Chicago on 7/9/1903. Motive: saloon stickup. Bohumil "Benjamin" LeGros (white, age 43) and Adolph Johnson (white, age 21) at Chicago on 8/1/1903. Motive: saloon stickup. Also Chicago police officers John Quinn (white, age 37) and Joseph D. Driscoll (white, age 33), on 11/21/1903 and 11/27/1903 respectively. Motive: resisting arrest and evading pursuit. Also a railroad brakeman named John Sovea (white, age 25) on 11/27/1903 when they tried to hijack a train at Whiting, IN. These three killers were hanged at Chicago on April 22, 1904. Source: *Daily Review* (Decatur, IL), 8/31/03 (1:4). *Chicago Tribune*, 4/23/04 (3:1). See also: 1903 Cook Co. death cert. nos. 787, 3506, 7627, 9525 & 14460; 1904 Cook Co. death cert. nos. 10532, 12059 & 18755. Also: 1903 *Register of Deaths* (Whiting, IN),. Lake County Health Office, Crown Point, IN. *Daring Detective*, 1/37 & 2/37. *Master Detective*, 7/32 & 3/55.

Frank Lewandowski (white, age 48). *Murder.* The crime was committed on 2/24/1904 in Cook County. Uxoricide. Executed for the murder of 62-year-old Frances Lewandowski (white), she having been nearly decapitated with a butcher knife. Motive: alcoholism. This wife-killer was hanged at Chicago on September 30, 1904. Source: *Chicago Tribune*, 10/1/04 (7:1). *Stevens Point (WI) Daily Journal*, 10/1/04 (2:4). See also: 1904 Cook Co. death cert. nos. 9577 & 9601.

1905

John Johnson (black, age 36). *Murder.* The crime was committed on 9/26/1903 in Cook County. Police killer. Fatal assault on the person of 50-year-old Dennis Fitzgerald (white), who was overpowered by two ruffians, beaten, kicked, stomped and shot with his own service revolver, which had been wrested from him. Motive: disorderly conduct. Fitzgerald succumbed to his injuries on 1/20/1904. John Johnson was hanged at Chicago exactly one year later on January 20, 1905. Source: *Chicago Tribune*, 1/21/05 (9:2). See also: 1904 Cook Co. death cert. no. 4332 and 1905 Cook Co. death cert. no. 7565.

Jim Festley, alias "Eli Bugg" (black, age 30). *Murder.* The crime was committed on 7/23/1904 in Pulaski County. Executed for complicity in the handgun slaying of Christopher Mathis (black, age not recorded), the actual killer not having been caught. Motive: grudge. Recidivist killer. Bugg had previously served 14 years in the Menard Correctional Facility for another murder that he had committed as a teenager. He is also reported to have killed a fellow inmate while incarcerated. He was hanged at Mound City on February 17, 1905. Source: *Paducah (KY) Sun*, 2/17/05 (1:5). See also: 1900 U.S. Census (Randolph Co., IL), which notes Bugg as a prison inmate.

Charles Otis Botts (white, age 21). *Murder.* The crime was committed on 1/6/1905 in Peoria County. Uxoricide. Strangulation of 19-year-old Gertrude Slagle Botts (white). Motive: because she had refused to sell herself for immoral purposes. Botts was also the prime suspect in the 5/1/1900 handgun death of 18-year-old Bertha "Birdie" Hoffman (white, another Peoria girl), which was originally attributed to suicide despite an autopsy report proving that she had had sexual intercourse on the same day that she died. This user, abuser and destroyer of young women was hanged at Peoria on June 16, 1905. Source: *Peoria (IL) Star*, 1/7/05 (10:1), 1/8/05 (20:4), 1/9/05 (10:1), 3/38/05 (16:1) & 6/16/05 (16:1).

1906

John Mueller (white, age 33). *Murder.* The crime was committed on 1/11/1905 in Cook County. Uxoricide, filicide and baby killer. Handgun slayings of 27-year-old Annie Mueller, 2-year-old Martha Mueller and 18-month-old Mary Mueller (whites, his wife and daughters), they having also been repeatedly slashed with a razor. Motive: a drunk and a loser who went berserk when refused money with which to buy liquor, He was hanged at Chicago on February 16, 1906. Source: *Eau Claire (WI) Leader*, 1/12/05 (1:4). *Chicago Tribune*, 2/17/06 (16:1). See also: 1905 Cook Co. death cert. nos. 10130, 10131 & 10132; 1906 Cook Co. death cert. no. 2937.

Robert Newcomb (black, age 52). *Murder.* The crime was committed on 10/10/1905 at Chicago. Police killer, etc. Executed for the handgun slaying of 42-year-old John Peter Shine (white). Motive: resisting arrest. Newcomb had also murdered two other persons that day, Florence Poore (black female, age 27) and Walter Blue (black, age 25), by the same means during a jealous rampage. He was hanged at Chicago on February 16, 1906. Source: *Stevens Point (WI) Daily Journal*, 10/11/05 (2:5). *Chicago Tribune*, 2/17/06 (16:1). See also: 1905 Cook Co. death cert. nos. 1534, 13834 & 16843; 1906 Cook Co. death cert. no. 11892.

Johann Otto Hoch (white, age 42). *Murder.* The crime was committed on 1/12/1905 at Chicago. Uxoricide. Serial killer. Executed for the deliberate and fatal poisoning of 46-year-old Marie Walcker Hoch (white). Motive: bunco. This man was by all accounts a professional marriage swindler who duped an indeterminate number of lovelorn women throughout the USA and perhaps his homeland of Germany as well. More than *forty* middle-aged females (all of them reportedly widows) accepted his fraudulent marriage proposals, only to be left abandoned, dead and/or financially ruined. An estimated dozen or so of these ladies were poisoned with arsenic when they began to suspect the true nature of their newly acquired husband. Several of these were said to have died by such means. A complete and accurate listing of them is impossible to compile based on available information. However, two can be identified for certain: Caroline Miller Hoch (white, age abt. 38), who died at Wheeling, WV, on 6/15/1895, and Martha Steinbucher Hoch (white, age 45), who died at Chicago on 2/14/1896. Additional homicide victims were said to be Barbara Brossert of San Francisco, CA, who married Hoch on 9/22/1896 and died of chagrin a short time later when her "husband" absconded with her life's savings. Also Clara Bartel Schmidt of Cincinnati, OH, who died in January of 1897. Also: Mary Schultz Buschberg and her daughter Nellie Schultz (white, age 15) of Argos, IN, who both vanished in the summer of 1900. Also Mary Becker (or "Decker") of St. Louis MO in 1902 and Lena Hoch of Milwaukee, WI, who died in June of 1904. Johann Hoch paid for his crimes on the gallows at Chicago on February 23, 1906. Source: *Chicago Tribune*, 2/24/06 (5:4). See also: 1896 Cook Co. death cert. no. 7662. See also: *Celebrated Criminal Cases of America* by Thomas Samuel Drake (San Francisco, CA: James H. Barry, 1910), 431–437. *Daring Detective*, 9/35. *Dynamic Detective*, 3/37. *Headline Detective*, 3/42.

Richard G. Ivins (white, age 24). *Murder.* The crime was committed on 1/12/1906 in Cook County. Strangulation of 30-year-old Bessie M. Hollister (white), she having had copper wire tightly twisted around her neck. Motive: sexual assault. Ivins was hanged at Chicago on June 22, 1906. Source: *Chicago Tribune*, 6/23/06 (4:1). See also: 1906 Cook Co. death cert. no. 6197.

Daniel R. Francis (black, age 47). *Murder.* The crime was committed on 10/27/1905 in Cook County. Uxoricide, etc. Handgun slayings of 46-year-old Maria Francis and 39-year-old Dorinda J. Scroggs (blacks). Motive: spousal alienation; he blamed the Scroggs woman for causing disharmony in his marriage. This double killer was hanged at Chicago on October 12, 1906. Source: *Daily Chronicle* (Marshall, MI), 10/13/06 (4:3). See also: 1905 Cook Co. death cert. nos. 4689 and 16844; 1906 Cook Co. death cert. no. 4627.

1907

Richard Walton (black, age 36). *Murder.* The crime was committed on 9/19/1907 in Cook County. Strangulation of 40-year-old Lillian W. Grant (white). Motive: burglary. This killer and complete disregarder of the rights and property of others was hanged at Chicago on December 13, 1907. Source: *Chicago Tribune*, 12/14/07 (5:1). See also: 1907 Cook Co. death cert. nos. 5423 and 20174.

Edward Clifford (white, age 23). *Murder.* The crime was committed on 11/25/1906 in Peoria County. Patricide. Shotgun slaying of 54-year-old Isaac Clifford (white), the victim having been blasted from behind. Motive: monetary dispute. The younger Clifford was hanged for what he did at Peoria on December 20, 1907. Source: *Oelwein (IA) Daily Register*, 11/26/06 (1:6) & 12/21/07 (1:2). See also: 1900 U.S. Census (Peoria Co., IL), which notes both parties.

1908

Joe James (black, age 23). *Murder.* The crime was committed on 7/3/1908 in Sangamon County. Fatal stabbing of 45-year-old Clergy A. Ballard (white).

Motive: physical altercation. Ballard had caught James in his daughter's bedroom. The incident precipitated a race riot in which seven people were killed and more than forty buildings burned. It also gave fuel to those who advised against interracial relationships. Joe James was hanged for the crime of murdering a man in his own home at Springfield on October 23, 1908. Source: *Chicago Tribune*, 10/24/08 (2:3). *Fort Wayne (IN) Sentinel*, 10/23/08 (1:5). See also: 1908 Sangamon Co. death cert. nos. 17972 and 18302.

Frank Bryant (white, age 25). *Murder.* The crime was committed on 8/24/1908 in Sangamon County. Ax murder of 65-year-old Thomas Brady (white). Motive: larceny. The killer was a lovesick fool hard up for money that would enable him to visit a girl in a neighboring city. He wound up going through the gallows trap at Springfield with a rope around his neck instead on December 18, 1908. Source: *Daily Review* (Decatur, IL), 12/17/08 (1:7), 12/18/08 (3:1) & 12/19/08 (8:2). See also: 1908 Sangamon Co. death cert. nos. 18133 and 18465. *Daring Detective*, 2/43.

1909

Andrew Williams (black, age 22). *Murder.* The crime was committed on 3/10/1908 in Cook County. Uxoricide. Handgun slaying of 20-year-old Ophelia Hardy Williams (black). Motive: marital estrangement. This black-on-black killer was hanged at Chicago on October 22, 1909. Source: *Chicago Tribune*, 10/23/09 (15:6). See also: 1908 Cook Co. death cert. no. 20181 and 1909 Cook Co. death cert. no. 20116.

1910

Willis Clark (black, age 22). *Murder.* The crime was committed on 12/18/1909 in St. Clair County. Handgun slaying of 34-year-old Eugene V. Goudey (white). Motive: robbery. Clark was hanged at Belleville on February 18, 1910. Source: *Semi Weekly Advocate* (Belleville, IL), 2/18/10 (1:1). See also: 1900 U.S. Census (St. Clair Co., IL), which notes Mr. Goudey.

Clinton St. Clair (white, age 40). *Murder.* The crime was committed on 1/20/1910 in Winnebago County. Mutilation murder of 79-year-old Mary E. McIntosh (white), she having been literally gutted like a fish. Motive: robbery and home invasion. The man responsible for this atrocity was hanged at Rockford on April 15, 1910. Source: *News-Palladium* (Benton Harbor, MI), 1/22/10 (4:4). *Cook County (IL) Herald*, 4/22/10 (3:4). See also: 1900 U.S. Census (Winnebago Co., IL), which notes the homicide victim, and 1900 U.S. Census (Baltimore, MD), which notes the killer.

Robert Martin (black, age 27). *Murder.* The crime was committed on 1/30/1910 in St. Clair County. Shotgun slaying of 19-year-old Floyd Harris (black), who was deliberately blasted in the back. Motive: suspicion of adultery. Robert Martin was hanged at Belleville on July 22, 1910. Source: *Semi Weekly Advocate* (Belleville, IL), 4/29/10 (7:4) & 7/22/10 (1:1). See also: 1900 U.S. Census (St. Louis, MO), which notes Harris.

1911

Alexander King (black, age 41). *Murder.* The crime was committed on

4/3/1911 in Saline County. Executed for the murder of 48-year-old James Mitchell (white), who had been clubbed on the head; his house was burned down around him. Motive: robbery and home invasion. The culprit was hanged at Harrisburg IL on June 16, 1911. Source: *Sheboygan (WI) Daily Press,* 4/7/11 (5:6). *The Pointer* (Riverdale, IL), 4/14/11 (6:3). *Indianapolis Star,* 6/17/11 (13:5). See also: *Saline County Death Certificates,* vol. 3, 46. See also: 1910 U.S. Census (Saline Co., IL), which notes the killer.

1912

Thomas Jennings (black, age 28). *Murder.* The crime was committed on 9/19/1910 in Cook County. Handgun slaying of 41-year-old Clarence D. Hiller (white), who was shot three times. Motive: burglary. The killer was hanged at Chicago on February 16, 1912. Source: *Waterloo (IA) Evening Courier,* 9/19/10 (1:7). *Chicago Tribune,* 2/17/12 (3:1). See also: 1910 Cook Co. death cert. no. 6597 and 1912 Cook Co. death cert. no. 17869.

Thomas W. Schultz (white, age 19), **Ewald Shiblawski** (white, age 21), **Frank Shiblawski** (white, age 23) and **Philip Somerling** (white, age 21). *Murder.* Their crime was committed on 10/20/1911 in Cook County. Fatal beating and stabbing of 23-year-old Frederick W. Guelzow (white). Motive: highway robbery. All four of these killers were hanged at Chicago on February 16, 1912. Source: *Waterloo (IA) Evening Courier,* 10/23/11 (1:6). *Chicago Tribune,* 2/17/12 (3:1). See also: 1911 Cook Co. death cert. no. 6293 and 1912 Cook Co. death cert. no. 17937.

George Engel (white, age 54). *Murder.* The crime was committed on 5/29/1912 in Perry County. Uxoricide, etc. Fatal stabbings of pregnant 41-year-old Rosa Yost Engel and 41-year-old Anna Yost (whites, they respectively being his wife and sister-in-law and apparently twins) by means of a butcher knife. Motive: marital estrangement. This grumpy husband, double killer and destroyer of his unborn child was hanged at Pinckneyville IL on October 18, 1912. Source: *Daily Free Press* (Carbondale, IL), 6/7/12 (2:1) & 7/12/12 (1:2). *Daily Review* (Decatur, IL), 10/19/12 (7:2). See also: *Perry County Death Register,* vol. 2, 88–89. See also: 1910 U.S. Census (Randolph Co., IL), which notes the Engels.

1914

Henry Spencer (white, age abt. 30). *Murder.* The crime was committed on 9/27/1913 in DuPage County. Handgun slaying of 35-year-old Mildred Allison Rexroat (white), her body having also been mangled by a train. Motive: dope addict; robbery. Spencer's compulsion brought him to the gallows at Wheaton on July 31, 1914. It is significant to note that the killer's narcotics addiction was disallowed as a mitigating factor because he had had plenty of opportunity to seek treatment and thereby rid himself of that driving force. The fact that he did not man up to doing so was taken as an aggravating factor. Source: *Washington (DC) Post,* 10/7/13 (1:3). *Janesville (WI) Daily Gazette,* 7/31/14 (1:6). *Chicago Tribune,* 8/1/14 (11:1). See also: 1910 U.S. Census (Chicago, IL), which notes the murdered woman as "Mildred Allison," the wife of Henry W. Allison. *Front Page Detective,* 10/37. *Intimate Detective,* 4/42. *Master Detective,* 3/45 & 2/49.

1915

Roswell C. Smith (white, age 26). *Murder*. The crime was committed on 7/7/1914 in Cook County. Child killer. Strangulation of 4-year-old Hazel Weinstein, a little Jewish girl. Motive: sexual assault. Further details of this atrocity are withheld for decency's sake. Roswell Smith was hanged for what he did on February 13, 1915. Source: *Chicago Tribune*, 2/14/15 (5:4). See also: 1914 Cook Co. death cert. no. 20621 and 1915 Cook Co. death cert. no. 17667.

Frank Repetto (white, age 26). *Murder*. The crime was committed on 9/17/1914 in Will County. Fatal stabbing of 21-year-old Charles Masters (white). Motive: prison violence. Repetto was hanged at Joliet on July 10, 1915. Source: *Daily Free Press* (Carbondale, IL), 7/17/15 (4:6). See also: 1910 U.S. Census (Chicago, IL), which notes Masters.

Joe DeBerry (black, age 21). *Murder*. The crime was committed on 7/30/1915 in Jackson County. Executed for the murder of 53-year-old Elizabeth Martin (white), she having been battered to death with an iron poker. Motive: base ingratitude. DeBerry had previously been jailed for stealing a valuable ring from Mrs. Martin. She mistook him for an object of compassion and obtained his parole. She also gave him a job around her upscale home. DeBerry repaid the lady's kindness by dashing her brains out. He also bore responsibility for the death of 62-year-old James H. Martin (husband of the murdered woman), who succumbed to a nervous breakdown two weeks later. The public hangman saw to DeBerry's rehabilitation at Murphysboro on October 16, 1915. Source: *Waterloo (IA) Evening Courier*, 8/10/15 (1:1). *Chicago Tribune*, 10/17/15 (1:4). See also: 1910 U.S. Census (Jackson Co., IL), which notes the Martins.

1917

Walter Murphy (black, age 24). *Murder*. The crime was committed on 11/10/1915 in Vermilion County. Handgun slayings of 30-year-old George Lang and 28-year-old Louis Lang (whites). Motive: armed robbery. Murphy paid with his life for this at Danville IL on February 16, 1917. Source: *Oelwein (IA) Daily Register*, 11/11/15 (2:6). *Daily Review* (Decatur, IL), 2/16/17 (1:4). *Chicago Tribune*, 2/17/17 (8:5).

1918

Harry Lindrum (white, age 21). *Murder*. The crime was committed on 8/23/1917 in Cook County. Police killer. Handgun slaying of 38-year-old Joseph Patrick Tiernan (white). Motive: resisting arrest. Lindrum plunged to his doom at the end of a rope for this at Chicago on February 15, 1918. Source: *Chicago Tribune*, 2/16/18 (8:4). See also: 1910 U.S. Census (Chicago, IL), which notes both parties.

Edward Wheed (white, age 48). *Murder*. The crime was committed on 8/28/1917 in Cook County. Handgun slayings of 26-year-old Barton O. Allen and 24-year-old Louis Osenberg (whites). Motive: armed robbery. Wheed was additionally found to have been a police killer. He had gunned down Chicago patrolman Peter R. Bulfin (white, age 39) during an unrelated robbery on 7/13/1917. He was hanged at Chicago on February 15, 1918. Source: *Daily Northwestern* (Oshkosh, WI), 8/28/17 (1:7). *Chicago Tribune*, 2/16/18 (8:4). See also: 1910 U.S. Census (Chicago, IL), which notes Bulfin, and 1910 U.S. Census (Leavenworth, KS), which notes Wheed as a federal prisoner. See also: 1900 U.S. Census (Greenup Co., KY), which notes Barton Allen as a minor. *Dynamic Detective*, 8/37.

Vincenzo Martellaro (white, age abt. 35). *Murder.* The crime was committed on 7/1/1916 in Will County. Handgun slaying of 40-year-old Antonio Carugati (white). Motive: saloon brawl. A hothead whose first instinct was to shoot, Martellaro paid the forfeit of his own life at Joliet on March 1, 1918. Source: *Joliet Herald Sunday News*, 7/2/16 (1:1). *Joliet Evening Herald News*, 3/1/18 (3:1). Appeal: 281 IL 300–310.

William Carter (black, age 35). *Murder.* The crime was committed on 11/4/1917 in Rock Island County. Handgun slaying of 50-year-old Peter Jelvek (white), the victim having been murdered in his bed. Motive: burglary. The gallows ended the criminal forays of William Carter at Rock Island on March 15, 1918. Source: *Rock Island Argus*, 11/5/17 (12:1) & 3/15/18 (13:1).

Dennis Anderson (white, age 21). *Murder.* The crime was committed on 10/29/1917 in Cook County. Police killer. Handgun slaying of 57-year-old Patrick Lavin (white), who was shot with his own service weapon, which had been wrested from him. Motive: employee pilferage and treachery. The guilty party was hanged at Chicago on July 19, 1918. Source: *Logansport (IN) Pharos-Reporter*, 10/30/17 (1:5). *Chicago Tribune*, 7/20/18 (13:8). See also: 1910 U.S. Census (Chicago, IL), which notes Lavin.

John Cloures (black, age 28). *Murder.* The crime was committed on 4/19/1917 in Will County. Executed for the murder of Henry Findley (black, age not recorded), who was bludgeoned with a heavy iron clamp. Motive: prison violence. Recidivist killer. Cloures was already serving a sentence of life imprisonment for another murder when he killed Findley. He is known to have also served time in Macon Co., IL for maliciously stabbing his landlord. He was hanged at Joliet on August 16, 1918. Source: *Joliet Evening Herald News*, 3/26/18 (1:1) & 8/16/18 (5:1). *Decatur (IL) Review*, 11/8/08 (5:4) & 3/11/09 (12:4). See also: 1918 Will Co. death cert. no. 22936.

Lloyd Bopp (white, age 22). *Murder.* The crime was committed on 6/14/1916 in Cook County. Police killer. Handgun slaying of 27-year-old Herman J. Malow (white). Motive: highway robbery gone awry. Bopp was hanged at Chicago on December 6, 1918. Source: *Lincoln (NB) Sunday Star*, 10/29/16 (5:3). *Chicago Tribune*, 12/7/18 (17:6). See also: 1910 U.S. Census (Cook Co., IL), which notes Malow.

1919

Albert Johnson (white, age 27). *Murder.* The crime was committed on 6/6/1917 in Cook County. Police killer. Handgun slaying of 39-year-old Martin J. Corcoran (white), who was shot in the groin and succumbed after two months of agony on 8/13/1917. Motive: evading arrest. The shooter was hanged at Chicago on February 28, 1919. Source: *Chicago Tribune*, 3/1/19 (9:2). See also: 1910 U.S. Census

(Chicago, IL), which notes the slain officer as "Corcorans." Appeal: 121 NE 246–248. See also: *Journal of the American Judicature Society*, June 1921, 56.

Earl Dear (white, age 25). *Murder.* The crime was committed on 1/19/1918 in Cook County. Handgun slaying of 24-year-old Rudolph Wolfe (white), the victim having been shot in the face at point-blank range. Motive: grand theft auto. Earl Dear was hanged at Chicago on June 27, 1919. Source: *Chicago Tribune*, 6/28/19 (11:1). *Evening Gazette* (Cedar Rapids, IA), 6/27/19 (6:1). See also: 1918 Cook Co. death cert. no. 6001983 and 1919 Cook Co. death cert. no. 6018707. *TRUE* (magazine) 2/41.

Thomas R. Fitzgerald (white, age 39). *Murder.* The crime was committed on 7/23/1919 in Cook County. Child killer. Executed for the deliberate murder of 6-year-old Janet Wilkinson (white), who was forcibly smothered and her body concealed in a coal pile. Motive: sexual assault. The culprit was hanged at Chicago on October 17, 1919. Source: *Sheboygan (WI) Press*, 7/28/19 (1:4). *Chicago Tribune*, 10/18/19 (17:8). *Actual Detective*, 5/42.

1920

Raffaelo Durrazio, alias "Durrage," "Durage," and "DiSozzo" (white, age 33). *Murder.* The crime was committed on 7/21/1919 in Cook County. Handgun slayings of 51-year-old Onofrio Gargano and 45-year-old Mary Gargano (whites), a married couple. Motive: landlord-tenant dispute. The killer was hanged at Chicago on January 2, 1920. Source: *Chicago Tribune*, 7/22/19 (5:5), 7/23/19 (11:2) & 1/3/20 (13:1). See also: Ellis Island Passenger Arrival Manifest, 2/22/96, which notes Onofrio Gargano, plus 1920 Cook Co. death cert. no. 6000074.

John O'Brien (white, age 21). *Murder.* The crime was committed on 6/16/1919 in Cook County. Police killer. Handgun slaying of 38-year-old Richard J. Burke (white). Motive: big attitude. Officer Burke (while in the course of his duty) had seen a saloon that was open past the legal hour. Entering the place, he announced that it was to be closed immediately. The tipplers resented this. O'Brien (who was among the latter) pulled a gun on the policeman and shot him dead. The price he paid was death by the rope on February 20, 1920. Source: *Chicago Tribune*, 2/21/20 (13:1). See also: 1910 U.S. Census (Chicago, 4th Ward), which notes Burke.

William Yancey Mills (black, age 19). *Murder.* The crime was committed on 10/12/1919 in Cook County. Executed for the murders of 40-year-old Antonio Brizzolara and 35-year-old Isadore Gansky (whites), they being a fruit-monger and a tailor, respectively. Both were fatally bludgeoned in their adjacent shops by means of an iron pipe wrapped in newspaper. Motive in each case: robbery. The killer was hanged at Chicago on April 16, 1920. Source: *Chicago Tribune*, 10/13/19 (1:7) & 4/17/20 (12:1). See also: 1910 U.S. Census (Chicago, IL), which notes Brizzolara.

Frank Campione (white, age 22). *Murder.* The crime was committed on 6/24/1919 in Cook County. Executed for the handgun slayings of 58-year-old Andrew P. Bowman (who was shot twice in the forehead) and 35-year-old Benjamin Wendell (whites). Motive:

armed robbery. Campione is confirmed to have also been an active accessory in the 11/15/1919 handgun slaying of 26-year-old Albert Kubalanza (white, also of Chicago) during an armed robbery. He was also the prime suspect in the gangland shooting of 33-year-old Santo Orlando (white) at Lockport IL on or about 12/1/1919, the victim having been shot fourteen times and his body submerged in an automobile that had been rolled into a canal. He was also a suspected accomplice in the 1/15/1920 handgun slaying of 47-year-old Antonio Varchetto (white, a Chicago bakery owner) while robbing his place of business. Campione was additionally suspected of shooting and severely wounding Officer James Carlin of the Chicago police department on 10/15/1919. He was hanged at the Cook County Jail on October 14, 1920. Source: *Chicago Tribune*, 10/15/20 (21:1). *Chicago Heights (IL) Star*, 8/19/20 (1:3). *Sheboygan (WI) Journal*, 10/14/20 (1:3). See also: 1910 U.S. Census (Chicago, IL), which notes Orlando. *Official Detective*, 3/15/37. *Front Page Detective*, 8/44 & 8/53. *Real Detective*, 2/38.

John Henry Reese (black, age 42). *Murder.* The crime was committed on 12/5/1919 in Cook County. Uxoricide. Executed for the hatchet killing of 40-year-old Mary Reese (black), whose decapitated corpse was then chopped into five parts that he wrapped in newspapers and secretly buried. Motive: henpecked husband. He was hanged at Chicago for this black-on-black butchery on October 14, 1920. Source: *Chicago Tribune*, 10/14/20 (1:7) & 10/15/20 (21:1). *Chicago Defender*, 12/20/19 (1:1).

Frank Zagar (white, age 20). *Murder.* The crime was committed on 4/15/1919 in Cook County. Executed for the handgun slaying of Polidaris Sardakis (white, age not recorded). Motive: armed robbery. Zagar is confirmed to have also murdered a second man named Paul Palipo (white, age not recorded) under identical circumstances that same night. He was hanged at Chicago on October 15, 1920. Source: *Chicago Tribune*, 5/1/20 (1:4) & 10/16/20 (7:5).

Arthur Haensel (white, age 27). *Murder.* The crime was committed on 2/4/1919 in Cook County. Uxoricide. Handgun slaying of 18-year-old Cecilia Lenarczyak Haensel (white). Motive: marital estrangement. This wrathful young man was hanged for what he did at Chicago on November 19, 1920. Source: *Fort Wayne (IN) News*, 2/5/19 (1:4). *Daily Northwestern* (Oshkosh, WI), 10/18/19 (13:5). *Chicago Tribune*, 11/20/20 (4:3).

Nicholas Viana (white, age 17). *Murder.* The crime was committed on 11/15/1919 in Cook County. Hanged on his 19th birthday for the handgun slaying of 26-year-old Albert Kubalanza (white). Motive: armed robbery. His execution was carried out at Chicago on December 10, 1920. Source: *Chicago Tribune*, 12/11/20 (14:6). See: Frank Campione (executed 10/14/20). See: Sam Cardinella (executed 4/15/21). *Official Detective*, 3/15/37. *Front Page Detective*, 8/44 & 8/53.

1921

Edward Brislane (white, age 26). *Murder.* The crime was committed on 3/11/1920 in Cook County. Handgun slaying of 38-year-old William A. Mills (white). Motive: attempted robbery. This killer was hanged at Chicago on

February 11, 1921. Source: *Chicago Tribune*, 2/12/21 (3:6). See also: 1920 U.S. Census (Chicago, IL), which notes both parties. *Crime Detective*, 5/50.

Settimi DeSantis (white, age 30). *Murder.* The crime was committed on 8/2/1920 in Williamson County. Executed for the murders of 17-year-old Amel Calcaterra and 19-year-old Peyton Roderick Hemphill (whites), they each having been shot execution-style (with a handgun) and slashed almost beyond recognition with a butcher knife. In addition, both were buried in shallow graves, Calcaterra with a knife protruding from his heart and Hemphill with one of his hands (which was purposely painted black) sticking up out of the ground. Motive: gangland shooting. DeSantis was hanged at Marion IL on February 11, 1921. Source: *Daily Free Press* (Carbondale, IL), 8/6/20 (1:5), 8/7/20 (1:5) & 2/11/21 (1:5). *Front Page Detective*, 1/39 & 6/70.

Samuel Cardinella (white, age 39). *Murder.* The crime was committed on 6/24/1919 in Cook County. Executed for masterminding the murders of 58-year-old Andrew P. Bowman and 35-year-old Benjamin Wendell (whites). Motive: robbery. Prime suspect in the gangland killing of 33-year-old Santo Orlando. Also regarded as the catalyst behind the robbery murders of Albert Kubalanza on 11/15/1919 and Antonio Varchetto on 1/15/1920, each at Chicago. This alleged gangster was hanged at the Cook County Jail on April 15, 1921. Source: *Chicago Tribune*, 4/16/21 (2:1). See: Frank Campione (executed 10/14/20). See: Nicholas Viana (executed 12/10/20). See: Joseph Costanzo (executed 4/15/21). *Official Detective*, 3/15/37. *Front Page Detective*, 8/44 & 8/53. *Real Detective*, 2/38 & 1/64.

Joseph Costanzo (white, age 21) and **Samuel Ferrera** (white, age 21). *Murder.* Their specific offense was committed on 1/15/1920 in Cook County. Both executed for the handgun slaying of 47-year-old Antonio Varchetto (white). Motive: armed robbery. Additionally suspected of participating in the gangland murders of Andrew P. Bowman, Benjamin Wendell, Santo Orlando and Albert Kubalanza. They were hanged along with their alleged boss Sam Cardinella on April 15, 1921. See: Frank Campione (executed 10/14/20). See: Samuel Cardinella (executed 4/15/21).

Frank Lowhone (white, age 35). *Murder.* The crime was committed on 4/4/1919 in White County. Handgun slaying of 34-year-old Max Nottingham (white). Motive: possibly deranged. Lowhone was hanged at Carmi IL on April 15, 1921. Source: *Iowa City (IA) Citizen*, 5/23/19 (4:4). *Freeport (IL) Journal-Standard*, 4/15/21 (10:3). Appeal: 292 IL 32–54. See also: 1920 U.S. Census (St. Clair Co., IL), which notes Lowhone as a prisoner, and 1910 U.S. Census (Breckinridge Co., KY), which notes the murdered man as "Mc. Nottingham."

Oscar McGavick (black, age abt. 22) and **Grover Cleveland Redding** (black, age 37). *Murder.* Their crimes were committed on 6/20/1920 in Cook County. Executed for the handgun slaying of 26-year-old Robert Lawson Rose (white), a sailor who had tried to stop them from desecrating the American flag. A second man named Joseph Hoyt (white, age 59) was slain in the same incident by means of a rifle volley that rioters had fired into his place of business. Motive: civil disorder and race riot. McGavick and Redding died on the Cook County gallows for these acts of hooliganism on June 24, 1921. Source: *Chicago Tribune*, 6/21/20 (1:8) & 6/22/20 (1:1). *Chicago Defender*, 6/26/20 (1:6), 7/3/20 (1:6) & 7/2/21 (2:4).

Antonio Lopez (white, age 19). *Murder.* The crime was committed on 1/15/1920 in Cook County. Accomplice in the handgun slaying of 47-year-old Antonio Varchetto (white). Motive: armed robbery. This young killer and reported member of the Cardinella gang was hanged by the neck until dead at Chicago on July 8, 1921. Source: *Chicago Tribune*, 7/8/21 (2:6). See: Joseph Costanzo (executed 4/15/21).

Harry Hollister Ward (white, age 23). *Murder.* The crime was committed on 10/23/1920 in Cook County. Executed for the handgun slaying of 35-year-old Frank Schwartz (white), who succumbed to his wound on 11/21/1920. Motive: attempted carjacking. Additionally sentenced to life imprisonment for fatally shooting Thomas Graney (white, age 60) in the same incident. Ward was further determined to have murdered Howard B. Rhodes (white, age 29) by the same means during a lovers' lane stickup at Evanston IL on 8/30/1920. He was hanged at Chicago on July 15, 1921. Source: *Chicago Tribune*, 7/16/21 (5:1). See also: 1920 U.S. Census (Cook Co., IL), which notes all three homicide victims. *Crime Detective*, 9/43. *Real Detective*, 4/32. *True* (magazine) 5/39.

Carl Otto Wanderer (white, age 24). *Murder.* The crime was committed on 6/21/1920 in Cook County. Uxoricide, etc. Executed for the handgun slaying of 22-year-old "John Doe" (white), a Skid Row vagabond whose true identity was never ascertained. Tried separately and sentenced to 25 years' imprisonment for the concomitant murder of pregnant 22-year-old Ruth Johnson Wanderer (white), his wife. The victims of this felony were shot thrice and two times respectively. Motive: desire for another woman, or so it was said. Disillusionment with the institution of marriage has also been cited as a factor. Further claims that Wanderer (a highly decorated World War I veteran) was a subliminal homosexual who wanted out of his wedded status are unproven. He had killed the nameless derelict in an effort to substitute his corpse for his own and thereby fake a scene of murder-suicide. He was hanged at Chicago on September 30, 1921. Source: *Janesville (WI) Daily Gazette*, 7/14/20 (11:3). *Chicago Tribune*, 10/1/21 (2:2). See also: 1920 U.S. Census (Chicago, IL), which notes Mr. & Mrs. Wanderer. *Official Detective*, 9/15/37. *Famous Detective Cases*, 12/35. *Front Page Detective*, 10/69. *Master Detective*, 12/49. *Crime Detective*, 9/51.

John Christmas (black, age 26). *Murder.* The crime was committed on 4/15/1921 in Champaign County. Uxoricide. Executed for the murder of 17-year-old Ada Christmas (black), she having been decapitated with a razor. This black-on-black butcher was hanged at Urbana on October 21, 1921. Source: *Decatur (IL) Daily Review*, 10/21/21 (1:7). *The Pointer* (Riverdale, IL), 10/28/21 (5:4).

Frank Ligregni (white, age 27). *Murder.* The crime was committed on 12/21/1920 in Cook County. Uxoricide. Handgun slaying of 23-year-old Genevieve Ligregni (white), she having been shot three times through the heart. Motive: marital estrangement. Her wrathful husband was hanged at Chicago on November 9, 1921. Source:

Chicago Tribune, 12/22/20 (1:7) & 11/10/21 (3:6). See also: 1921 Cook Co. death cert. no. 26208.

1922

Harvey Willard Church (white, age 23). *Murder.* The crime was committed on 9/8/1921 in Cook County. Executed for the deliberate killings of 24-year-old Carl Ausmus and 39-year-old Bernard Joseph Dougherty (whites), who had been handcuffed and battered to death with a baseball bat. Ausmus was then secretly buried. Dougherty's body was dumped in a river after being further mutilated. Motive: obsessive desire for a sporty new car. The victims in this case were automobile salesmen who had agreed to home delivery at the killer's request only to get murdered and robbed for their efforts. The guilty man was hanged at Chicago on March 3, 1922. Source: *Racine (WI) News Journal*, 9/10/21 (1:3). *New York Times*, 9/12/21 (1:5). *Chicago Tribune*, 3/4/22 (1:8). See also: 1920 U.S. Census (Chicago, IL), which notes Ausmus. Also: 1900 U.S. Census (Marquette Co., WI), which notes Church as a minor. See also: *1913 Harvard College Alumni Directory*, 228, which notes Dougherty and the correct spelling of his surname. *Master Detective*, 5/31. *Front Page Detective*, 2/46.

Myron Corbridge (white, age 20). *Murder.* The crime was committed on 6/15/1922 in Livingston County. Prison-guard killer. Executed for the murder of 38-year-old John Sullivan Jones (white), who was beaten about the head with a steel pipe. Motive: prison violence. The killer was hanged at Pontiac IL on December 15, 1922. Source: *Burlington (IA) Hawk-Eye*, 6/16/22 (1:6). *Edwardsville (IL) Intelligencer*, 12/15/22 (8:4). See also: 1920 U.S. Census (Livingston Co., IL), which notes Corbridge. Also: 1922 Livingston Co. death cert. no. 530186.

1923

Leroy Hollins (black, age 28) and **Ernest Williams** (black, age 23). *Murder.* Their crime was committed on 10/19/1922 in St. Clair County. Serial rapists and highwaymen. Executed for the handgun slaying of 21-year-old Alphonse de Hon (white). Motive: robbery of the male victim and sexual assault of his female companion. These predators were hanged at Belleville IL on February 21, 1923. Source: *Chillicothe (OH) Constitution*, 12/7/22 (1:3). *Cook County (IL) Herald*, 3/2/23 (3:7). See also: 1922 St. Clair Co. death cert. no. 3820577.

Casper Pastoni (white, age 31). *Murder.* The crime was committed on 7/29/1922 in Cook County. Child killer, etc. Handgun slayings of 32-year-old Elizabeth Witchell and 4-year-old Elizabeth Ann Witchell (whites), they being a mother and her daughter. Motive: because the elder victim had refused to be lured away from her husband. Pastoni was hanged at Chicago on June 15, 1923. Source: *Chicago Tribune*, 6/16/23 (7:2). See also: 1922 Cook Co. death cert. nos. 6020318 and 6020319.

1924

George Barber (black, age 23). *Murder.* The crime was committed on 11/26/1923 in Vermilion County. Handgun slaying of 59-year-old Edward Mourer (white). Motive: armed robbery. This killer was hanged at Danville

IL on April 11, 1924. Source: *Decatur (IL) Daily Review*, 11/28/23 (8:5) & 4/11/24 (1:4). See also: 1923 Vermilion Co. death cert. no. 2920548.

Lucius Dalton (black, age abt. 23) and **Henry Wilson** (black, age abt. 25). *Murder.* Their crime was committed on 1/7/1924 in Cook County. Police killers. Handgun slaying of 50-year-old Vincent Skiba (white). Motive: resisting arrest. They were hanged at Chicago on April 18, 1924. Source: *Chicago Tribune*, 1/8/24 (1:7), 1/9/24 (3:7) & 4/19/24 (6:6). See also: 1920 U.S. Census (Chicago, IL), which notes the slain officer. Also: 1924 Cook Co. death cert. no. 6011458.

Lester Kahl (white, age 24). *Murder.* The crime was committed on 9/25/1924 in Macoupin County. Uxoricide. Shotgun slaying of 21-year-old Margaret Sophia Slaughter Kahl (white, his bride of three weeks), whom he secretly buried in a cornfield. Motive: because she had chided him for having a roving eye. He was hanged at Carlinville on December 22, 1924. Source: *Edwardsville (IL) Intelligencer*, 12/1/24 (8:5) & 12/22/24 (1:4). *Daily Independent* (Murphysboro, IL), 12/22/24 (1:7). *Dynamic Detective*, 1/42. *Master Detective*, 10/46.

1925

Hess Connors (black, age 21). *Murder.* The crime was committed on 7/21/1924 in Pulaski County. Handgun slaying of 18-year-old Daisy Wilson (white). Motive: armed robbery. This killer was hanged at Mound City on January 16, 1925. Source: *Daily Independent* (Murphysboro, IL), 7/22/24 (1:6), 7/23/24 (1:1) & 1/16/25 (1:4). *Davenport (IA) Democrat*, 1/16/25 (1:4).

John Kammerer (white, age 37). *Murder.* The crime was committed on 6/27/1924 in DuPage County. Mass killer. Executed for the murders of 34-year-old Otto Eder and pregnant 34-year-old Frances Eder (whites, a married couple) together with their three young children, Roy Eder (age 11), Harvey Eder (age 6) and John Eder (age 3), they having all been clubbed to death. Motive: possibly deranged. The hangman made that question immaterial when he sent John Kammerer through the trap at Wheaton on February 13, 1925. Source: *Chicago Tribune*, 6/30/24 (1:7) & 2/14/25 (3:6). See also: 1920 U.S. Census (Chicago IL, Ward 13), which notes the Eders. *Official Detective*, 6/36.

John Stacey (white, age 34). *Murder.* The crime was committed on 11/25/1924 in Macon County. Handgun slaying of 53-year-old Hyman Rubenstein (white). Motive: armed robbery. This homicidal offender was hanged at Decatur IL on February 13, 1925. Source: *Decatur (IL) Daily Review*, 11/26/24 (1:7) & 2/13/25 (1:7). See also: 1920 U.S. Census (Joliet, IL), which notes Stacey as a prison inmate.

Lawrence Washington (black, age 32). *Murder.* The crime was committed on 9/14/1924 in Cook County. Handgun slaying of 42-year-old Nunzio Mascolino (white). Motive: armed robbery. He is confirmed to have also murdered a second man named William C. Fox (white, age 59) under similar circumstances on 9/27/1924. Washington legally paid the price of folly with a rope around his neck at Chicago on May 15, 1925. Source: *Chicago Tribune*, 9/15/24 (1:7), 10/7/24 (1:8) & 5/16/25 (4:1). See also: 1920 U.S. Census (Evanston, IL), which notes both of the murdered men, the former anglicized as "Nathaniel."

Willis Sams (black, age 29). *Murder.* The crime was committed on 8/24/1924 in Cook County. Police killer, etc. Executed for the handgun slaying of 44-year-old Cornelius Broderick (white), a Chicago policeman. Motive: evading arrest. Also convicted for the handgun slaying of 67-year-old Meyer Oppenheim (white, also of Chicago) in a separate incident on 8/7/1924. Sams dropped to his doom from the Cook County gallows on June 19, 1925. Source: *Chicago Tribune*, 6/20/25 (2:4). See also: 1910 U.S. Census (Chicago, IL), which notes Broderick and 1920 U.S. Census (Chicago, IL), which notes Oppenheim.

Frank Lanciano (white, age 29). *Murder.* The crime was committed on 3/27/1925 in Cook County. Handgun slaying of 32-year-old Rose Attila, alias "Rose Lanciano" (white), a woman who was posing as his wife. Motive: because she scolded him for coming home drunk. Lanciano was made to pay with his life for this on the Cook County gallows on October 16, 1925. Source: *Chicago Tribune*, 3/29/25 (2:1) & 10/17/25 (2:1).

1926

Campbell McCarthy (black, age 19). *Murder.* The crime was committed on 5/4/1925 in Cook County. Handgun slaying of 55-year-old Christian Getzen (white), who was shot five times. Motive: burglary. The hangman did his duty in this case at Chicago on January 29, 1926. Source: *Chicago Tribune*, 5/4/25 (1:3) & 1/30/26 (6:2). See also: 1925 Cook Co. death cert. no. 6013310.

Alva Grimmett (white, age 41). *Murder.* The crime was committed on 9/3/1925 in Morgan County. Handgun slaying of 50-year-old Robert William Steele (white), the victim having been shot in the back. Motive: armed robbery. Gallows-bound Grimmett met his end that way at Jacksonville IL on February 13, 1926. Source: *Jacksonville (IL) Daily Journal*, 9/4/25 (1:1) & 2/14/26 (1:1). See also: 1910 U.S. Census (Morgan Co., IL), which notes this killer.

Joseph Holmes (white, age abt. 25) and **Jack Wilson**, alias "Jack Woods" (white, age abt. 25). *Murder.* Their crime was committed on 7/29/1925 in Cook County. Handgun slaying of 52-year-old Frank Blair Rodkey (white). Motive: hotel robbery. Both men were hanged at Chicago on February 13, 1926. Source: *Lima (OH) News*, 7/30/25 (1:4). *Chicago Tribune*, 2/14/26 (10:1). See also: 1920 U.S. Census (Chicago IL, Ward 3), which notes Mr. Rodkey. See also: 1926 Cook Co. death cert. nos. 6004308 and 6004700. *Detective Tabloid*, 3/35.

Jose Ortiz (Latino, age 18). *Murder.* The crime was committed on 3/12/1925 in Peoria County. Handgun slaying of 17-year-old Emiliana Martinez (Latina), she having been shot three times. Motive: jealous suitor. The hangman ensured that there would be no further problems with this young killer by ending his life at Peoria on April 15, 1926. Source: *Decatur (IL) Daily Review*, 4/15/26 (1:2). Appeal: 320 IL 205–213.

Raymond Costello (white, age 21). *Murder.* The crime was committed on 7/10/1925 in Cook County. Strangulation of 16-year-old Madeline White (white). Motive: sexual assault. Costello found a permanent cure for his concupiscence at the end of the hangman's rope at Chicago on April 16, 1926. Source: *Stevens Point (WI) Daily Journal*, 7/10/25 (1:6). *Chicago Tribune*, 4/17/26 (16:1). *Actual Detective*, 3/23/38 & 7/43. *Famous Detective Cases*, 7/36. *Crime Detective*, 7/48. *Master Detective*, 12/47, *True Detective*, 1/33.

Emil Fricker (white, age 43). *Murder.* The crime was committed on 9/15/1924 in Madison County. Executed for orchestrating the murder of 23-year-old John Nungesser (white), the victim having been shot fourteen times with three different handguns. Motive: jealous obsession with a married woman. Fricker is additionally confirmed to have killed 30-year-old Robert Kehrli (white) of Clinton Co., IL on 5/10/1920 for the same reason, the decedent having been shot through the head with a handgun and made to look as though he had taken his own life. This two-time killer and coveter of other men's wives was hanged at Edwardsville IL on April 16, 1926. Source: *Decatur (IL) Daily Review*, 4/16/26 (1:8). See also: 1920 U.S. Census (Clinton Co., IL), which notes Fricker, and 1920 U.S. Census (Madison Co., IL), which notes the two murdered men. *Intimate Detective*, 11/40. *Dynamic Detective*, 12/37. *Headline Detective*, 9/39. *Crime Detective*, 7/50. *Master Detective*, 9/46.

Charles Hobbs (black, age 26). *Murder.* The crime was committed on 12/21/1925 in Cook County. Strangulation of 21-year-old Betty Barnett (black). Motive: larceny. Hobbs thought that Miss Barnett had a lot of money secreted about her, but he came away with less than a dollar. This money-hungry murderer was hanged at Chicago on April 16, 1926. Source: *Chicago Tribune*, 4/17/26 (16:1). See also: 1926 Cook Co. death cert. no. 6012506.

Richard Evans (white, age 19). *Murder.* The crime was committed on 3/27/1926 in Cook County. Police killer. Handgun slaying of 33-year-old Edward Finnegan (white). Motive: big attitude at having been stopped for a traffic violation. The gallows claimed this young hothead at Chicago on October 29, 1926. Source: *Chicago Tribune*, 3/28/26 (1:7) & 10/30/26 (2:1).

James Gricius (white, age 22) and **Thomas McWayne** (white, age 19). *Murder.* Their crime was committed on 7/12/1926 in Cook County. Both executed for the handgun killings of 25-year-old Frederick Hein and 23-year-old Marie Blang (whites). Motive: mugging. They were additionally condemned for the 7/12/1926 handgun slaying of 35-year-old Ludwig Rose (white) during a concomitant carjacking incident. These lawless young hoodlums were hanged at Chicago on December 31, 1926. Source: *Chicago Tribune*, 7/12/26 (1:7), 7/13/26 (1:8) & 1/1/27 (5:3).

1927

Joseph Peck Smith (white, age 50). *Murder.* The crime was committed on 11/2/1926 in Gallatin County. Uxoricide. Shotgun slaying of 49-year-old Orpha Smith (white), she having been blasted from behind as she sat in a rocking chair. Motive: insurance fraud. This wife-killer was hanged at Shawneetown on February 16, 1927. Source: *Decatur (IL) Daily Review*, 2/16/27 (1:6). See also: 1920 U.S. Census (Gallatin Co., IL), which notes both parties. *Actual Detective,* 4/40. *Crime Detective,* 4/47 & 4/62.

Oscar Quarles (black, age 21). *Murder.* The crime was committed on 4/2/1926 in Cook County. Handgun slaying of 39-year-old Morris Dushoff (white). Motive: armed robbery. The hangman added Quarles to his tally at Chicago on February 18, 1927. Source: *Chicago Tribune,* 4/3/26 (3:6) & 2/19/27 (7:3). *Chicago Defender,* 2/19/27 (1:8). See also: 1920 U.S. Census (Chicago, IL), which notes Mr. Dushoff.

John Walton Winn (white, age 37). *Murder.* The crime was committed on 12/29/1925 in Cook County. Executed for the killing of 63-year-old Albert Nusbaum (white), who was battered to death with a hammer; his body was dumped in a remote area. Motive: adultery and a female catalyst. Score another one for the Chicago hangman on April 15, 1927. Source: *Chicago Tribune,* 4/16/27 (6:3). *Intimate Detective,* 8/41. *Official Detective,* 12/35. *Master Detective,* 9/32.

Thomas Twine (black, age 35). *Murder.* The crime was committed on 11/11/1926 in Adams County. Executed for the murder of 22-year-old Lillian Jackson (black), she having been shot with a handgun and her head dashed in by a heavy gas pipe. Motive: lovers' quarrel. This black-on-black killer atoned for what he did by plunging through the gallows trap at Quincy IL on April 29, 1927. Source: *Quincy Herald-Whig,* 11/12/26 (16:1), 4/28/27 (20:4) & 4/29/27 (1:8).

Joseph Chesnas (white, age 21). *Murder.* The crime was committed on 8/8/1926 in Saline County. Handgun slaying of 68-year-old William A. Unsell (white). Motive: burglary prompted by a desire for personal revenge. This killer was hanged at Harrisburg IL on June 17, 1927. Source: *Decatur (IL) Evening Herald,* 6/17/27 (1:1). *Decatur (IL) Daily Review,* 6/17/27 (1:1). Appeal: 325 IL 361–370. See also: 1920 U.S. Census (Saline Co., IL), which notes the victim.

Elin Lyons (Latino, age 27). *Murder.* The crime was committed on 12/15/1926 in Cook County. Police killer. Handgun slaying of 38-year-old Julian Bonfield (white). Motive: armed robbery gone awry. This offender was hanged at Chicago on June 24, 1927. Source: *Chicago Tribune,* 12/16/26 (3:1), 12/17/26 (2:4) & 6/24/27 (1:5).

Charles Duschowski (white, age 28) and **Walter Stalesky** (white, age 28). *Murder.* Their crime was committed on 5/5/1926 in Will County. Prison-guard killers. Executed for the murder of 49-year-old Peter N. Klein (white), the deputy warden of Statesville Prison. He was slashed to death with contraband knives and specially sharpened scissors. Motive: jailbreak. Duschowski was also a Recidivist killer then serving a 25-year sentence for his part in the slaying of Chicago police sergeant Terrence Lyons (white, age 32) on 5/10/1922. He was also the prime suspect in the fatal shooting of a second Chicago police officer named Thomas J. Clark (white, age 30) on that same day. Both policemen were slain with handguns in separate incidents when they approached suspicious-looking automobiles with the intention of questioning their occupants. These condemned jailbirds were hanged at Joliet on July 15, 1927. Source: *Chicago Tribune,* 5/10/22 (1:8), 5/6/26 (1:8), 5/7/26 (1:8) & 7/16/27 (5:1). *Joliet Evening Herald-News,* 5/6/26 (1:1) &

5/7/26 (1:1). Appeal: 326 IL 145–166. *Daring Detective*, 9/40. *Front Page Detective*, 3/55.

Roberto Torrez (Latino, age 26). *Murder.* The crime was committed on 5/5/1926 in Will County. Prison-guard killer. Accomplice in the murder of 49-year-old Peter N. Klein (white), the deputy warden of Statesville Prison. Motive: jailbreak. He is confirmed to have also killed (by means of a handgun) Chicago police officer Leo A. Grant (white, age 30) on 3/12/1927 while resisting capture following another jailbreak. Recidivist killer. Torrez was already serving a life sentence for an earlier homicide when he murdered the Deputy Warden. The victim in that case was a Chicago Elevated Lines ticket agent named Charles H. Johnson (white, age 60), shot dead during a robbery of his transit booth on 11–3-1923. Roberto Torrez shared the same fate as the other assassins of Deputy Warden Klein at Joliet on July 15, 1927. Source: *Chicago Tribune*, 5/10/22 (1:8), 5/6/26 (1:8), 5/7/26 (1:8) & 7/16/27 (5:1). *Joliet Evening Herald-News*, 5/6/26 (1:1) & 5/7/26 (1:1). Appeal: 326 IL 145–166. *Daring Detective*, 9/40. *Front Page Detective*, 3/55. *Master Detective*, 10/59.

Rado Millich (white, age 35). *Murder.* The crime was committed on 10/25/1926 in Williamson County. Rifle slaying of 26-year-old Ward "Casey" Jones (white), the victim having been shot four times. Motive: gangland quarrel. The public hangman dispatched Rado Millich at Marion IL on October 21, 1927. Source: *Decatur (IL) Daily Review*, 10/27/26 (1:1) & 10/21/27 (1:7). See also: 1926 Gallatin Co. death cert. no. 300098. *Master Detective*, 11/42.

William Brown (black, age 44). *Murder.* The crime was committed on 12/17/1926 in Massac County. Ax murders of 38-year-old Sadie Harris and 80-year-old Georgia Ann Caldwell (black females). Motive: drunken temper tantrum. This double killer was stone sober when he plunged through the gallows trap at Metropolis IL on December 16, 1927. Source: *Republican-Herald* (Metropolis, IL), 12/23/26 (1:1), 12/14/27 (1:7) & 12/21/27 (1:2).

James Hayes (white, age 28). *Murder.* The crime was committed on 5/25/1927 in Sangamon County. Ax murder of 43-year-old Sarah "Dollie" Flatt (white). Motive: anger at having lost his job for a reason that was his own fault. He was hanged at Springfield IL on December 16, 1927. Source: *News-Palladium* (Benton Harbor, MI), 12/16/27 (1:7). *Daily Independent* (Murphysboro, IL), 12/16/27 (1:4). See also: 1910 U.S. Census (Sangamon Co., IL), which notes the murdered woman.

Herschel Andrews (black, age 34). *Murder.* The crime was committed on 12/25/1926 in Champaign County. Fatal stabbing of 65-year-old Thomas Tate (black). Motive: restaurant brawl. This black-on-black killer was hanged at Urbana on December 23, 1927. Source: *Decatur (IL) Daily Review*, 4/22/27 (1:3), 10/22/27 (7:7) & 12/23/27 (2:3).

1928

Charles Birger (white, age 46). *Murder.* The crime for which he was executed was committed on 12/12/1926 in Franklin County. Hanged for orchestrating the assassination of 36-year-old Joseph "Joe" Adams (white), the Mayor of West

City, IL. Motive: gangland killing. Birger was additionally determined to have been responsible for a bare minimum of fifteen other homicides, some by his own hands and some by his orders: Cecil Knighton (white, age 17) in Williamson Co., IL (by means of a handgun), on 11/14/1923. Motive: gangland discipline. James Elvin Stone (white, age abt. 20) in Williamson Co., IL on 12–1-1925 by means of a handgun, his body left propped up against a tree with a cigar in its mouth. Motive: rivalry for a female. Harry Walker (white, age 27) and Everett Smith (white, age 20) in Williamson Co., IL on 8/23/1926, they having been simultaneously gunned down from behind (with automatic rifles) in a drive-by shooting. Motive: gangland killing. William C. Holland (white, age 20) in Williamson Co., IL on 9/12/1926 by means of a Thompson submachine gun. Motive: gangland killing. Lyle Worsham (white, age 33) in Williamson Co., IL on 9/17/1926, the victim having been machine gunned and his dismembered torso found in the ruins of a barn that had been torched. Motive: gangland killing. William B. McQuay (white, age 23) in Williamson Co., IL on 10/26/1926, he having been machine gunned in his automobile. Motive: gangland killing. John Milroy (white, age abt. 20) and Jeff Stone (white, age 50) in Williamson Co., IL on 11-6-1926, they having been machine gunned to death. Motive: gangland violence. Steven George and Mary George (whites, a married couple, ages not recorded) along with James "Jimmy" Sims (white, age abt. 18) and Elmo Thompson (white, age 19) in Saline Co., IL on 1–8-1927, they having been killed in a house bombing contrived to put blame on Birger's enemies. Also: Illinois state policeman Lory L. Price (white, age 35) and his wife Ethel Prudence Price (white, age abt. 32) in Washington Co., IL on 1/17/1927. The man was shot three times with a handgun and raked further by machine gun fire as he lay on the ground, a total of eighteen bullets being found in his body. The woman was shot four times with a handgun, and her body was dumped in an old mineshaft, where it was found on 6/13/1927. Motive: gangland retribution. Charles Birger—the man responsible for all these crimes and undoubtedly many more—was hanged at Benton IL on April 19, 1928. Source: Williamson Co. death cert. nos. 1000547 (Knighton), 1000490 (Stone), 1000339 (Walker), 1000340 (Smith), 1000367 (Holland), 1000410 (McQuay), 1000453 (Jeff Stone) and 1000189 (Ethel Price). Also: Franklin Co., IL death cert. no. 280640 (Joe Adams) plus Washington Co., IL death cert. no. 950017 (Lory Price). See also: 1910 U.S. Census (Franklin Co., IL), which notes Worsham and Joe Adams. Also: 1920 U.S. Census (Williamson Co., IL), which notes Jeff Stone, Holland, Smith and McQuay. *Daily Independent* (Murphysboro, IL), 10/5/26 (1:2) & 12/15/27 (2:4). *Master Detective*, 11/42 & 3/55. *Front Page Detective*, 7/52, 8/52 & 9/52.

Charles Shader (white, age 23). *Murder.* The crime was committed on 5/5/1926 in Will County. Patricide, sororicide, police killer, and prison-guard killer. Recidivist killer. Executed for participating in the murder of 49-year-old Peter N. Klein (white), the deputy warden of Statesville Prison, who was fatally slashed with knives and scissors. Motive: jailbreak. Shader had committed at least three previous homicides as follows: that of his father William Shader (white, age 49) at Chicago on 11/11/1921 by means of a handgun. Motive: domestic violence. A verdict of justifiable homicide was rendered in that case based on a purported claim that the victim was beating Shader's mother at the time. Also the 3/13/1922 "honor killing" of his sister Margaret Shader (white, age 16) because she had had consensual sex with a black male. A verdict of suicide was returned, however, because the victim was found with the instrument of her demise (a handgun) clutched in her hand. Third, the 1/26/1922 handgun slaying of Chicago police officer Harry Joseph Busse (white, age 29) during the course of a mugging, the victim then being in civilian dress and off duty. Shader was serving a life sentence for this last offense when he attacked and killed Deputy Warden Klein. Allegations of additional killings by Shader are too vague to be accredited. He was hanged at Joliet on October 10, 1928. Source: *Edwardsville (IL) Intelligencer*, 10/10/28 (1:6). See Chas. Duschowski (executed 7/15/27). See also: 1910 U.S. Census (Chicago, IL), which notes Busse, and 1920 U.S. Census (Chicago, IL), which notes Shader's family. See also: 1921 Cook Co. death cert. no. 6026441 (W. Shader) and 1922 Cook Co. death cert. nos. 6004228 (Busse) and 6007457 (M. Shader).

Dominic Bressette (Native American, age 20), **John Brown** (black, age 31) and **Claude Clark** (black, age 47). *Murder.* Their crime was committed on 5/16/1928 in Lake County. All three executed for the handgun slaying of 36-year-old William Beck, Jr. (white). Motive: home invasion. Bressette was a Chippewa tribesman, to be precise. An electric chair put an end to the lives of this trio at Joliet Prison on December 15, 1928. Source: *Decatur (IL) Daily Review*, 5/17/28 (1:3) & 5/18/28 (1:3). *Edwardsville (IL) Intelligencer*, 12/15/28 (1:1).

1929

Charles Walz (white, age 17) and **Anthony Grecco** (white, age 18). *Murder.* Their crime was committed on 4/27/1928 at Chicago. Police killers. Both executed for the handgun slaying of 32-year-old Arthur Esau (white), who was shot three times. Motive: armed robbery gone awry. These teenage assassins of a law enforcement officer were put to death by electrocution at the Cook County Jail on February 20, 1929. Source: *Decatur (IL) Sunday Review*, 4/29/28 (1:3). *Edwardsville (IL) Intelligencer*, 2/20/29 (1:5). See also: 1910 U.S. Census (Chicago, IL), which notes Esau. *Daring Detective*, 10/39. *Real Detective*, 7/47.

Napoleon Glover (black, age 18) and **Morgan Swan** (black, age 22). *Murder.* Their crime was committed on 11/11/1928 at Chicago. Both executed for the handgun slaying of 48-year-old Charles O. Metlock (black). Motive: armed robbery. They had also shot dead another black man named Peter Lucas (age 45) three days later because he had scolded them for profaning the Sabbath. The Cook County electric chair ensured that they went no further on June 21, 1929. Source: *Chicago Defender*, 11/17/28 (1:8) & 6/22/29 (1:2). See also: 1928 Cook Co. death cert. nos. 6033770 (Metlock) and 6034977 (Lucas).

1930

Aaron Woodward (black, age 35). *Murder*. The crime was committed on 7/30/1928 at Chicago. Police killer, etc.

Executed for the handgun slaying of 38-year-old Jeremiah E. O'Connell (white). Motive: mugging gone awry. Woodward also bore responsibility for the concomitant death of a second man named George Petroloza (black, age 28), who was slain in the same incident when the killer (Woodward) used him as a human shield. The Cook County electric chair put a permanent end to Woodward's depredations on April 11, 1930. Source: *Chicago Defender*, 8/4/28 (2:3) & 4/12/30 (1:8).

August Vogel (white, age 20). *Murder.* The crime was committed on 10/13/1929 at Chicago. Handgun slaying of 26-year-old Lyle Perrenoud (white). Motive: road rage. The Cook County electric chair put an end to Vogel's temper-control problem as well as his life on May 9, 1930. Source: *Waterloo (IA) Evening Courier*, 10/17/29 (2:6) & 10/28/29 (2:2). *Southtown Economist* (Chicago, IL), 5/13/30 (4:1). See also: 1920 U.S. Census (Sioux Falls, SD), which notes Perrenoud.

Lafon Fisher (black, age 28) and **Leonard Shadlow** (black, age 23). *Murder.* Their crime was committed on 1/18/1929 at Chicago. Handgun slaying of 75-year-old Martin B. French (black). Motive: bank robbery. The end result was two more for the Cook County electric chair on October 3, 1930. Source: *Decatur (IL) Evening Herald*, 1/20/29 (1:4) & 10/3/30 (13:2). *Chicago Defender*, 1/26/29 (1:8) & 10/4/30 (1:5). See also: 1930 Cook Co. death cert. no. 6026614. Also: 1920 U.S. Census (Joliet, IL), which notes Fisher, and 1920 U.S. Census (Chicago, IL), which notes French, a retired policeman who was moonlighting as a bank guard.

Leon Brown (black, age 27). *Murder.* The crime was committed on 1/18/1929 at Chicago. Accomplice in the handgun slaying of 75-year-old Martin B. French (black), an elderly bank guard. Motive: armed robbery. Brown met the same fate as his two teammates on November 28, 1930. Source: *Alton (IL) Evening Telegraph*, 11/28/30 (1:7). See also: Lafon Fisher and Leonard Shadlow (executed 10/3/30).

William Lenhardt (white, age 21). *Murder.* The crime was committed on 6/20/1929 at Chicago. Handgun slaying of 52-year-old Miltos Valasopulos (white). Motive: armed robbery. The Cook County electric chair added this young man to its record on December 12, 1930. Source: *Decatur (IL) Daily Review*, 12/12/30 (1:5). See also: 1929 Cook Co. death cert. no. 6019430, which notes the homicide victim in this case.

1931

John E. Preston (white, age 32). *Murder.* The crime was committed on 10/12/1929 in DuPage County. Strangulation of 26-year-old Agnes Johnson (white). Motive: sexual assault. This pervert was executed at Joliet Prison on October 9, 1931. Source: *Decatur (IL) Evening Herald*, 10/15/29 (1:5). *Edwardsville (IL) Intelligencer*, 10/9/31 (1:2). *Crime Detective*, 8/49. *Master Detective*, 10/31 & 9/54.

Frank Jordan (white, age 29). *Murder.* The crime was committed on 4/30/1931 at Chicago. Police killer. Handgun slayings of 43-year-old Anthony L. Ruthy and 38-year-old Patrick Durkin (whites). Motive: evading arrest. Jordan was executed at the Cook County Jail on October 16, 1931. Source: *Decatur (IL) Daily Review*,

5/1/31 (1:6). *Wisconsin Rapids Daily Tribune,* 5/1/31 (1:8). *Daily Independent* (Murphysboro, IL), 10/16/31 (1:3). *Official Detective,* 8/41.

Charles Rocco (white, age 23) and **John Popescue** (white, age 23). *Murder.* Their crime was committed on 10/28/1930 at Chicago. Both executed for the fatal stabbing of 56-year-old Courtney Roy Merrill (white). Motive: mugging. These offenders had also murdered another person earlier that same evening at East Chicago, IN. Name: John Schweiger (white, age 45). Murder weapon: handgun. Motive: attempted carjacking. Rocco and Popescue were executed at the Cook County Jail on October 16, 1931. Source: *Decatur (IL) Evening Herald,* 10/31/30 (1:2). *Daily Independent* (Murphysboro, IL), 10/16/31 (1:3). *Daring Detective,* 8/39. *Master Detective,* 7/44.

Richard Sullivan (white, age 34). *Murder.* The crime was committed on 6/16/1930 at Chicago. Handgun slaying of 35-year-old Christo Patras. Motive: armed robbery. The killer paid with his life for this at the Cook County Jail on October 16, 1931. Source: *Daily Independent* (Murphysboro, IL), 10/16/31 (1:3). See also: 1930 U.S. Census (Chicago, IL), which notes Patras. See also: 1930 Cook Co. death cert. no. 6017477.

Merley James Johnson (white, age 25). *Murder.* The crime was committed on 5/20/1931 in Coles County. Baby killer, etc. Executed for the murders of 38-year-old Carrie Klanke Bowers and her two children, Joseph Bowers, Jr. (age 6) and Delmar Bowers (age 19, mo.). The woman was shot through the head with a handgun. Her little ones were shot as well but also had their heads smashed in with a tire jack, and ropes were tightly knotted around their necks. Motive: disillusioned lover gone loco. Johnson was put to death for this atrocity at the Menard Correctional Facility on October 20, 1931. Source: *Decatur (IL) Daily Review,* 5/20/31 (1:1), 5/21/31 (1:1) & 5/23/31 (1:4). *Edwardsville (IL) Intelligencer,* 10/20/31 (2:7).

Willie Green (black, age 30). *Murder.* The crime was committed on 1/31/1931 in St. Clair County. Handgun slaying of 38-year-old Max Newmark (white). Motive: armed robbery. An electric chair evened this matter with Willie Green at the Menard Correctional Facility on December 11, 1931. Source: *East St. Louis (IL) Daily Journal,* 2/1/31 (1:8) & 12/11/31 (1:1).

James Jackson, alias "Fat Sam" (black, age 32). *Murder.* The crime was committed on 4/5/1931 in St. Clair County. Uxoricide. Shotgun slaying of 24-year-old Albertha Jackson (black). Motive: marital estrangement. The wrathful husband was executed at Menard on December 11, 1931. Source: *East St. Louis (IL) Daily Journal,* 4/6/31 (1:1) & 12/11/31 (1:1). See also: 1930 U.S. Census (East St. Louis, IL), which notes both parties.

Hazel Johnson (black male, age 23). *Murder.* The crime was committed on 1/23/1931 in Macon County. Police killer. Handgun slaying of 38-year-old William D. Keller (white), a railroad policeman. Motive: resisting arrest. This miscreant paid the death penalty at Menard on December 11, 1931. Source: *Decatur (IL) Evening Herald,* 1/24/31 (1:7). *Carbondale (IL) Free Press,* 12/11/31 (1:7).

Henry Pannier (white, age 57). *Murder.* The crime was committed on

7/24/1931 in Randolph County. Shotgun slayings of 42-year-old Herman Schuline and 39-year-old Lillian Schuline (whites), a married couple. Motive: landlord-tenant dispute. Pannier paid with his life for this at the Menard Correctional Facility on December 11, 1931. Source: *Daily Independent* (Murphysboro, IL), 7/25/31 (1:3). *Carbondale (IL) Free Press*, 12/11/31 (1:7). See also: 1920 U.S. Census (Randolph Co., IL), which notes Mr. & Mrs. Schuline.

1932

Frank Bell (white, age 29). *Murder.* The crime was committed on 6/16/1930 at Chicago. Accomplice in the handgun slaying of 35-year-old Christo Patras. Motive: armed robbery. Bell suffered death for this in the Cook County electric chair on January 8, 1932. Source: *Wisconsin State Journal* (Madison, WI), 1/8/32 (6:1). See also: Richard Sullivan (executed 10/16/31).

Ben Norsingle (black, age 19) and **John Reed** (black, age 26). *Murder.* Their crime was committed on 8/3/1931 at Chicago. Handgun slaying of 37-year-old John Martin (white). Motive: armed robbery. The Cook County electric chair precluded any future criminal forays by this pair on January 15, 1932. Source: *Stevens Point (WI) Daily Journal*, 8/4/31 (8:8). *Chicago Defender*, 11/14/31 (7:1) & 1/16/32 (1:8).

Elmer Gray (white, age 41). *Murder.* The crime was committed on 12/28/1931 in Wayne County. Handgun slaying of 59-year-old Angus C. Moats (white). Motive: home invasion. Gray paid the forfeit of his life at the Menard Correctional Facility on August 27, 1932. Source: *Edwardsville (IL) Intelligencer*, 8/27/32 (5:7). See also: 1930 U.S. Census (Wayne Co., IL), which notes Mr. Moats. *Dynamic Detective*, 7/37.

James Smith (black, age 21). *Murder.* The crime was committed on 11/26/1931 in St. Clair County. Handgun slaying of 44-year-old Taras "Tom" Bogosian (white). Motive: armed robbery. Sentence of death was carried out on the person of James Smith at the Menard Correctional Facility on September 23, 1932. Source: *East St. Louis (IL) Daily Journal*, 11/27/31 (1:1) & 9/23/32 (1:1). See also: 1920 U.S. Census (East St. Louis, IL), which notes Mr. Bogosian.

1933

Morris Cohen (white, age 38). *Murder.* The crime was committed on 8/14/1933 at Chicago. Police killer. Handgun slaying of 36-year-old Joseph P. Hastings (white). Motive: armed robbery gone awry. The Cook County electric chair closed the case of *State vs. Morris Cohen* on October 13, 1933. Source: *Alton (IL) Evening Telegraph*, 8/15/33 (2:7) & 10/13/33 (10:1). See also: 1933 Cook Co. death cert. no. 6021456.

Ross King (white, age 29). *Murder.* The crime was committed on 7/8/1933 at Chicago. Police killer. Handgun slaying of 38-year-old Harry Redlich (white), the slain man having been shot three times in the back. Motive: armed robbery gone awry. The Cook County electric chair rid society of Ross King on October 16, 1933. Source: *Daily Globe* (Ironwood, MI), 7/8/33 (1:1) & 7/10/33 (5:4). *Chicago Daily Tribune*, 8/4/33 (4:3). *Sheboygan (WI) Press*, 10/16/33 (2:5).

John Allen (white, age 26) and **Harry Shelby** (white, age 46). *Murder.* Their crime was committed on 8/29/1933 in Jasper County. Both executed for the indescribable torture killing of 82-year-old Mary Schrader (white), who was sexually violated and otherwise mistreated for the space of five hours in an attempt to make her reveal the hiding place of her valuables. The particular details of what she endured are unprintable. Motive: home invasion. The sadistic killers of this defenseless old woman were put to death at Menard on December 22, 1933. Source: *Edwardsville (IL) Intelligencer*, 8/31/33 (2:4) & 12/22/33 (10:5).

Martin D. Gray (black, age 24). *Murder.* The crime was committed on 6/12/1933 in Marion County. Fatal stabbing of 50-year-old Susie Gregory (black). Motive: monetary dispute. This black-on-black killer was executed at the Menard Correctional Facility on December 22, 1933. Source: *Edwardsville (IL) Intelligencer*, 12/22/33 (10:5). See also: 1930 U.S. Census (Marion Co., IL), which notes Susie Gregory. See also: 1933 Marion Co. death cert. no. 2610077.

1934

George Dale (white, age 28). *Murder.* The crime was committed on 8/4/1933 at Chicago. Handgun slaying of 72-year-old Gustav Hoeh (white). Motive: armed robbery. Dale died in the Cook County electric chair on April 20, 1934. Source: *Chicago Daily Tribune*, 8/4/33 (3:1). *Wisconsin Rapids Daily Tribune*, 4/20/34 (2:5). See also: 1930 U.S. Census (Chicago Ward 27), which notes Mr. Hoeh. *Front Page Detective*, 11/47. *Detective Tabloid*, 2/35. *Master Detective*, 3/35. *Crime Detective*, 1/58. *Real Detective*, 11/62.

Joseph Francis (black, age 34). *Murder.* The crime was committed on 8/2/1933 at Chicago. Handgun slaying of 28-year-old Joseph Hartel (white). Motive: attempted robbery. The Cook County electric chair performed its designated function in this case on April 20, 1934. Source: *Chicago Daily Tribune*, 8/3/33 (15:4). *Wisconsin Rapids Daily Tribune*, 4/20/34 (2:5). See also: 1930 U.S. Census (Chicago, IL), which notes Mr. Hartel. See also: 1933 Cook Co. death cert. no. 6021054.

John Scheck (white, age 21). *Murder.* The crime was committed on 7/24/1933 at Chicago. Police killer, etc. Executed for the handgun slaying of 32-year-old John G. Sevic (white). Motive: attempt to escape from custody. Scheck was awaiting trial for an earlier murder when he made use of a smuggled pistol in the Sevic slaying. He had participated in a bank robbery at Niles Center IL on 4–7-1933 during which a cashier named Harry J. Mueller (white, age 35) was killed by a blast from a sawed-off shotgun. Identified as the assassin in that case, Scheck later tried to shoot his way out of the Chicago Criminal Courts Building and killed Officer Sevic in the process. He was electrocuted pursuant to law at the Cook County Jail on April 20, 1934. Source: *Wisconsin Rapids Daily Tribune*, 4/20/34 (2:5). See also: 1930 U.S. Census (Niles, IL), which notes Mueller. *Master Detective*, 9/45.

Warren Little (white, age 22). *Murder.* The crime was committed on 9/30/1933 in Hamilton County. Handgun slaying of 33-year-old Denver E. Carlton (white), the victim having been shot in the back. Motive: dispute over a petty debt. Carlton was a barber by trade. Little owed him fifty cents for haircuts done on credit, but murdered the barber rather than pay him that small amount. This niggardly act earned Little a seat in the electric chair at Menard on June 25, 1934. Source: *Alton (IL) Evening Telegraph*, 10/2/33 (1:8). *Hammond (IN) Times*, 6/26/34 (1:6). See also: 1930 U.S. Census (Hamilton Co., IL), which notes Mr. Carlton.

Alonzo McNeil (black, age 29) and **George Walker** (black, age 20). *Murder.* Their crime was committed on 4/13/1934 at Chicago. Police killers. Both executed for the handgun slaying of 46-year-old John R. Officer (white). Motive: armed robbery gone awry. The Cook County electric chair did double service in this case on October 12, 1934. Source: *Vidette-Messenger* (Valparaiso, IN), 10/12/34 (1:4). See also: 1920 U.S. Census (Chicago, Ward 2), which notes Officer. See also: 1934 Cook Co. death cert. no. 6015192.

Armando Boulan (Latino, age 39) and **Walter Dittman** (white, age 29). *Murder.* Their crime was committed on 9/1/1934 at Chicago. Police killers. Both executed for the handgun slaying of 30-year-old Earl Milton Jensen (white). Motive: traffic stop turned tragic. Again the Cook County electric chair did double duty when it ended the lives of these miscreants on December 15, 1934. Source: *Chicago Sunday Tribune*, 9/2/34 (1:5). *Chicago Daily Tribune*, 12/15/34 (1:7).

1935

Chester Novak (white, age 29). *Murder.* The crime was committed on 7/1/1934 at Chicago. Handgun slaying of 49-year-old Henry Mendelbaum (white). Motive: mugging. Novak paid with his life for this killing of an unarmed citizen at the Cook County Jail on March 21, 1935. Source: *Chicago Daily Tribune*, 7/2/34 (15:7). *Ironwood (MI) Daily Globe*, 3/21/35 (8:4). See also: 1920 U.S. Census (Chicago, Ward 27), which notes Mr. Mendelbaum.

Fred Blink (white, age 42). *Murder.* The crime was committed on 9/4/1934 in Whiteside County. Mass killer. Executed for the shotgun slayings of 62-year-old John Hamilton, 82-year-old Willoughby "Webb" Collier, 39-year-old Irene Corrick, 62-year-old Henry Menzie and 66-year-old Jennie Walters (whites). Motive: because he felt himself ill used. Blink was executed for this massacre at Joliet Prison on April 23, 1935. Source: *Thomson (IL) Review*, 9/6/34 (1:7). *Alton (IL) Evening Telegraph*, 4/23/35 (1:8). See also: 1930 U.S. Census (Whiteside Co., IL), which notes Blink and Hamilton. See also: 1934 Whiteside Co. death cert. nos. 980160 (Corrick), 980159 (Walters) and 980156 (Menzie).

Thomas J. Lehne (white, age 43). *Murder.* The crime was committed on 1/24/1934 in Madison County. Handgun slaying of 47-year-old Charles Puhse (white), the victim having been murdered in his bed. Motive: adultery. This midnight assassin was executed at the Menard Correctional Facility on April 23, 1935. Source: *Edwardsville (IL) Intelligencer*, 2/5/34 (1:4). *Alton (IL) Evening Telegraph*, 4/23/35 (1:8). See also: 1930 U.S. Census (Madison Co., IL), which notes the murdered man. *Actual Detective*, 7/40. *Master Detective*, 9/35.

Frederick Gerner (white, age 27), **John Hauff** (white, age 32) and

Arthur Thielen (white, age 42). *Murder.* Their crime was committed on 1/16/1935 in LaSalle County. Police killers, etc. All three executed for the handgun slaying of 46-year-old Josiah Charles Bundy (white). Motive: bank robbery. Gerner and his accomplices also killed two other men in a pistol battle that same day: Glen T. Axline (white, age 33) and Charles F. Seipp (white, age 59), they respectively being the sheriff of Marshall Co., IL and the town supervisor of Richland, IL. Motive: resisting arrest. The members of this death-dealing trio were themselves put to death (albeit legally) at Joliet Prison on May 10, 1935. Source: *Carbondale (IL) Free Press*, 1/16/35 (1:7) & 5/10/35 (1:7). See also: 1930 U.S. Census (LaSalle Co., IL, and Marshall Co., IL), which note the homicide victims.

Edward Balling (white, age 19). **Van Buren Dedmon** (white, age 25) and **John Krul** (white, age 21). *Murder.* Their crime was committed on 2/22/1935 in St. Clair County. Handgun slaying of 66-year-old William C. Moss (white). Motive: mugging. All three were held equally guilty by law because the two who did not shoot had made no effort to restrain the one who did. They were executed at the Menard Correctional Facility on July 9, 1935. Source: *Alton (IL) Evening Telegraph*, 7/9/35 (2:8).

Gerald Thompson (white, age 25). *Murder.* The crime was committed on 6/17/1935 in Peoria County. Serial rapist and pervert extraordinaire. Executed for the fatal beating and gross defilement of 19-year-old Mildred Hallmark (white). Motive: sexual assault. A more detailed description of what Thompson did would classify this book as pornography. He was executed at Joliet Prison on October 15, 1935. Source: *Alton (IL) Evening Telegraph*, 10/15/35 (12:1). *Daring Detective*, 2/36. *Famous Detective Cases*, 10/35. *Official Detective*, 10/35, 11/35 & 12/35. *Master Detective*, 10/42, 6/54, 7/68 & 3/77. *Real Detective*, 10/35 & 1/40.

1936

Andrew Bogacki (white, age 26) and **Frank Korczykowski** (white, age 27). *Murder.* Their crime was committed on 5/29/1936 at Chicago. Police killers. Both executed for the rifle slaying of 33-year-old Jerome M. McCauley (white). Motive: deadly pursuit. The Cook County electric chair ended the lives of these young men on October 21, 1936. Source: *Daily Independent* (Murphysboro, IL), 10/21/36 (1:2). *Daring Detective*, 4/37. *Front Page Detective*, 2/37. *Official Detective*, 3/50.

1937

Allen Mitchell (black, age 30). *Murder.* The crime was committed on 7/26/1935 in St. Clair County. Executed for the murder of 50-year-old Samuel Simpson (black), who was first shot with a handgun and then fatally pistol-whipped. Motive: insurance fraud. The killer paid with his own life for this at the Menard Correctional Facility on February 26, 1937. Source: *Freeport (IL) Standard-Journal*, 2/26/37 (2:1). *Edwardsville (IL) Intelligencer*, 2/26/37 (2:2). See also: 1935 St. Clair Co. death cert. no. 607.

Rufo Swain (black, age 27). *Murder.* The crime was committed on 8/16/1936 at Chicago. Executed for the murder of 24-year-old Mary Louise Trammell (white), she having been battered to death with a pewter water pitcher. Motive: sexual assault. The Cook County electric chair made short work of Rufo Swain on February 26, 1937. Source: *Carbondale (IL) Free Press*, 8/20/36 (1:1). *Freeport (IL) Standard-Journal*, 2/26/37 (2:1). *Front Page Detective*, 4/37. *Master Detective*, 6/37.

Joseph Rappaport (white, age 29). *Murder.* The crime was committed on 10/8/1935 in Cook County. Handgun slaying of 34-year-old Max Dent (white), who was chased down on a public sidewalk, shot multiple times and then finished off execution-style. Motive: gangland killing. The hit man met his own doom in the Cook County electric chair on March 2, 1937. Source: *Vidette-Messenger* (Valparaiso, IN), 10/11/35 (4:7). *Freeport (IL) Standard-Journal*, 3/2/37 (5:1). *Official Detective*, 1/45. *Front Page Detective*, 8/37 & 9/44. *Crime Detective*, 10/38.

Stanley Murawski (white, age 37) and **Frank Whyte** (white, age 47). *Murder.* Their crime was committed on 11–8-1936 at Chicago. Police killers. Handgun slaying of 32-year-old Michael Toth (white). Motive: resistance to being searched for concealed weapons, they feeling that they were being unduly violated. The fact that both had long criminal records counted heavily against them. Each took his final seat in the Cook County electric chair on April 16, 1937. Source: *Southtown Economist* (Chicago, IL), 12/20/36 (1:8). *Alton (IL) Evening Telegraph*, 4/16/37 (1:7). See also: 1936 Cook Co. death cert. no. 6032088.

Joseph Schuster (white, age 30). *Murder.* The crime was committed on 1/14/1937 at Chicago. Police killer. Handgun slaying of 38-year-old Arthur J. Sullivan (white). Motive: resisting arrest. The Cook County electric chair exacted payment for Schuster's transgression on April 16, 1937. Source: *Ironwood (MI) Daily Globe*, 1/15/37 (8:5). *Alton (IL) Evening Telegraph*, 4/16/37 (1:7). See also: 1930 U.S. Census (Pontiac, IL), which notes Schuster as a prison inmate.

Peter Chrisoulas (white, age 38). *Murder.* The crime was committed on 3/14/1936 in Cook County. Handgun slaying of 36-year-old Irving Fehlberg (white). Motive: big attitude. A theater manager (Fehlberg) had asked Chrisoulas if there was any truth in a complaint about his annoying a female moviegoer. The suspect's reply was to pull out a handgun and shoot the theater manager dead on the spot. The Cook County electric chair permanently cured Chrisoulas of his temper control problem on October 15, 1937. Source: *Oshkosh (WI) Northwestern*, 10/15/37 (16:1). See also: 1936 Cook Co. death cert. no. 6008170.

1938

Marie Kappen Porter (white, age 37) and **Angelo Ralph Giancola** (white, age 21). *Murder.* Their crime was committed on 7/3/1937 in St. Clair County. Fratricide in the woman's case. These unlikely lovers were respectively the catalyst and the triggerman in the handgun slaying of 38-year-old William Kappen (white) in a scheme to defraud an insurance company. The tabloid press had a field day with them because they were to all appearances a mismatched pair. They paid with their lives in the electric chair at Menard on January 28, 1938. Sources: *Freeport (IL) Journal-Standard*, 7/10/37 (9:4). *Edwardsville (IL) Intelligencer*, 1/28/38

(1:5). *Official Detective* (magazine) 3/16/38. *Front Page Detective*, 12/37 & 5/47. *Headline Detective*, 12/39 & 5/44. *Master Detective*, 3/47 & 10/75. *Real Detective*, 9/41.

J. C. Scott (full name not recorded, black, age 21). *Murder.* The crime was committed on 12/18/1937 in Cook County. Executed for the fatal beatings of two Romany women named Mary Ely (age 52) and Catherine Ely (age 26). Motive: robbery. Scott died by electrocution at the Cook County Jail on April 19, 1938. Source: *Hammond (IN) Times*, 4/19/38 (8:7). See also: 1937 Cook Co. death cert. nos. 6035812 and 6035813, which classify the homicide victims as white females probably because they did not fit a more specific ethnic grouping under the standards of that time. Scott's full name is not given in any known source, not even on his death certificate. He appears in both the 1920 and 1930 U.S. Censuses (Greenville Co., SC), as "J. C. Scott," the son of Jack and Maggie Scott.

John Henry Seadlund (white, age 26). *Murder.* The crime was committed on 9/25/1937. Executed under federal jurisdiction for the torture and handgun slaying of 72-year-old Charles S. Ross (white), who was found chained in an abandoned well. Motive: kidnapping for ransom. Seadlund also murdered his accomplice in this crime, James Atwood Gray (white, age 19), with the same handgun near Spooner, WI, because he (Seadlund) got greedy and wanted to keep all of the ransom money for himself. Seadlund was condemned under a federal statute that permitted the death penalty in cases of kidnapping with bodily harm rather than outright murder, even though he was equally guilty of that capital offense as well. He was electrocuted at the Cook County Jail on July 14, 1938. Source: *Alton (IL) Evening Telegraph*, 7/14/38 (1:1). *Official Detective*, 3/16/38, 3/30/38, 4/13/38, 4/27/38 and 5/11/38. *Front Page Detective*, 7/54. *Master Detective*, 1/45. *Crime Detective*, 4/53. *Real Detective*, 5/38 & 6/38.

John Jelliga (white, age 32). *Murder.* The crime was committed on 12/9/1937 in Will County. Torture and handgun slaying of 44-year-old Edward Pansa (white). Motive: home invasion. This remorseless killer was executed at Joliet Prison on October 21, 1938. Source: *Freeport (IL) Journal-Standard*, 10/21/38 (5:3). See also: 1930 U.S. Census (Will Co., IL), which notes Mr. Pansa. *Master Detective*, 11/40.

1939

Elvyn Wood (white, age 37). *Murder.* The crime was committed on 2/19/1939 in Grundy County. Handgun slaying of 38-year-old Abner Nelson (white), the victim having been shot five times in the back. His body was dumped in a river. Motive: kidnapping. Wood was not tried under the federal anti-kidnapping statute because no ransom demand had been made up to the time of his capture. He was executed at Joliet Prison on April 14, 1939. Source: *Logansport (IN) Pharos-Tribune*, 2/22/39 (1:1) & 4/14/39 (1:3). *Official Detective*, 5/39. *Dynamic Detective*, 6/39. *Real Detective*, 11/39.

Robert Nixon (black, age 24). *Murder.* The crime for which he was executed was committed on 5/27/1938 at Chicago. Serial killer. Electrocuted for the murder of 34-year-old Florence Johnson (white), whom he battered to death with a brick. Motive: burglary and sexual assault. Nixon is confirmed to have also murdered four other white females in the same way and for the same reason as follows: Florence Castle Thompson (age 24) at Chicago on 6/29/1936; Edna A. Worden (age 48) and Marguerite Worden (age 12), a mother and daughter, at Los Angeles, CA, on 4/4/1937; and Anita Kuchta (age 19) at Chicago on 8/21/1937. He was additionally the prime suspect in the identical murder of Rose G. Valdez (Latina, age 20) at Los Angeles, CA, on 3/2/1937. Nixon is further confirmed to have committed atrocious assaults on at least seven other women during the same period. News accounts of Nixon's being a teenager are incorrect; inquiry made in his hometown (Tallulah, LA), established that he was aged 24 when he murdered Mrs. Johnson. He was put to death at the Cook County Jail on June 16, 1939. Source: *Albuquerque (NM) Journal*, 4/5/37 (1:4). *Daily Independent* (Murphysboro, IL), 6/16/39 (2:7). *Master Detective*, 3/39, 4/39, 5/39, 6/39 & 7/39.

Stephen Cygan (white, age 24). *Murder.* The crime was committed on 4/5/1928 in Cook County. Police killer. Handgun slaying of 47-year-old John Chiska (white). Motive: armed robbery gone awry. Death in the electric chair was meted out to this killer at the Cook County Jail on October 13, 1939. Source: *Logansport (IN) Pharos-Tribune*, 4/6/28 (6:5). *Capital Times* (Madison, WI), 4/7/28 (2:6). *Oshkosh (WI) Daily Northwestern*, 10/13/39 (2:2). See also: 1920 U.S. Census (Chicago IL, Ward 34), which notes Chiska, and 1920 U.S. Census (Chicago IL, Ward 17), which notes Cygan.

Charles Price (black, age 26). *Murder.* The crime was committed on 3/30/1936 in Cook County. Executed for the handgun slaying of 35-year-old Nicholas Miller (white). Motive: mugging. Price is confirmed to have also participated in the 11/13/1937 murder of 50-year-old Harry Rubin (a kosher poultry man), who was gunned down in his place of business (at Chicago) during a holdup. The Cook County electric chair added Price to its score on October 27, 1939. Source: *Vidette-Messenger* (Valparaiso, IN), 3/31/36 (2:5). *Logansport (IN) Pharos-Tribune*, 12/2/37 (10:6). *LaCrosse (WI) Tribune and Leader-Press*, 10/27/39 (14:5). See also: 1930 U.S. Census (Chicago IL, Ward 24), which notes Mr. Rubin.

1940

Howard Poe (black, age 23). *Murder.* The crime was committed on 8/21/1938 in Cook County. Police killer. Handgun slaying of 32-year-old Patrick E. O'Malley (white). Motive: armed robbery gone awry. This ill-fated young man was executed at the Cook County Jail on April 19, 1940. Source: *Chicago Daily Tribune*, 8/22/38 (6:2) & 4/19/40 (14:2).

Victor Wnukowski (white, age 24) and **Frank Michalowski** (white, age 25). *Murder.* Their crime was committed on 10/13/1939 in Cook County. Both executed for the handgun slaying of 64-year-old Viggo Petersen (white). Motive: armed robbery. They met their legally mandated deaths at the Cook County Jail on May 17, 1940. Source: *Alton (IL) Evening Telegraph*, 5/17/40 (11:7). See also: 1939 Cook Co. death cert. no. 28994. *Dynamic Detective*, 8/40.

Robert Schroeder (white, age 26). *Murder.* The crime was committed on 7/17/1940 in Cook County. Child killer. Executed for the murder of 8-

year-old Maizie Smith (white), whom he beat to death with a wrought-iron furnace shaker. Motive: sexual assault. The electric chair dispatched this pervert on December 13, 1940. Source: *Freeport (IL) Journal-Standard*, 12/13/40 (11:4). See also: 1940 Cook Co. death cert. no. 20754. *Actual Detective*, 9/40.

1941

Edward Riley (white, age 37) and **Orville Watson** (white, age 28). *Murder.* Their crime was committed on 5/2/1939 in Cook County. Police killers, etc. Both executed for the handgun slayings of 35-year-old Philip J. Kelly (an off-duty police officer) and 57-year-old Alex Ferguson (whites). Motive: armed robbery gone awry. The electric chair rid society of these bandits on June 20, 1941. Source: *Appleton (WI) Post-Crescent*, 5/3/39 (1:4). *Wisconsin State Journal* (Madison, WI), 6/20/41 (12:4). *Headline Detective*, 1/43. *Crime Detective*, 7/39. *Real Detective*, 7/40. *True* (magazine) 11/39.

1942

Earl Parks (black, age 26). *Murder.* The crime was committed on 5/21/1941 in Cook County. Executed for the handgun slaying of 27-year-old Lawrence Murphy (white). Motive: mugging. He is also confirmed to have murdered 65-year-old Gustav R. Lindbloom (white) by the same means and for the same reason at Chicago on 4/26/1941. Parks was put to death on January 15, 1942. Source: *Southeast Economist* (Chicago, IL), 7/3/41 (3:1). *LaCrosse (WI) Tribune and Leader-Press*, 1/15/42 (2:4). *Official Detective*, 10/41.

Bernard Sawicki (white, age 18). *Murder.* The crime was committed on 6/30/1941 in Cook County. Police killer, etc. Executed for the handgun slaying of 54-year-old Charles J. Speaker (white), a Chicago parks policeman. Motive: carjacking gone awry. Sawicki had also murdered three other white males with the same handgun that same week: Henry E. Allain (age 73) in Kankakee Co., IL on 6/27/1941 because he blamed that man for having had him committed to a juvenile reformatory; Charles Kwasinski (age 17) at Chicago on 6/28/1941 out of sheer spite because the slain youth had refused to join him in an illegal foray; and John J. Miller (age 19) at Chicago on 6/29/1941. Motive: mugging. This teenage urban terrorist took his last seat in the electric chair on January 17, 1942. Source: *Freeport (IL) Journal-Standard*, 7/1/41 (2:1). *Daily Independent* (Murphysboro, IL), 1/17/42 (1:7). See also: 1941 Kankakee Co. death cert. no. 459 (Allain) and Cook Co. death cert. no. 19272 (Speaker). *Dynamic Detective*, 10/41. *Official Detective*, 9/41.

Leo Jordan (white, age 23). *Murder.* The crime was committed on 11–3-1941 in Whiteside County. Child killer. Executed for the murder of 5-year-old Warren Snyder (white), whose throat was slit with a razor blade. Motive: emotionally disturbed. Jordan had become enraged when some school children behaved disrespectfully toward him. Another account says that he had tried to sexually molest the little boy. Whatever the case, the motive proved immaterial to the outcome when Jordan died in the Joliet Prison electric chair on May 13, 1942. Source: *Sterling (IL) Daily Gazette*, 11/6/41 (6:1). *Daily Independent* (Murphysboro, IL), 5/13/42 (1:5). *Actual Detective*, 4/42.

John Pantano (white, age 19). *Murder.* The crime was committed on 12/10/1941 in Cook County. Police killer, etc. Executed for the handgun slaying of 51-year-old Charles H. Williams (white, a Chicago parks policeman), who was shot three times. Motive: armed robbery gone awry. Pantano was also a full accomplice in the 12/3/1941 handgun slaying of 40-year-old Nelton Scheuerman (white, a St. Louis MO saloonkeeper), who was shot four times during an attempted robbery of his establishment. The Cook County electric chair did for John Pantano on September 18, 1942. Source: *Sheboygan (WI) Press*, 4/16/42 (8:7). *Alton (IL) Evening Telegraph*, 9/18/42 (3:1). See also: 1941 Cook Co. death cert. no. 35608 (Williams) and 1942 Cook Co. death cert. no. 25527 (Pantano). See also: 1930 U.S. Census (St. Louis, MO), which notes Mr. Scheuerman.

1943

Ernest Wishon (white, age 34). *Murder.* The crime was committed on 6/28/1943 in Cook County. Handgun slaying of 79-year-old Joseph Schulte (white), a jeweler. Motive: armed robbery. Wishon was already dying of venereal disease on November 26, 1943, when the electric chair put him out of his misery. Source: *Daily Globe* (Ironwood, MI), 6/30/43 (3:6). *Freeport (IL) Journal-Standard*, 7/22/43 (6:6). *Wisconsin State Journal* (Madison, WI), 11/26/43 (14:4). See also: 1930 U.S. Census (Phelps Co., MO), which notes Wishon.

1944

Paul LeRoy Williams (white, age 24). *Murder.* The crime was committed on 9/19/1942 in Cook County. Handgun slaying of 45-year-old Thomas A. Papayanes (white). Motive: armed robbery. He was executed at the Cook County Jail on March 15, 1944. Source: *Freeport (IL) Journal-Standard*, 3/15/44 (11:4). See also: 1942 Cook Co. death cert. no. 25940.

Alvin Krause (white, age 29). *Murder.* The crime was committed on 6/18/1943 in Cook County. Executed for the handgun slaying of 50-year-old Walter Bush (white). Motive: armed robbery. Krause is confirmed to have also murdered a Chicago cashier named Agnes Olsen (white, age 54) on 7/3/1943 by spraying her with a poisonous chemical. Motive: robbery. He was executed at the Cook County Jail on September 15, 1944. Source: *Southtown Economist* (Chicago, IL), 6/20/43 (1:2). *San Antonio (TX) Light*, 7/7/43 (2:4). *Dixon (IL) Evening Telegraph*, 9/15/44 (10:6). *Front Page Detective*, 1/44. *Official Detective*, 2/44.

1945

Kermit Breedlove (black, age 33). *Murder.* The crime was committed on 12/16/1944 in Cook County. Uxoricide and double cop-killer. Handgun slayings of 35-year-old Goldine "Goldie" Breedlove (black, who was shot six times) and two black police officers named Samuel M. Black (age 53) and Ezra Caldwell (age 32). Motive: jealous husband gone berserk. This triple killer was executed on October 19, 1945. Source: *Chicago Sunday Tribune*, 12/17/44 (1:3). *Daily Journal-Gazette* (Mattoon, IL), 10/19/45 (1:5). See also: 1944 Cook Co. death cert. nos. 36567 (Black), 36568 (G. Breedlove) and 36569 (Caldwell). See also: 1930 U.S.

Census (Jefferson Co., AR), which notes Breedlove's origin.

1947

Charles Crosby (black, age 36). *Murder.* The crime was committed on 9/30/1946 in Cook County. Police killer. Handgun slaying of 45-year-old Herman Ziebel (white). Motive: evading arrest. The electric chair fulfilled its function in this case on June 20, 1947. Source: *Dixon (IL) Evening Telegraph,* 1/9/47 (8:7) & 6/20/47 (12:5). See also: 1930 U.S. Census (Cook Co., IL), which notes the murdered officer.

Ernest Gaither (black, age 23). *Murder.* The crime was committed on 2/9/1947 in Cook County. Handgun slaying of 49-year-old Max Baran (white). Motive: armed robbery. The hot seat claimed Ernest Gaither on October 24, 1947. Source: *Long Beach (CA) Independent,* 2/10/47 (12:2). *Daily Journal-Gazette* (Mattoon, IL), 10/24/47 (8:1). *Official Detective,* 8/47, 44–46.

1949

Herman Frederick Weber (white, age 24). *Murder.* The crime was committed on 12/3/1947 in Peoria County. Handgun slaying of 20-year-old Flavel Dean Fueger (white), the victim having been shot three times. Motive: grand theft auto. Weber paid with his life for this at Joliet Prison on September 16, 1949. Source: *Dixon (IL) Evening Telegraph,* 12/15/47 (1:3). *Daily Independent* (Murphysboro, IL), 12/20/47 (1:1). *Freeport (IL) Journal-Standard,* 9/16/49 (18:7). *Front Page Detective,* 6/48. *Crime Detective,* 12/48.

James Morelli (white, age 19). *Murder.* The crime was committed on 12/13/1947 in Cook County. Executed for the handgun slaying of 18-year-old Emil W. Schmeichel (white), the victim having been abducted, shot once in the gut, dumped from an automobile and then finished off by another shot through the head. Motive: gangland killing. Morelli is also confirmed to have murdered 30-year-old Theodore J. Callis (white) that same evening under similar circumstances, the only difference being an additional shot through the head. He was additionally proven to have been a full accomplice in the handgun slaying of John T. Kuesis (white, age 33) at Chicago earlier that same evening as part of a gangland vendetta. On November 26, 1949, the Cook County electric chair ensured that Morelli went no further. Source: *Logansport (IN) Press,* 12/14/47 (1:1). *Dixon (IL) Evening Telegraph,* 12/13/47 (1:1) & 11/26/49 (2:1).

1950

Alfonso Najera (Latino, age 25) and **Frederico Varela** (Latino, age 24). *Murder.* Their crime was committed on 4/13/1948 in Cook County. Both executed for the handgun slaying of 31-year-old Albert Brody (white, a cabbie), who was shot four times in the head. Motive: robbery. These killers paid the death penalty at the Cook County Jail on April 21, 1950. Source: *The Garfieldian* (Chicago), 4/22/48 (3:1) & 5/27/48 (4:6). *Dixon (IL) Evening Telegraph,* 4/21/50 (1:2). *Crime Detective,* 6/64. *Front Page Detective,* 6/49. *Master Detective,* 4/60.

Willard Truelove (black, age 31). *Murder.* The crime was committed on 10/26/1949 in Cook County. Fatal stabbing of 26-year-old Mary Salerno LoChirco (white), she having suffered multiple wounds. Motive: purse snatching. The sidewalks of Chicago became a wee bit safer when the electric chair permanently removed Willard Truelove from society on November 17, 1950. Source: *Ironwood (MI) Daily Globe*, 10/27/49 (1:2). *Austin (MN) Daily Herald*, 11/17/50 (13:4).

1952

Raymond Jenko (white, age 19). *Murder.* The crime was committed on 5/20/1950 in Cook County. Executed for the murder of 17-year-old Patricia Swartz (white), she having been stabbed twelve times with a butcher knife. Motive: purse snatching; dope addict. The electric chair permanently rehabilitated Raymond Jenko on January 25, 1952. Source: *Dixon (IL) Evening Telegraph*, 5/24/50 (2:8) & 1/25/52 (6:5). *Official Detective*, 11/50.

Harry Williams (black, age 19). *Murder.* The crime was committed on 8/20/1950 in Cook County. Serial rapist, woman-killer and prison-guard killer. Executed for the handgun slaying of 48-year-old Mary Gee Scott (black). Motive: sexual assault. Williams also murdered a guard at the Cook County Jail while on death row for the first killing. The date: 8/14/1951. The victim: George Turley (white, age 43), who was jumped from behind and battered to death with his own riot gun. Motive: attempted breakout. The electric chair finished off Harry Williams on March 14, 1952. Source: *Dixon (IL) Evening Telegraph*, 8/15/51 (6:2). *Daily Journal-Gazette* (Mattoon, IL), 3/14/52 (1:4). *Chicago Daily Tribune*, 8/15/51 (1:3). See also: 1950 Cook Co. death cert. no. 6057916, which notes Mary Gee Scott.

Bernice Davis, alias "Bernie Davis" (black male, age 22). *Murder.* The crime was committed on 7/14/1950 in Cook County. Police killer. Handgun slayings of 43-year-old Edward T. Crowley and 39-year-old Donald E. McCormick (whites, two Chicago police detectives), who were shot three times each. Motive: resisting arrest. Davis died in the electric chair on October 17, 1952. Source: *Logansport (IN) Press*, 7/15/50 (1:8). *Dixon (IL) Evening Telegraph*, 10/17/52 (3:2).

Leroy Lindsay (black, age 29). *Murder.* The crime was committed on 4/24/1950 in Cook County. Police killer. Handgun slaying of 52-year-old William B. Murphy (white), who was shot eight times. Motive: armed robbery gone awry. Lindsay paid with his life for this at the Cook County Jail on October 17, 1952. Source: *Tucson (AZ) Daily Citizen*, 4/25/50 (13:6). *Dixon (IL) Evening Telegraph*, 4/27/50 (1:8) & 10/17/52 (3:2).

1953

Emanuel Scott (black, age 24). *Murder.* The crime was committed on 4/24/1950 in Cook County. Police killer. Accomplice in the handgun slaying of 52-year-old William B. Murphy (white), who was shot eight times. Motive: armed robbery gone awry. Scott suffered the death penalty pursuant to law on March 19, 1953. Source: *Dixon (IL) Evening Telegraph*, 3/19/53 (5:6). See also: Leroy Lindsay (executed 10/17/52).

1958

Richard Carpenter (white, age 26). *Murder.* The crime was committed on

8/15/1955 in Cook County. Police killer. Handgun slaying of 34-year-old William J. Murphy (white). Motive: resisting arrest. Death in the electric chair was the fate of this assassin on December 19, 1958. Source: *Dixon (IL) Evening Telegraph*, 8/19/55 (1:5). *Edwardsville (IL) Intelligencer*, 12/19/58 (2:4). *Front Page Detective*, 8/57. *Official Detective*, 11/55 & 9/75.

1962

Vincent Ciucci (white, age 28). *Murder.* The crime was committed on 12/5/1953 in Cook County. Uxoricide and filicide. Rifle slayings of 28-year-old Anna Turco Ciucci (white) and their three children—Vincent Jr. (age 9), Virginia (age 8) and Angeline (age 4)—they having all been shot in their beds and partially cremated by an arson fire intended to destroy the crime scene. Motive: adultery. The killer had fathered a child with another woman and wanted to be free to further that relationship. Ciucci might have gotten away with it had not postmortem examination of the "house fire victims" shown that they had all been shot. This stupid man was executed at the Cook County Jail on March 23, 1962. Source: *Dixon (IL) Evening Telegraph*, 12/9/53 (7:2). *Southern Illinoisan* (Carbondale, IL), 3/23/62 (1:4). *Official Detective*, 3/54 & 11/75. *Master Detective*, 4/54, 3/68 & 9/70. *Real Detective*, 6/55. *Inside Detective*, 3/54.

James Dukes, alias "Jesse Welch" (black, age 31). *Murder.* The crime was committed on 6/16/1956 in Cook County. Police killer. Handgun slaying of 42-year-old John J. Blyth Jr. (white). Motive: obnoxious drunk. The electric chair at the Cook County Jail sent Dukes to regions unknown on August 24, 1962. Source: *Chicago Daily Tribune*, 6/16/56 (1:7), 6/17/56 (1:8) & 8/24/62 (1:8).

Indiana

1866

George Washington Sage (white, age 34). *Murder.* The crime was committed on 3/7/1866 in Jennings County. Baby killer. Executed for the murder of 2-year-old William Todd, Jr. (white), who was brutally battered to death with a brick. Motive: larceny gone awry. The culprit was hanged at Vernon IN on May 25, 1866. Source: *Fort Wayne (IN) Daily Gazette,* 3/17/66 (2:4). *Vernon (IN) Banner,* 5/31/66 (2:2). See also: Andrew R. Stoner, *Notorious 92: Indiana's Most Heinous Murders* (Bloomington, IN: Rooftop, 2007), 182–184. See also: *Louisville (KY) Daily Courier,* 5/30/66 (1:8), for an excellent account of this case.

1867

Milton White (white, age 25). *Murder.* The crime was committed on 4/8/1867 in Madison County. Executed for the murder of 20-year-old Isaac Hoppis (white), the victim having been clubbed to death. Motive: revelation of larceny. The killer was hanged at Anderson IN on November 1, 1867. Source: Samuel Harden, *History of Madison County Indiana* (Markleville, IN: 1874), 287–289. See also: 1860 U.S. Census (Madison Co., IN), which notes both parties.

1869

Oliver Anson Morgan (white, age 26). *Murder.* The crime was committed on 7/11/1869 in Vigo County. Handgun slaying of 40-year-old John Petri (white). Motive: burglary. This killer plunged through the gallows trap at Terre Haute on December 23, 1869. Source: *Fort Wayne (IN) Daily Gazette,* 12/28/69 (3:1). See also: 1860 U.S. Census (Fond du Lac Co., WI), which notes the victim's age and earlier whereabouts.

1871

Ben Sawyer (black, age abt. 37). *Murder.* The crime was committed on 2/2/1871 in Vanderburgh County. Uxoricide. Executed for the murder of Lizzie Pane Sawyer (black, age not recorded), she having been battered to death with a clothes iron. Motive: marital estrangement. The public hangman sent this wife-killer to a felon's death at Evansville on May 26, 1871. Source: *Titusville (PA) Herald,* 2/3/71 (2:5). *New York Herald,* 6/1/71 (8:2). See also: *Vanderburgh County Marriage Register,* vol. 6, 336. Appeal: 35 IN 80–88.

Jerome W. Brooks (white, age 21). *Murder.* The crime was committed on 4/20/1871 in Cass County. Hanged for the murder of 55-year-old Asher M. Slater (white), who was beaten to death with a wooden dray pin. Motive: robbery. Venue changed from Cass County to Carroll County. The killer swung to his doom at Delphi IN on October 27, 1871. Source: *Democratic Pharos* (Logansport, IN), 8/23/71 (1:3) & 11/1/71 (2:2). See also: 1870 U.S. Census (Cass Co., IN), which notes Mr. Slater's correct name and age.

1872

Thomas Camp (white, age 19). *Murder.* The crime was committed on 7/31/1871 in Gibson County. Executed for the murder of 31-year-old John Riley Bilderback (white), who was clubbed to death; his body was stripped naked. Motive: robbery. The killer was hanged at Princeton IN on November 22, 1872. Source: *Princeton (IN) Clarion*, 11/28/72 (2:2). *Fort Wayne (IN) Daily Sentinel*, 11/23/72 (1:3). See also: "Coroner's Report on the Death of J. R. Bilderback," dated 8/9/71, Genealogy Dept., Princeton (IN), Public Library.

1878

John W. Beavers (white, age 33). *Murder.* The crime was committed on 11/3/1877 in Jefferson County. Executed for the murder of 60-year-old J. W. Sewell (white, full name not recorded), who was bludgeoned with a stick and his body left in a burning church. Motive: robbery and gross perfidy. The killer was hanged at Madison IN on February 15, 1878. Source: *Logansport (IN) Daily Journal*, 11/8/77 (1:1) & 2/16/78 (1:2). *New York Herald*, 2/16/78 (10:1). *Chicago Tribune*, 1/30/79 (7:1).

1879

John Achey (white, age 42). *Murder.* The crime was committed on 7/16/1878 in Marion County. Handgun slaying of George Leggett (white, age not recorded). Motive: because the killer felt that the victim had swindled him. The former was hanged at Indianapolis on January 29, 1879. Source: *Daily Journal* (Logansport, IN), 1/30/79 (1:1). *New York Herald*, 1/30/79 (4:5). See also: 1870 U.S. Census (Marion Co., IN), which notes Achey.

William A. Merrick (white, age 34). *Murder.* The crime was committed on 9/14/1878 in Marion County. Uxoricide and infanticide. Fatal poisonings of 36-year-old Julia Paul Merrick (white) and an unnamed male newborn that was emitted from the former's womb during the convulsions that immediately preceded her death. The naked corpses of mother and child were found concealed beneath a brush pile. Motive: unwanted paternity. This feckless father was hanged at Indianapolis on January 29, 1879. Source: *Fort Wayne (IN) Daily Sentinel*, 12/16/78 (1:2). *New York Times*, 1/30/79 (5:1). *Daily Journal* (Logansport, IN), 1/30/79 (1:1). Appeal: 63 IN 327–337. See also: *Marion County Marriage Register* (1876–1880), which notes the nuptials of William A. Merrick and Julia A. Paul on 7/16/1878. See also: 1860 U.S. Census (Morgan Co., IN), which notes Miss Paul.

Walter Watson (white, age 27). *Murder.* The crime was committed on 1/9/1879 in Vermillion County. Handgun slaying of 34-year-old Ezra Compton (white). Motive: anger over a 25-cent store credit. The gallows made that quarter a very dear one to Walter

Watson at Newport, IN, on April 3, 1879. Source: *Fort Wayne (IN) Daily Sentinel*, 4/4/79 (1:2). *Daily Journal* (Logansport, IN), 4/4/79 (1:2). See also: 1870 U.S. Census (Wabash Co., IN), which notes the killer in this case. See also: 1860 U.S. Census (Middlesex Co., NJ), which notes Ezra Compton.

Louis Guetig (white, age 19). *Murder.* The crime was committed on 9/19/1878 in Marion County. Handgun slaying of 20-year-old Mary McGlew (white), she having been shot four times. Motive: jilted lover. Guetig paid for what he did at the end of a rope exactly one year later at Indianapolis on September 19, 1879. Source: *The Advocate* (Tipton, IN), 9/26/79 (3:2). *Fort Wayne (IN) Sentinel*, 9/19/79 (1:2). See also: 1870 U.S. Census (Marion Co., IN), which notes Mary McGlew.

1883

Joseph T. Stout (white, age 21). *Murder.* The crime was committed on 11/24/1882 in Parke County. Executed for the murder of 33-year-old Taylor Dunbar (white), who was shot twice with a rifle and had his head smashed in. Motive: robbery and treachery. The killer was hanged at Rockville IN on August 8, 1883. Source: *Logansport (IN) Daily Journal*, 11/28/82 (1:2) & 8/9/83 (2:1). *Fort Wayne (IN) Daily Gazette*, 8/9/83 (2:2). *Janesville (WI) Daily Gazette*, 8/9/83 (1:2). See also: 1880 U.S. Census (Montgomery Co., IN), which notes Mr. Dunbar.

Samuel McDonald (white, age 29). *Murder.* The crime was committed on 3/23/1883 in Allen County. Hatchet killing of 27-year-old Louis Laurent (white). Motive: robbery and deceitfulness. This miscreant was hanged at Fort Wayne on October 9, 1883. Source: *Fort Wayne (IN) Daily Sentinel*, 3/31/83 (1:5) & 10/9/83 (1:3). See also: 1880 U.S. Census (Kewaunee Co., WI), which notes Mr. Laurent.

1884

John Anderson (white, age 17) and **Zachary Snyder** (white, age 20). *Murder.* Their crime was committed on 8/17/1883 in Posey County. Both hanged for the murder of 17-year-old James van Wye (white), the victim having been felled with a club, his throat cut and his body dumped in a river. Motive: mugging. The killers were made to pay life for life at Mt. Vernon IN on January 25, 1884. Source: *Logansport (IN) Journal*, 1/26/84 (1:1).

Charles Butler (white, age 28). *Murder.* The crime was committed on 9/29/1883 in Whitley County. Uxoricide. Handgun slaying of 26-year-old Abigail Sheehan Butler (white), she having been shot twice in the back. Motive: marital estrangement. This wife-killer was hanged at Columbia City IN on October 10, 1884. Source: *Daily Gazette* (Ft. Wayne, IN), 10/11/84 (3:1).

1885

John Coffey (white, age 24). *Murder.* The crime was committed on 1/7/1885 in Montgomery County. Executed for the murders of 38-year-old James W. McMullen and 38-year-old Julia A. McMullen (whites, a married couple), they having each been shot with a handgun and their residence burned down upon them. Motive: plunder. The hangman performed his office in the case of John Coffey at Crawfordsville IN on October 16, 1885. Source: *Morning Review* (Decatur, IL), 1/14/85 (1:6). *Daily Gazette* (Ft. Wayne, IN), 10/17/85 (1:1). See also: 1880 U.S. Census (Montgomery Co., IN), which notes the McMullens.

1886

Weiburn Wartena (white, age 40+). *Murder.* The crime was discovered on 10/29/1884 in Jasper County. Executed for the murder of John Dregher (white, age not recorded), the victim having been battered to death with the butt of a shotgun and his weighted corpse dumped in a river. Motive: forgery and betrayal. The killer was hanged at Renssalaer IN on February 26, 1886. Source: *Logansport (IN) Pharos*, 12/6/84 (3:3). Appeal: 105 IN 445–450. *Chicago Tribune*, 2/27/86 (7:5). *The Tribune* (Chesterton, IN), 3/4/86 (1:7).

Robert G. Phillips (black, age 21). *Murder.* The crime was committed on 6/24/1885 in Marion County. Uxoricide. Hanged for the murder of 19-year-old Louise Smith Phillips (black), she having been slashed to death with a case knife. Motive: jealousy. This killer was executed at Indianapolis on April 8, 1886. Source: *Logansport (IN) Pharos*, 4/9/86 (3:5). See also: *Marion County Board of Health Death Register*, vol. H-2, 88. Also: *Marion County Marriage Register*, vol. 237, entry dated 3/24/85.

John C. Henning (white, age 55). *Murder.* The crime was committed on 10/24/1885 in Montgomery County. Handgun slaying of 54-year-old Charlotte Vollmer (white). Motive: jilted lover. Henning was hanged at Crawfordsville IN on May 27, 1886. Source: *Logansport (IN) Daily Journal*, 5/28/86 (1:4). Appeal: 106 IN 386–403. See also: 1880 U.S. Census (Miami Co., IN), which notes the murdered woman. See also: *Montgomery County Register of Deaths*, vol. H-37, 46.

Samuel Archer (white, age 24). *Murder.* The crime was committed on 7/11/1882 in Martin County. Participant in the gunshot slaying of Samuel Anderson Bunch (white, age not recorded), who was shot sixteen times with rifles and handguns; his body was burnt. Three co-defendants were lynched on 3/10/1886. Samuel Archer was legally hanged at Shoals IN on July 9, 1886. Source: *Logansport (IN) Daily Pharos*, 7/10/86 (1:2). *Northern Vindicator* (Estherville, IA), 7/23/86 (6:5). *Albany Law Journal*, vol. 34, 50–53. See also: 1870 U.S. Census (Martin Co., IN), which notes Archer.

Nathaniel Stillman Bates (white, age 26). *Murder.* The crime was committed on 3/23/1886 in Wayne County. Uxoricide. Executed for the murder of 23-year-old Kitty Hoover Bates (white), who was slashed to death with a finely honed knife. Motive: marital estrangement. The hangman accounted for this wife-killer at Richmond IN on August 26, 1886. Source: *Fort Wayne (IN) Gazette*, 8/27/86 (1:2). *New York Times*, 8/27/86 (3:3). See also: 1870 U.S. Census (Wayne Co., IN), which notes the victim as "Kattie Hoover."

1888

Macy Warner (white, age 25). *Murder.* The crime was committed on 4/15/1887 in Clark County. Executed for the fatal stabbing of 45-year-old Frank Harris (white). Motive: prison violence. Recidivist killer. Warner had first been sent to prison at the age of 14 for shooting an Indianapolis police officer. Released after five years, he turned up at Washington, IN (Daviess Co.), on 9/22/1883, where he fatally shot a saloon keeper named Jacob Mandery (white, age 34) and subsequently drew a 21-year prison sentence for first-degree manslaughter. He was three years into that term when he killed Frank Harris. He was hanged at Jeffersonville IN on March 9, 1888. Source: *Logansport (IN) Journal*, 9/30/83 (4:2). *Alton (IL) Daily Telegraph*, 1/28/84 (1:4). *Newark (OH) Daily Advocate*, 4/18/87 (3:5). *Logansport (IN) Daily Pharos*, 3/10/88 (3:4). Appeal: 16 NE 189–192. See also: 1880 U.S. Census (La Porte Co., IN), which notes Warner, and 1880 U.S. Census (Putnam Co., IN), which notes Harris. See also: 1870 U.S. Census (Brooklyn, NY), which notes Mandery.

1889

Sylvester Grubb (white, age 23). *Murder.* The crime was committed on 9/13/1888 in Gibson County. Handgun slaying of 18-year-old Gertrude Downey (white), she having been shot five times. Motive: frustrated suitor. Venue changed from Gibson County to Knox County. The killer was hanged at Vincennes on April 19, 1889. Source: *Daily Journal* (Logansport, IN), 4/20/89 (4:2). See also: 1880 U.S. Census (Gibson Co., IN), which notes Miss Downey, plus 1870 U.S. Census (Richland Co., IL), which notes Grubb.

1894

James E. Stone (white, age 40). *Murder.* The crime was committed on 9/19/1893 in Daviess County. Mass killer and child killer. Hanged for the deliberate slayings of 35-year-old Dillard Denson Wratten and 33-year-old Ada Wratten (whites, a married couple), along with 11-year-old Ethel Wratten, 6-year-old Stella Wratten and 3-year-old Henry Wratten (their three children), plus 61-year-old Elizabeth Wratten (white), the paternal grandmother of that family. All of them were hacked to death with a corn cutter. Motive: plunder. The man who butchered these six people was executed at the Indiana State Prison on February 16, 1894. Source: *Logansport (IN) Daily Reporter*, 9/20/93 (1:1). *Kokomo (IN) Daily Tribune*, 2/16/94 (1:4). See also: 1880 U.S. Census (Daviess Co., IN), which notes Stone as well as the slain couple as Denson Wratten and "Alley J. Wratten." See also: *Family Records Collection* (Wratten) located at the Daviess County Museum, Washington, IN. *Famous Detective Cases*, 2/36.

1897

Henry Jones (black, age 26). *Murder.* The crime was committed on 7/5/1896 in La Porte County. Fatal stabbing of 21-year-old Omer Thomas (black). Motive: prison violence. Recidivist killer. Jones was already serving a 21-year sentence for manslaughter when he murdered Thomas. He had previously been convicted in Marion County for killing a man in a saloon brawl. Additionally, on 3/9/1896 (about four months prior to the homicide for which he was executed) Jones had purposely chopped off four fingers of his left hand in order to avoid doing mandatory prison labor. The knife with which he killed Thomas was apparently wielded with the other hand. Jones was hanged at the Indiana

State Prison on May 7, 1897. Source: *Logansport (IN) Journal*, 3/10/96 (6:5) & 7/6/96 (1:6). *Fort Wayne (IN) Sentinel*, 5/6/97 (1:4) & 5/7/97 (1:2). See also: *La Porte County Register of Deaths*, vol. H-20, 122 & 136.

1901

Joseph Keith (white, age 39). *Murder.* The crime was committed on 4/2/1900 in Warrick County. Hanged for the murder of 18-year-old Nora Kifer (white), she having been beaten to death with cast-iron knuckles and her weighted body dumped in a creek. Motive: adultery gone bad. Venue changed from Warrick County to Gibson County. The killer was executed at the Indiana State Prison on November 15, 1901. Source: *Fort Wayne (IN) Weekly Sentinel*, 11/20/01 (13:1). *Master Detective*, 9/41. *Front Page Detective*, 4/41.

1902

John Rinkard (white, age 64). *Murder.* The crime was committed on 6/9/1900 in Grant County. Uxoricide. Handgun slaying of 50-year-old Laura Peeler Rinkard (white), she having been shot multiple times. Motive: chronic brutality. Venue changed from Grant County to Wabash County. John Rinkard was hanged at the Indiana State Prison on January 17, 1902. Source: *Logansport (IN) Daily Journal*, 6/10/00 (1:3). *Fort Wayne (IN) Journal-Gazette*, 1/17/02 (1:6).

Willis B. Wheeler (white, age 44). *Murder.* The crime was committed on 7/7/1901 in Warrick County. Hanged for the murder of 23-year-old Elias Burns (white, his son-in-law), who was shot first and then finished off with an axe. Motive: family flare-up. This killer was executed at the Indiana State Prison on June 6, 1902. Source: *Fort Wayne (IN) Sentinel*, 6/6/02 (2:3). See also: *Warrick County Death Register*, vol. H-20, 34, and *Michigan City (IN) Death Register*, vol. CH-10, 19.

Lewis Russell (black, age 34). *Murder.* The crime was committed on 4/27/1902 in Gibson County. Handgun slaying of 30-year-old Perry Stout (black). Motive: rivalry for a female. Russell suffered death by hanging for this black-on-black homicide at the Indiana State Prison on September 26, 1902. Source: *Fort Wayne (IN) Sentinel*, 9/26/02 (1:6). See also: *Gibson County Death Register*, vol. H-36, 6, and *La Porte County Death Register*, vol. H-23, 40.

1903

Matthew Alexander (black, age 27). *Murder.* The crime was committed on 9/7/1902 in Vigo County. Executed for the murder of 42-year-old Thomas Burke (white), who was slashed to death with a razor. Motive: attempted rape of the slain man's wife. The killer was hanged at the Indiana State Prison on April 16, 1903. Source: *The World* (New York), 9/9/02 (3:5). *Fort Wayne (IN) Gazette-Journal*, 4/16/03 (1:5). See also: *Vigo County Death Register*, vol. H-39, 28 and *La Porte County Death Register*, vol. H-24, 7.

Ora E. Copenhaver (white, age 25). *Murder.* The crime was committed on 9/8/1902 in Marion County. Uxoricide. Handgun slaying of 20-year-old Delia Ferguson Copenhaver (white), she having been shot three times despite the presence of a baby in her arms. Motive:

hubris. Ora Copenhaver was hanged at the Indiana State Prison on June 12, 1903. Source: *Fort Wayne (IN) Gazette-Journal*, 9/9/02 (5:3) & 6/12/03 (4:2). See also: *Marion County Death Register*, vol. H-10, 69.

William Jackson (black, age 51). *Murder.* The crime was committed on 1/25/1903 in Vanderburgh County. Executed for the murder of 39-year-old Allen Blankenship (black), who was bludgeoned with a piece of pig iron. Motive: robbery and perfidy. The gallows was the last thing this black-on-black killer saw at the Indiana State Prison on June 12, 1903. Source: *Fort Wayne (IN) Journal-Gazette*, 6/12/03 (4:2). See also: *Vanderburgh County Death Register*, vol. CH-4c, 135. Appeal: 161 IN 36–43. See also: 1900 U.S. Census (Vanderburgh Co., IN), which notes Blankenship's correct age and race.

Edward Hoover (white, age 28). *Murder.* The crime was committed on 5/12/1903 in Marion County. Handgun slaying of 49-year-old Frank Sutton (white, his father-in-law), who was shot four times. Motive: family problems. This imprudent act earned Edward Hoover a rope necklace at the Indiana State Prison on November 13, 1903. Source: *Fort Wayne (IN) Journal-Gazette*, 11/13/03 (1:5). Appeal: 68 NE 591–594. See also: 1860 U.S. Census (Tippecanoe Co., IN), which notes Mr. Sutton as a minor.

1904

Benjamin Springs (black, age 33). *Murder.* The crime was committed on 2/17/1904 in Vigo County. Fatal stabbing of 35-year-old Jesse Case (black). Motive: suspicion of adultery. The killer was hanged on July 1, 1904. Source: *Logansport (IN) Daily Reporter*, 7/1/04 (7:4). *Lincoln (NB) Evening News*, 7/1/04 (1:7). See also: *Vigo County Death Register*, vol. H-39, 31 and *Michigan City (IN) Death Register*, vol. CH-11, 2.

Jerry Duggins (white, age 29). *Murder.* The crime was committed on 2/23/1904 in Vigo County. Child killer, baby killer, etc. Hanged for the murders of 32-year-old Sarah Ramsey, 5-year-old Lewis Ramsey and 18-month-old Myrtle Ramsey (whites, a mother and her two children) who were all slashed to death with a razor. Motive: rebuffed suitor gone loco. He was executed on July 8, 1904. Source: *Fort Wayne (IN) Weekly Sentinel*, 2/24/04 (1:1). *Logansport (IN) Daily Reporter*, 7/8/04 (2:7). See also: *Vigo County Death Register*, vol. H-39, 32.

1905

Berkeley Smith (black, age 30). *Murder.* The crime was committed on 12/20/1904 in Marion County. Uxoricide. Handgun slaying of 21-year-old Harriet Smith (black). Motive: marital estrangement. This wife-killer was hanged on June 30, 1905. Source: *Logansport (IN) Reporter*, 12/21/04 (7:5). *Van Wert (OH) Daily Bulletin*, 6/30/05 (1:5). See also: 1900 U.S. Census (Fayette Co., KY), which notes both parties.

1907

George Williams (black, age 27). *Murder.* The crime was committed on 9/30/1906 in Marion County. Police killer. Handgun slayings of 35-year-old Charles J. Russell and 37-year-old

Edward J. Petticord (whites). Motive: big attitude. Williams legally paid the forfeit of his life at the end of a rope on February 8, 1907. Source: *Fort Wayne (IN) Journal-Gazette,* 10/1/06 (1:5). *Fort Wayne (IN) Daily News,* 2/8/07 (4:3). See also: *Marion County Death Register,* vol. H-13, 35 & 36.

1914

John Chirka (white, age 39). *Murder.* The crime was committed on 5/15/1913 in Lake County. Uxoricide. Handgun slaying of about 36-year-old Mary Skio Chirka (white), she having been shot three times. Motive: drunken brutality. The Indiana electric chair cured Chirka of his boorish ways on February 20, 1914. Source: *Lake County Times* (Hammond, IN), 5/15/13 (1:1) & 2/20/14 (1:7).

Henry Rasico (white, age 34). *Murder.* The crime was committed on 9/13/1913 in Vigo County. Uxoricide and filicide. Handgun slayings of 32-year-old Bertha Benton Rasico and 18-month-old Walter Rasico (whites). Motive: marital estrangement. This destroyer of his family died in the electric chair on February 20, 1914. Source: *Indianapolis Star,* 2/20/14 (1:7). See also: *Vigo County Death Register,* vol. CH-53, 60.

Robert Collier (black, age 34). *Murder.* The crime was committed on 6/14/1914 in Vanderburgh County. Police killer. Handgun slaying of 47-year-old John V. Cain Jr. (white). Motive: disorderly conduct. An electric chair exacted life for life in the case of Robert Collier on October 16, 1914. Source: *Kokomo (IN) Tribune,* 10/16/14 (2:3). See also: *Vanderburgh County Death Register,* vol. CH-4E, 339.

1916

Kelly Robinson (black, age 22). *Murder.* The crime was committed on 12/20/1914 in Marion County. Handgun slaying of 53-year-old John F. Roe (white), who succumbed to his wound after 27 days of agony. Motive: pesky panhandler. The killer pulled out a gun and shot Roe when the latter refused to give him a nickel. The electric chair rid society of this moocher-turned-killer on February 1, 1916. Source: *Fort Wayne (IN) Journal-Gazette,* 12/21/14 (10:7). *Kokomo (IN) Daily Tribune,* 2/1/16 (10:4).

1920

William Ray (black, age 19). *Murder.* The crime was committed on 4/19/1920 in Marion County. Child killer. Fatal stabbing of 14-year-old Martha Huff (white), she having been knifed 13 times and thrown into a swollen creek. Motive: attempted sexual assault. The killer was executed on August 5, 1920. Source: *Fort Wayne (IN) Journal-Gazette,* 4/23/20 (1:7) & 8/5/20 (7:6).

William Thornton (black, age 21). *Murder.* The crime was committed on 6/12/1920 in Lake County. Handgun slaying of 42-year-old Nicholas Kish (white). Motive: mugging. The streets of Gary IN became a little bit safer when this killer was put to death on December 10, 1920. Source: *Lake County Times* (Hammond, IN), 6/13/20 (1:3) & 12/10/20 (1:1). See also: World War I draft registration card no. 179 (East Chicago, IN), which notes Mr. Kish.

1922

William E. Donovan (white, age 40). *Murder.* The crime was committed on 7/21/1921 in Parke County. Uxoricide. Handgun slaying of 37-year-old Nora Donovan (white), she having been shot while holding a baby in her arms. Motive: habitual brutality. Venue changed from Parke County to Montgomery County. The electric chair took this character on June 1, 1922. Source: *News Sentinel* (Ft. Wayne, IN), 6/1/22 (1:3). See also: 1920 U.S. Census (Parke Co., IN), which notes both parties.

Ben Brooks (white, age 33). *Murder.* The crime was committed on 8/23/1921 in Jackson County. Torture and mutilation of 49-year-old Amazona Montgomery (white). Motive: feuding. Venue changed from Jackson County to Bartholomew County. The exact details of what Brooks did to this woman are too violent and obscene for publication. This hatred-fueled killer was executed on December 1, 1922. Source: *News Sentinel* (Ft. Wayne, IN), 12/1/22 (1:4). See also: 1920 U.S. Census (Jackson Co., IN), which notes both parties.

1924

Harry Diamond (white, age 24). *Murder.* The crime was committed on 2/14/1923 in Porter County. Uxoricide. Handgun slaying of 42-year-old Nettie Herscovitz Diamond (white). Motive: despoilment by a bridegroom who played her false. Venue changed from Porter County to La Porte County. Double-dealing Diamond died in the electric chair on November 14, 1924. Source: *Lake County (IN) Times,* 5/26/23 (1:5). *Kokomo (IN) Daily Tribune,* 11/14/24 (3:2).

1925

Peter Vergolini (white, age 30). *Murder.* The crime was committed on 9/22/1924 in Lake County. Child killer. Strangulation of 10-year-old Annie Tomicik (white). Motive: sexual assault. This pervert was executed on January 30, 1925. Source: *Logansport (IN) Morning Press,* 9/26/24 (1:5) & 1/30/25 (1:1). *Actual Detective,* 6/41.

John Koval (white, age 31). *Murder.* The crime was committed on 4/2/1925 in Lake County. Executed for the murder of 33-year-old Martha Egelski (white), who was slashed to death with a razor. Motive: drunken quarrel. The killer was completely sober when he went to the electric chair on October 16, 1925. Source: *Lake County Times* (Hammond, IN), 4/3/25 (1:5) & 10/16/25 (1:4).

1926

Edward Stewart (black, age 24). *Murder.* The crime was committed on 2/11/1925 in Marion County. Executed for the murder of 35-year-old Ralph Cunningham (white), who had been struck on the head with an iron bar. Motive: robbery. Stewart met death at the hands of the State on January 16, 1926. Source: *Logansport (IN) Pharos-Tribune,* 2/12/25 (2:4) & 1/16/26 (1:7).

Peter Jankowski (white, age 27). *Murder.* The crime was committed on 4/20/1925 in Lake County. Handgun slaying of 21-year-old Andrew Hritzu (white), the victim having been shot in the back. Motive: mugging. This thug was electrocuted on January 22, 1926. Source: *Gary (IN) Post-Tribune,* 4/21/25 (2:2), 4/22/25 (2:1) & 4/24/25 (1:9). *Gary (IN) Evening Times,* 1/22/26 (1:8).

Henry Smith (black, age not recorded). *Murder.* The crime was committed on 6/27/1925 in Lake County. Handgun slaying of Martin Smith (black, no relation, age not recorded). Motive: irate cuckold. Venue changed from Lake County to Porter County. Henry Smith was also determined to have been a fugitive from Memphis, TN, where he had murdered his wife in 1916. He was executed for his Indiana offense on March 26, 1926. Source: *Gary (IN) Post-Tribune*, 6/29/25 (1:2) & 12/11/25 (5:1). *Lake County (IN) Times*, 3/26/26 (11:1).

1927

Roosevelt Hicks (black, age 21). *Murder.* The crime was committed on 7/26/1925 in Marion County. Uxoricide. Handgun slaying of about 19-year-old Esther Lewis Hicks (black). Motive: disobedience to her husband's wishes. The young wife-killer was executed on July 29, 1927. Source: *Logansport (IN) Pharos-Tribune*, 7/29/27 (3:1). See also: *Marion County (IN) Marriage Index* (1920–1925), vol. 125, 78.

1928

John Grzyb, alias "John Hall," alias "John Gray" (white, age 21). *Murder.* The crime was committed on 3/29/1926 in St. Joseph County. Handgun slaying of 53-year-old Louis Kreidler (white). Motive: robbery. Venue changed from St. Joseph County to Elkhart County. This killer was executed on April 10, 1928. Source: *Logansport (IN) Pharos-Tribune*, 4/10/28 (9:5). *Master Detective*, 4/39. See also: 1920 U.S. Census (St. Joseph Co., IN), which notes Mr. Kreidler.

1930

James Britt (black, age 41). *Murder.* The crime was committed on 10/7/1929 in Lake County. Handgun slaying of 32-year-old Samuel Goldberg (white), who was shot three times. Motive: suspected gangland killing. The gunman (James Britt) was himself executed (albeit legally) on March 21, 1930. Source: *Gary (IN) Post-Tribune*, 10/8/29 (1:8). *Chicago Daily Tribune*, 10/8/29 (8:3). *Lake County Times*, 10/8/29 (1:8). *Logansport (IN) Press*, 3/21/30 (1:4).

1931

Ignacio Saragoza (Latino, age 27). *Murder.* The crime was committed on 12/14/1930 in La Porte County. Police killer, etc. Executed for the handgun slaying of 58-year-old Charles L. Glafke (white). Motive: resisting arrest. Saragoza had also murdered a fellow Mexican named Manuel Sisneros (with the same handgun) about four hours prior to killing the policeman. Motive: gambling dispute. He was not tried in that case. The State of Indiana put him to death on June 24, 1931. Source: *Vidette-Messenger* (Valparaiso, IN), 12/15/30 (3:7). *Rushville (IN) Republican*, 6/24/31 (1:6). *Dynamic Detective*, 8/39. *Official Detective*, 9/39.

1932

Herbert Johnson (white, age 33). *Murder.* The crime was committed on 6/5/1931 in La Grange County. Shotgun (sawed off) slaying of 50-year-old Bertram Charles Fry (white). Motive: robbery. The electric chair accounted for Herbert Johnson on February 12, 1932. Source: *La Grange (IN) News*,

6/11/31 (1:7). *Logansport (IN) Press*, 10/13/31 (1:7). *Logansport (IN) Pharos-Tribune*, 2/12/32 (1:8).

Ulysses McKnezzer, alias "Ulysses Mack" (black, age 28). *Murder.* The crime was committed on 3/17/1929 in Lake County. Incipient serial killer. Executed for the hatchet murder of 20-year-old Josephine Odoriczzi (white). Motive: sexual assault. He is also confirmed to have perpetrated at least two other murders at Gary IN within the same week: Mary Gigl (white, age 16) by means of a hatchet on 3/13/1929 (motive: sexual assault), and James Welsh (black, age abt. 45) on 3/15/1929, who he had bludgeoned with a steel bar. Motive: robbery. Venue changed from Lake County to Porter County. This hatchet man was executed by high voltage on July 1, 1932. Source: *Gary (IN) Post-Tribune*, 3/15/29 (24:1) & 3/16/29 (1:4). *Lake County (IN) Times*, 3/16/29 (1:2). *Vidette-Messenger* (Valparaiso, IN), 5/18/29 (1:4). *Logansport (IN) Pharos-Tribune*, 7/1/32 (9:2). *Master Detective*, 2/30.

Glen Donald Shustrom (white, age 23). *Murder.* The crime was committed on 4/10/1932 in Lake County. Child killer. Strangulation of 12-year-old Alberta Knight (white). Motive: sexual assault. The electric chair settled matters with this aberrant young man on July 28, 1933. Source: *Vidette-Messenger* (Valparaiso, IN), 4/11/32 (3:7). *Gary (IN) Evening Times*, 7/28/33 (1:6). *Actual Detective*, 10/40.

Charles Vernon Witt (white, age 26). *Murder.* The crime was committed on 5/27/1931 in Marion County. Handgun slaying of 67-year-old Lafayette A. Jackson (white), a grocery store magnate. Motive: attempted robbery. Venue changed from Marion County to Boone County. The Indiana electric chair added Charles Witt to its count on November 24, 1933. Source: *Logansport (IN) Pharos-Tribune*, 5/29/31 (2:6). *Tipton (IN) Daily Tribune*, 11/24/33 (8:2). See also: 1930 U.S. Census (Marion Co., IN), which notes Mr. Jackson. *Official Detective*, 5/45. *Master Detective*, 2/49.

1933

John Edward Moore (white, age 29). *Murder.* The crime was committed on 11/11/1932 in Blackford County. Shotgun slayings of 65-year-old Charles A. Moore and 61-year-old Violet Ann Moore (whites), a married couple. Motive: robbery. The killer was Charles Moore's nephew. He was executed for this act of turpitude on March 2, 1933. Source: *Charleston (WV) Daily Mail*, 11/13/32 (5:2). *Vidette-Messenger* (Valparaiso, IN), 11/16/32 (1:4). *Gary (IN) Evening Times*, 3/2/33 (14:3). See also: 1920 U.S. Census (Blackford Co., IN), which notes Mr. & Mrs. Moore.

1934

Harley Edwards (white, age 37). *Murder.* The crime was committed on 7/23/1932 in Lawrence County. Uxoricide. Handgun slaying of 32-year-old Lillian B. Edwards (white). Motive: marital discord. Venue changed from Lawrence County to Jackson County. The killer paid the death penalty on March 2, 1934. Source: *Hammond (IN) Times*, 1/24/34 (7:3). *Tipton (IN) Daily Tribune*, 3/2/34 (8:2). See also: 1930 U.S. Census (Summit Co., OH), which notes both parties.

Louis Hamilton (white, age 25). *Murder.* The crime was committed on

5/27/1931 in Marion County. Accomplice in the handgun slaying of 67-year-old Lafayette A. Jackson (white), a grocery store magnate. Motive: attempted robbery. Venue changed from Marion County to Boone County. Hamilton met the same fate as his partner on September 28, 1934. Source: *Vidette-Messenger* (Valparaiso, IN), 9/28/34 (2:8). See also: Charles Witt (executed 11/24/33).

Richard Perkins (black, age 29). *Murder.* The crime was committed on 1/3/1931 in Marion County. Police killer. Handgun slaying of 27-year-old Carl W. Heckman (white). Motive: robbery gone awry. Venue changed from Marion County to Hancock County. The electric chair finished off Richard Perkins on October 1, 1934. Source: *Logansport (IN) Press*, 1/4/31 (1:6). *Logansport (IN) Pharos-Tribune*, 3/10/32 (7:3) & 10/1/34 (5:7). See also: 1930 U.S. Census (Marion Co., IN), which notes Heckman.

Edward Coffin (white, age 21). *Murder.* His crimes were committed on 6/4/1934. Police killer. Handgun slayings of 25-year-old Harold Amick and 38-year-old John Pfaffenberger (whites) in separate incidents in Scott County and Jackson County, respectively. Motive: evading pursuit. Venue changed to Clark County. An electrocuted Edward Coffin was lowered into his coffin at the Indiana State Prison on October 9, 1934. Source: *Vidette-Messenger* (Valparaiso, IN), 6/7/34 (1:3) & 10/9/34 (2:3).

1935

Olivett Griggs (black, age 31). *Murder.* The crime was committed on 5/30/1934 in Lake County. Handgun slaying of 50-year-old Vugo Orescan (white). Motive: robbery. Death in the electric chair was the fate of Olivett Griggs on June 14, 1935. Source: *Hammond (IN) Times*, 6/14/35 (1:1). *Greensburg (IN) Daily News*, 6/14/35 (1:2). See also: 1930 U.S. Census (Gary, IN), which notes Mr. Orescan.

Richard Chapman (white, age 20). *Murder.* The crime was committed on 12/31/1934 in Lake County. Shotgun slaying of 42-year-old Henry Nolte (white). Motive: robbery. This young killer was made to pay with his life at the Indiana State Prison on October 19, 1935. Source: *Vidette-Messenger* (Valparaiso, IN), 12/31/34 (1:3) & 1/5/35 (1:8). *Greensburg (IN) Daily News*, 10/19/35 (1:2).

1936

George W. Barrett (white, age 54). *Murder.* The crime was committed on 8/16/1935. Police killer. Executed under federal authority for the handgun slaying of 37-year-old Nelson B. Klein (white), an F.B.I. agent. Motive: resisting arrest. Barrett was hanged at Indianapolis on March 24, 1936. Source: *Kokomo (IN) Tribune*, 3/24/36 (1:3). *Front Page Detective*, 10/36. *Master Detective*, 5/39 & 8/55.

Gaston Slaughter (black, age 35). *Murder.* The crime was committed on 8/3/1934 in Vigo County. Police killer. Handgun slaying of 45-year-old Walter Lanfair (white). Motive: burglary gone awry. This offender was executed at the Indiana State Prison on April 17, 1936. Source: *Vidette-Messenger* (Valparaiso, IN), 9/5/34 (4:8). *Logansport (IN) Press*, 9/30/34 (8:5). *Kokomo (IN) Tribune*, 4/17/36 (1:6).

Clarence E. Thomas (white, age 31). *Murder.* The crime was committed on 7/3/1936 in Whitley County. Executed for the murder of 21-year-old Harry Zumbrun (white), who was felled by a hammer blow to the head and then finished off by having his throat cut. Motive: robbery. The price this killer paid was death in the electric chair on October 19, 1936. Source: *Logansport (IN) Pharos-Tribune,* 10/19/36 (1:1).

Harry Singer (white, age 25). *Murder.* The crime was committed on 7/21/1936 in Wabash County. Child killer, etc. Executed for the handgun slayings of 56-year-old John Wesley Caufman and 36-year-old Viola Caufman (whites, a married couple), and the fatal pistol-whipping of 12-year-old Marjorie Caufman, their daughter. Motive: disgruntled employee. Singer is also confirmed to have perpetrated the 7–3-1936 carjack killing of 20-year-old Joseph F. Bryant (white) in Wabash IN with the same handgun. He was put to death on December 26, 1936. Source: *Logansport (IN) Pharos-Tribune,* 8/8/36 (1:6), 12/24/36 (2:8) & 12/26/36 (1:1). *Front Page Detective,* 4/37. *Dynamic Detective,* 6/37. *Headline Detective,* 2/43. *Master Detective,* 8/44. *Real Detective,* 5/37.

1937

Chester Arkuszewski (white, age 23). *Murder.* The crime was committed on 7/27/1936 in La Porte County. Handgun slaying of 67-year-old Ignatz Pazuchoski (white). Motive: robbery. The killer was executed on March 12, 1937. Source: *Vidette-Messenger* (Valparaiso, IN), 7/29/36 (7:5) & 3/12/37 (1:8). *Dynamic Detective,* 5/39.

William A. Kuhlman (white, age 27), **John Joseph Poholsky** (white, age 34) and **Frank Gore Williams** (white, age 23). *Murder.* Their crime was committed on 6/9/1936 in Franklin County. Fatal beating and complete dismemberment of 65-year-old Harry R. Miller (white). Motive: murder-for-hire. All three killers were put to death on June 10, 1937. Source: *Vidette-Messenger* (Valparaiso, IN), 6/10/37 (1:3). *Front Page Detective,* 12/36. *Daring Detective,* 4/37, *Crime Detective,* 8/39. *Master Detective,* 12/54 & 8/76. *Real Detective,* 1/37. See also: Heber L. Hicks (executed 5/6/38).

Raymond Fortune (white, age 25). *Murder.* The crime was committed on 2/29/1936 in Allen County. Handgun slaying of 27-year-old Oris M. Dokken (white), who was shot eight times. Motive: robbery. Venue changed from Allen County to Huntington County. The killer was executed on September 17, 1937. Source: *Logansport (IN) Pharos-Tribune,* 3/2/36 (2:5). *Kokomo (IN) Tribune,* 9/17/37 (1:2). See also: 1930 U.S. Census (Sheboygan Co., WI), which notes Dokken.

1938

Willis Fuller (white, age 27). *Murder.* The crime was committed on 7/16/1936 in Vigo County. Police killer. Handgun slaying of 45-year-old J. Paul Mankin (white). Motive: resisting arrest. The Indiana electric chair evened the score with Willis Fuller on January 14, 1938. Source: *Logansport (IN) Pharos-Tribune,* 7/17/36 (8:3), 7/18/36 (5:4) & 1/14/38 (5:1).

Monroe White (black, age 32). *Murder.* The crime was committed on 8/2/1937 in Lake County. Handgun slaying of 42-year-old Michael Pappas (white). Motive: robbery. Venue changed from Lake County to Newton County. The killer was executed on May 3, 1938. Source: *Hammond (IN) Times*, 8/2/37 (1:6). *Kokomo (IN) Tribune*, 5/3/38 (14:1).

Heber L. Hicks (white, age 38). *Murder.* The crime was committed on 6/9/1936 in Franklin County. Catalyst in the fatal beating and dismemberment of 65-year-old Harry R. Miller (white), a grocery store magnate. Motive: financial gain. On May 6, 1938, Hicks became the fourth man to suffer capital punishment at the hands of the State for the part he played in this tragedy. Source: *Logansport (IN) Pharos-Tribune*, 5/6/38 (1:4). See: William Kuhlman et al. (executed 6/10/37).

John Dee Smith (white, age 19). *Murder.* The crime was committed on 8/13/1935 in Allen County. Handgun slaying of 42-year-old Arlie Foster (white). Motive: robbery. Venue changed from Allen County to Whitley County. The killer was executed on June 1, 1938. Source: *Logansport (IN) Pharos-Tribune*, 7/16/37 (2:2). *Kokomo (IN) Tribune*, 2/19/38 (3:2). *Logansport (IN) Press*, 6/1/38 (1:1). *Master Detective*, 4/46.

Robert Shaw (white, age 27). *Murder.* The crime was committed on 12/3/1937 in La Grange County. Police killer. Handgun slaying of 44-year-old Harry E. Spice (white). Motive: resisting arrest. Shaw was a Canadian by birth but officially a British subject. He was executed at the Indiana State Prison on June 28, 1938. Source: *Kokomo (IN) Tribune*, 12/3/37 (1:2). *Logansport (IN) Pharos-Tribune*, 6/28/38 (1:1). *Official Detective*, 1/15/38. *Daring Detective*, 12/39.

Vurtis Neal (white, age 21) and **Hugh Marshall** (white, age 19). *Murder.* Their crime was committed on 1/4/1937 in Shelby County. Handgun slaying of 31-year-old William C. Bright (white), who was shot four times. Motive: carjacking. The Indiana electric chair dealt with these young hooligans pursuant to law on July 8, 1938. Source: *Logansport (IN) Press*, 1/9/37 (1:8). *Logansport (IN) Pharos-Tribune*, 7/8/38 (1:4). See also: 1930 U.S. Census (Marion Co., IN), which notes Mr. Bright. *Front Page Detective*, 11/37. *Daring Detective*, 2/39. *Master Detective*, 3/50.

Henry Noelke (white, age 31). *Murder.* The crime was committed on 8/29/1937 in Warrick County. Uxoricide and filicide. Handgun slayings of 29-year-old Hazel Noelke and 18-month-old Rita Jo Noelke (whites), the former having been shot three times while holding the latter in her arms. Motive: ungovernable temper. Venue changed from Warrick County to Vanderburgh County. The Indiana electric chair did the rest in this case on September 30, 1938. Source: *Charleston (WV) Daily Mail*, 8/30/37 (7:8). *Kokomo (IN) Tribune*, 8/31/37 (7:4). *Logansport (IN) Press*, 9/30/38 (1:1). *Greensburg (IN) Daily News*, 9/30/38 (8:6).

Rhuel James Dalhover (white, age 31). *Murder.* The crime was committed on 5/25/1937. Police killer. Executed under federal authority for the machine-gun murder of 33-year-old Paul Vincent Minneman (white), an Indiana state trooper. Dalhover is also confirmed to have either perpetrated outright or to have participated in three other homicides as follows: the 11/25/1935 handgun killing of Anderson IN policeman Frank M. Levy (white, age 57) while evading pursuit; the 3/21/1936 handgun slaying of Edward Lindsay (white, age 22), a Piqua, OH, grocery clerk, during the course of a robbery; and the 4/27/1936 machine-gun slaughter of Indianapolis IN policeman Richard Rivers (white, age 44) while evading pursuit. The Indiana electric chair put an end to Dalhover and his evil antics on November 18, 1938. Source: *Logansport (IN) Pharos-Tribune*, 11/18/38 (1:1). *Actual Detective*, 3/9/38. *Master Detective*, 11/44, 12/44 & 3/69. *Official Detective*, 10/1/37, 10/15/37, 11/1/37, 11/15/37, 12/1/37, 12/15/37, 1/1/38 and 4/76. *Real Detective*, 1/38. *True* (magazine) 1/38.

1939

Orelle Easton (white, age 25). *Murder.* The crime was committed on 6/26/1938 in La Porte County. Police killer. Handgun slaying of 28-year-old William Raymond Dixon (white). Motive: resisting arrest. Easton was executed for what he did on June 3, 1939. Source: *Logansport (IN) Pharos-Tribune*, 6/27/38 (1:7) & 6/3/39 (1:3). *Official Detective*, 10/38. *Crime Detective*, 11/46.

James Swain (black, age 20). *Murder.* The crime was committed on 11/23/1937 in Vanderburgh County. Handgun slaying of 68-year-old Christ H. Bredenkamp (white). Motive: attempted robbery. This killer was executed on June 23, 1939. Source: *Kokomo (IN) Tribune*, 11/27/37 (16:3). *Hammond (IN) Times*, 12/31/37 (3:6). *Logansport (IN) Pharos-Tribune*, 6/23/39 (9:7). See also: 1920 U.S. Census (Vanderburgh Co., IN), which notes Mr. Bredenkamp.

Adrian Miller (white, age 31). *Murder.* The crime was committed on 10/13/1938 in Allen County. Strangulation of 17-year-old Alice Mae Girton (white). Motive: sexual assault. This predator was put to death on August 16, 1939. Source: *Logansport (IN) Pharos-Tribune*, 10/14/38 (1:7) & 8/16/39 (1:3). *Actual Detective*, 1/39. *Master Detective*, 6/49 & 5/57. *Real Detective*, 9/74 & 12/77.

1941

Milton Leonard Hawkins (white, age 24). *Murder.* The crime was committed on 5/20/1940 in Clark County. Executed for the murder of 38-year-old Edmund J. Davis (white), a taxi driver who was bludgeoned with a lead pipe, bound with wire and thrown from his moving cab. Motive: carjacking. Venue changed from Clark County to Floyd County. The electric chair claimed this killer on November 14, 1941. Source: *Hammond (IN) Times*, 5/27/40 (11:6). *Kokomo (IN) Tribune*, 11/14/41 (1:5). *Official Detective*, 9/40. *Crime Detective*, 5/41. *Master Detective*, 3/48. *Real Detective*, 3/41.

1942

Virginius Carter (white, age 32). *Murder.* The crime was committed on 5/16/1941 in Dearborn County. Shotgun slayings of 59-year-old Johnston Agrue and 63-year-old Nina Agrue (a married couple), 22-year-old Leo Agrue, 33-year-old William Agrue and 12-year-old Mary Elizabeth Breeden (whites). Motive: resentment at having been forced to marry a girl that he had put in the family way. This playboy-turned-mass-killer was executed on February 10, 1942. Source: *Kokomo*

(IN) Tribune, 2/10/42 (2:4). *Official Detective*, 8/41. *Headline Detective*, 9/41.

1945

Cleveland Greathouse (black, age 63). *Murder.* The crime was committed on 4/28/1945 in Lake County. Fatal stabbing of 38-year-old Rebecca Cortland, a.k.a. "Rebecca Holding" (black). Motive: because he could no longer endure her nagging, or so he said. The Indiana electric chair closed his life's account on November 26, 1945. Source: *Hammond (IN) Times*, 6/24/45 (1:3) & 11/26/45 (1:6). *Vidette-Messenger* (Valparaiso, IN), 11/26/45 (1:8).

1946

Frank James Quarles (black, age 44). *Murder.* The crime was committed on 11/29/1944 in Vanderburgh County. Strangulation of 68-year-old Julia Gottman (white). Motive: disgruntled employee. Quarles was put to death for this on April 2, 1946. Source: *Kokomo (IN) Tribune*, 12/22/44 (2:8). *Vidette-Messenger* (Valparaiso, IN), 4/2/46 (2:3). See also: 1930 U.S. Census (Evansville, IN), which notes Julia Gottman.

1949

Robert O. Brown (white, age 36) and **Frank Badgley** (white, age 49). *Murder.* Their crime was committed on 1/11/1947 in Lake County. Police killers. Handgun slayings of 29-year-old John J. Gerka Jr., and 21-year-old Donald B. Cook (whites). Motive: resisting arrest. Venue changed from Lake County to Jasper County. These double murderers were executed on February 23, 1949. Source: *Logansport (IN) Pharos-Tribune*, 1/29/47 (14:5) & 2/23/49 (19:6). *Official Detective*, 6/48. *Real Detective*, 1/76.

Thomas Kallas (white, age 57). *Murder.* The crime was committed on 9/4/1947 in Lake County. Fatal stabbing of 23-year-old George Stocks (white). Motive: sexual assault. No conclusions are drawn concerning his romantic inclinations. It was the homicide that brought Kallas to the electric chair on March 29, 1949. Source: *Daily Register* (Harrisburg, IL), 9/6/47 (4:5). *Daily Independent* (Murphysboro, IL), 1/16/48 (8:7). *Vidette-Messenger* (Valparaiso, IN), 3/29/49 (4:5).

1950

Franklin Click (white, age 24). *Murder.* The crime was committed on 8/4/1944 in Allen County. Possible serial killer. Executed for the beating and strangulation of 17-year-old Phyllis Conine (white). Motive: sexual assault. Prime suspect in two other Allen County sex slayings: Wilhelmina Haaga (white, age 38) on 2/2/1944 and Anna Kuzeff (white, age 19) on 5/22/1944. Franklin Click was executed on December 30, 1950. Source: *Kokomo (IN) Tribune*, 12/30/50 (1:6). *Official Detective*, 5/50, 6/50, 7/50, 8/50 & 9/50. *Crime Detective*, 8/61. *Real Detective*, 12/56.

1951

Robert Austin Watts (black, age 25). *Murder.* The crime was committed on 11/12/1947 in Marion County. Shotgun slaying of 39-year-old Mary Lois Burney (white). Motive: attempted sexual assault. Prime suspect in the 10/30/1947 butcher-knife killing of 68-year-old Mabel Merrifield (white), an Indianapolis woman. Venue changed from Marion County to Bartholomew County. Robert Watts went to his death in the electric chair on January 16, 1951. Source: *Vidette-Messenger* (Valparaiso, IN), 11/18/47 (1:1). *Logansport (IN) Pharos-Tribune*, 1/16/51 (9:6). *Official Detective*, 3/48. *Front Page Detective*, 3/48.

1961

Richard Allen Kiefer (white, age 36). *Murder*. The crime was committed on 1/15/1957 in Allen County. Uxoricide and filicide. Hammer killings of 36-year-old Pearl Kiefer and 5-year-old Dorothy Kiefer (whites), his wife and daughter, respectively. Motive: ungovernable temper. The Indiana electric chair solved that problem for him permanently on June 15, 1961. Source: *Logansport (IN) Pharos-Tribune*, 1/17/57 (1:4) & 6/15/61 (2:2).

Iowa

1887

Chester Bellows (white, age 27). *Murder.* The crime was committed on 7/8/1886 in Floyd County. Handgun slaying of 16-year-old Alice Waterman (white), his niece. Motive: sexual obsession. This twisted uncle was hanged at Charles City on December 16, 1887. Source: *Jackson Sentinel* (Maquoketa, IA), 7/22/86 (2:7) & 11/25/86 (6:8). *Iowa State Reporter* (Waterloo, IA), 12/22/87 (2:1).

1888

Henry Schmidt (white, age 18). *Murder.* The crime was committed on 9/4/1886 in Fayette County. Hanged for the murders of 72-year-old Abraham Peek and 61-year-old Lucretia Peek (whites, a married couple), the woman having been fatally wounded by a rifle shot and the man battered to death with the butt of that weapon. Motive: dispute over wages. This killer's execution was carried out at West Union on January 13, 1888. Source: *Sumner (IA) Gazette*, 9/9/86 (6:1) & 1/19/88 (4:1). See also: 1880 U.S. Census (Fayette Co., IA), which notes Mr. & Mrs. Peek.

1894

James C. Dooley (white, age 16). *Murder.* The crime was committed on 5/13/1892 in Adams County. Handgun slayings of 45-year-old Lucinda Coons and 10-year-old Nellie Coons (whites, his aunt and cousin respectively), the latter having also been badly beaten. Motive: uncontrollable anger. Dooley had been scolded for neglecting his chores and he reacted violently. It was a tantrum that brought him to the gallows at the Iowa State Penitentiary on October 19, 1894. Source: *Pocahontas County Sun* (Laurens, IA), 5/19/92 (1:2). *Oxford (IA) Mirror*, 11/1/94 (3:3). See also: 1880 U.S. Census (Adams Co., IA), which notes Mrs. Coons.

1895

Jacob Cumberland (white, age 42). *Murder.* The crime was committed on 9/24/1889 in Shelby County. Hanged for the murders of 72-year-old James Robertson and 40-year-old Jasper Robertson (whites, a father and son), the elder man having been struck on the head with a blunt instrument and the younger one shot with a handgun. Their bodies (or what was left of them) were found two years later. Motive: robbery and despoilment. **Recidivist killer.** On 4–2-1883 this same offender had murdered his own son (Curtis Cumberland, white, age 14) in Neosho Co., KS, by shooting him in the gut with a handgun when the lad presumably balked at being separated from his mother and five siblings. Convicted and sentenced to death in that case,

Cumberland somehow wheedled both a commutation and a pardon. He was then turned loose on society with the aforesaid result. He was executed at the Iowa State Penitentiary on February 8, 1895. Source: *Alton (IL) Daily Telegraph*, 4/9/83 (2:2). *Cedar Rapids (IA) Evening Gazette*, 11/12/91 (1:5). *Carroll (IA) Sentinel*, 2/9/95 (4:3). *Waterloo (IA) Daily Courier*, 9/28/91 (2:3). See also: 1880 U.S. Census (Montgomery Co., IA), which notes the Robertsons.

1906

Joseph C. Smith (black, age 39). *Murder.* The crime was committed on 10/16/1903 in Monroe County. Handgun slaying of Ida Canady (black, age not recorded), she having been shot twice and severely beaten as well. Motive: jilted lover gone wild. Smith was executed for this black-on-black killing on April 20, 1906. Source: *Sioux Valley (IA) News*, 4/19/06 (2:2). *Iowa State Register and Farmer*, 4/27/06 (7:2).

1910

John Junkins (black, age 27). *Murder.* The crime was committed on 2/5/1909 in Wapello County. Hanged for the murder of 29-year-old Clara Rosen (white), she having been bludgeoned with a rock. Motive: mugging. Venue changed from Wapello County to Appanoose County. The execution of this offender was carried out on July 29, 1910. Source: *Iowa City Daily Press*, 3/1/09 (1:1). *Atlantic (IA) Evening News*, 7/29/10 (1:1). See also: 1900 U.S. Census (Hardin Co., IA), which notes Junkins as a reformatory inmate, and 1880 U.S. Census (Wapello Co., IA), which notes Clara Rosen as a minor.

1918

Fred Allen (black, age 22), **Nelson Johnson** (black, age 30) and **Stanley Tramble** (black, age 33). *Rape.* Their crime was committed on 5/24/1918. All three condemned under military authority for indecently assaulting a 17-year-old white girl named Jessie Barnes. The attack took place on the grounds of a U.S. military base when this roving trio overpowered the girl's male escort. They then proceeded to force themselves on her. All three were tried by a wartime court-martial. They paid the price of folly when they were hanged at Camp Dodge on July 5, 1918. Source: *Muscatine (IA) Journal*, 7/5/18 (1:3). See also: Copy of court-martial proceedings in this case, Gold Star Museum, Camp Dodge, IA.

1922

Ira Pavey (white, age 28). *Murder.* The crime was committed on 3/28/1919 in Sioux County. Handgun slaying of 37-year-old Claude Letner (white). Motive: highway robbery and gangland rivalry. The killer was hanged at the Iowa State Penitentiary on September 8, 1922. Source: *Sioux City (IA) Index*, 1/30/20 (1:2), 3/18/21 (1:4) & 9/15/22 (1:5). See also: 1910 U.S. Census (Sioux City, IA), which notes the murdered man.

Eugene Weeks (white, age 26). *Murder.* The crime was committed on 2/5/1921 in Polk County. Handgun slaying of 58-year-old George Fosdick (white). Motive: armed robbery. Weeks took his last walk up the 13 steps of the gallows on September 15, 1922. Source: *Des Moines (IA) Capitol*, 9/15/22 (1:5). See also: 1920 U.S. Census (Polk Co., IA), which notes both parties.

Orrie Loren Cross (white, age 22). *Murder.* The crime was committed on 2/5/1921 in Polk County. Accomplice in the handgun slaying of 58-year-old George Fosdick (white). Motive: armed robbery. He was hanged on November 24, 1922. Source: *Evening Gazette* (Cedar Rapids, IA), 11/24/22 (1:6). See also: Eugene Weeks (executed 9/15/22).

1923

Earl Throst (white, age 24). *Murder.* The crime was committed on 12/12/1921 in Allamakee County. Executed for the murder of 21-year-old Inga Magnusson (white), who was clubbed to death. Motive: because she had rebuffed the killer's advances. He was hanged on March 9, 1923. Source: *Postville (IA) Herald*, 12/15/21 (1:2). *Davenport (IA) Democrat*, 3/9/23 (1:1).

William Olander (white, age 24). *Murder.* The crime was committed on 3/12/1921 in Webster County. Handgun slaying of 54-year-old Berthold Halfpap (white). Motive: armed robbery. The gallows at the Iowa State Prison was the last thing this killer saw, on September 7, 1923. Source: *West Bend (IA) Journal*, 3/17/21 (1:2). *Davenport (IA) Democrat*, 9/7/23 (1:8). See also: 1920 U.S. Census (Webster Co., IA), which notes both parties.

1924

Roy Maupin (black, age 24). *Murder.* The crime was committed on 1/20/1922 in Polk County. Executed for the murder of 27-year-old Joseph Hayes (white), who was struck on the head with a 2' × 4'. Motive: mugging. The killer was hanged on January 18, 1924. Source: *Davenport (IA) Democrat*, 1/23/22 (1:1) & 1/18/24 (1:4). See also: 1910 U.S. Census (Macon Co., MO), which notes Maupin, and 1920 U.S. Census (Polk Co., IA), which notes the murdered man as "J. J. Hayes."

1925

Archie Burris (black, age 28). *Murder.* The crime was committed on 12/17/1921 in Wapello County. Handgun slaying of 20-year-old Hattie Renfro Bates (black), she having been blasted with a .45 automatic. Motive: lovers' imbroglio. The killer was hanged on January 2, 1925. Source: *Davenport (IA) Democrat*, 2/8/22 (17:5) & 1/2/25 (1:3).

Harlan Simons (white, age 28). *Murder.* The crime was committed on 7/12/1924 in Scott County. Executed for the murder of 38-year-old Orton Ferguson (white), who was battered to death with a heavy gas pipe. Motive: robbery. The killer stole the pants right off the victim's body and was found to be wearing them when he was arrested. He was hanged on November 16, 1925. Source: *Davenport (IA) Democrat*, 7/14/24 (1:2) & 11/16/25 (1:7).

1931

Joseph Altringer (white, age 22). *Murder.* The crime was committed on 10–4-1930 in Dubuque County. Child killer. Executed for strangling 12-year-old Earl Fuller, Jr. (white) by means of wire twisted tightly around the boy's neck. Motive: sexual assault. This pervert had his own life wrung out of him when he was legally hanged on November 6, 1931. Source: *Charles City (IA) Press*, 10/6/30 (4:1). *Ames (IA) Daily Tribune-Times*, 11/6/31 (1:6).

1935

Elmer Brewer (white, age 38) and **Patrick Griffin** (white, age 34). *Murder.* Their crime was committed on 12/16/1932 in Black Hawk County. Police killers. Handgun slaying of 38-year-old Wendell F. Dilworth (white). Motive: resisting arrest. These assassins of a law enforcement officer were hanged on June 5, 1935. Source: *Ames (IA) Daily Tribune-Times*, 12/17/32 (1:7) & 6/5/35 (1:5). See also: 1930 U.S. Census (Waterloo, IA), which notes Dilworth.

Reginald Tracy (white, age 53). *Murder.* The crime was committed on 10/3/1934 in Delaware County. Uxoricide. Catalyst in the handgun slaying of 53-year-old Mabel Tracy (white), she having been shot in the back. Motive: adultery on his part and murder-for-hire. The actual triggerman avoided capture. Reginald Tracy died twitching at the end of a rope on November 29, 1935. Source: *Oelwein (IA) Daily Register*, 11/29/35 (1:1). See also: 1930 U.S. Census (Delaware Co., IA), which notes the Tracys. *Crime Detective*, 3/40. *Master Detective*, 10/46. *Real Detective*, 6/58.

1938

John Milton Mercer (white, age 22). *Murder.* The crime was committed on 8/8/1930 in Cedar County. Handgun slaying of 57-year-old Robert G. Sproat (white, a posse man), who was shot three times with a .45 automatic. Motive: resisting arrest. The gunman was hanged on January 24, 1938. Source: *Atlantic (IA) News-Telegraph*, 8/9/30 (1:4). *Oelwein (IA) Daily Register*, 1/24/38 (1:1). See also: 1930 U.S. Census (Cedar Co., IA), which notes Mr. Sproat. *Front Page Detective*, 2/37. *Master Detective*, 2/39. *Real Detective*, 12/47.

Allen Wheaton (white, age 19). *Murder.* The crime was committed on 6/11/1936 in Pottawattamie County. Handgun slaying of 38-year-old Henry Plummer (white), the victim having been abducted from his place of employment and shot four times. The initial shot was in the back; it was followed by three more fired into the back of his head execution-style. Motive: abduction and robbery. The killer was himself executed (by hanging) on January 24, 1938. Source: *Oelwein (IA) Daily Register*, 6/13/36 (1:1) & 1/24/38 (1:1).

Marlo Heinz (white, age 29). *Murder.* The crime was committed on 7/23/1935 in Dubuque County. Child killer. Strangulation of 6-year-old David Fox (white, his nephew), whose little body was later found in a creek. Motive: sexual assault. This death-row inmate who was hated by even his fellow death-row inmates was hanged by the neck until dead on April 19, 1938. Source: *Oelwein (IA) Daily Register*, 7/24/35 (1:1) & 4/19/38 (1:1).

Franz Jacobsen (white, age 29). *Murder.* The crime was committed on 11/30/1936 in Wapello County. Handgun slaying of 25-year-old Catherine Elizabeth Leahy (white). Motive: jilted lover. Jacobsen was hanged for what he did on April 19, 1938. Source: *Oelwein (IA) Daily Register*, 12/1/36 (1:2) & 4/19/38 (1:1). *Daring Detective*, 10/37.

1940

Walter Rhodes (white, age 29). *Murder.* The crime was committed on

2/9/1937 in Johnson County. Uxoricide. Booby-trap bomb killing of 31-year-old Mabel Rhodes (white). Motive: insurance fraud and adultery on his part. This assassin (and defiler of his marriage vows) was hanged at the Iowa State Penitentiary on May 7, 1940. Source: *Carroll (IA) Daily Record*, 3/30/37 (1:4). *Iowa City Press-Citizen*, 5/7/40 (1:1). *Official Detective*, 5/1/37. *Daring Detective*, 9/37. *Real Detective*, 7/51.

1941

Ivan Leon Sullivan (white, age 28). *Murder.* The crime was committed on 7/8/1940 in Lee County. Prison-guard killer. Sniper slaying of 75-year-old Robert Hart (white) at the Iowa State Penitentiary. Motive: conspiracy to break out of prison. His efforts earned him a one-way walk onto the gallows platform on November 12, 1941. Source: *Iowa City Press-Citizen*, 7/9/40 (6:1). *Mason City (IA) Globe-Gazette*, 7/25/40 (12:6) & 11/12/41 (1:8). See also: 1930 U.S. Census (Lee Co., IA), which notes Robert Hart. *Headline Detective*, 11/40.

1944

Stanley Kaster (white, age 35). *Murder.* The crime was committed on 9/25/1943 in Bremer County. Shotgun slaying of 38-year-old Glenn Winchell (white), a security guard who literally had his face blown off. Motive: because the killer coveted the victim's sidearm. Kaster wound up with a rope around his neck and a certification of death by hanging on December 29, 1944. Source: *Waterloo (IA) Daily Courier*, 9/27/43 (5:3). *Daily Times Herald* (Carroll, IA), 12/29/44 (1:2).

1945

William Jarrett (white, age 53). *Murder.* The crime was committed on 1/11/1944 in Webster County. Executed for the murder of 48-year-old Everett Warden (white), who was beaten to death with an iron bar. Motive: because the killer coveted the victim's wife. The only prize that Jarrett gained from this was death by hanging. He collected that prize at the Iowa State Prison on February 23, 1945. Source: *Daily Times-Herald* (Carroll, IA), 1/12/44 (1:4) & 2/23/45 (1:4). *Front Page Detective*, 8/44.

1946

Philip Heincy (white, age 71) and **William Henry Heincy** (white, age 45). *Murder.* Their crime was committed on 12/16/1944 in Dickinson County. Handgun slaying of 63-year-old Robert W. Raebel (white). The homicide victim and his wife were also severely battered with a blackjack and a hammer. Motive: robbery and home invasion. The killers were hanged pursuant to law on March 29, 1946. Source: *Beatrice (NB) Daily Sun*, 12/18/44 (2:5). *Ames (IA) Daily Tribune*, 1/8/45 (8:7). *Daily Times-Herald* (Carroll, IA), 3/29/46 (1:3).

1949

Corliss Bruntlett (white, age 50). *Murder.* The crime was committed on 12/8/1947 in Pottawattamie County. Rifle slaying of 57-year-old Percy J. Smith (white), whose body was then destroyed in a bonfire. Motive: extortion. The killer had forced Mr. Smith to write him a check for a large amount of money just prior to pulling the trigger. Bruntlett was made to pay a much higher price when he was hanged at the Iowa State Penitentiary on July 6, 1949. Source: *Oelwein (IA) Daily Register*, 12/15/47 (1:6). *Council Bluffs (IA) Nonpareil*, 7/6/49 (9:8). *Master Detective*, 9/48.

1952

Edward James Beckwith (white, age 28). *Murder.* The crime was committed on 6/22/1949 in Grundy County. Mutilation murder of 22-year-old Irma Jean Klenzman Stahlhut (white). Motive: rebuffed suitor gone berserk. Venue changed from Grundy County to Black Hawk County. The killer paid the death penalty at the Iowa State Penitentiary on August 4, 1952. Source: *The Democrat* (Davenport, IA), 6/23/49 (1:8). *Oelwein (IA) Daily Register*, 8/4/52 (1:4). *Front Page Detective*, 11/49. *Real Detective*, 11/49. *Crime Detective*, 9/59. *Master Detective*, 12/59.

1962

Charles Noel Brown (white, age 28). *Murder.* The crime was committed on 2/22/1961 in Pottawattamie County. Spree killer. Executed for the handgun slaying of 54-year-old Alvin Koehrsen (white), who was shot seven times. His body was dumped on a public street. Motive: carjacking. Brown and his accomplice (Charles Edwin Kelley) are confirmed to have also murdered two other men as follows: Howard Trowbridge (white, age 52) during a tavern holdup at Minneapolis, MN, on 2/20/1961 and Harry Goldberg (white, age 60) during a liquor store robbery at Omaha, NB, the following day, all with the same weapons. Charles Noel Brown was hanged at the Iowa State Penitentiary on July 24, 1962. Source: *Mason City (IA) Globe-Gazette*, 2/23/61 (1:7). *Carroll (IA) Daily Times-Herald*, 7/24/62 (1:4). *Front Page Detective*, 6/61. *Master Detective*, 6/71. See also: Charles Edwin Kelley (executed 9/6/62).

Charles Edwin Kelley (white, age 20). *Murder.* The crime was committed on 2/22/1961 in Pottawattamie County. Spree killer. Executed for participating in the handgun slaying of 54-year-old Alvin Koehrsen (white), who was shot seven times. His body was dumped on a public road. Motive: carjacking. Kelley is confirmed to have also been a full accomplice in two other murders that same week in Minnesota and Nebraska. His trial for the Iowa murder was taken on a change of venue from Pottawattamie County to Mills County. He was hanged for his part in that crime on September 6, 1962. Source: *Cedar Rapids (IA) Gazette*, 9/6/62 (1:1). See also: Charles Noel Brown (executed 7/24/62).

1963

Victor Henry Feuger (white, age 24). *Murder.* The crime was committed on 7/11/1960. Executed under federal authority for the abduction and handgun killing of 34-year-old Edward Bartels (white, a physician), whom he shot execution-style. Motive: robbery and carjacking. Feuger was prosecuted under a federal kidnapping statute because he had abducted Dr. Bartels in one State (Iowa) but murdered him in another (Illinois). He was hanged at the Iowa State Penitentiary on March 15, 1963. Source: *Carroll (IA) Daily Times-Herald*, 3/15/63 (1:4). *Official Detective*, 11/60. *Master Detective*, 12/60, 4/71 & 8/74.

Kentucky

1866

George McMurray (black, age not recorded). *Murder.* The crime was committed on 4/28/1866 in McCracken County. Ax murder of Silas Manley (black, age not recorded). Motive: robbery. This black-on-black killer was hanged at Paducah on June 22, 1866. Source: McCracken County Circuit Court Criminal Case Files (1862–1866) Box 9, File 35, KY State Archives. *Louisville Daily Courier*, 6/27/66 (1:10).

Samuel Gaines (white, age not recorded). *Murder.* The crime was committed on 6/24/1865 in Marshall County. Handgun slaying of 45-year-old Benjamin F. McNabb (white). Motive: a grudge about a horse. The killer was hanged at Benton KY on July 13, 1866. Source: Circuit Court Case File (*Commonwealth vs. Gaines*), office of the Clerk of Court, Marshall County Courthouse. See also: *Louisville Daily Courier*, 7/20/66 (2:3). Also: 1850 U.S. Census (Calloway Co., KY), which notes McNabb.

George Sheridan (black, age not recorded). *Murder.* The crime was committed on 4/12/1866 in Warren County. Executed for the murder of Patrick Donovan (white, age not recorded), the victim having been felled with a rock and his throat cut. Motive: robbery. The killer was hanged at Bowling Green on July 13, 1866. Source: *Louisville Daily Courier*, 4/16/66 (1:6) & 7/16/66 (1:6).

Allen Eggleston (white, age 25). *Murder.* The crime was committed on 6/6/1866 in Campbell County. Handgun slaying of 45-year-old Almon P. Menter (white). Motive: burglary. The killer was hanged at Newport KY on September 28, 1866. Source: *Louisville Daily Courier*, 6/8/66 (3:4) & 9/29/66 (4:3). See also: 1850 U.S. Census (Onondaga Co., NY), which notes Eggleston as a minor. See also Mr. Menter's tombstone inscription in Greenlawn Cemetery, Columbus, OH.

1867

William Price King (white, age 30) and **Abram Owens** (white, age 23). *Murder.* Their crime was committed on 11/11/1866 in Simpson County. Fratricide in King's case. Both executed for the handgun slaying of 28-year-old John Harvey King (white). Motive: gangland killing. These men were train robbers who feared that J. H. King might inform on them. The victim's body was found partially devoured by hogs. His killers were hanged at Franklin KY on June 28, 1867. Source: *Kentucky Gazette* (Lex.), 6/29/67 (2:1). *Louisville Daily Courier*, 7/6/67 (4:6). See also: Original Case File *(Commonwealth vs. Wm. King et al.)*, Dept. of Special Collections (Call no. SC 1744), Western Kentucky University Library. See also: 1860 U.S. Census (Simpson Co., KY), which notes all parties.

William F. Diggs, alias "Pudd Diggs" (white, age abt. 23). *Murder.* The crime was committed on an unspecified date in 1863 or 1864 in Calloway County. War criminal. Executed for the murder of George W. Miller (white, age uncertain), who was called to his door one night and assassinated there. Motive: wartime marauding. Diggs came from Henry Co., TN. He reportedly killed a deputy sheriff named Irvan there while resisting arrest in 1865. He was hanged at Murray KY on September 27, 1867. Source: *Louisville Daily Courier,* 10/3/67 (4:6).

1868

Negress Susan (black, age 12). *Murder.* The crime was committed on 8/15/1867 in Henry County. Child killer. Executed for the murder of 3-year-old Walter S. Graves (white), who had been battered to death with rocks. Motive: petulance. According to one account, she "took the child from the house to a tobacco patch in the rear of the stable about 50 yards from the house. Here, it appears from her own confession, she made the child lay down on the ground and after crossing its hands on its breast and making it bid its pa and ma good-bye, seized a stone and crushed its head almost to a jelly. She then seized it by an ankle and dragged it over the stubble to some thick undergrowth where it was concealed from human view." The killer's age was not accepted as a mitigating factor. She was hanged at Newcastle KY on February 7, 1868. Source: *Louisville Daily Courier,* 10/4/67 (3:4), 2/9/68 (2:3) & 2/12/68 (2:3). *Evening Star* (Wash., D.C.), 9/17/67 (4:1) & 2/18/68 (1:7).

Pleasant W. Shields (white, age abt. 17). *Murder.* The crime was committed on 5/1/1866 in Grayson County. Executed for the murder of about 17-year-old Henry Hocker (white), who was "shot while laying off corn ground in a field." Motive: not specified. The killer was hanged at Leitchfield KY on June 26, 1868. Source: *Louisville Daily Courier,* 5/30/68 (1:6) & 7/9/68 (1:7).

George Johnson (black, age not recorded). *Rape.* The crime was committed on 3/20/1868 in Hopkins County. Indecent assault on the person of about 8-year-old Minerva A. Keen (white). The price he paid for this was death on the gallows at Madisonville KY on July 17, 1868. Source: *Louisville Daily Courier,* 7/28/68 (3:5), reprinted from a lost issue (7/23/68) of the *Madisonville (KY) Times.* See also: Original Case File *(Commonwealth vs. Johnson),* Hopkins County Circuit Court Criminal Case File no. 1941, Kentucky State Archives.

1870

William Kriel (white, age 46). *Murder.* The crime was committed on 3/7/1868 in Jefferson County. Uxoricide. Executed for the killing of 38-year-old Margaret Evans Kriel (white), she having been manually choked and then finished off with shots fired from a handgun. Motive: because the killer thought that the woman was planning to leave him. Kriel was hanged at Louisville on January 21, 1870. Source: *Louisville Daily Courier,* 3/8/68 (3:5). *Louisville Courier-Journal,* 1/22/70 (4:2).

1872

John Ryan (white, age not recorded). *Murder.* The crime was committed on or about 8/15/1863 in Graves County. Executed for the murder of 15-year-old Sarah Jane Owen (white), who was shot with a handgun and then pistol-whipped almost beyond recognition. Motive: home invasion. The killer was caught nearly 8 years later. He was hanged at Mayfield KY on May 31, 1872. Source: *Louisville Courier Journal*, 5/24/71 (2:1) & 12/14/71 (2:1). *Mayfield (KY) Monitor*, 6/14/93 (2:3) in retrospect.

Thomas Guthrie (black, age not recorded). *Murder.* The crime was committed on 3/7/1872 in Boyle County. Ax murder of 76-year-old Joseph McNeil (white). Motive: hooliganism. This killer was hanged at Danville KY on July 5, 1872. Source: *Louisville Courier Journal*, 3/10/72 (3:3). *Edwardsville (IL) Intelligencer*, 7/18/72 (2:3).

William Ayres (white, age not recorded). *Murder.* The crime was committed on an unspecified date in 1864 or 1865 in Wayne County. War criminal. Executed for the gunshot slaying of about 26-year-old Morgan Daffron (white male). Motive: marauding. Ayres was a Union guerrilla during the War of the Rebellion. Daffron was a disabled CSA veteran. The trial record for this case was presumably lost in an 1898 courthouse fire. William Ayres was hanged at Monticello KY on August 30, 1872. Source: *Louisville Courier Journal*, 12/4/71 (2:1) & 9/4/72 (1:2). *Monticello (KY) Signal*, 1/13/87 in retrospect. See also: 1860 U.S. Census (Wayne Co., KY), which notes Daffron.

Will Twyman (black, age 23). *Murder.* The crime was committed on 4/10/1872 in Woodford County. Executed for the murder of 53-year-old Richard Tyson (white), who was bludgeoned with a rock. Motive: highway robbery. The killer was hanged at Versailles KY on November 29, 1872. Source: *Louisville Courier Journal*, 4/15/72 (2:1) & 12/2/72 (3:5). See also: 1870 U.S. Census (Woodford Co., KY), which notes both parties.

1873

Thomas Smith (black, age 27). *Murder.* The crime was committed on 5/10/1871 in Jefferson County. Handgun slaying of 44-year-old Joseph Bradner (white). Motive: robbery. Smith suffered death on the gallows for this at Louisville on March 28, 1873. Source: *Louisville Courier Journal*, 3/29/73 (4:2). *New York Herald*, 3/29/73 (3:3). See also: 1870 U.S. Census (Van Wert Co., OH), which notes Mr. Bradner.

Joseph Duncan (black, age 48). *Murder.* The crime was committed on 4/27/1872 in Bourbon County. Rifle slaying of John Hawkins (black, age not recorded), whose brains were also dashed out with the butt of that weapon. Motive: personal animosity. The killer was hanged at Paris KY on June 13, 1873. Source: *Louisville Courier Journal*, 5/1/72 (2:1) & 6/14/73 (1:2). See also: 1870 U.S. Census (Bourbon Co., KY), which notes Duncan.

Lindsay Brown (black, age 33) and **Levi Clapp** (black, age not recorded). *Rape.* Their crime was committed on 8/13/1873 in Ballard County. Both executed for indecently assaulting "a married white woman" named Nancy

Warden, age not recorded. The circumstances were such that they were toned down in the press. The condemned men were hanged at Blandville KY on December 5, 1873. Source: *Louisville Courier Journal*, 12/6/73 (1:3) & 12/8/73 (1:6). See also: 1870 U.S. Census (Graves Co., KY), which notes Brown.

1874

George Miller (black, age 22). *Murder.* The crime was committed on or about 5/27/1873 in Washington County. Ax murder of 63-year-old Granville C. Alfred (white). Motive: adultery with the victim's 34-year-old wife. It is impossible to determine to what extent (if any) the interracial aspect of this case may have influenced the trial court, since the homicide was enough to hang George Miller in its own right. He was executed at Springfield KY on May 1, 1874. Source: *Louisville Courier Journal*, 5/1/74 (3:6) & 5/2/74 (1:5).

1877

Richard Schuck (white, age 26). *Murder.* The crime was committed on 7/26/1876 in Owen County. Handgun slaying and partial cremation of 66-year-old Nelson Parrish (white), his father-in-law. Motive: forgery and despoilment. This impatient heir was hanged at Owenton KY on July 27, 1877. Source: *Elyria (OH) Constitution*, 8/10/76 (4:7). *Louisville Courier Journal*, 7/28/77 (3:3). Appeal: 9 KY Opin. 440–444. See also: 1850 U.S. Census (Owen Co., KY), which notes Mr. Parrish, and 1870 U.S. Census (Henry Co., KY), which notes the killer as "Richard H. Shuck."

1878

Philip Watson (black, age 63). *Murder.* The crime was committed on 9/2/1877 in Kenton County. Uxoricide. Executed for the hatchet killing of 54-year-old Eda Watson (black). Motive: marital discord. The hangman did his duty in this case at Covington on February 1, 1878. Source: *Louisville Courier Journal*, 2/2/78 (1:1). *New York Herald*, 2/2/78 (6:2). See also: 1870 U.S. Census (Kenton Co., KY), which notes both parties.

John W. Parker (black, age 19). *Murder.* The crime was committed on 3/9/1878 in Pulaski County. Fatal stabbing of George Franklin (black, age not recorded). Motive: dispute over protocol. Parker had tipped his hat to Franklin, a gesture that was highly insulting when done between males. This black-on-black provocateur was hanged at Somerset KY on June 12, 1878. Source: *Atlanta Constitution*, 3/14/78 (3:2). *Louisville Courier Journal*, 6/13/78 (1:5).

1879

George Washington (black, age 21). *Rape.* The crime was committed on 10/19/1878 in Jefferson County. Indecent assault (at knifepoint) on the person of 11-year-old Frances Otte (white). Death by hanging was legally meted out to this offender at Louisville on February 21, 1879. Source: *Louisville Courier Journal*, 10/21/78 (4:2), 10/25/78 (4:2), 10/26/78 (4:2) & 2/22/79 (4:2). See also: Charles Webster (executed 4/2/80).

1880

Robert Anderson (white, age 46). *Murder.* The crime was committed on 4/18/1878 in Jefferson County. Uxoricide. Fatal stabbing of 45-year-old Margaret Anderson (white). Motive: alcoholism. The murdered woman had refused to turn her pay (which she had earned as a laundress) over to her husband, knowing full well that he would squander it on liquor. A temper tantrum ensued, with fatal consequences for both parties. Anderson was a self-centered inebriate of the common variety. He was hanged at Louisville on April 2, 1880. Source: *Louisville Courier Journal,* 4/3/80 (5:2). See also: 1870 U.S. Census (Louisville, KY, Ward 10), which notes this ill-fated couple.

Charles Webster (black, age 21). *Rape.* The crime was committed on 10/19/1878 in Jefferson County. Accomplice and full participant in the knifepoint sexual violation of 11-year-old Frances Otte (white). He was executed at Louisville on April 2, 1880. Source: *Louisville Courier Journal,* 4/3/80 (5:2). See: George Washington (executed 2/21/79).

1881

John von der Heide (white, age 22). *Murder.* The crime was committed on 7/21/1880 in Shelby County. Child killer. Executed for the murder of 13-year-old Rebecca Johnson (black), whose head he smashed with rocks. Motive: an act of desperation by a fugitive. This cruel and unnecessary deed brought young von der Heide to the gallows at Shelbyville on February 25, 1881. Source: *Louisville Courier Journal,* 2/26/81 (2:2). *New York Herald,* 2/26/81 (5:2).

1882

John Major Hicks (black, age 18). *Murder.* The crime was committed on 12/15/1880 in Kenton County. Executed for the murder of 24-year-old Henry Murray Williams (white), who was beaten on the head with an iron rod. Motive: mugging. The killer was hanged at Covington on February 24, 1882. Source: *Louisville Courier Journal,* 2/25/82 (2:7). *New York Herald,* 2/25/82 (4:4). *Daily Journal* (Logansport, IN), 2/25/82 (1:2).

John Bridges (black, age 49). *Murder.* The crime was committed on 8/22/1881 in Trigg County. Uxoricide. Musket slaying of 41-year-old Clarry Bridges (black). Motive: marital breakdown. This luckless husband was hanged at Cadiz KY on June 30, 1882. Source: *Louisville Courier Journal,* 7/1/82 (4:5). See also: 1880 U.S. Census (Trigg Co., KY), which notes both parties.

Isaac Turner (black, age 23). *Murder.* The crime was committed on 6/10/1881 in Fayette County. Handgun slaying of 26-year-old Abe Ray (black). Motive: supposedly because Ray had bullied the killer's mother. Whatever the circumstances, they were deemed heinous enough to bring black on black killer Isaac Turner to the gallows at Lexington on July 28, 1882. Source: *Louisville Courier Journal,* 7/29/82 (6:1).

William Austin (white, age 24). *Murder.* The crime was committed on 1/19/1882 in Garrard County. Mutilation murder of 77-year-old Elizabeth "Betsy" Bland (white, his great-aunt), she having been repeatedly kicked in the face with heavy boots, sodomized with an ax handle and then hacked to death. Motive: sheer depravity. Austin was described as one of the nastiest killers that Kentucky ever produced. He was hanged at Lancaster on October 13, 1882. Source: *Louisville Courier Journal,* 10/14/82 (4:5). *New York Herald,* 10/14/82 (4:5). See also: 1880 U.S. Census (Garrard Co., KY), which notes Betsy Bland.

1883

David Timberlake (black, age 43). *Rape.* The crime was committed on 5/5/1883 in Fayette County. Indecent assault on the person of 9-year-old Maggie Lamson (black), who was severely mauled in the process. This condemned pervert was excoriated by his fellow blacks, they having no reservations about capital punishment so long as it was kept among themselves. The gallows marked his last earthly utterances at Lexington on July 20, 1883. Source: *Louisville Courier Journal,* 7/21/83 (4:6). *New York Herald,* 7/21/83 (4:5).

Samuel Bulger (black, age 41). *Rape.* The crime was committed on 6/21/1883 in Mason County. Indecent assault on the person of 11-year-old Hannah Belle McAuliffe (white), she having been violated at gunpoint as she was walking home from school. Her attacker was legally hanged at Maysville KY on September 4, 1883. Source: *Daily Evening Bulletin* (Maysville, KY), 6/22/83 (3:2). *Louisville Courier Journal,* 9/5/83 (4:6). See also: 1850 U.S. Census (Mason Co., KY), which notes the culprit as a minor, and 1880 U.S. Census (Mason Co., KY), which notes the injured girl.

Ellis Craft (white, age 28). *Murder.* The crime was committed on 12/23/1881 in Boyd County. Executed for the killings and partial cremations of 17-year-old Robert Gibbons, 14-year-old Fannie Gibbons and 15-year-old Emma Carrico Thomas (whites), they having all been hacked and bludgeoned with a hatchet and a crowbar prior to being left in a burning house. Motive: sexual assault. Venue changed from Boyd County to Carter County. The killer was hanged at Grayson KY on October 12, 1883. Source: *Stevens Point (WI) Daily Journal,* 12/31/81 (7:2). *Louisville Courier Journal,* 10/13/83 (1:6). *New York Times,* 10/13/83 (3:3). See also: 1880 U.S. Census (Boyd Co., KY), which notes the Gibbons family. See also: William Neil (executed 3/27/85).

1884

Frank Slagel (white, age 20). *Murder.* The crime was committed on 8/13/1883 in Pulaski County. Ax murders of 28-year-old James Adair and 22-year-old John Adair (whites, brothers), and a third young white man named Joseph Claibourne (white, age uncertain), their mutilated bodies having also been "riddled with bullets" and rolled off a cliff. Motive: robbery and gross perfidy. This gory triple killer was hanged at Somerset KY on March 14, 1884. Source: *Louisville Courier Journal,* 8/15/83 (5:1) & 3/15/84 (4:5). *New York Herald,* 3/15/84 (5:5). Appeal: 81 KY 485–489. See also: 1880 U.S. Census (Wayne Co., KY), which notes the Adairs.

Champ Fitzpatrick (white, age 23) and **Rudolph Fitzpatrick** (white, age 32). *Murder.* Their crime was committed on 8/6/1883 in Adair County.

Both executed for the murder of 40-year-old Miller Brewster (white), who was first attacked with a knife and then finished off by shots fired from two handguns in the middle of a public street. Motive: personal animosity based on petty jealousy. These brazen killers were hanged at Columbia KY on March 21, 1884. Source: *Louisville Courier Journal*, 3/22/84 (1:4). *Daily Journal* (Logansport, IN), 3/22/84 (1:3). See also: 1880 U.S. Census (Taylor Co., KY), which notes the murdered man.

Wash Fletcher (black, age 48). *Murder.* The crime was committed on 6/19/1883 in McCracken County. Fatal stabbing of 38-year-old Amanda Jackson (black). Motive: because she had objected to his beating her daughter. Wash Fletcher was hanged for this at Paducah on October 3, 1884. Source: *Louisville Courier Journal*, 10/4/84 (5:5). See also: 1880 U.S. Census (McCracken Co., KY), which notes both parties.

John Bush (black, age 31). *Murder.* The crime was committed on 1/13/1879 in Fayette County. Handgun slaying of 17-year-old Annie van Meter (white). Motive: ramifications of gossip. Bush was hanged at Lexington on November 21, 1884. Source: *Louisville Courier Journal*, 11/22/84 (5:1). *Daily Evening Bulletin* (Maysville, KY), 11/22/84 (1:2). See also: 1880 U.S. Census (Lexington, KY), which notes the killer as a prisoner.

1885

William Neil (white, age 23). *Murder.* The crime was committed on 12/23/1881 in Carter County. Accomplice in the murders of 17-year-old Robert Gibbons, 14-year-old Fannie Gibbons and 15-year-old Emma Carrico Thomas (whites). Motive: sexual assault. Neil was hanged at Grayson KY on March 27, 1885. Source: *Louisville Courier Journal*, 3/28/85 (1:7). See: Ellis Craft (executed 10/12/83). See also: 1880 U.S. Census (Boyd Co., KY), which notes Neil.

John Sexton (white, age 26). *Murder.* The crime was committed on or about 7/15/1884 in Knox County. Handgun slaying of 26-year-old George Rowden (white), the victim having been shot in the back. Motive: robbery and gross perfidy. Sexton was hanged for this foul play at Barbourville on March 27, 1885. Source: *Louisville Courier Journal*, 3/28/85 (2:2). *New York Herald*, 3/28/85 (6:6). See also: 1880 U.S. Census (Knox Co., KY), which notes the killer, and 1880 U.S. Census (Garrard Co., KY), which notes George Rowden.

Augustus Finley (white, age abt. 20). *Murder.* The crime was committed on 8/4/1883 in Floyd County. Handgun slaying of 19-year-old James Hunt (white). Motive: saloon brawl. Young Finley got more than he bargained for when he found himself dancing at the end of a rope at Prestonsburg on April 17, 1885. Source: *Logansport (IN) Daily Journal*, 4/18/85 (1:5). See also: KY Ct. of Appeals case no. 1565 (original manuscript), KY State Archives. See also: 1880 U.S. Census (Floyd Co., KY), which notes James Hunt as a pauper.

Moses Caton (white, age 45). *Murder.* The crime was committed on 2/21/1885 in Union County. Uxoricide. Hanged on his 46th birthday for the fatal abuse of 28-year-old Hester Taylor Peters Caton (white), whose ordeal was described in the following words:

Caton, a widower with three children (two sons and a daughter) was married to a widow possessed of considerable property. It was due to this latter fact that the subsequent tragedy was traceable. Caton, backed by his children, desired his wife to deed her land to him, and upon her refusal, he at once began a series of abuses and bodily tortures which were inflicted upon her for four years. The sick and feeble woman was driven like a brute from labor in the fields to stand by while the others ate. Then still starving [unless other hands than those of her stepchildren gave her bread], she was driven back to the fields. When the day's toil was over she was hurried to the miserable quarters in which the Catons lived. This was only a log house. The upper floor was a lot of loose planks. There was only one door to the house and no windows or chimneys but the house was well-pierced with loopholes. Caton said when he built it: "I intend it to be law proof and bullet proof!" The smoke having no outlet, it would settle in the upper part of the house and into this dingy and suffocating place his wife found her only resting place. Her bed consisted of an old straw tick upon the floor and for covering she was supplied with an old feather (quilt) containing about ten pounds of feathers. She often complained of the smoke but no attention was paid her. She was at times half frozen but upon complaining to her persecutors they removed her only covering, leaving her to endure the cold as best she might. She was not allowed to eat with the family nor drink from the family gourd, not sit at the table but was given an old tin plate, an oyster can for a drinking vessel and a box to sit on. Her food consisted of the scraps left by the family. She was compelled to do all of the menial labor about the house. Besides this, she was compelled to cut and pile brush. All of the members of the family took turns at whipping her. For the amusement of the family, Moses Caton and Josephine Fritz [who was living in adultery with the Catons] in February last made Mrs. Caton a pair of pants and a body [suit] out of old coarse sailcloth sewed with shoe thread. This they compelled her to wear with a thin shirt under it and also provided her with a crownless hat and one boot and one shoe. Thus attired, they drove her about like an ox. John Caton [her stepson] beat her about the head and shoulders with a hickory pole despite her pleadings not to treat her so cruelly. Wesley Caton [her other stepson] on one occasion compelled the woman to present herself in a nude condition to the farmhands and then outraged [i.e., raped] her in a most brutal manner. On the day before she was murdered an attempt was made to poison her by mixing arsenic with an egg which the woman was compelled to eat. She became sick and moaned and groaned through the entire night but none of the family paid any attention to her. On Saturday February 21st the inhuman family seemed to have tired of the sport with their victim and while the farmhands were out in the fields, Moses Caton and his two sons took Mrs. Caton out, beat her most brutally and finally hanged her. Her neck was broken and her body black with bruises. In this condition the body was piled into a rude box and taken into the house. It was only by accident that one woman living nearby learned of Mrs. Caton's demise and visited the house so that then the facts came out. Upon an attempt being made to arrest the miscreants, Caton and his sons barricaded themselves in the house. A brisk fire took place between them and the sheriff's posse resulting in the death of the 12-year-old daughter of Caton and the shooting of his son John through the lungs.

This man who hanged his wife was himself hanged at Morganfield KY on May 8, 1885. The circumstances speak for themselves. Source: *Louisville Courier Journal,* 5/9/85 (1:5). *Daily Leader* (Eau Claire, WI), 5/10/85 (4:4).

Jordan Taylor (black, age 36). *Murder.* The crime was committed on 10/8/1884 in Christian County. Ax murder of about 40-year-old Sally Saunders (black). Motive: wrathful lover. This ax man was hanged at Hopkinsville on June 26, 1885. Source: *Louisville Courier Journal,* 6/27/85 (2:1). *New York Herald,* 6/27/85 (5:5). See also: 1880 U.S. Census (Christian Co., KY), which notes the killer.

Henry Freese (black, age not recorded). *Murder.* The crime was committed on 5/2/1885 in Boyd County. Handgun slaying of 26-year-old Chester Honaker (white). Motive: whorehouse brawl. The penalty was death by hanging at Catlettsburg on August 14, 1885. Source: *Louisville Courier Journal,* 8/15/85 (4:3). *New York Herald,* 8/15/85 (5:5). See also: 1870 U.S. Census (Boyd Co., KY), which notes young Honaker.

Floyd Williams (white, age 19). *Murder.* The crime was committed on 6/21/1884 in Wolfe County. Handgun slaying of 38-year-old Payton Stricklin (white). Motive: adultery and a female catalyst. This sexual initiation proved fatal when country boy Williams was hanged at Campton KY on September 4, 1885. Source: *Louisville Courier Journal,* 9/5/85 (4:7). *Hazel Green (KY) Herald,* 9/9/85 (2:2). See also: 1880 U.S. Census (Wolfe Co., KY), which notes both parties.

Joseph Early (black, age 23). *Murder.* The crime was committed on 10/20/1885 in Whitley County. Handgun slaying of 18-year-old Leander Lawson (white). Motive: fracas in a rural schoolhouse. Early had strode into a black schoolhouse uninvited and verbally abused Lawson (the tutor) for some perceived slight. Lawson then ejected Early from the premises. Early came back a short time later brandishing a pistol with murderous intent. He ended up with a rope around his neck and a trap door beneath his feet at Williamsburg, KY, on December 7, 1885. Source: *Daily Evening Bulletin* (Maysville, KY), 10/23/85 (3:3). *Louisville Courier Journal,* 12/8/85 (2:3). See also: 1880 U.S. Census (Whitley Co., KY), which notes Lawson.

1886

Robert Smith (black, age 19). *Murder.* The crime was committed on 11/28/1885 in Jessamine County. Ax murder of 55-year-old James Sea (black, his stepfather), the victim having been attacked in his sleep, his mutilated body wrapped in a blanket and then dumped in a nearby river. Motive: theft of $12. This act cost its doer much more than that when he paid with his life at Nicholasville on April 17, 1886. Source: *Louisville Courier Journal,* 4/18/86 (7:4). *New York Herald,* 4/18/86 (12:2). See also: 1870 U.S. Census (Jessamine Co., KY), which notes James Sea.

Robert Fowler (white, age 24). *Murder.* The crime was committed on 8/16/1885 in Union County. Executed for the murder of 18-year-old Lydia Burnett (white), she having been waylaid by a knife wielding assailant and raped; her throat was cut with such force as to nearly decapitate her. Motive: frustrated suitor. Life for life was the price paid by Fowler when he was hanged at Morganfield KY on April 23, 1886. Source: *Logansport (IN) Daily Pharos,* 8/19/85 (2:3) & 4/24/86 (2:3). *Louisville Courier Journal,* 4/24/86 (3:1).

Harvey Pash (black, age 23). *Murder.* The crime was committed on 6/4/1885 in Nelson County. Shotgun slaying of 17-year-old Felix Adams (black). Motive: suspicion of adulterous intent. Hothead Harvey was hanged for this at Bardstown on December 10, 1886. Source: *Louisville Courier Journal,* 12/11/86 (5:3). See also: 1880 U.S. Census (Bardstown, KY), which notes the killer, and 1870 U.S. Census (Nelson Co., KY), which notes a very young Felix Adams.

1887

Granville Prewitt (white, age 23). *Murder.* The crime was committed on 10/30/1886 in Wayne County. Executed for the murders of 41-year-old Jarvis Buck and 35-year-old Mary Ellen Buck (whites, siblings), the man having been lured from his home and slashed to death with knives (wielded by three thugs) and the woman likewise slain with knives (inside her home) plus having her skull smashed by a heavy washboard. Motive: plunder. Prewitt was the one who didn't get away. He was hanged at Monticello KY on January 12, 1887. Source: *Galveston (TX) Daily News,* 11/1/86 (1:5). *Louisville Courier Journal,* 1/13/87 (5:5). See also: 1870 U.S. Census (Wayne Co., KY), which notes John and Mary Ellen Buck, and 1880 U.S. Census (Monroe Co., KY), which notes Prewitt.

James Marcum (white, age 24). *Murder.* The crime was committed on 2/10/1886 in Lawrence County. Sniper slaying of 38-year-old Henry Fisher Marcum (white), his uncle. Motive: family problems. Death by hanging was the fate of the nephew at Louisa KY on April 28, 1887. Source: *Big Sandy News* (Louisa, KY), 4/28/87 (3:3). *Louisville Courier Journal,* 4/30/87 (3:1). See also: 1880 U.S. Census (Lawrence Co., KY), which notes both parties, the murdered man as "H. F. Marcum."

James McElroy (black, age 20). *Murder.* The crime was committed on 9/29/1886 in Henderson County. Executed for the murder of 49-year-old Walter Mart (white), who was slashed to death (nearly beheaded) with a knife. Motive: robbery and deceitfulness. Death on the gallows was meted out to James McElroy at Henderson KY on July 1, 1887. Source: *Louisville Courier Journal,* 7/2/87 (6:4). *New York Herald,* 7/2/87 (10:1). See also: 1880 U.S. Census (Henderson Co., KY), which notes Mr. Mart.

Albert Turner (black, age 26). *Murder.* The crime was committed on 4/21/1887 in Jefferson County. Hanged for the murder of 24-year-old Jennie Bowman (white), she having been beaten, kicked and fatally battered with a wrought iron poker. Motive: burglary. The killer paid the death penalty at Louisville on July 1, 1887. Source: *Louisville Courier Journal,* 7/1/87 (1:5) & 7/2/87 (6:1). *New York Herald,* 7/2/87 (10:1). See also: William Patterson (executed 6/22/88).

James Tucker Agee (white, age 32). *Murder.* The crime was committed on 9/22/1886 in Fayette County. Handgun slaying of 30-year-old James Falconer (white, his brother-in-law). Motive: a stupid argument about the ownership of 24 ears of corn. It is uncertain whether this killer was served an extra helping of corn with his final meal before being led to the gallows at Lexington on November 4, 1887. Source: *Lexington (KY) Daily Press*, 9/24/86 (1:3). *Louisville Courier Journal*, 11/5/87 (4:6). See also: 1880 U.S. Census (Lex., KY), which notes both parties.

1888

William Patterson (black, age 32). *Murder.* The crime was committed on 4/21/1887 in Jefferson County. Accomplice in the fatal beating of 24-year-old Jennie Bowman (white), who succumbed to her injuries after 18 days in intensive care. Motive: burglary. Patterson paid with his own life at Louisville on June 22, 1888. Source: *Louisville Courier Journal*, 6/22/88 (6:1) & 6/23/88 (6:1). See also: Albert Turner (executed 7/1/87).

1889

James Ross (black, age 29). *Murder.* The crime was committed on 4/6/1888 in Meade County. Ax murder of 42-year-old Benedict Rhodes (white). Motive: burglary. The transgressor was hanged for what he did at Brandenburg on February 8, 1889. Source: *Louisville Courier Journal*, 2/9/89 (2:5). See also: 1880 U.S. Census (Meade Co., KY), which notes the murdered man as "Ben Rhodes."

Monroe Wilkerson (black, age not recorded). *Murder.* The crime was committed on 9/22/1888 in Allen County. Handgun slaying of 40-year-old Berry Manion (black), the victim having been shot in the back. Motive: obnoxious drunk. This black-on-black killer was hanged at Scottsville on March 22, 1889. Source: *Louisville Courier Journal*, 9/25/88 (4:4) & 3/23/89 (5:1). Appeal: 88 KY 29–34. See also: 1870 U.S. Census (Allen Co., KY), which notes Manion.

Charles Dilger (white, age 29). *Murder.* The crime was committed on 8/16/1888 in Jefferson County. Police killer. Fatal stabbings of 40-year-old James W. Jones and 43-year-old Joseph Rosenberg (whites). Motive: obnoxious drunk. Death on the gallows was the fate of Charles Dilger at Louisville on July 31, 1889. Source: *Louisville Courier Journal*, 7/31/89 (1:2) & 8/1/89 (1:2). See also: *Jefferson County Mortuary Record* (August 1888), which notes the victims of this lethal knife attack.

Harry Smart (white, age 26). *Murder.* The crime was committed on or about 7/5/1888 in Jefferson County. Hanged for the murders of about 25-year-old Meisner Green and about 35-year-old Mary J. Rannells, alias "Belle Ward" (whites), who were last seen alive on 7/5/1888 and whose bodies were later found in the Ohio River with their throats cut. Motive: rivalry between pimps. Harry Smart (who was smart in nothing but his name) legally paid the forfeit of his life at Louisville on July 31, 1889. Source: *Louisville Courier Journal*, 7/10/88 (6:7), 7/11/88 (6:4), 7/31/89 (1:2) & 8/1/89 (1:2).

Patrick Hunt (white, age 35). *Murder.* The crime was committed on 2/27/1889 in Bourbon County. Handgun slaying of 29-year-old James C. Abnee (white), who was shot three times. Motive: revenge. Abnee had testified against Hunt's wife in a court case that resulted in her imprisonment. Patrick Hunt's actions resulted in his execution at Paris KY on December 18, 1889. Source: *Louisville Courier Journal*, 12/19/89 (5:1). *Eau Claire (WI) Daily Leader*, 12/19/89 (1:7). See also: 1880 U.S. Census (Bourbon Co., KY), which notes Hunt, and 1880 U.S. Census (Nicholas Co., KY), which notes Abnee.

1890

Ellison Mounts, alias "Cotton Top" (white, age 24). *Murder.* The crime was committed on 1/1/1888 in Pike County. Executed for the rifle slaying of 29-year-old Alifair McCoy (white female). Motive: clan rivalry. A male sibling of Miss McCoy named Calvin McCoy (age abt. 25) was fatally wounded in the same incident, but the exact identity of the person who shot him was never made clear. "Cotton Top" (so called because of his fair hair) was one of a party of wrathful mountaineers who had staked out the McCoy cabin early on the above date and shot at anything that moved. He was legally hanged at Pikeville on February 18, 1890. Source: *Louisville Courier Journal*, 2/19/90 (2:4). *Hamilton (OH) Daily Democrat*, 2/19/90 (1:3). See also: 1860 U.S. Census (Pike Co., KY), which notes Miss McCoy as a minor. For an excellent account of this case and the events surrounding it see *The Hatfields and the McCoys*, by Virgil Carrington Jones (University of NC Press, 1948). *Master Detective*, 12/32.

Thomas O'Brien (white, age 26). *Murder.* The crime was committed on 3/31/1889 in Fayette County. Hanged for the murder of pregnant 26-year-old Betty Shea (white), she having been battered about the head with brass knuckles. Motive: unwanted paternity and its ramifications. Thomas O'Brien—who liked to play but not to pay—went to his death on the gallows at Lexington on February 27, 1890. Source: *Lexington (KY) Press*, 4/2/89 (2:3) & 2/27/90 (1:3). Appeal: 89 KY 354–366.

1891

Levi James (black, age 20). *Murder.* The crime was committed on 11/10/1889 in Fulton County. Handgun slaying of about 35-year-old James Garvin (white). Motive: mistaken identity. This proved to be a costly mistake indeed when Levi James was hanged for it at Hickman KY on June 10, 1891. Source: *Hickman (KY) Courier*, 6/12/91 (3:2). *Louisville Courier Journal*, 6/11/91 (6:3). *The World* (New York), 6/11/91 (12:2). *Fort Wayne (IN) Sentinel*, 12/18/89 (1:4).

1892

Jesse Brown (black, age 24). *Murder.* The crime was committed on 1–3-1891 in McCracken County. Handgun slaying of 33-year-old John Larry, a.k.a. "John Lowrie" (black). Motive: rivalry for a female. This self-described asserter of this male prerogative asserted himself right onto the gallows at Paducah on January 15, 1892. Source: *Louisville Courier Journal*, 1/16/92 (2:5). *Owensboro (KY) Daily Messenger*, 1/16/92 (1:4). Appeal: 13 KY Law Rep. 372–373. See also: 1880 U.S. Census (Lyon Co., KY), which notes the murdered man.

Simpson Bush (white, age 22). *Murder.* The crime was committed on 6/23/1890 in Powell County. Uxoricide. Handgun slaying of about 20-year-old Annie Rogers Bush (white), she having been asleep at the time with their 4-month-old baby in her arms. Motive: none apparent. Whatever the killer's reasons, they became immaterial when he was hanged at Stanton KY on February 5, 1892. Source: *Louisville Courier Journal*, 2/6/92 (1:2). *Saturday Evening Telegraph* (Alton, IL), 2/6/92 (1:4).

Robert Charlton (black, age 19). *Murder.* The crime was committed on 11/27/1890 in Henderson County. Hanged for the murder of 25-year-old Minnie Hoskins (black), she having been slashed across the face with a knife and shot three times with a handgun. Motive: because she had refused to give Charlton money with which to gamble. The only stake that he accrued was a death sentence. It was carried out at Henderson KY on February 5, 1892. Source: *Louisville Courier Journal*, 2/6/92 (1:2). *Saturday Evening Telegraph* (Alton, IL), 2/6/92 (1:4).

William Puckett, alias "Rug Back Bill" (white, age 50). *Murder.* The crime was committed on 11/4/1890 in Estill County. Hanged for the murder of 53-year-old William Hall (white), who was fatally clubbed in a drunken brawl. "Rug Back Bill" was presumably sober when he felt the noose pull tight around his neck at Irvine KY on February 5, 1892. Source: *Louisville Courier Journal*, 2/6/92 (1:2). *Newark (OH) Daily Advocate*, 9/23/91 (1:4). See also: 1870 U.S. Census (Estill Co., KY), which notes the killer as the father of Ambrose Puckett so as not to confuse him with other relatives of the same name. See also: 1870 & 1880 U.S. Censuses (Estill Co., KY), which note the murdered man as "William T. Hall."

Henry S. Smith (black, age 28). *Murder.* The crime was committed on 1/18/1891 in Jefferson County. Handgun slaying of 42-year-old Louis Specht (white), who was shot three times. Motive: disgruntled employee. The result of this was the loss of both his job and his life when Smith was hanged at Louisville on March 25, 1892. Source: *Louisville Courier Journal*, 1/19/91 (2:8) & 3/26/92 (12:2). See also: *Jefferson County Mortuary Record* (March 1892, p. 79, line 44), which notes the killer.

Oscar Jones (black, age 46). *Murder.* The crime was committed on 12/24/1891 in Bath County. Police killer. Fatal stabbing of 25-year-old Taylor Vice (white). Motive: interfering with a police officer. This Christmas Eve killer was hanged at Owingsville on November 4, 1892. Source: *Newark (OH) Daily Advocate*, 3/7/92 (1:2). *Louisville Courier Journal*, 11/5/92 (4:4). See also: 1880 U.S. Census (Bath Co., KY), which notes both parties.

Stephen R. Hite (white, age 36). *Murder.* The crime was committed on 9/20/1891 in Jefferson County. Fatal stabbing of 28-year-old Albert Baumann (white). Motive: drunken brawl. The penalty for this was death by hanging. Hite tendered payment at Louisville on December 9, 1892. Source: *Louisville Courier Journal*, 9/21/91 (8:5) & 12/9/92 (1:8). Appeal: 14 KY Law Rep. 308–310. See also: *Jefferson County Mortuary Record* (September 1891, p. 17, line 38), which notes the slain man by his correct name.

Nelson Lewis (black, age 27). *Murder.* The crime was committed on

11/28/1891 in Jefferson County. Handgun slaying of 16-year-old George Dean (black). Motive: personal animosity. The killer paid full measure on the gallows at Louisville on December 9, 1892. Source: *Louisville Courier Journal*, 12/9/92 (1:8). *Daily Advocate* (Newark OH), 12/10/92 (1:3).

Dennis McCarthy (white, age 33). *Murder.* The crime was committed on 9/7/1891 in Jefferson County. Uxoricide. Handgun slaying of pregnant 30-year-old Ellen McCarthy (white). Motive: indiscernible based on surviving accounts. The killer was hanged at Louisville on December 9, 1892. Source: *Louisville Courier Journal*, 12/9/92 (1:8). *Newark (OH) Daily Advocate*, 12/10/92 (1:3). See also: *Jefferson County Mortuary Record* (September 1891, p. 14, line 55), which notes the slain woman.

Grant Thomas (black, age 19). *Murder.* The crime was committed on 2/9/1892 in Jefferson County. Strangulation of 17-year-old Birdie Coleman (black). Motive: adultery turned deadly. Exit Grant Thomas on the gallows stage at Louisville on December 9, 1892. Source: *Louisville Courier Journal*, 12/9/92 (1:8). *Daily Advocate* (Newark OH), 12/10/92 (1:3).

1893

Bob Brown (black, age 29). *Murder.* The crime was committed on 12/10/1892 in Graves County. Handgun slaying of Albert Colley (white, age not recorded). Motive: fracas in a whorehouse. Bob Brown knew only the company of men thereafter. He was hanged at Mayfield KY on June 9, 1893. Source: *Hamilton (OH) Daily Republican*, 12/12/92 (1:4). *Louisville Courier Journal*, 6/10/93 (7:7). *Mayfield (KY) Monitor*, 6/14/93 (2:3).

Elijah Henry Hall (white, age abt. 33). *Murder.* The crime was committed on 6/17/1892 in Pike County. Fratricide. Handgun slaying of 35-year-old Randall Hall (white), the victim having been shot twice in the head. Motive: gambling dispute. This killer—who had blown away his own brother for a handful of coins—was hanged by the neck until dead at Pikeville on August 11, 1893. Source: *Louisville Courier Journal*, 8/12/93 (1:4). Appeal: 94 KY 322–327. See also: 1860 U.S. Census (Letcher Co., KY), which notes Randall Hall as a minor, son of Reuben and Nancy Hall.

George Armstrong (black, age 35). *Murder.* The crime was committed on 9/24/1892 in Spencer County. Executed for the murder of pregnant 27-year-old Arie "Kate" Downs (black), she having been felled with a sledgehammer and then finished off with a rock. Motive: unwanted paternity. This player and slayer was hanged at Taylorville KY on December 1, 1893. Source: *Louisville Courier Journal*, 12/2/93 (1:6). See also: KY Court of Appeals case no. 22251, original manuscript, KY State Archives. See also: 1880 U.S. Census (Spencer Co., KY), which notes both parties.

1894

Phil Evans (black, age 20). *Rape.* The crime was committed on 10/15/1893 in Nelson County. Indecent assault on the person of 12-year-old Mary E. Hall (white) under circumstances that cannot be further described without descending into the realm of pornography. Suffice it to say that the perpetrator of this misdeed was legally hanged at Bardstown on January 5, 1894. Source: *Titusville (PA) Morning Herald*, 10/17/93 (2:3). *Louisville Courier Journal*, 1/6/94 (1:8). See also: 1900 U.S. Census (Nelson Co., KY), which notes the violated girl who had by long odds survived until then.

Robert Marler (white, age 22). *Murder.* The crime was committed on 8/28/1893 in Bell County. Sniper slaying of Mary E. Bowden (white, age not recorded). Motive: mistaken identity. A rope necklace was this killer's reward at Pineville KY on February 9, 1894. Source: *Louisville Courier Journal*, 8/29/93 (2:2) & 2/10/94 (1:6). See also: 1880 U.S. Census (Bell Co., KY), which notes Marler as a minor.

Beverly Adams (black male, age 22). *Murder.* The crime was committed on 5/9/1894 in Christian County. Handgun slaying of Otto Campbell, age 60+ (black). Motive: because the killer disliked the older man's intimacy with his grandmother. The public hangman became the final arbiter of this family tiff at Hopkinsville on September 14, 1894. Source: *Louisville Courier Journal*, 9/15/94 (2:5). *Sandusky (OH) Register*, 9/15/94 (2:5).

1895

William Taylor (black, age 27). *Murder.* The crime was committed on 12/7/1894 in Madison County. Handgun slaying of 36-year-old David C. Doty (white), who was shot four times in the back of the head execution-style. Motive: mule stealing. Taylor was led to his own execution at Richmond KY on January 11, 1895. The bluegrass hemp did its job quite effectively. Source: *Galveston (TX) Daily News*, 12/10/94 (1:4). *Louisville Courier Journal*, 1/12/95 (3:1). See also: 1870 U.S. Census (Madison Co., KY), which notes Doty as a minor.

George Magee (black, age 18). *Murder.* The crime was committed on 7/3/1894 in Franklin County. Fatal stabbing of Charles Thomas (black, age not recorded), who was knifed in the back. Motive: prison violence. This teenage terror of the state penitentiary was executed at Frankfurt on March 1, 1895. His fellow blacks were ambivalent about his fate. Source: *Daily Capitol* (Frankfurt, KY), 7/4/94 (1:2). *Frankfurt (KY) Roundabout*, 3/2/95 (7:1).

Thomas Smith, alias "Bad Tom" (white, age 36). *Murder.* The crime was committed on 2/5/1895 in Breathitt County. Executed for the handgun slaying of 38-year-old John E. Rader (white), the victim having been shot in his sleep. Motive: robbery in a whorehouse. Smith was a mountain man and feudist with at least seven other murders to his discredit: Joseph Hurt (white, age 27), who was slain during a drunken row (by unspecified means) in Perry Co., KY circa 1887. Also the bushwhack killings of Joseph C. Eversole (white, age 34) and Nicholas Combs (white, age 21) in Perry Co. (the latter of whom had his eyeballs deliberately shot out) on 4/15/1888. Also the sniper slayings of Shadrach Combs (white, age 53) and Ambrose Amburgey (white, age 34), the former in Perry Co., KY on 7/21/1888 and the latter in Knott Co., KY on or about 10/15/1888. Also the rifle slaying of Jacob McKnight (white, age 34) during a battle between feuding factions in Hazard KY (Perry Co.) on 11/8/1889. Lastly the sniper killing of another Perry County man named Robin Cornett (white, age not recorded) on or about 7/15/1890. "Bad Tom" got his neck stretched pursuant to law at Jackson KY on June 28, 1895. Source: *Louisville Courier Journal,* 6/29/95 (1:2). *Sandusky (OH) Register,* 2/8/95 (4:4). *Perry (IA) Daily Chief,* 3/17/95 (1:3). See also: *Kentucky's Famous Feuds and Tragedies,* by Charles G. Mutzenberg (NY: R. F. Fenno, 1917), 187–233.

John Johnson (black, age 28). *Murder.* The crime was committed on 6/15/1895 in Montgomery County. Police killer. Handgun slaying of Charles Evans (white, age not recorded). Motive: resisting arrest. The subsequent sentence of death in this case was carried out on the convicted man at Mount Sterling on August 16, 1895. Source: *Mt. Sterling (KY) Advocate,* 6/18/95 (1:3). *Sandusky (OH) Register,* 8/17/95 (1:3). See also: 1880 U.S. Census (Montgomery Co., KY), which notes the culprit.

1896

James DeWitt (white, age 25). *Murder.* The crime was committed on 11/14/1895 in Carter County. Uxoricide. Hanged for the murder of 36-year-old Elizabeth DeWitt (white), she having been strangled and clubbed; her body was dumped in a wooded ravine. Motive: because she had dared to ask for a divorce. Apparently her younger spouse had fallen short of her expectations. He was executed at Grayson KY on May 21, 1896. Source: *Louisville Courier Journal,* 5/22/96 (1:6). *The World* (New York), 5/22/96 (14:6). *Daily Herald* (Delphos, OH), 5/23/96 (6:5).

Henry Mitchell Smith (black, age 24). *Rape.* The crime was committed on 8/14/1895 in Fayette County. Indecent assault on the person of 52-year-old Mary Hudson (white), the published details of which had to be toned down to forestall civil unrest. The ravisher was legally hanged at Lexington on June 2, 1896. Source: *Sandusky (OH) Register,* 8/17/95 (1:6). *Lexington (KY) Morning Herald,* 6/3/96 (2:1). Appeal: 17 KY Law Rep. 1162–1165.

Buford Overton (white, age 18). *Murder.* The crime was committed on 6/21/1895 in Harlan County. Rifle slayings of Gustave Loeb, age 60+, and Julia Loeb, age 60+ (whites), a married couple of the Jewish ethnicity. Motive: murder-for-hire, or so it was alleged. What is certain aside from the murders themselves is the fact that this nefarious deed brought its teenage perpetrator to the gallows at Harlan KY on October 12, 1896. Source: *Louisville Courier Journal,* 10/13/96 (7:8). *Times-Democrat* (Lima, OH), 10/13/96 (1:4). See also: 1880 U.S. Census (Hancock Co., TN), which notes the killer as a small child.

1897

Robert H. Laughlin (white, age 37). *Murder.* The crime was committed on 2/14/1896 in Bracken County. Uxoricide and child killer. Executed for the murders of about 37-year-old Sarah Ann Laughlin, a.k.a. "Emma Laughlin," and 13-year-old Mary Jones (whites), they respectively being his wife and that lady's niece. Both had their brains beaten out with an iron poker and their house burned down around them. Motive: sexual assault of the younger victim. This unconscionable husband had his neck wrung on the gallows at Brookville KY on January 9, 1897.

Source: *Louisville Courier Journal*, 2/16/96 (4:1) & 1/10/97 (2:1). *Newark (OH) Daily Advocate*, 2/17/96 (2:4). *Daily Republican* (Decatur, IL), 2/19/96 (1:5). Appeal: 18 KY Law Rep. 640–645.

Scott Jackson (white, age 27) and **Alonzo Walling** (white, age 20). *Murder.* Their crime was committed on 1/31/1896 in Campbell County. Both executed for the murder of pregnant 22-year-old Pearl Bryan (white), she having first been drugged and then having had her head cut off with a surgical saw. Motive: unwanted paternity. The killers were hanged at Newport KY on March 20, 1897. Source: *The Mysterious Murder of Pearl Bryan: The Headless Horror* (Cincinnati, OH: Barclay, 1897). Harvard Law School Library. See also: 1880 U.S. Census (Putnam Co., IN), which notes Miss Bryan as a minor. *Actual Detective*, 11/37. *Dynamic Detective*, 4/37. *Crime Detective*, 6/49. *Master Detective*, 4/42 & 6/47.

George Winston (black, age 31). *Murder.* The crime was committed on 4/22/1897 in McCracken County. Executed for the murder of Vina Stubblefield (black, age not recorded), she having been stabbed and slashed (with a knife) numerous times in a deep and rending manner. Motive: temper tantrum in a brothel. The killer was hanged at Paducah on November 19, 1897. Source: *Paducah (KY) Daily Sun*, 4/23/97 (1:5) & 11/19/97 (1:1).

1898

Thomas Hayden (black, age abt. 23). *Murder.* The crime was committed on 10/20/1897 in Ohio County. Handgun slaying of 16-year-old Bena Logan (black female). Motive: because she had declined his advances. Hayden succeeded in wooing his way only onto the gallows at Hartford KY on July 11, 1898. Source: *Hartford (KY) Herald*, 10/27/97 (3:7), 12/15/97 (3:4) & 7/13/98 (3:4). *Hartford (KY) Republican*, 10/22/97 (2:3).

Clarence Vinegar (black, age 22). *Murder.* The crime was committed on 4/11/1897 in Scott County. Uxoricide. Handgun slaying of 23-year-old Etta Belle Vinegar (black), she having been shot three times. Motive: marital estrangement. This wife-killer was hanged at Georgetown KY on July 18, 1898. Source: *Georgetown (KY) Times*, 7/20/98 (3:3). *Louisville Courier Journal*, 7/19/98 (3:2). Appeal: 19 KY Law Rep. 840–844.

George Stephenson (black, age 17). *Murder.* The crime was committed on 7/4/1898 in Lincoln County. Child killer. Handgun slaying of 13-year-old Joseph Tilford (white), who was shot five times. Motive: a dispute about a baseball bat. He was hanged pursuant to law at Stanford KY on August 18, 1898. Source: *Louisville Courier Journal*, 8/19/98 (3:4). *Semi Weekly Interior Journal* (Stanford, KY), 8/19/98 (1:1).

William Cato (white, age 21). *Murder.* The crime was committed on 9/16/1897 in Lyon County. Ax murder of David Askew, age 60+ (white), the victim having been attacked while asleep and his weighted body dumped in a river. Motive: robbery and gross perfidy. William Cato was hanged at Eddyville on November 25, 1898. Source: *Hartford (KY) Herald*, 9/22/97 (2:5). *Louisville Courier Journal*, 11/26/98 (5:3).

1899

William Miller (black, age 16). *Rape.* The crime was committed on 9/1/1898 in Oldham County. Indecent assault on the person of 24-year-old Lena Gertrude Leet (white), the further details of which cannot be described within the parameters of decency. William Miller was a precocious sex fiend. He was legally hanged at LeGrange KY on February 3, 1899. Source: *Louisville Courier Journal,* 2/4/99 (3:3). See also: 1900 U.S. Census (Oldham Co., KY), which notes the prosecutrix.

Johnson Franklin (white, age 42). *Murder.* The crime was committed on 9/19/1898 in Barren County. Sniper slaying of about 40-year-old Hannah Bowles (white), his mother-in-law. Motive: because he blamed her for the failure of his marriage. Franklin had previously eloped with the woman's 16-year-old daughter, a spark that ignited a family feud. This cradle-robber-turned-killer was hanged by the neck until dead at Glasgow KY on March 10, 1899. Source: *Louisville Courier Journal,* 3/11/99 (2:1). *Owensboro (KY) Daily Messenger,* 3/11/99 (1:6).

Robert Brown (white, age 33). *Murder.* The crime was committed on 11/10/1898 in Barren County. Handgun slaying of 65-year-old Alonzo McClelland (white), his father-in-law. Motive: because the killer felt indignant at having been suspected of sexual impropriety. He was hanged at Glasgow KY on April 3, 1899. Source: *Louisville Courier Journal,* 4/4/99 (5:6). Appeal: 20 KY Law Rep. 1552–1555.

William Tutt (black, age 25). *Murder.* The crime was committed on 8/23/1897 in Graves County. Uxoricide. Handgun slaying of about 22-year-old Estella Tutt (black). Motive: male hubris. The slain woman had gone to a baseball game in direct disobedience of her husband's orders. He didn't like that. He was hanged at Mayfield KY on April 13, 1899. Source: *Louisville Courier Journal,* 4/14/99 (2:3). *Owensboro (KY) Daily Messenger,* 8/24/97 (1:2) & 4/14/99 (1:6).

Robert Blanks (black, age 36). *Rape.* The crime was committed on 1/12/1898 in Graves County. Indecent assault on the person of 11-year-old Tennie Bailey (white). Further details are omitted because they are too obscene for publication. The culprit was legally hanged at Mayfield KY on April 18, 1899. Source: *Louisville Courier Journal,* 4/19/99 (2:2). *Dubuque (IA) Herald,* 4/21/99 (2:4). See also: 1880 U.S. Census (McCracken Co., KY), which notes this miscreant.

Clarence Williams (black, age 26). *Murder.* The crime was committed on 3/26/1899 in Bourbon County. Handgun slaying of about 21-year-old Josie Tillman (black), she having been shot in the back. Motive: jealous lover. Williams legally paid the price of folly with a rope around his neck at Paris KY on December 11, 1899. Source: *The Bourbon News* (Paris, KY), 12/11/99 (1:1). *Louisville Courier Journal,* 12/12/99 (4:7).

1901

Thomas Cole (black, age 23). *Murder.* The crime was committed on 1/19/1901 in Hickman County. Shotgun slaying of about 25-year-old Emma McCrory (black), the blast having decapitated her. Motive: adultery turned deadly. The killer was hanged at Clinton KY on April 26, 1901. Source: *Louisville Courier Journal*, 4/27/01 (2:7). *Xenia (OH) Daily Gazette*, 4/27/01 (1:5). See also: 1900 U.S. Census (Hickman Co., KY), which notes Cole.

Reuben Quinn (black, age 49). *Murder.* The crime was committed on 4/10/1901 in Boyle County. Police killer. Handgun slaying of 43-year-old John T. Crum (white). Quinn was executed at Danville, KY, on December 20, 1901. Motive: resisting arrest. Source: *Louisville Courier Journal*, 12/21/01 (6:5). Appeal: 23 KY Law Rep. 1302–1306. See also: 1900 U.S. Census (Boyle Co., KY), which notes both parties.

1902

Frank Lewis (white, age 19). *Murder.* The crime was committed on 5/20/1902 in Harlan County. Gunshot slaying of 39-year-old Henry Dixon (white), his father-in-law. Motive: family fallout. The exact make of the murder weapon is not specified in any known news account. The killer was hanged at Harlan KY on December 12, 1902. Source: *Louisville Courier Journal*, 12/13/02 (1:7). *Hazel Green (KY) Herald*, 12/18/02 (1:6). See also: 1900 U.S. Census (Harlan Co., KY), which notes the murdered man.

1903

John Black (black, age 44). *Murder.* The crime was committed on 5/28/1902 in Jefferson County. Executed for the murder of 64-year-old Archie James (black, his uncle), who was fatally slashed with a butcher knife. Motive: because the older man had reproached the younger one for carousing. The latter was hanged for killing his uncle at Louisville on May 15, 1903. Source: *Louisville Courier Journal*, 5/29/02 (10:2) & 5/15/03 (1:8). See also: *Jefferson County Mortuary Record*, 1902, 220–221, and May 1903, no page number.

Claude O'Brien (white, age 20) and **Earl Whitney** (white, age 17). *Murder.* Their crime was committed on 10/11/1902 in Fayette County. Handgun slaying of 68-year-old Addison B. Chinn (white). Motive: burglary gone awry. These two bad boys were hanged at Lexington on July 24, 1903. No circumstances were found in their favor. Source: *Louisville Courier Journal*, 7/25/03 (2:2). *Lexington (KY) Morning Herald*, 7/24/03 (1:1) & (5:1). See also: 1902 Fayette Co. death cert. no. 6333 and 1903 Fayette Co. death cert. nos. 618 and 619.

1904

Elijah Custer Gardner (white, age 26). *Murder.* The crime was committed on 11/30/1903 in Hart County. Shotgun slayings of 54-year-old Squire W. Osborne and 21-year-old David Osborne (whites), a father and son. Motive: because Gardner suspected them of thwarting his romantic interests. This killer paid the death penalty when he was hanged at Munfordville on July 28, 1904. Source: *Louisville Courier Journal*, 7/29/04 (1:8). See also: 1900 U.S. Census (Hart Co., KY), which notes the older victim. *Daring Detective*, 2/42.

1905

John Hathaway (black, age 33). *Murder.* The crime was committed on

1/4/1904 in Clark County. Handgun slaying of 25-year-old Etta Thomas (black, a known prostitute), she having been shot multiple times. Motive: lovers' quarrel. The life of a whore was just as valuable as that of anyone else, at least in the eyes of the law. John Hathaway learned this the hard way when he was hanged for his misdeed at Winchester KY on January 3, 1905. Source: *Louisville Courier Journal*, 1/4/05 (3:6). Appeal: 26 KY Law Rep. 630–634. See also: 1900 U.S. Census (Clark Co., KY), which notes the victim.

James W. Bess (white, age 46). *Murder.* The crime was committed on 3/6/1903 in Fayette County. Strangulation of 36-year-old Martha McQuinn Martin (white) and illegal disposal of her body in a reservoir. Motive: adultery turned deadly. A common perjurer (because he had broken his marriage vow to forsake all others) as well as a murderer, James Bess met a fate as disgraceful as his conduct when he was hanged at Lexington on January 13, 1905. Source: *Lexington (KY) Morning Herald*, 1/13/05 (1:1). *Louisville Courier Journal*, 1/14/05 (3:1). Appeals: 25 KY Law Rep. 1092–1100 and 26 KY Law Rep. 839–842. See also: 1903 Fayette Co. death cert. no. 6656. *Daring Detective*, 1/42.

Roy Green (black, age 17). *Murder.* The crime was committed on 7/31/1904 in Daviess County. Executed for the killing of 39-year-old James E. Coomes (white), who was battered with a jagged piece of wood after which a large splinter thereof was deliberately driven through his neck and left protruding from the wound. Motive: robbery and beguilement. The hangman performed his duty in this case at Owensboro on February 17, 1905. Source: *Louisville Courier Journal*, 2/18/05 (10:1). Appeal: 26 KY Law Rep. 1221–1229. See also: 1900 U.S. Census (Webster Co., KY), which notes Mr. Coomes.

George Holland (black, age 20). *Murder.* The crime was committed on 11/14/1903 in Christian County. Executed for the mutilation murder of an unknown white man whose name and age were never determined. The victim was a lone wayfarer who had camped beneath a roadside tree. An eight-man gang of black ruffians stalked him. These included George Holland. They pounced on the stranger as he slept. His brains were beaten out with an ax handle. One of the attackers also used a knife to methodically carve all of the flesh from the dead man's face. The body was also stripped and castrated. What remained of it was found three days later partially devoured by hogs. Motive: robbery. George Holland was the one who didn't get away. He was hanged at Hopkinsville on July 7, 1905. Source: *Louisville Courier Journal*, 7/8/05 (7:4). Appeal: 26 KY Law Rep. 789–799. See also: 1900 U.S. Census (Christian Co., KY), which notes Holland.

Robert Mathley (white, age 35). *Murder.* The crime was committed on 6/26/1904 in Daviess County. Handgun slayings of 25-year-old James Gregson and 18-year-old Emma Watkins (whites), a courting couple. Motive: thwarted lover. Mathley was hanged for this jealous misdeed at Owensboro on July 7, 1905. Source: *Fort Wayne (IN) News*, 7/7/05 (12:1). *Louisville Courier Journal*, 7/8/05 (7:4). Appeal: 27 KY Law Rep. 785–788. See also: 1900 U.S. Census (Daviess Co., KY), which notes Mathley and Gregson.

Samuel Hisle (black, age 19). *Rape.* The crime was committed on 8/14/1905 in Clark County. Indecent assault on the person of a married white woman named Mary Case (age not recorded), who was attacked in her own home shortly after Hisle had attempted to do likewise at another nearby residence. He was legally hanged for this at Winchester KY on October 19, 1905. Source: *Bourbon News* (Paris, KY), 8/18/05 (1:1). *Winchester (KY) Democrat,* 8/18/05 (3:5). *Louisville Courier Journal,* 10/20/05 (3:6).

1906

William Van Dalsen (white, age 23). *Murder.* The crime was committed on 9/19/1904 in Jefferson County. Hanged for the murder of 30-year-old Fannie Porter (white), she having been slashed to death with a razor. Motive: lovers' quarrel. This killer suffered the extreme penalty of the law at Louisville on January 19, 1906. Source: *Louisville Courier Journal,* 1/20/06 (3:1). See also: 1904 *Jefferson County Mortuary Record,* p. 221, which notes the slain woman.

Garth Thompkins (black, age 21). *Murder.* The crime was committed on 12/24/1902 in Hopkins County. Rifle slaying of 32-year-old James Brame (black). Motive: jealous ex-husband. This Christmas Eve killer had his wounded machismo assuaged when he was hanged for his crime at Madisonville on March 16, 1906. Source: *Louisville Courier Journal,* 3/17/06 (3:8). Appeal: 28 KY Law Rep. 642–646. See also: 1900 U.S. Census (Christian Co., KY), which notes the homicide victim, and 1900 U.S. Census (Lyon Co., KY), which notes the killer as a prison inmate.

James Pearsall (black, age 17). *Rape.* The crime was committed on 1/21/1905 in Fayette County. Indecent assault on the person of a married white woman named Lizzie Wagner (age not recorded), the culprit having broken into her home for that purpose and shot her husband, albeit not fatally. Precocious Pearsall was legally hanged for this at Lexington on July 6, 1906. Source: *Lexington (KY) Herald,* 7/6/06 (1:2). Appeal: 29 KY Law Rep. 222–224. See also: 1906 Fayette Co. death cert. no. 469.

Cornelius Johnson (black, age 18). *Murder.* The crime was committed on 5/28/1905 in Jefferson County. Handgun slaying of Conrad Kaiser (white, age not recorded), a saloon owner. Motive: brawling and a big attitude. All this got him was an invitation to his own hanging at Louisville on July 27, 1906. Source: *Louisville Courier Journal,* 5/29/05 (3:8) & 7/28/06 (5:6). Appeal: 29 KY Law Re. 442–447.

Allen Mathis (black, age 16). *Rape.* The crime was committed on 7/25/1906 in Graves County. Indecent assault on the person of 18-year-old Ethel McClain (white). He had mugged her first, but finding no money in her purse, he raped Miss McClain as an act of spitefulness. The price he paid was death by hanging at Mayfield KY on July 31, 1906. Source: *Paducah (KY) Evening Sun,* 7/26/06 (1:4) & 8/1/06 (1:1). *Louisville Courier Journal,* 8/1/06 (1:2).

Joseph Johnson (black, age 42). *Murder.* The crime was committed on 12/9/1904 in Jefferson County. Uxoricide. Hanged for the murder of Alice Johnson (black, age not recorded), she having been severely beaten and her head completely severed with a corn knife. Motive: marital estrangement. This wife-killer was executed at Louisville on August 17, 1906. Source: *The Times* (Louisville, KY), 12/10/04 (2:6), 12/19/04 (6:6) & 8/17/06 (2:4). Appeal: 29 KY Law Rep. 675–678. See also: Case no. 26377 (December 1904), Circuit Court Criminal Division, Jefferson County Archives, original case file.

Thomas Stout (black, age 27). *Murder.* The crime was committed on 3/25/1905 in Fayette County. Shotgun slaying of about 25-year-old Simeon Lee (black). Motive: a quarrel over how to handle a tobacco crop that they jointly owned. The only ones who profited from its sale were the lawyer and the undertaker. The latter carried Stout's legally throttled corpse away from the Lexington jail on November 23, 1906. Source: *Semi Weekly Interior Journal* (Stanford, KY), 3/28/05 (2:2). *Louisville Courier Journal*, 11/24/06 (3:3).

1907

Jesse Fitzgerald (black, age 27). *Murder.* The crime was committed on 7/25/1906 in Knox County. Hanged for the murder of a married white woman named Martha Broughton (age not recorded), whose throat was cut as she slept in her own bed. Motive: burglary. This nocturnal nemesis was legally put to death at Barbourville on February 15, 1907. Source: *Louisville Courier Journal*, 7/28/06 (1:6) & 2/16/07 (1:2). Appeal: 30 KY Law Rep. 349–351.

Polk Fletcher (white, age 59) and **Guy Lyon** (white, age not recorded). *Rape.* Their crime was committed on 5/22/1905 in Logan County. Both executed for an indecent assault on the person of 23-year-old Mary E. Gladder (white), she and her physically infirm father (neither of whom could speak English) having been robbed and assaulted by four unwashed vagabonds as they camped along a rural roadside. The female victim of this outrage was gang-raped by all four assailants. Fletcher and Lyon were the two that didn't get away. They seem to have been particularly rum characters from the sub-basement of society. Two nooses changed their social status from marginally existent to nonexistent at Russellville on February 15, 1907. Source: *Louisville Courier Journal*, 5/24/05 (1:5) & 2/16/07 (1:2). *Hopkinsville Kentuckian*, 10/20/06 (1:6).

Benjamin Huffaker (black, age 27). *Murder.* The crime was committed on 5/2/1905 in Lyon County. Executed for the fatal stabbing of Edward Shirley (black, age not recorded). Motive: prison violence. Recidivist killer. Huffaker was already serving a sentence of life imprisonment in the Kentucky State Penitentiary for a previous murder when he killed Shirley. He had entered the former state prison at Frankfurt on 4/29/1898 (having been convicted of killing his wife in Pulaski County) and been transferred to Eddyville in 1904. He was hanged at the Lyon County jail on February 15, 1907. Source: *Hopkinsville Kentuckian*, 5/9/05 (2:3). *Louisville Courier Journal*, 2/16/07 (1:2). Appeal: 30 KY Law Rep. 334–336. See also: 1900 U.S. Census (Franklin Co., KY), which notes Huffaker as a prisoner.

Harrison Alexander (black, age 18). *Rape.* The crime was committed on 6/2/1906 in Muhlenberg County. Indecent assault on the person of about 30-year-old Florence Whitehouse (white), a mentally retarded woman. He also tried to cut out her tongue (so that she could not speak against him), thereby inflicting additional injuries on her. Alexander plunged through the gallows trap at Greenville, KY on August 9, 1907. He committed no more atrocities thereafter. Source: *Hartford (KY) Herald*, 6/6/06 (5:4). *Louisville Courier Journal*, 8/10/07 (3:8). *Daily Free Press* (Carbondale, IL), 8/10/07 (1:3).

1908

Clarence Sturgeon (white, age 18). *Murder.* The crime was committed on 6/13/1906 in Jefferson County. Handgun slayings of 22-year-old Ira Bruner, 50-year-old James Blackerly and 21-year-old Wilfred McMichael (whites). Motive: whorehouse brawl. Had he been left to himself, young Sturgeon might have cleaned up the Louisville red light district single-handed. He was hanged instead at the County jail there on January 3, 1908. Source: *Louisville Courier Journal*, 1/4/08 (12:2). See also: *Jefferson County Mortuary Record*, June 1906, 138–139.

1909

William Carter (black, age 27). *Murder.* The crime was committed on 5/20/1907 in Jefferson County. Executed for the murder of 36-year-old Joseph M. Walker (white), who was struck down from behind with an iron pipe. Motive: workplace dispute. This killer was hanged at Louisville on April 16, 1909. Source: *Louisville (KY) Times*, 4/16/09 (1:3). *Louisville Courier Journal*, 4/17/09 (12:5). Appeal: 131 KY Law Rep. 240–248. See also: *Jefferson County Mortuary Record*, 1907, 259.

1910

Earl Thompson (black, age 18). *Rape.* The crime was committed on 11/16/1909 in Grant County. Indecent assault on the person of 25-year-old Hattie Roberts (white), the full details of which were censored. The attacker was legally hanged at Williamstown, KY on January 7, 1910. Source: *Louisville Courier Journal*, 1/8/10 (9:6). See also: 1910 U.S. Census (Grant Co., KY), which notes the victim of this sex crime.

Floyd Frazier (white, age 21). *Murder.* The crime was committed on 5/21/1907 in Letcher County. Mutilation murder of 30-year-old Ellen Flannery (white), she having been stabbed multiple times and stripped naked, had her throat cut (among other gross defilements of the Jack the Ripper genre) and her remains hidden beneath a rock pile. Motive: presumed sexual assault. This young maniac was hanged at Whitesburg KY on May 19, 1910. Source: *Berea (KY) Citizen*, 5/30/07 (7:5). *Mountain Eagle* (Whitesburg, KY), 5/26/10 (1:1). *Daring Detective*, 6/42.

1911

James White (black, age 14). *Rape.* The crime was committed on 7/29/1909 in Bell County. Indecent assault on the person of 8-year-old Mossie Woodward (white) under circumstances that were deemed heinous enough to warrant his legal execution at Pineville, KY on January 30, 1911. Source: *Louisville Courier Journal*, 1/31/11 (1:3). Appeal: 140 KY 9–11. See also: 1910 U.S. Census (Bell Co., KY), which notes this incipient pervert as a prisoner.

Roger Warren (black, age 23). *Murder.* The crime was committed on 3/21/1910 in Franklin County. Hanged for the murder of Melvin Ratcliffe (black, age not recorded), whose throat was cut from behind. Motive: prison violence. Recidivist killer. Warren had reportedly killed another black man at Louisville. He had entered the Frankfurt Penitentiary on 7/6/1906 under a 12-year sentence for manslaughter. He was executed at the Franklin County jail on May 25, 1911. Source: *Frankfurt (KY) News Journal,* 5/25/11 (1:1). Appeal: 143 KY 54–56.

James Buckner (black, age 17). *Murder.* The crime was committed on 5/7/1911 in Marion County. Police killer. Executed on his 18th birthday for the fatal stabbing of 55-year-old John Austin Robey (white), the murdered man having been pierced 19 times all told. Motive: hooliganism. A newly installed electric chair rid society of James Bucker at the Kentucky State Prison on July 8, 1911. Source: *Louisville Courier Journal,* 5/8/11 (1:6) & 7/9/11 (3:8). See also: 1911 Marion Co. death cert. no. 13225 (Robey) and 1911 Lyon Co. death cert. no. 18858 (Buckner).

Shay Pellman (black, age 34). *Rape.* The crime was committed on 9/5/1910 in Lincoln County. Indecent assault on the person of 11-year-old Nancy Jane Rankin (white). This sex offender was executed by high voltage on August 5, 1911. Source: *Interior Journal* (Stanford, KY), 9/6/10 (1:1). See also: 1911 Lyon Co. death cert. no. 21556.

Oliver Locks (black, age 52). *Murder.* The crime was committed on 9/16/1910 in Jefferson County. Uxoricide. Executed for the murder of 33-year-old Lulie Locks (black), a knife having been used to cut her throat from ear to ear. Motive: a heated argument over how to treat their kids. Death in the electric chair was the fate of Oliver Locks on August 22, 1911. Source: *Louisville Courier Journal,* 9/17/10 (12:6). See also: *Jefferson County Mortuary Record,* September 1910, 105, and 1911 Lyon Co. death cert. no. 21559.

Matthew Kelley (black, age 37). *Murder.* The crime was committed on 5/20/1911 in Jefferson County. Hatchet murders of 22-year-old Pearl Miller (black, his sister-in-law) and 20-year-old Clara Hamilton (black), their throats having also been slit with a razor. Motive: suspected infidelity and gossip. Recidivist killer. On 6/6/1901 this same Matthew Kelley had shot dead his then-girlfriend Artie Smith (black, age 16) during a lovers' quarrel. He was sentenced to a term of life imprisonment for that offense but was paroled in 1909. The Kentucky electric chair righted all of these wrongs when it rendered Kelley incapable of murdering any more people on September 28, 1911. Source: *Louisville Courier Journal,* 5/21/11 (2:3:7). See also: *Jefferson County Mortuary Register,* May–June 1901. Also: 1911 Jefferson Co. death cert. no. 12640 and 1911 Lyon Co. death cert. no. 23933. See also: 1910 U.S. Census (Louisville, KY), which notes Miss Hamilton.

1912

Charles Howard (black, age 21). *Murder.* The crime was committed on 8/27/1910 in Franklin County. Fatal stabbing of about 30-year-old Edward Rice (white), who he reportedly attacked for no other reason than "sheer viciousness." The electric chair successfully tamed him on January 31, 1912. Source: *Frankfort (KY) News*, 8/29/10 (4:4), 1/4/11 (1:6) & 1/20/11 (1:7). *Louisville (KY) Times*, 1/31/12 (11:5). See also: 1912 Lyon Co. death cert. no. 2117.

Willard Richardson (white, age 38). *Murder.* The crime was committed on 2/17/1912 in Carlisle County. Handgun slaying of 55-year-old John B. Violett (white). Motive: obnoxious drunk. Violett had accidentally bumped into the inebriated killer on a sidewalk and the latter didn't like it. So he pulled out a gun and started shooting. The price he paid was death in the electric chair on April 19, 1912. Source: *Louisville Courier Journal*, 2/18/12 (1:7) & 4/20/12 (3:3). See also: 1912 Carlisle Co. death cert. no. 3478 and 1912 Lyon Co. death cert. no. 10751.

Calvin Miracle (white, age 39). *Murder.* The crime was committed on 8/27/1911 in Bell County. Handgun slayings of 51-year-old Matthew Jones and 31-year-old Dulcie E. Partin (white male and female), who were shot execution-style thrice and two times, respectively. Motive: another obnoxious drunk. This one sat in the chair of death on August 30, 1912. Source: *Thousandsticks* (Middleboro, KY), 8/31/11 (1:1), 11/30/11 (1:3) & 1/4/12 (1:5). See also: 1910 U.S. Census (Bell Co., KY), which notes Jones and Miracle, plus 1900 U.S. Census (Bell Co., KY), which notes Mrs. Partin. See also: 1912 Lyon Co. death cert. no. 20443 which notes Miracle but misstates his age.

Charles Smith (black, age 26) and **James Smith** (black, age 23). *Murder.* Brothers and suspected serial killers. Their crime was committed on 7/7/1911 in Mason County. Both executed for murdering a wayfaring black man known only as "Ed" (age not recorded), who was beaten on the head and thrown down a railroad embankment. Motive: robbery. The electric chair claimed this pair on September 27, 1912. Source: *Lexington Leader*, 9/27/12 (6:5). Appeal: 148 KY 60-73. Also 1912 Lyon Co. death cert. nos. 23036 and 23037.

James Ellis (white, age 31). *Murder.* The crime was committed on 7/14/1911 in Pulaski County. Magistrate killer. Handgun slaying of 45-year-old Andrew Jackson Beatty (white) who was shot three times in the back. Ellis had been arraigned for bootlegging. He pulled out a concealed pistol in the courtroom and opened fire. The Kentucky electric chair closed this case on November 22, 1912. Source: *Lexington Herald*, 7/18/11 (1:3). Also: 1911 Pulaski Co. death cert. no. 19408 and 1912 Lyon Co. death cert. no. 28499.

1913

Silas Williams (black, age 16). *Murder.* The crime was committed on 3/1/1913 in Woodford County. Executed for the murder of 68-year-old Susan Black (white), she having been bludgeoned with a heavy gridiron. Motive: attempted rape gone awry. The killer had assaulted the victim's niece in the kitchen of her home, severely beating her on the head with a rolling pin. The older woman was slain when she tried to intervene. Williams also used coal oil to set the house on fire, but the younger woman escaped to summon help. Silas Williams suffered a searing death by electrocution for what he did on March 21, 1913. Source: *Xenia (OH)*

Gazette, 3/3/13 (7:5). See also: 1910 U.S. Census (Woodford Co., KY), which notes Susan Black. See also: 1913 Lyon Co. death cert. no. 8151.

William Wilson, alias "Carroll," alias "Lem Carroll" (black, age 27). *Murder.* The crime was committed on 11/16/1912 in Jefferson County. Handgun slaying of 54-year-old Gerhard Henry Heuermann (white). Motive: armed robbery. A death sentence being imposed in this case, it was carried out on March 24, 1913. Source: *Louisville Courier Journal*, 11/17/12 (1:8) & 11/18/12 (1:6). See also: 1912 Jefferson Co. death cert. no. 28036 and 1913 Lyon Co. death cert. no. 8152. See also: Case no. 34968, Circuit Court Criminal Branch, original case file, Jefferson County Archives.

John H. Bowman (white, age 29). *Rape.* The crime was committed on 2/26/1911 in Marion County. Indecent assault on the person of 18-year-old Minnie Deering, a.k.a. "Minnie Lamb" (white), she having been abducted by two men, forced to drink whiskey and then violated by both. Bowman got caught. He paid with his life in the Kentucky electric chair on April 11, 1913. Source: Marion County Circuit Court Criminal Case File no. 3375, KY State Archives. See also: 1913 Lyon Co. death cert. no. 10906. *News Leader* (Springfield, KY), 3/9/11 (1:6). *Louisville (KY) Evening Post*, 4/11/13 (5:5).

Isom Taliaferro (black, age 21). *Rape.* The crime was committed on 4/3/1912 in Todd County. Indecent assault on the person of 17-year-old Rosa Robertson (white), she having been attacked in her own home while tending her 6-week-old infant. The predator in this case was put to death on April 18. 1913. Source: Todd County Circuit Court Criminal Case File (*Commonwealth vs. Taliaferro*), Summer Term, 1912, KY State Archives. See also: 1913 Lyon Co. death cert. no. 10909.

Jim Brown, alias "Ben Jenkins" (black, age 22). *Murder.* The crime was committed on 11/23/1912 in Clark County. Police killer. Handgun slaying of 49-year-old George M. Hart (white). Motive: resisting arrest. The electric chair permanently removed this assassin from the society of his fellow man on April 25, 1913. Source: *Louisville Courier Journal*, 11/29/12 (4:5) & 4/26/13 (3:4). See also: 1912 Clark Co. death cert. no. 27285 and 1913 Lyon Co. death cert. no. 10910.

Thomas Warren Lawson (black, age 18) and **Thomas Edgar Martin** (black, age 23). *Murder.* Their crime was committed on 10/28/1911 in Shelby County. Both executed for the fatal stabbing of 19-year-old Bennie Hardin Engrum, a.k.a. "Hardin Ingham" (white). Motive: a racial incident. The homicide victim had shoved a black girl off a sidewalk because she had sassed some white girls. Seeing this, Lawson and his accomplice intervened on the black girl's behalf and stabbed the white boy to death. This negligible act of chivalry cost them their lives. The end came for them at the Kentucky State Prison on June 20, 1913. Source: *Louisville Courier Journal*, 6/21/13 (4:5). See also: 1911 Shelby Co. death cert. no. 23701 and 1913 Lyon Co. death cert. nos. 16506 and 16507.

General May (white, age 39). *Murder.* The crime was committed on 3/5/1911 in Clay County. Handgun slayings of Sherman Merideth (age not recorded) and 30-year-old Belle Hensley Merideth (whites), a married couple. Motive: boundary dispute. Venue changed from Clay County to Laurel County. The killer sat in the hot seat on June 27, 1913. Source: *Louisville Courier Journal*, 6/28/13 (4:1). See also: 1911 Clay Co. death cert. nos. 5950 and 5951. See also: 1913 Lyon Co. death cert. no. 16508. Also: 1900 U.S. Census (Clay Co., KY), which notes the female homicide victim by her maiden name.

1915

Turner Graham (white, age 23). *Murder.* The crime was committed on 12/12/1914 in Hardin County. Police killer. Executed for the handgun slaying of 36-year-old Robert Terry McMurtry (white). Motive: resisting arrest. Two days prior to this, Graham had fatally shot a rural mail carrier named James Wood (white, age 22) with the same weapon. An indictment in that case was held in abeyance pending resolution of the other one. Turner Graham went to the electric chair on July 30, 1915. Source: *Ancestral News Quarterly*, Summer 2003, 56 (Ancestral Trails Hist. Soc., Vine Grove, KY). See also: 1914 Hardin Co. death cert. nos. 31478 and 31482. Also: 1915 Lyon Co. death cert. no. 17717. *Louisville Courier Journal*, 7/30/15 (1:5).

Will Lane (black, age 23). *Murder.* The crime was committed on 1/30/1914 in Bell County. Uxoricide. Executed for the murder (by unspecified means) of Mary Lane (black, age not recorded). Motive: marital estrangement. Missing records inhibit further study of this case. Lane the wife-killer paid the extreme penalty of the law on July 30, 1915. Source: *The Sun* (Pineville, KY), 2/20/14 (1:1) & 8/6/15 (1:3). See also: 1915 Lyon Co. death cert. no. 17718.

Wallace Smothers (black, age 41). *Rape.* The crime was committed on 7/11/1915 in Clark County. Indecent assault on the person of 7-year-old Georgia Baird (white), the details being too repulsive for repetition. This child rapist was legally put to death on September 3, 1915. Source: *Winchester (KY) Democrat*, 7/27/15 (4:4), 7/30/15 (1:1) & 9/7/15 (8:2).

John Henry, alias "Black Texas" (black, age 29). *Murder.* The crime was committed on 9/9/1915 in Boyd County. Handgun slaying of 34-year-old Joseph C. Gibson (white). Motive: attempted train robbery. This killer suffered death in the Kentucky electric chair on November 19, 1915. Source: *Valley Sentinel* (Portsmouth, OH), 9/22/15 (3:1). *Bluefield (WV) Daily Telegraph*, 11/20/15 (6:3). See also: 1915 Boyd Co. death cert. no. 21243 and 1915 Lyon Co. death cert. no. 27725.

1916

Harry Garrison (black, age 19). *Rape.* The crime was committed on 7/28/1915 in Campbell County. Indecent assault on the person of 19-year-old Luella Crowder (white), she having been attacked in her own home at knifepoint. The culprit was legally executed on November 17, 1916. Source: *Louisville Courier Journal*, 7/29/15 (3:6). Appeal: 183 SW 473–475. See also: 1916 Lyon Co. death cert. no. 28620.

1917

John Henry Blue (black, age 46). *Murder.* The crime was committed on

5/29/1915 in Jefferson County. Hatchet killing of 59-year-old Adam Oster (white). Motive: landlord-tenant dispute. This hatchet man paid the penalty of death by electrocution on August 10, 1917. Source: *Louisville Courier Journal*, 5/30/15 (1:4). See also: 1915 Jefferson Co. death cert. no. 12665 and 1917 Lyon Co. death cert. no. 23188.

1918

Melvin Collins (white, age 21). *Murder.* The crime was committed on 5/25/1918 in Carter County. Handgun slayings of 60-year-old Declu Vincent Carpenter, 44-year-old John Anthony Howard and 35-year-old Grover Cleveland Sparks (whites). Motive: fury because they had reported him to the local draft board. This triple killer died without honor in the Kentucky electric chair on July 12, 1918. Source: *Gettysburg (PA) Times*, 5/27/18 (2:2). See also: 1918 Carter Co. death cert. nos. 12582, 12583 and 12584. Also: 1918 Lyon Co. death cert. no. 330.

1919

Patrick Kearney (white, age 31) and **James Lawler** (white, age 31). *Murder.* Their crime was committed on 3/5/1918 in Kenton County. Handgun slayings of 67-year-old Andrew Nordmeyer and 82-year-old John Rehm (whites). Motive: armed robbery. These men shot, robbed and murdered their way right into the arms of the electric chair on February 21, 1919. Source: 1918 Kenton Co. death cert. nos. 7938 and 7940. See also: 1919 Lyon Co. death cert. nos. 7264 and 7265. *Daring Detective*, 9/41.

Lewis Alexander Harris (black, age 23). *Murder.* The crime was committed on 12/22/1917 in Mason County. Uxoricide. Handgun slaying of 22-year-old Betina Miner Harris (black), she having been shot six times. Motive: marital estrangement. This wife-killer was made to sit in the chair of death on June 6, 1919. Source: *Maysville (KY) Daily Bulletin*, 12/24/17 (1:1). See also: 1917 Mason Co. death cert. no. 34233 and 1919 Lyon Co. death cert. no. 19193.

James Howard (black, age 19). *Murder.* The crime was committed on 8/12/1917 in McCracken County. Police killer. Handgun slaying of 35-year-old William Romaine (white), who was shot three times. Motive: disorderly conduct. Howard paid with his life for this on June 6, 1919. Source: *Paducah (KY) Evening Sun*, 6/6/19 (1:6). See also: 1917 McCracken Co. death cert. no. 23229 and 1919 Lyon Co. death cert. no. 19191.

Lube Martin (black, age 31). *Murder.* The crime was committed on 12/9/1916 in Calloway County. Police killer. Handgun slaying of 54-year-old Guthrie Duiguid (white). Motive: personal vendetta. The slain man was a deputy constable assigned to the Calloway County chain gang. The killer's grudge probably had something to do with that. It was enough to put him in the electric chair on July 25, 1919. Source: 1916 Calloway Co. death cert. no. 29566 and 1919 Lyon Co. death cert. no. 21659. Appeal: 199 SW 603–610.

1920

Charles Music (white, age 23). *Murder.* The crime was committed on 3/31/1919 in Boyd County. Police killer.

Handgun slaying of 41-year-old Charles West Hatfield (white). Motive: armed robbery gone awry. The Kentucky electric chair saw duty in this case on March 10, 1920. Source: *Big Sandy News* (Louisa, KY), 4/4/19 (1:4). See also: 1919 Boyd Co. death cert. no. 8737 and 1920 Lyon Co. death cert. no. 9234.

Will Lockett (black, age 33). *Murder.* The crime was committed on 2/4/1920 in Fayette County. Child killer. Executed for the murder of 10-year-old Geneva Hardeman (white), she having been bludgeoned with a rock. Motive: sexual assault. Lockett was also (to at least some extent) responsible for the deaths of five white men who were killed in a riot on 2–9-1920 at the Fayette County courthouse when he was brought there for trial. Those additional fatalities were: Benjamin Carrier (age 27), John L. Thomas (age 46), Major King (age 46), William Hiram Ethrington (age 31) and John M. Rogers (age 61). In addition to this, Lockett may or may not have been a serial killer. He claimed to have raped and strangled a white girl in Todd Co., KY in 1905; a white woman at Carmi IL in 1911; a black woman at Evansville IND in 1917 and another black woman near Baton Rouge, LA, in 1918 when he was a soldier stationed at Camp Zachary Taylor. So horrific were the unpublished details of what befell prepubescent Geneva Hardeman at the hands of Will Lockett that they prompted Kentucky lawmakers to reinstitute public hanging in such cases. As for Lockett himself, the electric chair broiled him to death on March 11, 1920. Source: *Lexington (KY) Leader*, 2/5/20 (1:8), 2/6/20 (1:6), 2/10/20 (1:1) & 3/11/20 (1:3). See also: 1920 Fayette Co. death cert. nos., 3663, 3657, 3654, 3661, 3660 and 3658. Also: 1920 Lyon Co. death cert. no. 9235.

1921

Lee Ellison (black, age 45). *Murder.* The crime was committed on 11/5/1920 in Hopkins County. Police killer. Shotgun slaying of 38-year-old Richard Scott Hunter (white). Motive: resisting arrest. Death by electrocution was Ellison's fate on January 31, 1921. Source: *Daily Republican* (Rushville, IN), 11/6/20 (1:1). See also: 1920 Hopkins Co. death cert. no. 27226 and 1921 Lyon Co. death cert. no. 1775.

1922

Dave Brown (white, age 26). *Murder.* The crime was committed on 5/30/1921 in Pike County. Baby killer, etc. Handgun slayings of 41-year-old James H. Brumfield and his infant child (name and gender not specified), whom he was holding in his arms at the time. Motive: adultery turned deadly. Brumfield had reclaimed his wife after she had absconded with Brown. Resenting this lawful repossession of a lawful spouse, Brown bushwhacked Brumfield as he was walking the woman homeward along a rural road. This homicidal home-wrecker suffered death in the electric chair on November 16, 1922. Source: *Middleboro (KY) Daily News*, 11/16/22 (1:7). Appeal: 195 KY 166–176. See also: 1922 Lyon Co. death cert. no. 27932. See also: 1920 U.S. Census (Mingo Co., WV), which notes Mr. Brumfield.

1923

Benny Bibbs (black, age 28). *Murder.* The crime was committed on

8/4/1922 in Christian County. Handgun slaying of 28-year-old Robert Lee Armstrong (black, a taxi driver), who was shot in the back. Motive: robbery. Bibb's actions secured a seat for him in the electric chair on January 26, 1923. Source: *Kingsport (TN) Times*, 1/26/23 (1:6). See also: 1922 Christian Co. death cert. no. 17479 and 1923 Lyon Co. death cert. no. 16651.

Thomas Nichols (black, age 29). *Murder.* The crime was committed on 8/6/1922 in Christian County. Executed for the murder of about 50-year-old B. H. Robey (white, full name not recorded), who was struck down with a sledgehammer. Motive: disgruntled employee. Score another one for the Kentucky electric chair on January 26, 1923. Source: *Louisville Courier Journal*, 1/26/23 (11:2). See also: 1922 Christian Co. death cert. no. 17480 and 1923 Lyon Co. death cert. no. 16650.

Henry S. Banks (black, age 22). *Murder.* The crime was committed on 4/11/1922 in Scott County. Police killer. Handgun slaying of 44-year-old William Owens Barkley (white). Motive: burglary gone awry. Having tried and failed to shoot his way out of a bad situation, Banks wound up in a far worse one when he took his final seat in the electric chair on May 15, 1923. Source: *Louisville Courier Journal*, 4/12/22 (5:2). See also: 1922 Scott Co. death cert. no. 12350 and 1923 Lyon Co. death cert. no. 16644.

James Powers (white, age 21). *Murder.* The crime was committed on 1/22/1922 in Kenton County. Handgun slaying of 25-year-old Mannie Lee (white male). Motive: robbery. The penalty for this was death by electrocution and thus ended the life of young James Powers on June 15, 1923. Source: *Lima (OH) News*, 6/15/23 (1:4). See also: 1922 Kenton Co. death cert. no. 1741 and 1923 Lyon Co. death cert. no. 21677.

1924

Will Chambers (black, age 20). *Murder.* The crime was committed on 12/21/1923 in Barren County. Handgun slaying of 27-year-old Charles Henry Bybee (white), the victim having been shot in the head. His body was dumped in a creek. Motive: carjacking. Death by high voltage was meted out to Will Chambers at the Kentucky State Prison (Eddyville) on March 7, 1924. Source: *Park City (KY) Daily News*, 1/9/24 (3:7) & 1/25/24 (1:7). See also: 1923 Barren Co. death cert. no. 10942 and 1924 Lyon Co. death cert. no. 7263.

Charles Miller (black, age 22). *Murder.* The crime was committed on 10/4/1922 in Breckenridge County. Handgun slayings of 58-year-old Samuel Haycraft and 41-year-old Edward Sago (whites). Motive: evading pursuit. Prime suspect in the 10–2-1922 handgun slaying of 57-year-old Abe Wilson (black) at Orell, KY. Miller made it a threesome for the Kentucky electric chair on May 9, 1924. Source: *Middleboro (KY) Daily News*, 10/6/22 (1:2). See also: 1922 Breckenridge Co. death cert. no. 21289. Also: 1922 Jefferson Co. death cert. nos. 22073 and 22090 plus 1924 Lyon Co. death cert. no. 14544.

Frank Thomas (white, age 66). *Murder.* The crime was committed on 11/26/1921 in Jefferson County. Executed for the handgun slaying of 58-year-old Lee Arbegust (white). Motive: because the slain man had stopped him from shooting up a polling place. Recidivist killer. Thomas was—of all things—a former Jefferson County police chief. On 5/16/1916 he shot dead his successor in that position: Edward Holman "Frank" Powell (white, age 35). A watered-down conviction for manslaughter came next. Lee Arbegust reportedly helped this killer to secure a pardon. Thomas had also shot dead a black man named Bert Skaggs in 1905 but is alleged to have cooked up a story to make it look justifiable. This fallen lawman met the fate of a condemned criminal at the Eddyville Penitentiary on May 9, 1924. Source: *Louisville Courier Journal,* 11/27/21 (1:1) & 5/9/24 (1:8). See also: 1916 Jefferson Co. death cert. no. 13345 and 1921 Jefferson Co. death cert. no. 26807, plus 1924 Lyon Co. death cert. no. 14543.

George Weick (white, age 41). *Murder.* The crime was committed on 10/7/1922 in Jefferson County. Executed for the murder of 39-year-old William E. Oelke (white), who was shot from ambush with a rifle as he was riding a bicycle and then finished off with a coup de grace from a handgun. Motive: adultery turned deadly. Weick paid the death penalty on May 9, 1924. Source: 1922 Jefferson Co. death cert. no. 22071 and 1924 Lyon Co. death cert. no. 14542. Appeal: 201 KY 632–642.

1925

Sid Davis (black, age 37). *Murder.* The crime was committed on 10/28/1923 in Fayette County. Handgun slaying of 31-year-old John H. Johnson (white), who was shot multiple times. Motive: rivalry for a female. Chalk up another one for the Kentucky electric chair on March 20, 1925. Source: *Lexington (KY) Leader,* 10/29/23 (6:5). Appeal: 204 KY 601–606. See also: 1923 Fayette Co. death cert. no. 25349 and 1925 Lyon Co. death cert. no. 7324.

Leonard Griffin (black, age 24). *Murder.* The crime was committed on 3/31/1924 in Harlan County. Police killer. Handgun slaying of 39-year-old James Valentine Gross (white). Motive: resisting arrest. The much-maligned County of Harlan—known to many as "Bloody Harlan"—saw to it that Griffin had a fair trial. The verdict, however, was inevitable thanks to Griffin himself. He went to the electric chair on March 20, 1925. Source: 1924 Harlan Co. death cert. no. 9007 and 1925 Lyon Co. death cert. no. 7325. Appeal: 204 KY 783–792.

George Farrell (white, age 24), **Elmer Hall** (white, age 25) and **Richard Newhouse** (white, age 22). *Murder.* Their crime was committed on 6/11/1924 in Bourbon County. Handgun slaying of 61-year-old Frank Buchanan (white). Motive: bank robbery. No mitigating factors being found in this case, the guilty trio were ordered for execution. They paid the penalty on June 26, 1925. Source: *Middleboro (KY) Daily News,* 6/11/24 (1:2). *Portsmouth (OH) Daily Times,* 6/26/25 (1:4). See also: 1924 Bourbon Co. death cert. no. 13142 and 1925 Lyon Co. death cert. nos. 17434, 17436 and 17437.

Harry Armond (black, age 23). *Murder.* The crime was committed on 3/1/1924 in Jefferson County. Handgun slaying of 44-year-old Ambrose K. Witten (white). Motive: robbery. It was an act that cost the shooter his own life on July 3, 1925. Source: 1924 Jefferson Co. death cert. no. 6854 and 1925 Lyon

Co. death cert. no. 17435. Appeal: 207 KY 652–654.

Ray Ross (black, age 22). *Rape.* The crime was committed on 7/3/1924 in Fayette County. Indecent assault on the person of 9-year-old Willie Mae Young (black female) under circumstances that were deemed compelling enough to order his public execution pursuant to the Act of 1920. This was a change in Kentucky law mandating that condemned rapists be publicly hanged in the county where they were convicted rather than by means of the electric chair. This lasted until 1938. A huge crowd saw black on black child rapist Ray Ross legally strung up at Lexington on August 28, 1925. Source: *Lexington Herald,* 8/28/25 (1:8). Appeal: 208 KY 52-54. Also 1925 Fayette Co. death cert. no. 18763.

1926

Edward Harris (black, age 45). *Rape.* The crime was committed on 1/19/1926 in Fayette County. Sex maniac, child killer, etc. Executed for an indecent assault on the person of 31-year-old Margaret Bryant (white), whom he battered with the butt of a shotgun after first murdering her husband and two children with that same weapon. The slain were Clarence W. Bryant (white, age 29), Ethel Bryant (white, age 8) and Wilburn Bryant (white, age 6). Homicide charges were held in abeyance pending prosecution on the rape charge, a capital felony in itself. Harris was legally hanged at Lexington on March 5, 1926. Source: *Logansport (IN) Pharos-Tribune,* 1/20/26 (1:1). *Lexington Herald,* 1/21/26 (1:7) & 3/5/26 (1:7). See also: 1920 U.S. Census (Fayette Co., KY), which notes Mr. & Mrs. Bryant. See also: 1926 Fayette Co. death cert. nos. 830, 831 and 832 (which bear incorrect ages), plus cert. no. 6322.

John Baker (black, age 31). *Murder.* The crime was committed on 7/10/1924 in Jefferson County. Uxoricide. Handgun slaying of 22-year-old Marie Hall Baker (black), she having been shot five times. Recidivist killer. Baker had slain a previous wife at Kansas City in 1915. He was freed after serving barely a year in jail. Kentucky proved less lenient when it sent him to the electric chair on May 28, 1926. Source: 1924 Jefferson Co. death cert. no. 16104 and 1926 Lyon Co. death cert. no. 13584. Appeal: 210 KY 525–532.

Edward Lake (white, age 30). *Murder.* The crime was committed on 7/19/1924 in Jefferson County. Uxoricide, etc. Handgun slayings of 36-year-old Matha Peavler Lake and 36-year-old Mary A. Smith (whites), they respectively being his wife and a family friend. Motive: marital estrangement. The Kentucky electric chair put down this killer on May 28, 1926. Source: *Sunday Times-Signal* (Zanesville, OH), 7/20/24 (2:3). See also: 1924 Jefferson Co. death cert. nos. 16125 and 16131. Also: 1926 Lyon Co. death cert. no. 13581.

Elisha Sloan (white, age 29). *Murder.* The crime was committed on 2/7/1925 in Perry County. Handgun slaying of 28-year-old Marvin Jackson Kingins (white). Motive: possibly deranged. Sloan was an unemployed miner who had been disabled by work-related injuries. His situation drove him to distraction. The murdered man was a physician then in the act of making a house call, as was common in those days. Sloan blamed Dr. Kingins for what he saw as ineffective treatment. Sloan was no longer in need of medical assistance when his electrocuted corpse was carried from the Eddyville Penitentiary on May 28, 1926. Source: 1925 Perry Co. death cert. no. 4902 and 1926 Lyon Co. death cert. no. 13583. Appeal: 211 KY 318–323.

Roger Brannon (white, age 20). *Murder.* The crime was committed on 12/26/1925 in Fayette County. Handgun slaying of 32-year-old William Nelson Fant (white). Motive: robbery. No chance was given this young killer to get out of jail and perhaps offend anew. The Kentucky electric chair made sure of that on December 17, 1926. Source: *Hamilton (OH) Evening Journal*, 1/18/26 (2:3), 1/18/26 (14:3) & 12/17/26 (1:1). See also: 1925 Fayette Co. death cert. no. 772 and 1926 Lyon Co. death cert. no. 31916. See also: Raymond C. Davis (executed 9/16/27).

Samuel Harris, alias "Smokey Harris" (black, age 34). *Murder.* The crime was committed on 4/29/1925 in Christian County. Uxoricide. Executed for the killing of 21-year-old Leona Clark Harris (black), she having been clubbed to death and her body dumped in a river. Motive: unclear. Harris suffered capital punishment at the Eddyville penitentiary on December 17, 1926. Source: 1925 Christian Co. death cert. no. 11290 and 1926 Lyon Co. death cert. no. 31915. Appeal: 214 KY 787–793.

1927

Raymond C. Davis (white, age 26). *Murder.* The crime was committed on 12/26/1925 in Fayette County. Accomplice in the handgun slaying of 32-year-old William Nelson Fant (white). Motive: robbery. Davis was executed on September 16, 1927. Source: *Evening Independent* (Massillon, OH), 9/16/27 (8:8). See also: Roger Brannon (executed 12/17/26).

Nathan Bard (black, age 40) and **Bunyan Fleming** (black, age 30). *Rape.* Their crime was committed on 4/7/1926 in Hopkins County. Both executed for indecent assaults on the person of 16-year-old Nell Catherine Breithhaupt (white), she and her 24-year-old male companion having also been robbed when three assailants jumped them on the grounds of an upscale country club. Bard and Fleming were legally hanged at Madisonville KY on November 25, 1927. Source: *Louisville Courier Journal*, 4/11/26 (1:8). *Hamilton (OH) Daily News*, 4/29/26 (1:3). See also: 1927 Hopkins Co. death cert. nos. 25314 and 25315.

1928

Hascue Dockery (white, age 25). *Murder.* The crime was committed on 3/25/1926 in Harlan County. Executed for the rifle slaying of pregnant 28-year-old Esther M. Howard (white). Motive: estranged husband gone loco. Dockery also murdered a married couple named Joseph Jenkins (white, age 31) and Judie Creech Jenkins (white, age 28) at the same time by the same means but was not tried in those cases pending resolution of the initial prosecution. The Kentucky electric chair ended the life of this three-time killer on July 13, 1928. Source: *Louisville Courier Journal*, 4/4/26 (1:7). See also: 1926 Harlan Co. death cert. no. 6618 and 1928 Lyon Co. death cert. no. 20638. See also: 1920 U.S. Census (Harlan Co., KY), which notes Mr. &

Mrs. Jenkins. Note also that the killer's death certificate bears an incorrect date of birth.

James Howard (black, age 21). *Murder.* The crime was committed on 4/17/1926 in Jefferson County. Fatal stabbing of 28-year-old Lucy Buckner (black), also known as "Lucy King Howard." Motive: atavistic male jealousy. This killer was executed on July 13, 1928. Source: 1926 Jefferson Co. death cert. no. 10013 and 1928 Lyon Co. death cert. no. 20639. Appeal: 224 KY 224–229.

Milford Lawson (white, age 31). *Murder.* The crime was committed on 7/29/1926 in Whitley County. Handgun slaying of 45-year-old John Ira Stansbury (white), the victim having been shot down in his own doorway. Motive: obnoxious drunk. Life for life was exacted in the case of *Commonwealth vs. Lawson* on July 13, 1928, in the manner prescribed by law. Source: 1926 Whitley Co. death cert. no. 19085 and 1928 Lyon Co. death cert. no. 20636. Appeal: 222 KY 614–621.

Clarence McQueen (black, age 36). *Murder.* The crime was committed on 4/25/1927 in Harrison County. Shotgun slaying of 74-year-old Lewis Williams (black), the victim having been blasted twice in the back. Motive: because the killer thought that Williams had reported him for making illegal liquor. McQueen wound up with far worse problems when he had to answer for a capital offense. The Kentucky electric chair took his life on July 13, 1928. Source: 1927 Harrison Co. death cert. no. 8415 and 1928 Lyon Co. death cert. no. 18083. Appeal: 224 KY 89–96.

Charles Paul Mitra (white, age 22). *Murder.* The crime was committed on 12/13/1926 in Jefferson County. Handgun slaying of 59-year-old Marion A. George (white male). Motive: armed robbery. Death by electrocution was the price this killer paid on July 13, 1928. Source: 1926 Jefferson Co. death cert. no. 31183 and 1928 Lyon Co. death cert. no. 20637. *Master Detective,* 7/32. See also: Carl Hord (executed 9/13/29).

Willie Moore (black, age 47). *Murder.* The crime was committed on 12/8/1926 in Jefferson County. Executed for the murder of 30-year-old Anna Eslick (black), she having had her skull shattered by a thick glass beer bottle and her brains literally beaten out. Motive: lovers' quarrel. This uncouth male of the species went to his death in the electric chair on July 13, 1928. Source: 1926 Jefferson Co. death cert. no. 31125 and 1928 Lyon Co. death cert. no. 20640. Appeal: 223 KY 128–135.

Orlando Seymour (white, age 18). *Murder.* The crime was committed on 4/3/1926 in Jefferson County. Handgun slaying of 33-year-old William A. Schanzenbacher (white). Motive: armed robbery. A callous disregard for human life being seen in this young killer along with a proclivity toward violence, no convincing reason could be found to spare him. He was accordingly put to death on July 13, 1928. Source: *Louisville Courier Journal,* 4/10/26 (1:4) & 7/13/28 (1:7). See also: 1926 Jefferson Co. death cert. no. 9997 and 1928 Lyon Co. death cert. no. 20635.

1929

Carl Hord (white, age 18). *Murder.* The crime was committed on

12/13/1926 in Jefferson County. Accomplice in the handgun slaying of 59-year-old Marion A. George (white male). Motive: armed robbery. Hord was executed pursuant to sentence on September 13, 1929. Source: 1929 Lyon Co. death cert. no. 24659. See: Charles Mitra (executed 7/13/28).

Ivan Hutsell (white, age 23). *Murder.* The crime was committed on 5/29/1927 in Oldham County. Shotgun slayings of 47-year-old John A. Ditchler and 28-year-old Jessie Zimmerman Ditchler (whites), a married couple. Motive: revenge. The homicide victims had testified against Hutsell in a court case, thereby incurring his wrath. Hutsell wound up in the electric chair on September 13, 1929. Source: *Gettysburg (PA) Times*, 9/13/29 (2:2). See also: 1927 Oldham Co. death cert. nos. 14224 and 14225, plus 1929 Lyon Co. death cert. no. 24660.

1930

Richard Edmonds (black, age 25). *Murder.* The crime was committed on 11/14/1928 in Jefferson County. Electrocuted for the murder of 54-year-old Harry S. Long (white), who had been beaten on the head with a heavy gas pipe. Motive: burglary. Exit Edmonds from this world by due process of law on June 13, 1930. Source: *Piqua (OH) Daily Call*, 6/13/30 (1:1). See also: 1928 Jefferson Co. death cert. no. 27567 and 1930 Lyon Co. death cert. no. 20507.

Ballard Ratcliffe (white, age 39). *Murder.* The crime was committed on 5/23/1928 in Jefferson County. Hammer slaying of 64-year-old William A. Muse (white), who was attacked from behind as he was praying at his wife's grave. Motive: mugging. The dastardliness of this killing struck a chord with the public that put it in a class by itself. The American Society for the Abolition of Capital Punishment (a well-known organization of that era) apparently wrote Ratcliffe off as being bad for business. He was executed on June 13, 1930. Source: *Piqua (OH) Daily Call*, 6/13/30 (1:1). See also: 1928 Jefferson Co. death cert. no. 12563 and 1930 Lyon Co. death cert. no. 20508. *Master Detective*, 8/30.

1932

Auburn E. Cooksey (black, age 23). *Murder.* The crime was committed on 11/24/1929 in Hopkins County. Police killer. Handgun slaying of 61-year-old John H. Ashby (white), who was shot in the back. Motive: resisting arrest. The Kentucky electric chair rid the world of Auburn Cooksey on April 29, 1932. Source: *Portsmouth (OH) Times*, 4/29/32 (1:8). See also: 1932 Lyon Co. death cert. no. 19724. See also: 1910 U.S. Census (Hopkins Co., KY), which notes the killer by his actual name and his parents as the same persons identified as such on his death certificate. See also: 1920 U.S. Census (Hopkins Co., KY), which notes Ashby.

Walter Holmes (black, age 31) and **Charles Rogers** (black, age 22). *Murder.* Their crime was committed on 4/8/1931 in Hardin County. Handgun slaying of 57-year-old Thomas Dye Tillery (white). Motive: home invasion. This pair of killers—whose hallmark was an utter disregard for the lives, rights and property of others—suffered death by electricity according to law on April 29, 1932. Source: *Kingsport (TN) Times*, 4/9/31 (5:3) & 4/10/31 (8:7). See also: 1931 Hardin Co. death cert. no. 9805 and 1932 Lyon Co.

death cert. nos. 9623 and 19723. See also: Walter Dewberry (executed 11/10/33).

Sam Jennings (black, age 36). *Rape.* The crime was committed on 10/6/1930 in Breckenridge County. Indecent assault on the person of 22-year-old Mabel Downs (white), she having been accosted with a shotgun as she walked across a field. Her attacker was legally hanged at Smithland KY on June 17, 1932. Source: *Hancock (KY) Clarion*, 10/31/30 (1:3). *Louisville Courier Journal*, 10/25/30 (1:2), 6/17/32 (1:1) & 6/18/32 (1:2). See also: 1932 Breckenridge Co. death cert. no. 13043. See also: 1930 U.S. Census (Breck. Co., KY), which notes the victim of this sex crime.

Jeff Covington (black, age 29). *Murder.* The crime was committed on 12/25/1931 in Madison County. Police killer, etc. Handgun slayings of 59-year-old James Turner (white, a railroad detective) and 23-year-old Howard Smith (black). Motive: vendetta. Covington resented Turner for a previous brush with the law. It had cost him two years in jail. Howard Smith was in the wrong place at the wrong time. Two killings on Christmas Day made Covington's defense a hard sell. He was executed on December 17, 1932. Source: *Louisville Courier Journal*, 12/17/32 (1:4). See also: 1932 Madison Co. death cert. no. 1946 and 1932 Lyon Co. death cert. no. 30140.

1933

Frank Carson (white, age 16). *Murder.* The crime was committed on 2/23/1931 in Nelson County. Handgun slaying of 58-year-old Carl B. James (white). Motive: carjacking. A trial court concluded that society would be better protected from possible future depredations by this juvenile delinquent if he was put to death rather than being locked up for an uncertain length of time. Post-conviction reviewers of this case (including the governor of Kentucky) could find no grounds to disagree. So Frank Carson had his misspent life cut short at the hands of the State on April 7, 1933. Source: *Hammond (IN) Times*, 4/7/33 (19:8). See also: 1931 Nelson Co. death cert. no. 5195 and 1933 Lyon Co. death cert. no. 9798.

Sam McGee (black, age 28). *Murder.* The crime was committed on 1/17/1931 in McCracken County. Handgun slaying of 19-year-old Charles Clark (white). Motive: armed robbery. Paducah residents shed few tears for Sam McGee when he paid for his crime in the electric chair on April 7, 1933. Source: *Appleton (WI) Post-Crescent*, 1/21/31 (7:1). See also: 1931 McCracken Co. death cert. no. 2195 and 1933 Lyon Co. death cert. no. 9799.

Richard Gaines (black, age 26). *Murder.* The crime was committed on 8/16/1930 in Caldwell County. Gunshot slaying of 42-year-old George "Bud" Wilson (black). Motive: monetary dispute. Records are vague as to the exact type of firearm that was used in this case. It mattered little to Richard Gaines by the time he went to the electric chair on April 14, 1933. Source: *Louisville Courier Journal*, 4/14/33 (1:8). See also: 1930 Caldwell Co. death cert. no. 18858 and 1933 Lyon Co. death cert. no. 9795.

Kermit Roosevelt Pope (black, age 32). *Murder.* The crime was committed on 11/23/1931 in Jefferson County. Uxoricide. Handgun slaying of 27-year-old Lula Mae Pope (black).

Motive: jealous ex-spouse. It was enough to secure that man a seat in the electric chair on April 14, 1933. Source: 1931 Jefferson Co. death cert. no. 26824 and 1933 Lyon Co. death cert. no. 9797. *Louisville Courier Journal*, 4/14/33 (1:8).

John Young (white, age 35). *Murder.* The crime was committed on 4/12/1932 in Jefferson County. Police killer. Handgun slayings of 40-year-old William L. Mulligan and 39-year-old Edward E. Parr (whites). Motive: resisting arrest. A lethal dose of electricity administered at the hands of the State removed John Young from the ranks of the living on April 14, 1933. Source: *Louisville Courier Journal*, 4/13/32 (1:8) & 4/14/33 (1:8). See also: 1932 Jefferson Co. death cert. nos. 8949 and 8951 plus 1933 Lyon Co. death cert. no. 9796.

Ishmael Scott (white, age 23). *Murder.* The crime was committed on 8/7/1932 in Floyd County. Handgun slaying of 34-year-old Martin Stephens (white), who was holding a baby in his arms at the time. Motive: because the killer suspected the murdered man of harboring his estranged wife. Scott is confirmed to have also shot dead Charles "Red" Burnette (white, age abt. 20) at Wayland KY on 7/30/1932. He was executed on November 3, 1933. Source: *Floyd County Times*, 8/5/32 (1:4) & 8/12/32 (1:1). *Pike County (KY) News*, 11/9/33 (1:5). Appeal: 250 KY 70–73. See also: 1930 U.S. Census (Floyd Co., KY), which notes Scott and Stephens. Also: 1933 Lyon Co. death cert. no. 26927. Death certificates for Burnette and Stephens are missing.

William Waters, alias "Bad Bill" (white, age 46). *Murder.* The crime was committed on 7/13/1932 in Menifee County. Police killer, etc. Executed for the shotgun slaying of 26-year-old Stanley Cole Helton (white), who succumbed after 12 days of agony. Motive: resisting arrest. Venue changed from Menifee County to Montgomery County. Waters had also murdered two other men in relation to the same incident. They were: Charles Neil (white, age 56) on 7/11/1932 and Marion Stapleton (white, age 40) on 7/13/1932, they having respectively been a farmer and a law enforcement officer. Waters went to his own death in the Kentucky electric chair on November 3, 1933. Source: *Vidette-Messenger* (Valparaiso, IN), 11/3/33 (3:8). See also: 1932 Menifee Co. death cert. nos. 17376 and 22107. Also: 1932 Montgomery Co. death cert. no. 17425 and 1933 Lyon Co. death cert. no. 26926. See also: 1930 U.S. Census (Menifee Co., KY), which notes Mr. Neil.

Harve Burton (white, age 46). *Murder.* The crime was committed on or about 5/1/1932 in Elliott County. Uxoricide. Executed for the murder of 46-year-old Virgie Skaggs Burton (white), she having been struck on the head with a hoe and then decapitated by means of an axe. Motive: unspecified. This sanguine wife-killer went to the chair on November 10, 1933. Source: *Big Sandy (KY) News-Record*, 11/3/33 (1:4). *Daily News* (Middlesboro, KY), 11/10/33 (1:4). See also: 1920 U.S. Census (Elliott Co., KY), which notes both parties.

Walter Dewberry (black, age 22). *Murder.* The crime was committed on 4/8/1931 in Hardin County. Accomplice in the handgun slaying of 57-year-old Thomas Dye Tillery (white). Motive: home invasion. He was put to death on November 10, 1933. Source: 1933 Lyon Co. death cert. no. 29973.

See: Walter Holmes and Charles Rogers (executed 4/29/32).

1934

Will Chaney (black, age 46). *Murder.* The crime was committed on 12/24/1932 in Jefferson County. Shotgun slaying of 21-year-old George Bottoms (black). Motive: gambling dispute. Will Chaney went to the Kentucky electric chair on August 24, 1934. Source: *Louisville Courier Journal,* 12/25/32 (12:4). See also: 1932 Jefferson Co. death cert. no. 29194 and 1934 Lyon Co. death cert. no. 23153.

George W. Tincher (white, age 36). *Murder.* The crime was committed on 11/28/1932 in Scott County. Handgun slaying of 58-year-old Ben Michele Keenon (white). Motive: bank robbery. The death penalty was exacted from this bandit on August 24, 1934. Source: 1934 Lyon Co. death cert. no. 23157. Also: 1932 Franklin Co. death cert. no. 28658, which notes Keenon's demise in Frankfurt Hospital. Appeal: 253 KY 623–630. *Daring Detective,* 10/41. See also: Francis Glenday (executed 12/7/34).

Francis Glenday (white, age 27). *Murder.* The crime was committed on 11/28/1932 in Scott County. Accomplice in the handgun slaying of 58-year-old Ben Michele Keenon (white). Motive: bank robbery. This miscreant met the same fate as George Tincher on December 7, 1934. Source: 1934 Lyon Co. death cert. no. 2117. See also: George W. Tincher (executed 8/24/34).

1935

Wiley Graves (black, age 28). *Murder.* The crime was committed on 3/1/1934 in Fayette County. Handgun slaying of 30-year-old Charles W. Taylor (white), who was shot three times in the head. His body was dumped from his own automobile. Motive: murder-for-hire. This callous disregard for human life cost Wiley Graves his own life. He was electrocuted pursuant to court order on February 22, 1935. Source: 1934 Fayette Co. death cert. no. 6009 and 1935 Lyon Co. death cert. no. 7651. Appeal: 256 KY 777–786. *Famous Detective Cases,* 9/36. *Front Page Detective,* 5/41. *Intimate Detective,* 7/40.

Charlie Williams (black, age 26). *Murder.* The crime was committed on 12/16/1933 in Christian County. Handgun slaying of 38-year-old Grant E. Lane (white). Motive: mugging. The Kentucky electric chair did its job in this case on March 1, 1935. Source: 1933 Christian Co. death cert. no. 28183 and 1935 Lyon Co. death cert. no. 7652. Appeal: 257 KY 175–191.

Willard DeBoe (white, age 22). *Rape.* The crime was committed on 5/16/1934 in Livingston County. Legally hanged for the knifepoint rape of pregnant 31-year-old Marjorie Johnson (white) during the course of a robbery and home invasion. His execution took place at Smithland KY on April 19, 1935. Source: *Carbondale (IL) Free Press,* 4/19/35 (1:1). Appeal: 257 KY 792–803. *Master Detective,* 1/37.

James Smith (black, age 27). *Murder.* The crime was committed on 1/12/1932 in Fayette County. Firearm slaying of 53-year-old Leslie Poyntz (black male), who was first blasted by a shotgun and then finished off with a pistol. Motive: adultery turned deadly. The Kentucky electric chair was the last stop for James Smith on May 24,

1935. Source: 1935 Lyon Co. death cert. no. 17829. Appeal: 258 KY 482–484. See also: 1920 U.S. Census (Fayette Co., KY), which notes Leslie Poyntz and his disloyal wife.

Bill Young (white, age 25). *Murder.* The crime was committed on 12/25/1934 in Harlan County. Handgun slaying of 36-year-old Joe Wheeler Cawood (white). Motive: because the killer feared that Cawood might have him arrested for shoplifting. Another Christmas killer, this one was made to pay a much stiffer penalty than that of a thief when he sat in the Kentucky electric chair on June 28, 1935. Source: 1934 Harlan Co. death cert. no. 1119 and 1935 Lyon Co. death cert. no. 22849. Appeal: 258 KY 766–768.

Eulie Lotheridge (white male, age 25). *Murder.* The crime was committed on 12/5/1931 in Carroll County. Executed for the murder of 56-year-old Theodore Fitschen (white), who was battered with a tire jack and then immolated with gasoline taken from his own automobile. Motive: robbery and gross perfidy. The young man who did this suffered a searing death of his own in the Kentucky electric chair on December 6, 1935. Source: 1931 Jefferson Co. death cert. no. 29604 and 1935 Lyon Co. death cert. no. 31002. Appeal: 260 KY 500–508.

1936

Neal Bowman (white, age 30). *Murder.* The crime was committed on or about 4/1/1934 in Mercer County. Handgun slaying of 17-year-old Comer Franklin (white), who was shot execution-style; his weighted body was dumped in a lake. Motive: dishonor among thieves. The slain youth had voiced his intention to quit a robbery gang headed by Bowman. It was also determined that Bowman had murdered a storekeeper at Camp Nelson KY on 3/8/1934. The homicide victim in that case was George Kaufman (white, age 46), who was shot in the back. Motive: armed robbery. Neal Bowman was made to suffer death by high voltage on January 10, 1936. Source: 1934 Jessamine Co. death cert. no. 9667 and 1936 Lyon Co. death cert. no. 8566. Appeal: 261 KY 215–223. *Crime Detective*, 12/43.

Willard Hall (white, age 32) and **Calvin Tate** (white, age 20). *Murder.* Their crime was committed on 6/15/1934 in Jefferson County. Handgun slayings of 65-year-old John Bernard Schroering, 40-year-old Cecil Carter and 71-year-old Samuel Horine (whites). Motive: robbery with violence. Both of these felons met their doom at the hands of the State on January 17, 1936. Source: 1934 Jefferson Co. death cert. nos. 14531, 14532 and 14533. Also: 1936 Lyon Co. death cert. nos. 2311 and 5490. Appeal: 258 KY 685–697.

James Matthews (white, age 17). *Murder.* The crime was committed on or about 3/20/1935 in McCreary County. Rifle slaying of 24-year-old Cleve Spradlin (white), who was shot from behind. The killer then stripped his body and tumbled it over a cliff. Motive: highway robbery. Matthews was held fully responsible for what he did. He met an untimely death of his own in the electric chair on January 31, 1936. Source: *Daily News* (Middlesboro, KY), 11/27/35 (1:8). Appeal: 261 KY 484–491. See also: 1936 Lyon Co. death cert. no. 5489. Also: 1930 U.S. Census (McCreary Co., KY), which notes Spradlin.

Bennie Lee (black, age 26). *Murder.* The crime was committed on 5/4/1935 in Bell County. Ax murder of 56-year-old James Robert Townes (black). Motive: robbery and false pretense. Another black-on-black killer, this one suffered death for his crime on February 21, 1936. Source: 1935 Bell Co. death cert. no. 13790 and 1936 Lyon Co. death cert. no. 8565. Appeal: 262 KY 15–19. See also: 1930 U.S. Census (Bell Co., KY), which notes Townes.

Erleon Whitehead (white, age 33). *Murder.* The crime was committed on 3/19/1934 in Barren County. Handgun slaying of 68-year-old John Allen (black). Motive: home invasion. The killer died in the electric chair on March 20, 1936. Source: *Louisville Courier Journal,* 3/20/36 (Sec. 4) (12:4). See also: 1934 Barren Co. death cert. no. 5369 and 1936 Lyon Co. death cert. no. 8568.

Alfred Drake (black, age 31). *Murder.* The crime was committed on 4/14/1935 in Jefferson County. Police killer. Handgun slaying of 60-year-old James Edward Simpson (black). Motive: resisting arrest. The killer went to the electric chair on May 15, 1936. Source: 1935 Jefferson Co. death cert. no. 9846 and 1936 Lyon Co. death cert. no. 14425. Appeal: 263 KY 109–119.

Roy Simmons (black, age 22). *Murder.* The crime was committed on 5/30/1935 in McCracken County. Police killer. Handgun slaying of 31-year-old Richard Kelly (white), a railroad detective. Motive: boxcar break-in gone awry. Death in the electric chair befell Roy Simmons on May 15, 1936. Source: 1935 McCracken Co. death cert. no. 12961 and 1936 Lyon Co. death cert. no. 14414. Appeal: 263 KY 171–177.

James Russell Woodford (black, age 19). *Murder.* The crime was committed on 11/5/1933 in Fayette County. Handgun slaying of 62-year-old John M. Anderson (white), a trolley motorman. Motive: attempted robbery. Lexington residents knew there to be one less hoodlum in their midst when this one died in the electric chair on May 29, 1936. Source: *Daily News* (Middlesboro, KY), 5/29/36 (1:8). See also: 1933 Fayette Co. death cert. no. 25727 and 1936 Lyon Co. death cert. no. 14413. *Lexington Leader,* 5/29/36 (1:7).

Homer Young (black, age 38). *Murder.* The crime was committed on 8/1/1935 in Bell County. Handgun slaying of 28-year-old Enoch Beeler (white), who was shot in the back. Motive: unclear. The fact that both men had walked by each other on the street in a seemingly peaceable manner moments before the shooting confuted a plea of self defense. The killer was executed on June 5, 1936. Source: 1935 Bell Co. death cert. no. 18738 and 1936 Lyon Co. death cert. no. 17066. Appeal: 263 KY 683–693.

Rainey Bethea (black, age abt. 25). *Rape.* The crime was committed on 6/7/1936 in Daviess County. Legally hanged for indecently assaulting 70-year-old Lishia Edwards (white), who was also strangled to death in the course of the same incident. Separate indictments for burglary and murder were held in abeyance pending the outcome of the rape charge. This nocturnal marauder and pervert met death at the end of a rope at Owensboro on August 14, 1936. Source: 1936 Daviess Co. death cert. nos. 15728 and 24001. *Official Detective,* 12/1/36. See also: *The Last Public Execution in America,* by Perry T. Ryan (KY: P.T. Ryan, 1992) for an excellent account of this case.

1937

George Underwood (white, age 22). *Murder.* The crime was committed on 4/29/1936 in Bullitt County. Police killer. Handgun slaying of 55-year-old Wallace van Fleet (white). Motive: obnoxious drunk. Underwood had reacted violently to being ejected from a restaurant. He was executed on February 19, 1937. Source: 1936 Bullitt Co. death cert. no. 9756 and 1937 Lyon Co. death cert. no. 8678. Appeal: 266 KY 613–622.

Sam Franklin (black, age 23). *Armed robbery with violence.* The crime was committed on 11/17/1935 in Jefferson County. Executed for the gunpoint mugging of 45-year-old John C. O'Connor (white), the victim having suffered a concussion after being knocked to the ground and robbed of the following items: his lunch box, a Thermos bottle, a small clock, a pair of eyeglasses and $1.40 in silver. Two co-defendants were sentenced to life imprisonment. The draconian aspect of the punishments in this case suggest an underlying cause. This researcher makes no rush to judgment. Sam Franklin was executed on March 19, 1937. Source: *Kingsport (TN) Times*, 3/19/37 (5:3). Appeal: 266 KY 833–839. See also: 1937 Lyon Co. death cert. no. 14292.

Arnold Clift (white, age 23). *Murder.* The crime was committed on 5/30/1936 in Laurel County. Handgun slayings of 58-year-old Reed A. Taylor and 50-year-old Effie Cox Taylor (whites), a married couple. The body of the woman was found to have been partially devoured by swine. Motive: armed robbery. The killer was executed on July 16, 1937. Source: 1936 Laurel Co. death cert. nos. 19752 and 19753 plus 1937 Lyon Co. death cert. no. 21969. Appeal: 268 KY 573–585.

Perry Marion (white, age 27). *Murder.* The crime was committed on 5/30/1936 in Laurel County. Accomplice in the handgun slayings of 58-year-old Reed A. Taylor and 50-year-old Effie Cox Taylor (whites), a married couple. Motive: armed robbery. The Kentucky electric chair cleaned up what was left of this case on November 12, 1937. Source: 1937 Lyon Co. death cert. no. 29073. See also: Arnold Clift (executed 7/16/37).

John Peter Montjoy (black, age 21). *Rape.* The crime was committed on 3/22/1935 in Kenton County. Legally hanged for an indecent assault on the person of 27-year-old Irene Cummings (white), she having also been robbed of her purse at gunpoint—a concomitant capital crime in itself, constituting robbery with violence. Montjoy was sent through the gallows trap at Independence KY on December 17, 1937. Source: *Piqua (OH) Daily Call*, 8/20/36 (1:6). Appeals: 262 KY 426–436 and 270 KY 470–476. See also: 1937 Kenton Co. death cert. no. 31905.

1938

Troy Triplett (white, age 21). *Murder.* The crime was committed on 7/17/1937 in Letcher County. Handgun slaying of 40-year-old Dolph Hall (white), who was shot six times from behind. Motive: revenge. Hall had previously testified against Triplett in a court matter. An appellate report says that the victim was a 13-year-old boy, whereas his death certificate says that he was a 40-year-old man—a shocking disparity in official records. Troy

Triplett was executed on May 20, 1938. Source: 1937 Letcher Co. death cert. no. 19246 and 1938 Lyon Co. death cert. no. 15071. Appeal: 272 KY 714–719.

Harold van Venison (black, age 30). *Rape.* The crime was committed on 8/16/1937 in Kenton County. Legally hanged for an indecent assault on the person of 25-year-old Eleanor Nieberding (white), she having been abducted at gunpoint together with her 28-year-old white male companion (named Robert Steidel), the latter of whom was pistol whipped and robbed of his valuables, a capital crime in itself. The culprit died dangling at Covington KY on June 3, 1938. Source: *The Bee* (Danville, VA), 10/11/37 (9:1). Appeal: 273 KY 83–91. See also: 1938 Kenton Co. death cert. no. 14846.

Parkie Denny (white, age 42). *Murder.* The crime was committed on 9/14/1936 in Madison County. Uxoricide. Executed for the murder of 49-year-old Ethel Yates Denny (white), she having been battered to death with a hammer and her decapitated body dumped in a farmer's field. Motive: desire for a younger woman. The electric chair cured this killer's wanderlust on September 2, 1938. Source: 1936 Madison Co. death cert. no. 30813 and 1938 Lyon Co. death cert. no. 22756. Appeals: 271 KY 608–613 and 274 KY 419–425. *Dynamic Detective,* 1/38. *Headline Detective,* 7/42. *Master Detective,* 6/49.

Leonard Mosley (black, age 43). *Rape.* The crime was committed on 9/3/1938 in Meade County. Indecent assault on the person of 57-year-old Beulah Fontaine Hook (white), she having been attacked in her own home, beaten with fatal consequences and robbed. She died in Louisville Hospital on 2/17/1939. The electric chair settled matters with Leonard Mosley on October 28, 1938. Source: *Kingsport (TN) Times,* 9/8/38 (1:4). See also: 1938 Lyon Co. death cert. no. 25452 and 1939 Jefferson Co. death cert. no. 4114.

1939

Sylvester Warner (white, age 24). *Murder.* The crime was committed on 12/3/1933 in Casey County. Executed for the murders of 81-year-old John D. White and 51-year-old Clay White (whites, a father and son), who were tied up with wire and clubbed to death. Their bodies were dumped in a river. Motive: home invasion. The killer paid the death penalty on February 10, 1939. Source: *Daily News* (Middlesboro, KY), 12/5/33 (1:3). *Kingsport (TN) Times,* 2/10/39 (1:5). See also: 1933 Casey Co. death cert. nos. 21713 and 21714 plus 1939 Lyon Co. death cert. no. 4857. *Daring Detective,* 10/42. *Real Detective,* 4/46.

Bonnie Griffin (white male, age 22) and **Arnold Powell** (white, age 21). *Murder.* Their crime was committed on 1/5/1937 in Estill County. Both executed for the murders of 75-year-old Marion Francis Short and 40-year-old Martha Bremer Short (whites, a married couple), who were clubbed unconscious and had their house burned down upon them. Motive: robbery and home invasion. The killers went to the chair on March 3, 1939. Source: 1937 Estill Co. death cert. nos. 763 and 764 plus 1939 Lyon Co. death cert. nos. 7928 and 7929. Appeal: 276 KY 234–246.

Willie Waters (black, age 45). *Murder.* The crime was committed on 1/10/1938 in Jefferson County. Uxoricide. Fatal stabbing of 42-year-old Ella Caldwell Waters (black), the attack being so frenzied that the knife blade broke off in the wound. Motive: because she had dared to have a peace warrant sworn out against him. Waters took his last seat in the death chair on March 24, 1939. Source: 1938 Jefferson Co. death cert. no. 1488 and 1939 Lyon Co. death cert. no. 7927. Appeal: 276 KY 315–321.

Arvil Rice (white, age 19). *Murder.* The crime was committed on 7/20/1938 in Bell County. Handgun slaying of 23-year-old Walter Ludwig Dorfman (white). Motive: carjacking. This momentous mistake propelled Arvil Rice to an untimely death in the electric chair on July 7, 1939. Source: 1938 Bell Co. death cert. no. 15992 and 1939 Lyon Co. death cert. no. 18281. Appeal: 128 SW (2nd) 219–223.

Charles H. Smith (white, age 40). *Murder.* The crime was committed on 6/13/1938 in Lyon County. Executed for the fatal stabbing and decapitation of 22-year-old Clayton Sloan (white). Motive: prison violence. Recidivist killer. This was the second murder perpetrated by Smith since he had been initially sentenced to a term of life imprisonment 19 years earlier for another homicide, thereby making three in all. The first one had reportedly occurred at Ashland KY in 1919, the victim being a railroad detective. Then on 2/28/1925 Smith fatally stabbed a fellow prison inmate named Arthur Cunningham (white, age 28) with a butcher knife that he had stolen while on kitchen detail. The victim died ten days later and Smith had 21 years added to his sentence following conviction on a watered-down charge of manslaughter. The murder of Clayton Sloan could have been easily prevented had a meaningful sentence been imposed on this killer after his first or even second conviction. He was finally executed on July 14, 1939. Source: *Louisville Courier Journal,* 6/14/38 (8:8). Appeal: 128 SW (2nd) 590–592. See also: 1925 Lyon Co. death cert. no. 7327. Also: 1938 Lyon Co. death cert. no. 18059 and 1939 Lyon Co. death cert. no. 18279.

Jack Davis, alias "Berry Brewer" (white, age 48). *Murder.* The crime was committed on 7/8/1938 in Leslie County. Executed for the murder of 30-year-old Abram Combs (white), who was battered about the head with a large iron bolt wrapped in brown paper. His neck was also broken. Motive: carjacking. This slungshot killer was himself killed in the Kentucky electric chair on July 21, 1939. Source: *Kingsport (TN) Times,* 8/31/38 (3:1) & 7/21/39 (5:2). Appeal: 129 SW (2nd) 1030–1033. See also: 1939 Lyon Co. death cert. no. 2591. *Master Detective,* 7/48.

Edward Higgins (black, age 26). *Rape.* The crime was committed on 4/10/1939 in Mercer County. Indecent assault on the person of a 76-year-old white female (name withheld) together with the forcible detention of a second although younger white female who was insulted and terrorized at the same time. The exact details are too obscene for repetition. This sex maniac was legally put to death on July 25, 1939. Source: *Kingsport (TN) Times,* 4/11/39 (5:6). See also: 1939 Lyon Co. death cert. no. 18282.

1940

Henry Phillips (black, age 46). *Murder.* The crime was committed on

5/25/1939 in Jefferson County. Handgun slaying of 46-year-old Ellie P. Williamson (black). Motive: lovers' quarrel. The subsequent sentence of death by electrocution was carried out on the person of Henry Phillips on July 26, 1940. Source: 1939 Jefferson Co. death cert. no. 12839 and 1940 Lyon Co. death cert. no. 17602. Appeal: 140 SW (2nd) 1014–1015.

Ernest Houston (black, age 20). *Murder.* The crime was committed on 1/24/1940 in Jefferson County. Hatchet killing of 27-year-old Arnold Smith (white). Motive: robbery. This homicidal hatchet wielder had his own life cut short on August 30, 1940, when he paid for his crime in the electric chair. Source: 1940 Jefferson Co. death cert. no. 1524 and 1940 Lyon Co. death cert. no. 19966. Appeal: 142 SW (2nd) 150–151.

1941

Columbus Richardson (black, age 26). *Murder.* The crime was committed on 2/5/1939 in McCracken County. Handgun slaying of 64-year-old Tom McNary (black). Motive: obnoxious drunk. Richardson was not the first person to face the executioner due to the pernicious effects of alcoholism. Nor would he be the last. He paid the price pursuant to law on January 3, 1941. Source: 1939 McCracken Co. death cert. no. 4862 and 1941 Lyon Co. death cert. no. 2592. Appeal: 144 SW (2nd) 492–495.

Grover Chism (white, age 47). *Murder.* The crime was committed on 10/31/1939 in Hardin County. Shotgun slaying of 68-year-old Schuyler McClure (white). Motive: obnoxious drunk. This inebriate suffered death for his transgression on July 4, 1941. Source: 1939 Jefferson Co. death cert. no. 27729 and 1941 Lyon Co. death cert. no. 18105. Appeal: 150 SW (2nd) 694–696.

William Smiddy (white, age 35). *Murder.* The crime was committed on or about 6/15/1940 in Whitley County. Uxoricide. Fatal stabbing of 17-year-old Faye Meadows Smiddy (white, his child bride, who was already the mother of three children), she having been pierced in 16 different places. Motive: because she did not instantly comply with her husband's sexual demands. This killer was also the prime suspect in the 3/20/1933 handgun slaying of Alfred Sharp (white, age 47) near Jellico, TN. He was executed on August 29, 1941. Source: *LaFollette (TN) Press,* 3/23/33 (1:3). Appeal: 152 SW (2nd) 949–952. See also: 1941 Lyon Co. death cert. no. 20510. See also: 1930 U.S. Census (Campbell Co., TN), which notes Mr. Sharp. See also: Correspondence of Elizabeth Smiddy (a relative of the executed man) at Ancestry.com, ref. no. 20040601022606.73149.

1942

James Satterfield (black, age 34). *Murder.* The crime was committed on 12/25/1940 in Jefferson County. Fatal stabbing of 23-year-old John Wesley Hall, Jr. (black). Motive: fracas in a dance hall. This Christmas Day killer paid the forfeit of his life in the Kentucky electric chair on February 20, 1942. Source: 1940 Jefferson Co. death cert. no. 28827 and 1942 Lyon Co. death cert. no. 4389. Appeal: 157 SW (2nd) 89–92.

Eugene Burnam (black, age 15). *Rape.* The crime was committed on

4/6/1939 in Fayette County. Incipient serial rapist. Specifically executed for an indecent assault on the person of 22-year-old Hazel Perkins (white). He had also attacked two other young women that week. On March 27, 1942, the Kentucky electric chair ensured that Burnam would never do so again. Source: *Lexington (KY) Herald*, 4/7/39 (1:1), 4/8/39 (3:7) & 3/27/42 (1:2). Appeals: 141 SW (2nd) 282–284 and 158 SW (2nd) 131–134. See also: 1942 Lyon Co. death cert. no. 7269.

Robert Williams (black, age 22). *Rape.* The crime was committed on 4/16/1941 in Fayette County. Indecent assault on the person of 23-year-old Virgie Wigginton (white) amid circumstances of such a depraved nature that they cost the perpetrator his life. Williams died in the Kentucky electric chair on June 5, 1942. Source: *Lexington (KY) Herald-Leader*, 4/17/41 (12:5). Appeal: 160 SW (2nd) 585–587. See also: 1942 Lyon Co. death cert. no. 14290.

James Lee Robertson (black, age 25). *Murder.* The crime was committed on 5/15/1942 in Perry County. Executed for the killing of 27-year-old Bertha Lehman (white), she having been strangled and her head smashed in with a rock. Motive: sexual assault. Venue changed from Perry County to Fayette County. Robertson was executed on August 7, 1942. Source: *Kingsport (TN) Times*, 5/17/42 (1:4) & 8/7/42 (1:6). See also: 1942 Perry Co. death cert. no. 12356 and 1942 Lyon Co. death cert. no. 18797.

Jess Sanders (black, age 56). *Murder.* The crime was committed on 4/13/1941 in Jefferson County. Uxoricide. Handgun slaying of 44-year-old Katriona Motley Sanders (black), she having been shot eight times. Motive: acrimonious divorce. This wife-killer was executed on August 28, 1942. Source: 1941 Jefferson Co. death cert. no. 10221 and 1942 Lyon Co. death cert. no. 18795. Appeal: 163 SW (2nd) 493–496.

Otis Peter Smith (black, age 28). *Murder.* The crime was committed on 11/23/1940 in Jefferson County. Handgun slaying of 54-year-old Edward B. Hite (white). Motive: armed robbery. The sentence of death by electrocution was carried out in the case of *Commonwealth vs. Otis Peter Smith* on August 28, 1942. Source: 1940 Jefferson Co. death cert. no. 28887 and 1942 Lyon Co. death cert. no. 18796. Appeal: 157 SW (2nd) 79–81.

1943

McCoy Combs (white, age 19) and **Burnett Sexton** (white, age 17). *Murder.* Their crime was committed on 8/18/1941 in Perry County. Both executed for the murder of 50-year-old Robert McIntyre (white), the victim having been beaten to death with metal pipes and his body dumped in a culvert. Motive: robbery and carjacking. Clemency being denied in this case due to their callous indifference to human life, these young killers were electrocuted on January 15, 1943. Source: 1941 Perry Co. death cert. no. 23094 and 1943 Lyon Co. death cert. nos. 1968 and 1969. Appeal: 165 SW (2nd) 832–837.

Robert Anderson (white, age 36), **Raymond Baxter** (white, age 27) and **Thomas Penney** (white, age 32). *Murder.* Their crime was committed on 9/28/1941 in Fayette County. Handgun slayings of 52-year-old Elsie

Ego Miley and 27-year-old Marion Ego Miley (whites, a mother and daughter) in the main building of an upscale country club. Motive: burglary. The offending trio suffered death by electrocution for this sensational misdeed on February 26, 1943. Source: 1941 Fayette Co. death cert. nos. 23889 and 21734. Also: 1943 Lyon Co. death cert. nos. 4438, 4435 and 4437. *True* (magazine) 1/42. *Actual Detective*, 12/41. *Master Detective*, 7/54 & 6/60.

Ernest Trent (white, age 24). *Murder.* The crime was committed on 1/14/1942 in Breathitt County. Police killer. Handgun slaying of 35-year-old Hiram Smith (white). Motive: resisting arrest. The electric chair removed Ernest Trent from the ranks of the living on February 26, 1943. Source: 1942 Breathitt Co. death cert. no. 272 and 1943 Lyon Co. death cert. no. 4436. Appeal: 166 SW (2nd) 1002–1005.

William Carson Gray (black, age 17) and **Archie Simpson** (black, age 20). *Murder.* Their crime was committed on 1/31/1942 in Fayette County. Both executed for the needless killing of 66-year-old Byrd Taulbee (white), who had his head caved in with a brick. Motive: mugging. The young ruffians who did this underwent the extreme penalty of the law on June 25, 1943. Source: 1942 Fayette Co. death cert. no. 3195 and 1943 Lyon Co. death cert. nos. 14077 and 14078. Appeal: 170 SW (2nd) 869–873.

1945

Thomas Bass (black, age 26). *Murder.* The crime was committed on 6/17/1942 in Jefferson County. Hammer killing of 60-year-old John Thomas Brown. Motive: possibly deranged. This black-on-black killer went to the chair on March 16, 1945. Source: *Louisville Courier Journal*, 3/16/45 (Sec. 2) (4:5) & 3/17/45 (2:5). See also: 1942 Jefferson Co. death cert. no. 13786 and 1945 Lyon Co. death cert. no. 6400.

Tommie Nelson (white, age 35). *Murder.* The crime was committed on 10/7/1943 in Letcher County. Handgun slaying of 55-year-old Frelin Estepp (white). Motive: drunken quarrel. Venue changed from Letcher County to Pike County. The killer suffered death by electrocution pursuant to court order on March 16, 1945. Source: *Charleston (WV) Daily Mail*, 3/16/45 (9:7). See also: 1943 Letcher Co. death cert. no. 22895 and 1945 Lyon Co. death cert. no. 6399.

Carl Fox (black, age 16). *Rape.* The crime was committed on 8/23/1943 in Campbell County. Indecent assault on the person of 16-year-old Myrtle Barnes (white), she and her male escort having been attacked and beaten by four knife-wielding blacks as they cuddled on a park bench. Carl Fox was one of that foursome. He was executed on April 6, 1945. Source: *Lima (OH) News*, 3/11/44 (3:2). Also: 1945 Lyon Co. death cert. no. 8694. Appeals: 185 SW (2nd) 394–399 and 186 SW (2nd) 628–632. See also: Ed Hambrick (executed 5/25/45).

Ed Hambrick (black, age 25). *Rape.* The crime was committed on 8/23/1943 in Campbell County. Accomplice and full participant in the same gang assault for which Carl Fox was executed the preceding month. Hambrick was another one that didn't get away. He sat in the electric chair on May 25, 1945. Source: 1945 Lyon Co. death cert. no. 10784. See also: Carl Fox (executed 4/6/45).

1946

Anderson Adkins (white, age 33). *Murder*. The crime was committed on 2/11/1945 in Pike County. Handgun slayings of 50-year-old Jettie Johnson, 34-year-old Vernie Bentley Long and 29-year-old Clarence Blackburn (whites). Motive: divorced man gone loco. A fourth victim was left permanently blinded when Adkins shot her four times. He was executed for triple murder on March 15, 1946. Source: *Morning Herald* (Hagerstown, MD), 2/12/45 (3:8). *Daily News* (Middlesboro, KY), 2/14/45 (8:6). Appeal: 191 SW (2nd) 935–941. See also: 1945 Pike Co. death cert. nos. 4477, 4478 and 4480. Also: 1946 Lyon Co. death cert. no. 7145.

Arthur Jones (black, age 15) and **Thomas Earl Warner** (black, age 18). *Murder*. Their crime was committed on 3/20/1944 in Mason County. Both executed for the killing of 80-year-old Samuel Oliver Greenlee (white), who was bludgeoned with an iron bar. Motive: mugging. These teenage offenders having abrogated their right to existence (at least in the eyes of the law), through their own misconduct, they suffered capital punishment on March 22, 1946. Source: 1944 Mason Co. death cert. no. 7854. Also: 1946 Lyon Co. death cert. nos. 7144 and 7147. Appeal: 192 SW (2nd) 96–97.

Edward Calhoun (white, age 21). *Murder*. The crime was committed on 6/10/1945 in Garrard County. Executed for the killing of 43-year-old John Hager (white), the victim having been slashed to death with a barlow knife. Motive: robbery and carjacking. Calhoun paid a heavy price for his misdeeds when he died by high voltage at the hands of the State on May 24, 1946. Source: 1945 Garrard Co. death cert. no. 12201 and 1946 Lyon Co. death cert. no. 11741. Appeal: 193 SW (2nd) 420–422.

1947

Earl Lonnie Tungett (white, age 23). *Murder*. The crime was committed on 12/17/1945 in Lyon County. Executed for the handgun slaying of 61-year-old Luther R. Gumm (white), the deputy warden of the Eddyville Penitentiary. Motive: attempted breakout. Recidivist killer. Tungett was already serving a life sentence for an unrelated murder when he killed Luther Gumm. He was also an escape artist of sorts. On 7/4/1944 he broke out of the LaGrange (KY), Reformatory, where he had been serving a 5-year sentence for robbery. Then as a fugitive from justice on 10/28/1944 he murdered a Louisville nightclub bouncer named John William Westbrook (white, age 33) by shooting him in the forehead with a handgun. Next, on 12/26/1944 this miscreant escaped from the Jefferson County Jail. He was awaiting trial in the Westbrook case at that time. He was caught at Hamilton, OH, on 2/7/1945 and sentenced to life at Eddyville. He subsequently paid the death penalty there on July 11, 1947. Source: *Hamilton (OH) Daily News-Journal*, 2/7/45 (14:1) & 12/18/45 (14:8). Appeal: 198 SW (2nd) 785–789. See also: 1944 Jefferson Co. death cert. no. 22824. Also: 1945 Lyon Co. death cert. no. 26792 and 1947 Lyon Co. death cert. no. 16177.

1948

Luther Williams (black, age 27). *Murder*. The crime was committed on

9/15/1947 in Pulaski County. Executed for the killing of 55-year-old Mary Ada Hughes (white), who was abducted from her home at gunpoint and raped, and then had her head smashed in by the butt of a rifle. Motive: robbery and sexual assault. The killer was executed on February 27, 1948. Source: 1947 Pulaski Co. death cert. no. 23094 and 1948 Lyon Co. death cert. no. 3654. Appeal: 206 SW (2nd) 922–924.

Jasper Nease (white, age 22). *Armed robbery with violence.* The crime was committed on 3/13/1947 in Perry County. Executed for the carjacking (and murder) of 26-year-old Vernon L. Hodge (white), the victim having been garroted with a handkerchief, stripped naked, forcibly lashed to a rock and then dumped into a river, where he drowned. A separate indictment for murder was held in abeyance pending adjudication of the concomitant capital felony. Venue changed from Perry County to Jefferson County. The killer was executed on July 30, 1948. Source: 1947 Perry Co. death cert. no. 7166 and 1948 Lyon Co. death cert. no. 15057. Appeal: 211 SW (2nd) 826–829. *Master Detective,* 3/57. See also: Daniel McPeak (executed 11/5/48) and Herbert H. Workman (executed 3/4/49).

Daniel McPeak (white, age 21). *Armed robbery with violence.* The crime was committed on 3/13/1947 in Perry County. Accomplice in the carjacking and murder of 26-year-old Vernon L. Hodge (white). Venue changed from Perry County to Jefferson County. McPeak was executed on November 5, 1948. Source: 1948 Lyon Co. death cert. no. 23582. See also: Jasper Nease (executed 7/30/48) and Herbert H. Workman (executed (3/4/49).

1949

Charlie Pool (black, age 41). *Murder.* The crime was committed on 4/26/1945 in Christian County. Executed for the killing of 29-year-old Virginia Gray Harris (white), who was beaten to death with a wooden plank in the presence of her two small children, ages 2 and 5. Motive: because she had demurred when he made indecent proposals to her. The electric chair served its purpose in the case of Charlie Pool on January 28, 1949. Source: 1945 Christian Co. death cert. no. 7350 and 1949 Lyon Co. death cert. no. 1333. Appeals: 192 SW (2nd) 490–492 and 213 SW (2nd) 603–607. *Official Detective,* 6/48.

Herbert H. Workman (white, age 17). *Armed robbery with violence.* The crime was committed on 3/13/1947 in Perry County. Another accomplice in the carjack murder of 26-year-old Vernon L. Hodge (white). Venue changed from Perry County to Jefferson County. This one was executed on March 4, 1949, despite his comparative youth. He was held to be equally guilty under the law of accomplices because no effort had been made by him to dissuade his more bloodthirsty partners. Source: 1949 Lyon Co. death cert. no. 5773. See also: Jasper Nease (executed 7/30/48) and Daniel McPeak (executed 3/4/49).

Lawrence Benjamin Lightfoot (white, age 26). *Murder.* The crime was committed on 5/12/1947 in Campbell County. Executed for the killing of 84-year-old William Harvey Childers (white), the octogenarian victim having had a bottle smashed over his head before being mercilessly beaten and battered with a wrought iron poker. Motive: burglary. The needless brutality of this crime sealed the fate of its perpetrator. He was executed on June 24, 1949. Source: 1947 Campbell Co. death cert. no. 10417 and 1949 Lyon Co. death cert. no. 12495. Appeal: 219 SW (2nd) 984–990.

1950

Raymond Ellison (white, age 37). *Murder.* The crime was committed on 3/26/1948 in Muhlenburg County. Child killer and uxoricide. Executed for the killing of 12-year-old Imogene Sims Ellison (white), she having been strangled by means of a rag tightly knotted around her throat; her head was knocked in and her body dumped in a river, where it was found ten days later. Motive: because the perp resented his forced marriage to this minor, whom he had previously defiled. The Kentucky electric chair functioned flawlessly in this case on February 24, 1950. Source: 1948 Muhlenburg Co. death cert. no. 8670 and 1950 Lyon Co. death cert. no. 3323. Appeal: 225 SW (2nd) 470–475.

Columbus Webb (white, age 41). *Murder.* The crime was committed on 9/29/1948 in Martin County. Handgun slaying of 36-year-old Elijah Davis (white), the victim having been shot three times and having had his head stove in with a piece of timber. Motive: robbery. The killer was pronounced dead from a lethal dose of electricity on June 16, 1950. Source: 1948 Martin Co. death cert. no. 19285 and 1950 Lyon Co. death cert. no. 12726. Appeal: 229 SW (2nd) 455–458.

1951

Albert Shelkels (black, age 18). *Armed robbery with violence.* The crime was committed on 12/23/1948 in Jefferson County. Executed for the robbery (and murder) of 29-year-old Milton Zimmerman (white), the victim having been blasted by a shotgun; his cash drawer was plundered, his merchandise (consisting of several bottles of whiskey) was stolen, and his wallet and wedding ring were snatched from his dead body. A separate indictment for murder was held in abeyance pending the outcome of prosecution for the concomitant felony. Albert Shelkels was ordered for execution. The sentence was carried out on June 8, 1951. Source: 1948 Jefferson Co. death cert. no. 25742 and 1951 Lyon Co. death cert. no. 12589. Appeal: 229 SW (2nd) 465–470.

1952

James I. Robinson (white, age 31). *Murder.* The crime was committed on 7/8/1950 in Jefferson County. Child killer. Strangulation of 3-year-old Joyce Joan Shouse (white). Motive: necrophilia. A rare breed by any description, this convict was executed on January 18, 1952. Source: 1950 Jefferson Co. death cert. no. 14268 and 1952 Lyon Co. death cert. no. 1274. Appeal: 243 SW (2nd) 673–675. *Official Detective,* 4/51.

Earl David Bircham (white, age 46). *Murder.* The crime was committed on 8/14/1949 in Jefferson County. Police killer. Handgun slaying of 30-year-old John Harold Tennyson (white). Motive: resisting arrest. The penalty was death by electrocution on February 1, 1952. Source: 1949 Jefferson Co. death cert. no. 16454 and 1952 Lyon Co. death cert. no. 3348. Appeals: 238 SW (2nd) 1008–1016 and 245 SW (2nd) 932–934. *Crime Detective,* 3/50.

Jessie Lee Quarles (black, age 27). *Murder.* The crime was committed on 6/22/1950 in Christian County. Handgun slaying of 34-year-old James Everett Grady (white), a cabbie. Motive: robbery. Score another one for the Kentucky electric chair on April 1, 1952. Source: 1950 Christian Co. death cert. no. 11530 and 1952 Lyon Co. death cert. no. 8097. Appeal: 245 SW (2nd) 947–949.

1953

Roosevelt Spears (black, age 44). *Murder.* The crime was committed on 1/24/1949 in Campbell County. Handgun slaying of 27-year-old Charles Edward Thompson (black), who was shot three times. Motive: rivalry for a female. This otherwise unremarkable killer—whose motive was as old as mankind itself—was executed on February 27, 1953. Source: 1949 Campbell Co. death cert. no. 191 and 1953 Lyon Co. death cert. no. 3673. Appeal: 253 SW (2nd) 566–574.

1954

William Thomas Reed (black, age 36). *Murder.* The crime was committed on or about 12/27/1943 in Jefferson County. Executed for the killing of 30-year-old Louise Young (black), whom he had beaten to death with a chair and secretly buried. Her skeletal remains were found on 7/21/1948. Motive: obsessive male jealousy. Reed was also determined to have murdered a second woman named Lena Lewis (black, age 32), who had disappeared in April 1944 and whose bones were found along with those of Louise Young. She had been battered to death with an iron poker. William Thomas Reed had no further opportunities to murder women after he sat in the electric chair on June 4, 1954. Source: *Hamilton (OH) Daily Journal*, 6/4/54 (1:7). Appeals: 226 SW (2nd) 513–515 and 261 SW (2nd) 9–11. See also: 1948 Jefferson Co. death cert. nos. 27833 and 27834. See also: 1930 U.S. Census (Spencer Co., KY), which notes Louise Young.

1955

Roy Tarrence (white, age 46) and **Leonard Tarrence** (white, age 22). *Murder.* Their crime was committed on 2/28/1952 in Jefferson County. Both executed for the killing of 53-year-old Francis J. McCormack (white, a lawyer), who was abducted from his home, severely beaten and thrown into a creek with a large chunk of concrete lashed to him by means of barbed wire. Motive: revenge. The victim had represented the younger Tarrence's wife in a divorce proceeding. According to the Tarrence way of thinking this was something that no man could do and live. The killers met their own fate—albeit legally—on March 18, 1955. Source: *Dixon (IL) Evening Telegraph*, 3/7/52 (3:4). *Kingsport (TN) Times*, 3/18/55 (3:3). *Official Detective*, 3/73 & 2/84. *Front Page Detective*, 6/52. *Master Detective*, 8/63. *Crime Detective*, 7/52.

Ed Milam (black, age 26). *Murder.* The crime was committed on 7/15/1954 in Christian County. Handgun slaying of 61-year-old Stephen Farmer (white), a liquor store clerk. Motive: armed robbery. The killer was executed on September 16, 1955. Source: *Lexington (KY) Herald*, 9/17/55 (16:5). *Kingsport (TN) Times-News*, 7/18/54 (2:6). Appeal: 275 SW (2nd) 921-924.

Chester Merrifield (white, age 34). *Murder.* The crime was committed on 11/8/1952 in Jefferson County. Police killer. Handgun slaying of 34-year-old Alvin L. Keown (white). Motive: resisting arrest. Merrifield—a convicted armed robber—had been paroled from a life sentence in February 1952. He then went on to head up a gang specializing in the armed stickup of highbrow social gatherings. Merrifield and his merry men made themselves particularly notorious at Indianapolis IN and Nashville, TN. They overplayed their hands when they added Louisville, KY to their itinerary. Chester Merrifield paid the death penalty on December 23, 1955. Source: *Kingsport (TN) Times*, 11/16/52 (7:3) & 12/23/55 (2:1). See also: 1952 Jefferson Co. death cert. no. 23517.

David Nichols (black, age 53). *Murder.* The crime was committed on 5/21/1954 in Jefferson County. Fatal stabbing of 38-year-old Mary Georgia Roberts (black). Motive: wrathful ex-lover. This one died in the Kentucky electric chair on December 23, 1955. Source: *Kingsport (TN) Times*, 12/23/55 (2:1). Appeal: 283 SW (2nd) 184–187.

1956

James Franklin Bowman (black, age 45). *Murder.* The crime was committed on 8/29/1954 in Jefferson County. Executed for the gory killing of 72-year-old Roberta Busby (white), who was stabbed multiple times in the throat with a pair of scissors. Motive: sexual assault. The culprit paid with his life for this atrocity on November 30, 1956. Source: *Lima (OH) News*, 11/30/56 (31:3). Appeal: 290 SW (2nd) 814–820. See also: 1930 U.S. Census (Louisville, KY), which notes the murdered woman.

Charles DeBerry (black, age 19). *Murder.* The crime was committed on 1/2/1955 in Jefferson County. Handgun slaying of 54-year-old Richard V. Eddins (white). Motive: burglary. The young killer had his own life jolted out of him by a lethal dose of electricity on November 30, 1956. Source: *Lima (OH) News*, 11/30/56 (31:3). See also: 1955 Jefferson Co. death cert. no. 1022 and 1956 Lyon Co. death cert. no. 26148.

Robert Lee Sheckles (black, age 20). *Rape.* The crime was committed on 12/16/1954 in Jefferson County. Indecent assault on the person of a 28-year-old white female (name withheld), she having been carjacked by three thugs and driven to a park where they all took turns forcing themselves on her. Sheckles was the one who didn't get away. He was executed on November 30, 1956. Source: *Louisville Courier Journal*, 12/17/54 (18:3), 12/18/54 (13:3) & 11/30/56 (1:4). See also: 1956 Lyon Co. death cert. no. 26150.

1962

James Kelly Moss (white, age 43). *Murder.* The crime was committed on 11/6/1957 in Henderson County. Executed for the killing of 74-year-old Charles Abbitt (white, his stepfather), whom he had battered to death with a chromium pipe. Motive: family tension. Moss had been released from the Eddyville Penitentiary six weeks earlier, having served time there for a fourth felony conviction. He then added murder to his list of shameful acts. Back to Eddyville he went with a death sentence this time. That sentence was carried out on March 2, 1962. Source: *Middlesboro (KY) Daily News*, 3/2/62 (2:4). Appeal: 332 SW (2nd) 650–653.

Missouri

1866

Green Willis (black, age abt. 35). *Murder.* The crime was committed on 11/9/1865 in Buchanan County. Executed for the ax murder of Jacob Kuhn (white, age not recorded). Motive: highway robbery. Confirmed to have also murdered John L. Lahr (white, age 40) in a separate Buchanan County incident, the man having been struck down from behind with a stone and left unconscious to drown in a puddle. His frozen corpse was found on 12/20/1865. Motive: mugging. The culprit in both cases was hanged at St. Joseph MO on March 1, 1866. Source: *Iowa State Weekly Register*, 1/10/66 (1:9). *Morning Herald* (St. Joseph, MO), 3/2/66 (2:2). *Cedar Falls (IA) Gazette*, 3/16/66 (1:3). See also: 1860 U.S. Census (K.C., MO), which notes Mr. Lahr.

Ezekiel Hart (white, age 20). *Murder.* The crime was committed on or about 2/1/1865 in Morgan County. Gunshot slaying of Ross Saltimer (white, age not recorded). Motive: home invasion. This killer was hanged at Versailles MO on October 19, 1866. Source: *Daily Missouri Democrat* (St. Louis), 10/23/66 (1:2). *Jefferson City (MO) State Times*, 10/26/66 (3:3) & 10/31/66 (2:7). *Cleveland (OH) Plain Dealer*, 10/4/66 (1:4), reports the trial of Ezekiel's brother (Thomas M. Hart) for a separate offense in Miller County.

1867

Thomas Blue, alias "Tom Dooley" (black, age abt. 20). *Murder.* The crime was committed on 12/26/1866 in Monroe County. Executed for the gunshot slayings of 59-year-old William Madison Vandeventer and 46-year-old Sarah Cowherd Vandeventer (whites, a married couple), the latter of whom succumbed to her wounds on 5/6/1867. Motive: home invasion. The killer was hanged at Paris MO on June 21, 1867. Source: *Jefferson City (MO) State Times*, 7/5/67 (1:7). *Columbia (MO) Statesman*, 1/18/67 (2:1) & 5/10/67 (2:2). *Jefferson City (MO) People's Tribune*, 1/2/67 (3:1). See also: 1860 U.S. Census (Monroe Co., MO), which notes Mr. & Mrs. Vandeventer.

Peter Chrisman (white, age abt. 19). *Murder.* The crime was committed on 6/7/1867 in St. Louis County. Child killer, etc. Executed for the ax murders of 30-year-old Edward Ross and 4-year-old Moses Ross (whites), a father and son. Motive: uncertain. Chrisman was a vagabond youth described as a "half idiot" in the vernacular of that time. He did steal clothing from the homicide victims. He also fled with their horse and wagon. A sentence of death by hanging was pronounced in this case irrespective of the killer's mental aptitude. Chrisman met that fate at St. Louis on December 6, 1867.

Source: *Daily Missouri Democrat* (St. Louis), 12/6/67 (4:4) & 12/7/67 (4:3). See also: *St. Louis Municipal Registry of Deaths* for the week ending 6/14/67, lines 6–7.

1868

Alfred Hughes (black, age not recorded). *Murder.* The crime was committed on 11/12/1867 in Platte County. Gunshot slaying of about 25-year-old Daniel W. Jenkins (white). Motive: disgruntled employee. Venue changed from Platte County to Clinton County. Hughes was hanged at Plattsburg MO on July 24, 1868. Source: *Liberty (MO) Tribune*, 11/15/67 (2:3). *Daily Missouri Democrat* (St. Louis), 11/19/67 (1:2) & 8/5/68 (2:3). *Philadelphia Inquirer*, 8/4/68 (8:3), reprinted from the 7/30/68 issue of the *St. Joseph (MO) Gazette*, which is lost.

1869

William Edwards (black, age 23). *Murder.* The crime was committed on 12/4/1868 in St. Louis County. Fatal stabbing of 26-year-old Louis Wilson (black). Motive: fracas in a dance hall. Edwards ended up as dead as the man he killed when he was hanged for his crime at St. Louis on July 23, 1869. Source: *Missouri Republican* (St. Louis), 7/24/69 (2:4). *New York Herald*, 7/24/69 (7:2) & 7/26/69 (3:5). See also: *St. Louis Municipal Report of Interments*, 1868, p. 192, line 10, which says that Wilson was a white man, contrary to newspaper reports. Wilson was probably a black man albeit light toned. The dance halls were racially segregated in those days.

1870

John H. Skaggs (white, age 33). *Murder.* The crime was committed on 1/5/1870 in Dunklin County. Shotgun slaying of 49-year-old Robert Vinkler Richardson (white). Motive: business deal gone sour. Note that the homicide victim in this case had been nominated to the rank of brigadier general in the Confederate Army. Venue changed from Dunklin County to Stoddard County. The killer was hanged at Bloomfield, MO on August 6, 1870. Source: *New York Herald*, 9/1/70 (5:3). *Janesville (WI) Gazette*, 9/2/70 (1:5). See also: *Generals in Gray: Lives of the Confederate Commanders*, by Ezra J. Warner (Baton Rouge, LA: Louisiana State University Press, 1959), 256. See also: 1870 U.S. Census (Cape Girardeau Co., MO), which notes "Scaggs."

John Newton Grable (white, age 32). *Murder.* The crime was committed on 1/2/1870 in Buchanan County. Executed for the killing of 36-year-old Joel Drake (white, his brother-in-law) who was battered to death with a wooden animal yoke. Motive: drunken argument. Drake was a wastrel who had come into a significant amount of money. It rankled Grable to learn that the other man was squandering those funds in a brothel instead of using them to support his wife and children. Drake's conduct may have been shameful but it did not give Grable a right to kill him—at least not in the eyes of the law. Grable learned this the hard way when he walked up the 13 steps of the gallows at St. Joseph MO on September 9, 1870. Source: *New York Herald*, 9/13/70 (5:2). *Weekly Herald* (St. Joseph, MO), 1/13/70 (2:4) & 9/9/70 (4:3). See also: *History of Gentry and Worth Counties, Missouri* (St.

Joseph, MO: National Historical Co., 1882), at chapter "Crimes & Incidents." Also see: *Gentry County Civil War Draft Registrations*, 1863–1865, which notes Drake.

Jeremiah Bailey (white, age 20). *Murder.* The crime was committed on 3/25/1868 in New Madrid County. Handgun slaying of 24-year-old James Brock (white), who was shot three times. Motive: drunken brawl. Bailey was hanged for this at New Madrid on December 13, 1870. Source: *New York Times*, 12/19/70 (2:6), reprinted from the 12/15/70 issue of the *Daily Missouri Democrat* (St. Louis, MO), which is lost.

1871

John Armstrong (black, age 35) and **Charles Jolly** (black, age 35). *Murder.* Their crime was committed on 11/19/1870 in Washington County. Mass killers and baby killers. Both executed for the slaughter of 50-year-old David Lepine (white, a Quebecois by birth), who was shot four times with a handgun (before being literally hacked to pieces with an ax), plus that man's two female housemates and their respective offspring who were apparently of some unknown racial mix. The adult females were sisters named Louisa and Mary Christopher (ages not specified), alleged prostitutes. Both had their heads chopped off. The latter was also shot. Their presumably illegitimate children (whose paternities were known only to God) were a boy aged 18 months and a girl aged about one year, names not recorded. The male tot was swung about by its ankles with force enough to dash its brains out against a wall. The female baby was literally broiled in the cabin's hearth before also having its brains beaten out by the repeated pounding of its little head against the stone sill of the fireplace. Motive: attempted sexual assault of the two murdered women. The killers were hanged at Potosi on January 27, 1871. Source: *Weekly Public Ledger* (Memphis, TN), 11/29/70 (1:5). *Cincinnati Daily Gazette*, 11/29/70 (1:4). *Dubuque (IA) Herald*, 11/22/70 (1:4). *New York Herald*, 1/28/71 (9:5). See also: 1850 U.S. Census (Washington Co., MO), which notes Jolly, and 1860 U.S. Census (Washington Co., MO), which notes Armstrong and David "Lapeen."

1872

Charles Waller (white, age 42). *Murder.* The crime was committed on or about 9-1-1867 in Webster County. Triple killer and baby killer. Executed for the murders of William and Hannah Nowlan (whites, a married couple, ages not recorded) and their 18-month-old baby, whose name and gender are not specified in surviving accounts. The decomposed body of the woman was found by hunters lying in the woods with its throat cut on or about 12/1/1867. The remains of William Nowlan were found on 4/13/1869. His skeleton had been decapitated and bore evidence of gunshot wounds. The murdered baby was never found, it having been buried somewhere nearby. Motive: robbery and despoilment. The Nowlans had been headed westward in a covered wagon, intent on starting life anew. They had originally come from Indiana. The killer somehow learned that Mr. Nowlan had $1,000 (presumably in gold), with which he meant to buy land. Waller treacherously hired himself to Nowlan as a guide and later lured him into a forest on the pretense of hunting deer. It was there where he shot the man dead. Then on the following day he went to where the wife and baby were encamped, murdered them, and stole the aforesaid money. Eventually tracked down, this miscreant was legally hanged at Marshfield MO on May 17, 1872. Source: *History of Webster County, 1855–1955*, by Floy Watters George (pp. 18–22), has what appears to be the most accurate account of this case. The original court papers are long lost. *Chicago Tribune*, 5/21/72 (6:8). See also: 1860 U.S. Census (Bartholomew Co., IN), which notes Waller.

1873

Robert Champion (black, age 42). *Murder.* The crime was committed on 7/21/1872 in Howard County. Uxoricide. Executed for the killing of 47-year-old Rachel Champion (black), she having first been shot with a handgun and then beheaded by means of a large knife. Her remains were found in a pig pen partially devoured by swine. Motive: acrimonious divorce. Robert Champion found himself at the end of a rope for this (legally) at Fayette MO on February 21, 1873. Source: *Sedalia (MO) Daily Democrat*, 2/22/73 (1:2). *The World* (New York), 2/25/73 (2:4). See also: 1870 U.S. Census (Howard Co., MO), which notes both parties.

1874

Samuel Walker (black, age not recorded). *Murder.* The crime was committed on 10/14/1873 in Clay County. Uxoricide. Shotgun (?) slaying of Katie Walker (black, age not recorded). Motive: suspected infidelity. This wife killer was hanged at Liberty MO on May 15, 1874. Source: *Liberty (MO) Tribune*, 5/22/74 (2:2).

John T. Carlisle (white, age 20). *Murder.* The crime was committed on 7/10/1872 in Saline County. Executed for the killing of George Wecker (white, age not recorded), who was slashed to death with a large-bladed knife. Motive: personal grudge and robbery. Carlisle was hanged for this at Marshall MO on July 24, 1874. Source: *Daily Democrat* (Sedalia, MO), 7/15/72 (4:4). *St. Louis Post-Dispatch*, 7/24/74 (1:1). *The World* (New York), 7/25/74 (5:2).

Joseph P. Hamilton (white, age 17). *Murder.* The crime was committed on 7/14/1871 in Mercer County. Handgun slaying of 48-year-old Elisha W. Halleck (white). Motive: adultery with the dead man's wife. Venue changed from Mercer County to Harrison County. This smitten youth (who was reportedly lured to his doom by a female catalyst) paid a terrible price for his mistake when he was hanged at Bethany MO on October 30, 1874. Source: *St. Louis Dispatch*, 11/3/74 (1:3). *Boonville (MO) Weekly Eagle*, 11/6/74 (2:4). *St. Louis Daily Globe*, 11/9/74 (1:1). *Leavenworth (KS) Weekly Times*, 11/19/74 (1:4). See also: 1870 U.S. Census (Mercer Co., MO), which notes Mr. Halleck.

1875

Patrick J. O'Shea (white, age 35). *Murder.* The crime was committed on 3/18/1874 in St. Louis County. Uxoricide. Hanged for the fatal stabbing of 34-year-old Eliza Walsh O'Shea (white). Motive: boorish drunkard. The sentence was carried out at St.

Louis on April 9, 1875. Source: *St. Louis Dispatch*, 4/9/75 (1:1). *New York Herald*, 4/10/75 (3:2).

Travis Harris (white, age 39). *Murder.* The crime was committed on 11/3/1874 in Scott County. Handgun (derringer) slaying of 56-year-old Squire Masterson (white), his father-in-law. Motive: brawling and a smoldering grudge over the fact that the murdered man had opposed the killer's marriage. Travis had also killed another white man called "Buck McLeod" right in front of the Scott County courthouse. This was in the autumn of 1865 and stemmed from animosity during wartime. Harris seems to have escaped prosecution for that homicide even though McLeod was shot in the back. The gallows eventually claimed him at Benton MO on April 16, 1875. Source: *St. Louis Dispatch*, 4/16/75 (1:1). See also: 1870 U.S. Census (Scott Co., MO), which notes both parties.

Henry Brown (black, age 25). *Murder.* The crime was committed on 5/25/1875 in St. Louis County. Executed for the killing of 54-year-old Philip Pfarr (white), he having been clubbed to death; his wife was raped and his cabin ransacked. The hangman sent Henry Brown out of this world at St. Louis on October 22, 1875. Source: *Galveston (TX) News*, 6/2/75 (2:2). *St. Louis Dispatch*, 10/22/75 (1:1).

Henry Hallenschied (white, age 54). *Murder.* The crime was committed on 6/16/1875 in Gasconade County. Executed for the killing of 28-year-old Christian Albrand (white, his son-in-law), who was battered to death with a club. His body was rolled into a gully, where it was left to be devoured by dogs. Motive: family flare-up. The end came on December 17, 1875, when Hallenschied was hanged at Hermann, MO. Source: *Hermann (MO) Advertiser*, 12/17/75 (5:1). *St. Louis Dispatch*, 12/17/75 (1:6). *New York Herald*, 12/18/75 (6:4).

1876

Antonio Catalano (white, age abt. 40), **Dominic Damina** (white, age abt. 28) and **Bastiano Lombardo** (white, age abt. 21). *Murder.* Their crime was committed on 3/13/1875 in St. Louis County. All three executed for the handgun slaying of 25-year-old Francisco Palermo (white). Motive: feud among Sicilian immigrants. A triple hanging wrapped up this matter at St. Louis on February 18, 1876. Source: *Missouri Republican* (St. Louis) 2/19/76 (3:1). *New York Herald*, 2/19/76 (3:6). See also: *City of St. Louis Registry of Deaths*, 1876, 67–68.

William Foster (white, age 25). *Murder.* The crime was committed on 8/28/1875 in Warren County. Shotgun slaying of a wayfaring black man whose name and age were never ascertained. Motive: highway robbery. Foster met his court-ordered end at Warrenton, MO on June 19, 1876. Source: *Chicago Tribune*, 6/20/76 (5:6). *St. Louis Globe-Democrat*, 6/20/76 (1:3).

1877

Daniel Price (black, age 33). *Murder.* The crime was committed on 7/20/1876 in Warren County. Hanged for the murder of Samuel Taylor (black, age not recorded), who was battered about the head with the butt of a musket and slashed repeatedly with a dirk; his body was dumped in a river.

Motive: adultery with the victim's wife. Price paid the price at Warrenton, MO on January 18, 1877. Source: *St. Louis Dispatch*, 1/18/77 (4:4). *New York Herald*, 1/19/77 (8:1). *Daily Gazette & Bulletin* (Williamsport, PA), 1/20/77 (1:3).

William Pintz (white, age 30). *Murder.* The crime was committed on 11/15/1875 in Bollinger County. Child killer. Hanged for the ax murder of 9-year-old Catherine Burr (white). Motive: sexual assault. A gallows became the last earthly stage for this character at Marble Hill, MO on April 27, 1877. Source: *New York Herald*, 4/29/77 (7:3). See also: Harriet C. Frazier, *Death Sentences in Missouri, 1803–2005* (Jefferson, NC: McFarland, 2006), 62.

Samuel Orr (white, age 20). *Murder.* The crime was committed on 12/11/1873 in Christian County. Handgun slaying of 55-year-old George Davis (white). Motive: alleged murder-for-hire. Venue changed from Christian County to Lawrence County. The killer was hanged at Mt. Vernon, MO on May 18, 1877. Source: *St. Louis Dispatch*, 5/18/77 (1:3). *New York Herald*, 5/19/77 (5:6). Appeal: 64 MO 339–345. See also: 1870 U.S. Census (Christian Co., MO), which notes George Davis and 1870 U.S. Census (Greene Co., MO), which notes Orr.

Poindexter Edmundson (white, age 24). *Murder.* The crime was committed on 10/2/1876 in Stoddard County. Handgun slaying of 39-year-old William Shaw (white). Motive: tenant-landlord dispute. The killer was hanged at Bloomfield, MO on July 13, 1877. Source: *New York Herald*, 7/14/77 (3:5). Appeal: 64 MO 398–401. See also: 1870 U.S. Census (Stoddard Co., MO), which notes Mr. Shaw, and 1860 U.S. Census (Stoddard Co., MO), which notes Edmundson as a minor.

1878

William Wieners (white, age 21). *Murder.* The crime was committed on 1/29/1877 in St. Louis County. Handgun slaying of 27-year-old Americus Vespucius Lawrence (white). Motive: because the decedent had taunted him after he (Wieners) had been duped into marrying a worn-out prostitute. A public-laughing-stock-turned-killer, William Wieners was hanged at St. Louis on February 1, 1878. It was a calamitous fall for a young man just entering adulthood. Source: *St. Louis Dispatch*, 2/1/78 (2:4). *New York Herald*, 2/2/78 (6:1). See also: *City of St. Louis Deaths Registry*, 1877, 275–276.

John Ables (white, age 58). *Murder.* The crime was committed on 4/16/1874 in McDonald County. Handgun slaying of 24-year-old John L. Lane (white), the victim having been lured into a secluded area and shot twice. Motive: because Ables suspected that Lane had meddled with his wife. Venue changed from McDonald County to Jasper County. The killer was hanged at Carthage, MO on February 15, 1878. Source: *St. Louis Dispatch*, 2/15/78 (1:5). *New York Herald*, 2/16/78 (10:1). See also: 1870 U.S. Census (McDonald Co., MO), which notes John Lane.

John William Daniel (white, age 35). *Murder.* The crime was committed on 2/23/1877 in Pettis County. Executed for the killing of about 35-year-old Jesse R. Miller (white), who was struck down from behind with an unknown blunt instrument and stabbed multiple times, and had his throat cut from ear to ear. Motive: robbery and dirty dealing. Venue changed from Pettis County to Johnson County. Daniel was hanged at Warrensburg, MO on March 1, 1878. Source: *Sedalia (MO) Weekly Bazoo*, 3/5/78 (2:4). *St. Louis Dispatch*, 3/1/78 (1:2). *St. Louis Globe-Democrat*, 3/2/78 (1:8).

Edward McFarren, alias "Richard Green" (white, age 27). *Murder.* The crime was committed on 2/10/1877 in Jackson County. Police killer. Handgun slaying of Henry H. Hughes (white, age not recorded). Motive: resisting arrest. The gallows claimed this transgressor at Kansas City on March 1, 1878. Source: *St. Louis Dispatch*, 3/1/78 (1:2). *New York Herald*, 3/2/78 (8:1). *St. Louis Globe-Democrat*, 2/12/77 (1:6) & 3/2/78 (1:5).

Richard T. Isaacs (white, age 36). *Murder.* The crime was committed on 8/28/1878 in Cass County. Handgun slaying of 35-year-old Henderson B. Clark (white), the victim having been shot three times in the back and his head cut off. Motive: bunco and cattle rustling. The killer was legally swung from a gallows beam at Harrisonville, MO on October 25, 1878. Source: *New York Herald*, 10/26/78 (7:5). *Freeborn County (MN) Standard*, 11/14/78 (4:4). See also: 1860 U.S. Census (Van Buren Co., TN), which notes Clark as a teenager.

1879

John Isaac West (white, age 23). *Murder.* The crime was committed on 10/4/1878 in Cooper County. Hanged for the killing of about 28-year-old Frank Shinn (white), whose head was mashed with a rock. Motive: robbery. The killer fled from the scene wearing the dead man's clothes. Both were reportedly vagabonds. West was wearing a noose around his neck in addition to his clothes when he was executed at Boonville, MO on May 16, 1879. Source: *St. Louis Post-Dispatch*, 5/16/79 (1:4). *New York Herald*, 5/17/79 (5:4). Appeal: 69 MO 401–405.

John Blan (white, age 23). *Murder.* The crime was committed on 9/30/1878 in St. Charles County. Handgun slaying of 38-year-old Elijah Warren (white, his brother-in-law), who was murdered in his bed. Motive: hard to discern. Blan had blabbed to a third party about Warren's financial standing, or perhaps lack thereof. Warren resented this. A heated argument had ensued. Blan furtively entered Warren's home with homicidal intent at 3:00 a.m. the following day and presumably settled the matter with a gun. He was hanged at St. Charles, MO on June 6, 1879. Source: *Alton (IL) Daily Telegraph*, 10/1/78 (3:3). *St. Louis Post-Dispatch*, 6/6/79 (1:4).

Monroe Guy (black, age 21). *Murder.* The crime was committed on 12/25/1878 in Jefferson County. Handgun slaying of Aaron McPete (black, age not recorded). Motive: rivalry for a female. This black-on-black Christmas Day killer was hanged for his misdeed at Hillsboro, MO on June 6, 1879. Source: *St. Louis Post-Dispatch*, 6/6/79 (1:6).

Frank Davidson (white, age 23). *Murder.* The crime was committed on 9/21/1878 in Johnson County. Handgun slaying of 24-year-old William Haggerty (white), who was shot three times. Motive: drunken brawl. Davidson had insulted Haggerty's wife. He then opened fire on her husband when he objected. This ill-mannered young man was hanged at Warrensburg, MO on July 9, 1879. Source: *St. Louis Post-Dispatch*, 7/9/79 (1:4). See also: 1870 U.S. Census (Johnson Co., MO), which notes Haggerty.

1880

Charles H. Hardin (white, age 21). *Murder.* The crime was committed on 10/26/1879 in St. Francois County. Executed for the killing of 34-year-old Robert Ferguson (white), who was clubbed from behind as he sat by a camp fire and then rolled into a creek. Motive: robbery and gross perfidy. The hangman performed his office in this case at Farmington, MO on January 23, 1880. Source: *Sedalia (MO) Daily Democrat*, 10/31/79 (1:4). *Iola (KS) Register*, 1/30/80 (6:5). *National Police Gazette*, 2/14/80. See also: 1870 U.S. Census (Cherokee Co., KS), which notes Ferguson, and 1870 U.S. Census (Henry Co., KY), which notes Hardin.

Joseph Core (white, age 34). *Murder.* The crime was committed on 1/21/1879 in Laclede County. Shotgun slaying of 52-year-old George E. King (white), the victim's head having also been mashed by the butt of that weapon. Motive: dispute between neighbors. The killer was hanged at Lebanon, MO on March 5, 1880. Source: *New York Herald*, 3/6/80 (3:6). See also: 1870 U.S. Census (Laclede Co., MO), which notes both parties.

John Kilgore (white, age 22). *Murder.* The crime was committed on 1/27/1879 in Audrain County. Shotgun slaying of 39-year-old Lorenzo Dow Willingham (white). Motive: dispute between neighbors. The killer was hanged at Mexico, MO on March 5, 1880. Source: *St. Louis Post-Dispatch*, 3/5/80 (1:3). Appeal: 70 MO 546–550. See also Willingham's Civil War draft registration record (1863), which notes his age and place of residence.

William Barton (black, age 15). *Murder.* The crime was committed on 2/15/1879 in St. Charles County. Shotgun slaying of 26-year-old James Clatterbuck (white). Motive: disgruntled employee. The killer's youth did not save him. He was hanged at St. Charles, MO on March 26, 1880. Source: *St. Louis Post-Dispatch*, 3/26/80 (1:3). *St. Louis Globe-Democrat*, 3/27/80 (2:3). Appeal: 71 MO 288–293.

Nathan Faucett (black, age 34) and **Jacob Muldrow** (black, age 19). *Murder.* Their crime was committed on 9/30/1879 in Audrain County. Shotgun slaying of 29-year-old Octave Lewis Inlow (white). Motive: conspiracy with a white whore. Both of the killers were hanged for this offense at Mexico, MO on April 16, 1880. Source: *New York Herald*, 4/17/80 (4:5). See also Mr. Inlow's tombstone inscription recorded in *Cemetery Records of Calloway County, Missouri*, vol. 1, compiled by Elizabeth Ellsberry (1965).

Edward Nugent (white, age 42). *Murder.* The crime was committed on 8/20/1876 in St. Louis County. Uxoricide. Handgun slaying of about 40-year-old Ella Nugent (white). Motive: alcoholism and self pity. This wife-killing drunkard was hanged at St. Louis on April 23, 1880. Source: *St. Louis Post-Dispatch*, 4/23/80 (1:7). *New York Herald*, 4/24/80 (4:6).

Henry J. Redemeier (white, age 29). *Murder.* The crime was committed on 6/19/1878 in St. Louis County. Handgun slaying of 55-year-old Franz

Vosz (white). Motive: possibly deranged. The subsequent sentence of death by hanging was carried out in this case at St. Louis on April 23, 1880. Source: *St. Louis Post-Dispatch*, 4/23/80 (1:8). *New York Herald*, 4/24/80 (5:1). See also: *City of St. Louis Register of Deaths*, 1878, 187.

John Cropp (black, age abt. 25). *Murder.* The crime was committed on 12/25/1879 in Chariton County. Shotgun slaying of 24-year-old Noah Forrest (white). Motive: retaliation for racially charged harassment, or so it was alleged. This Christmas Day killer was hanged at Keytesville, MO, on June 11, 1880. Source: *St. Louis Post-Dispatch*, 6/11/80 (1:4). *New York Herald*, 6/12/80 (10:1). See also Forrest's tombstone inscription in Forest Green Cemetery, Chariton Township, MO.

James Hayden Brown (white, age 20). *Murder.* The crime was committed on 7/23/1877 in Randolph County. Shotgun slaying of 58-year-old Martha E. Parish (white), his mother-in-law. Motive: because she had given refuge to his estranged wife. This ireful young husband was hanged at Huntsville, MO on June 25, 1880. Source: *St. Louis Post-Dispatch*, 6/25/80 (1:2). *New York Herald*, 6/26/80 (5:1). See also: 1860 U.S. Census (Randolph Co., MO), which notes Mrs. Parish.

Thomas Benton Hopper (white, age 36). *Murder.* The crime was committed on 8/27/1879 in Cedar County. Handgun slaying of 23-year-old Samuel C. Ham (white). Motive: attempted robbery. Venue changed from Cedar County to Dade County. Hopper was swung from a gallows beam at Greenfield, MO on June 25, 1880. Source: *Burlington (IA) Hawk-Eye*, 9/2/79 (1:1) & 6/27/80 (1:7). Appeal: 71 MO 425–429. See also: 1870 U.S. Census (Fleming Co., KY), which notes Ham, and 1880 U.S. Census (Jasper Co., MO), which notes Hopper.

1881

Frank Brown (white, age not recorded) and **Jesse Meyers** (white, age not recorded). *Murder.* Their crime was committed on 5/9/1881 in New Madrid County. Police killers, etc. Both executed for the shotgun slaying of 24-year-old Robert D. LaFarge (white), a posse man. Motive: resisting arrest. They are confirmed to have also killed (with handguns) Wayne County, MO, sheriff John Thomas Davis (white, age 25) on 5/19/1881 while resisting arrest. Two-time killers Frank Brown and Jesse Meyers were hanged at New Madrid on July 15, 1881. Source: *Fort Wayne (IN) Daily Gazette*, 5/13/81 (1:1). *St. Louis Post-Dispatch*, 7/15/81 (1:3). *Sedalia (MO) Weekly Bazoo*, 7/19/81 (4:3).

John W. Patterson (white, age abt. 19). *Murder.* The crime was committed on 12/1/1868 in Henry County. Hatchet killing of about 50-year-old James G. Clark (white). Motive: highway robbery and mendacity. The culprit was eventually hunted down, there being no statute of limitations for crimes of this nature. He was hanged at Clinton, MO on July 22, 1881. Source: *Warrensburg (MO) Standard*, 12/10/68. *St. Louis Post-Dispatch*, 7/22/81 (1:4). *Sedalia (MO) Weekly Bazoo*, 7/26/81 (3:1).

Charles E. Talbott (white, age 16) and **Albert P. Talbott** (white, age 21). *Murder.* Their crime was committed on 9/18/1880 in Nodaway County.

Patricide. Sniper slaying of 53-year-old Perry H. Talbott (white). Motive: family tension. No mitigating factors being found, these not-so-filial offenders were hanged at Maryville, MO on July 22, 1881. Source: *St. Louis Post-Dispatch*, 7/22/81 (1:1). *Kansas City Times*, 7/23/81 (1:1). *New York Herald*, 7/23/81 (3:5). *Master Detective*, 6/38. See also: 1870 U.S. Census (Nodaway Co., MO), which notes all parties.

William Henry Erb (white, age 47). *Murder*. The crime was committed on 6/19/1879 in St. Louis County. Fatal stabbing of 47-year-old Rose Mion, alias "Rosalie Erb" (white), his common-law wife. Motive: alcoholism and romantic estrangement. This knife-wielder found himself standing on a gallows at St. Louis on December 30, 1881. He did not survive the experience. Source: *St. Louis Post-Dispatch*, 12/30/81 (1:4). *New York Herald*, 12/31/81 (9:4). See also: *City of St. Louis Register of Deaths*, 1879, 637.

1882

Charles Ellis (black, age 22). *Murder*. The crime was committed on 5/9/1880 in St. Louis County. Handgun slaying of 21-year-old Mack Sanders (black). Motive: gambling dispute. The hangman tendered his services to this black-on-black killer at St. Louis on January 6, 1882. Source: *St. Louis Post-Dispatch*, 1/6/82 (1:3). *New York Herald*, 7/16/81 (3:5) & 1/7/82 (3:5). See also: *City of St. Louis Deaths Register*, 1880, 187, and 1882, 449. Note that the 1881 news report of this execution was published prematurely and probably cost its author his job.

Joseph Michael Kotovsky (white, age 21). *Murder*. The crime was committed on 10/10/1878 in St. Louis County. Handgun slaying of 19-year-old Augusta Simon (white). Motive: because she had declined his advances. This young "fool in love" who could not take "no" for an answer was hanged for what he did at St. Louis on January 6, 1882. Source: *St. Louis Post-Dispatch*, 1/6/82 (1:3). See also: *City of St. Louis Deaths Register*, 1878, 420, and 1882, 449.

John A. Phelps (white, age 22). *Murder*. The crime was committed on 4/23/1881 in Saline County. Ax murder of 62-year-old Elijah Keyton (white). Motive: because the homicide victim had denied the killer permission to woo his daughter. This tragedy of young love versus parental authority was brought to a close when Johnny Phelps was cut down from the gallows at Marshall, MO on January 6, 1882. Source: *St. Louis Post-Dispatch*, 1/6/82 (4:4). *New York Herald*, 1/7/82 (3:5). See also: 1870 U.S. Census (Saline Co., MO), which notes Mr. Keyton.

Thaddeus Baber (white, age 29). *Murder*. The crime was committed on 8/14/1879 in St. Louis County. Handgun slayings of 52-year-old Fredericka Schuendler and 23-year-old Lena Schuendler (whites), a mother and daughter. Motive: anger and disgust. Baber had fathered an illegitimate child by the younger woman when she was aged 17. They all lived together for the next six years. Baber earned honest pay as a gas pipe fitter during that time and supported both the baby and its mother through such means. However, after six years of this the child's maternal grandmother (Fredericka Schuendler) induced her daughter (Lena Schuendler) to abandon Baber and work as a courtesan instead, both women living off the proceeds there from instead of what Baber earned through creditable labor. This infuriated Baber beyond the point of endurance and he reacted violently. Public opinion ran heavily in his favor, but the law drew no distinctions. Let the record show that Baber met his fate with a sense of self respect at St. Louis on January 13, 1882. Source: *St. Louis Post-Dispatch*, 1/13/82 (1:2). See also: *City of St. Louis Deaths Register*, 1879, 707, which notes the slain women as "Frederica Scheimler" and "Louisa Scheimler," alias "Lizzie Baber."

William Henry Ward (black, age 25). *Murder.* The crime was committed on 8/31/1879 in St. Louis County. Child killer. Handgun slaying of 15-year-old Annie Lewis (black). Motive: jilted lover. This unwise wooer lost his own life through due process of law at St. Louis on January 13, 1882. Source: *St. Louis Post-Dispatch*, 1/13/82 (1:2). See also: *City of St. Louis Deaths Register*, 1879, 722, and 1882, 458.

George Bohannon (white, age 18). *Murder.* The crime was committed on 8/5/1881 in Phelps County. Handgun slaying of 21-year-old William Light (white). Motive: big attitude. Both parties had argued at a picnic. Bohannon could not bear the affront. He wound up bearing something a whole lot worse when he plunged to his death through the gallows trap at Rolla, MO on April 21, 1882. Source: *St. Louis Post-Dispatch*, 4/21/82 (2:1). See also: 1880 U.S. Census (Phelps Co., MO), which notes the aforesaid persons.

Albert Sanders (black, age not recorded). *Murder.* The crime was committed on 11/19/1881 in Mississippi County. Executed for the killing of 25-year-old Moses Wing (black), who was stabbed four times in the back. Motive: rivalry for a female. The situation went from deadly to deadlier when Albert Sanders was hanged at Charleston, MO on December 8, 1882. Source: *St. Louis Post-Dispatch*, 12/8/82 (2:4). *New York Herald*, 12/9/82 (3:6). See also: 1880 U.S. Census (Mississippi Co., MO), which notes Wing.

1883

Howard Underwood (black, age 48). *Murder.* The crime was committed on 8/6/1881 in Mississippi County. Rifle slaying of 36-year-old Isabelle Lucas (black), she having also had her brains dashed out. Motive: adultery turned lethal. The killer was hanged at Charleston, MO on April 6, 1883. Source: *St. Louis Post-Dispatch*, 4/6/83 (2:6). *New York Herald*, 4/7/83 (3:2). See also: 1880 U.S. Census (Mississippi Co., MO), which notes both parties.

William Fox (white, age 22). *Murder.* The crime was committed on 5/19/1883 in Vernon County. Handgun slaying of 36-year-old William Thomas Howard (white), who was shot four times, initially in the back. Motive: robbery and betrayal. Fox realized that this was the worst mistake that he had ever or would ever make when the law wrung his neck at Nevada, MO on December 28, 1883. Source: *St. Louis Post-Dispatch*, 12/28/83 (1:3). *New York Herald*, 12/29/83 (3:3).

1884

Matthew Lewis (black, age 31). *Murder.* The crime was committed on 10/13/1876 in St. Louis County. Uxoricide. Executed for the killing of 22-year-old Mary Ann Lewis (black), who was stabbed multiple times. Motive:

infidelity on her part. It was no excuse for murder. Lewis paid the penalty with a noose around his neck at St. Louis on March 14, 1884. Source: *St. Louis Post-Dispatch*, 3/14/84 (1:6). See also: *City of St. Louis Deaths Register*, 1876, 223, and 1884, 466.

Thomas Dickson (white, age not recorded). *Murder.* The crime was committed on 3/10/1880 in Stoddard County. Executed for the deliberate murder of James McNabb (white, age not recorded) by undetermined means, the victim's skeletal remains having been found hidden beneath a log pile one year after his disappearance. Motive: business partnership gone bad, plus robbery and despoilment. The killer was hanged at Bloomfield, MO on May 2, 1884. Source: *St. Louis Post-Dispatch*, 5/2/84 (2:5).

Charles Malskey, alias "Charlie Hamilton" (white, age 20) and **Edward Altman**, alias "Billy Hamilton" (white, age 26). *Murder.* Their crime was committed on 3/30/1884 in Johnson County. Both executed for the murder of 25-year-old Carl Steidle (white), who was bludgeoned with a railroad lug wrench; his body was placed on tracks where it was mangled by a passing train. Motive: robbery and dirty dealing. The killers were hanged side by side at Warrensburg, MO on July 11, 1884. Source: *St. Louis Post-Dispatch*, 7/11/84 (2:1).

Oliver Bateman (white, age 19). *Murder.* The crime was committed on 8/31/1884 in Andrew County. Child killer. Hanged for the mutilation killings of 9-year-old Austie McLaughlin and 7-year-old Adella McLaughlin (whites), sisters. Motive: sexual assault. Further description of the crime scene is too abhorrent for publication—even at this distance in time. The teenage perpetrator was executed at Savannah, MO on November 21, 1884. Source: *Galveston (TX) Daily News*, 9/7/84 (4:2). *St. Louis Post-Dispatch*, 11/21/84 (2:6). See also: 1880 U.S. Census (Andrew Co., MO), which notes all parties.

1885

Samuel W. Collins (white, age 23). *Murder.* The crime was committed on 9/24/1883 in Pike County. Rifle slaying of 39-year-old Owen Utterback (white). Motive: because the killer thought that the victim had slandered his wife. This self-righteous young husband was hanged for capital felony at Bowling Green, MO on August 28, 1885. Source: *St. Louis Post-Dispatch*, 8/28/85 (2:2). See also: 1880 U.S. Census (Pike Co., MO), which notes Utterback, and 1880 U.S. Census (Montgomery Co., MO), which notes Collins.

1886

Henry S. Stair (white, age abt. 35). *Murder.* The crime was committed on 8/6/1885 in Vernon County. Executed for the ax murders of about 55-year-old Jacob Sewell and 16-year-old Mack Sewell (whites), a father and son. Motive: robbery. Absolutely nothing could be found in this man's favor. He was hanged at Nevada, MO on January 15, 1886. Source: *Daily Herald-Tribune* (Lawrence KS), 8/8/85 (1:1). *Kansas City Star*, 1/16/86 (1:1). *St. Louis Post-Dispatch*, 1/15/86 (7:4).

Charles Wilson (black, age 21). *Murder.* The crime was committed on 7/31/1882 in St. Louis County. Executed for the killing of 24-year-old Willie A. David (white), who was purposefully hit on the head with a rock. Motive: disgruntled employee. Death by hanging was the court-mandated fate of this transgressor at St. Louis on January 15, 1886. Source: *St. Louis Post-Dispatch*, 1/15/86 (7:2). *Reno (NV) Evening Gazette*, 1/15/86 (4:4). See also: *City of St. Louis Deaths Register*, 1882, 77, and 1886, 340.

Jeff Wilson (black, age 26). *Murder.* The crime was committed on 7/31/1884 in Lafayette County. Handgun slaying of about 27-year-old Jennie Sanford (black), she having been shot three times. Motive: because she had had sex with white men. This self-appointed guardian of African American womanhood atoned with his life for that self-imagined cause when he was hanged for the crime of black-on-black murder at Lexington, MO on April 2, 1886. Source: *St. Louis Post-Dispatch*, 4/2/86 (5:3). See also: 1880 U.S. Census (Lafayette Co., MO), which notes Wilson.

Joseph Jump (white, age 19). *Murder.* The crime was committed on 12/29/1885 in Daviess County. Executed for the killing of 40-year-old William C. Gladson (white), who was bludgeoned with an iron bar and had his body dumped down a well. Motive: robbery. The penalty for this was death by hanging. Joseph Jump made full payment on those terms at Gallatin, MO on July 23, 1886. Source: *St. Louis Post-Dispatch*, 7/23/86 (1:6). *Daily Journal* (Freeport, IL), 7/24/86 (1:5). *Galveston (TX) Daily News*, 7/25/86 (5:3). See also: 1880 U.S. Census (Monroe Co., IA), which notes Gladson, and 1880 U.S. Census (Daviess Co., MO), which notes Jump. See also: John T. Smith (executed 8/6/86).

John T. Smith (white, age 21). *Murder.* The crime was committed on 12/29/1885 in Daviess County. Accomplice in the killing of 40-year-old William C. Gladson (white). Motive: robbery. He was hanged at Gallatin, MO on August 6, 1886. Source: *Galveston (TX) Daily News*, 8/7/86 (2:4). See: Joseph Jump (executed 7/23/86).

Robert Grayor (black, age 22). *Murder.* The crime was committed on 7/6/1883 in St. Louis County. Executed for the killing of 35-year-old Berry Evans (black), who was beaten on the head with a wooden hay fork. Motive: workplace dispute. The services of the hangman were called upon to wrap up this case at St. Louis on December 10, 1886. Source: *St. Louis Post-Dispatch*, 12/10/86 (8:2). See also: *City of St. Louis Deaths Register*, 1883, 473, and 1886, 139.

1887

Edward F. Clum (white, age 52). *Murder.* The crime was committed on 7/8/1886 in Barry County. Shotgun slayings of 48-year-old John J. White and 17-year-old Ella Bowe (whites). Motive: male jealousy. This brooding double killer was hanged at Cassville, MO on April 15, 1887. Source: *Belleville (KS) Telescope*, 4/21/87 (1:3). *St. Louis Post-Dispatch*, 4/16/87 (9:7). See also: 1880 U.S. Census (Ontario Co., NY), which notes the ages and origins of the male actors in this tragedy.

Daniel Jewell (black, age 21). *Murder.* The crime was committed on 12/30/1884 in St. Louis County. Uxoricide. Handgun slaying of 16-year-old Ellen Jewell (black), she having succumbed to her wound after 121 days. Motive: marital estrangement. The errant young husband was hanged for the crime of capital murder at St. Louis on April 15, 1887. Source: *St. Louis Post-Dispatch*, 4/15/87 (8:2). *Belleville (KS) Telescope*, 4/21/87 (1:3).

Alfred Blunt (black, age 31). *Murder.* The crime was committed on 5/21/1886 in St. Louis County. Uxoricide. Executed for the killing of 24-year-old Mary Blunt (black), she having been slashed with a razor and then finished off with a hatchet. Motive: marital estrangement. This sanguine wife-killer was hanged for his crime at St. Louis on June 24, 1887. Source: *St. Louis Post-Dispatch*, 6/24/87 (5:1). See also: *City of St. Louis Deaths Register*, 1886, 482, and 1887, 188.

Edward Sneed (white, age 29). *Murder.* The crime was committed on 7/26/1884 in Jackson County. Handgun slaying of 19-year-old Orleans Harrison Loomis (white). Motive: obnoxious drunk. Sneed's past criminal record probably had a lot to do with the decision of the trial court to hang him. He was executed at Independence, MO on June 24, 1887. Source: *Sedalia (MO) Democrat*, 10/8/76 (2:3), which describes Sneed and his family as the dregs of society. Also: *Atchison (KS) Globe*, 7/28/84 (2:3). *Sedalia (MO) Weekly Bazoo*, 6/28/87 (1:5). Appeals: 88 MO 138–145 and 4 SW 411–413. See also: 1870 U.S. Census (Cole Co., MO), which notes Sneed as a juvenile delinquent.

1888

Peter Hronek (white, age abt. 31). *Murder.* The crime was committed on 4/17/1887 in Buchanan County. Uxoricide. Handgun slaying of "Jane Doe" Hronek (white, age and first name not recorded), who was shot three times while in the act of rocking their baby's cradle. Motive: alcoholism and atavistic male jealousy. This wife-killer was hanged at St. Joseph, MO on June 29, 1888. Source: *Kansas City Star*, 4/19/87 (1:4). *Kansas City Times*, 4/19/87 (1:5). *Sedalia (MO) Weekly Bazoo*, 6/28/87 (1:2). *St. Louis Post-Dispatch*, 6/29/88 (2:4). Although contemporary sources go into considerable detail about this case, none of them specify the first name or maiden name of the murdered woman. Hronek was a Bohemian immigrant who came to Missouri in 1878. He saved his money until he felt that he had enough to send for his fiancé in the old country. This was a common practice. Once reunited, the couple wed at Easton, MO circa 1885. They were survived by a 2-year-old daughter. They were buried side by side in the "Polish Cemetery" at St. Joseph, MO. Efforts to ascertain Mrs. Hronek's first name through marriage, birth and burial records have been unavailing.

George Mart Rider (white, age 25). *Murder.* The crime was committed on 7/23/1885 in Saline County. Shotgun slaying of 34-year-old Rousey Peter Tallent (white). Motive: because the homicide victim had aided the flight of Rider's physically abused girlfriend. Wrathful Rider was hanged for this crime at Marshall, MO on July 13, 1888. Source: *St. Louis Post-Dispatch*, 7/13/88 (2:3). See also: 1860 U.S. Census (Clinton Co., KY), which notes "Rowsey P. H. Talent" and 1880 U.S. Census, which notes his presence in Carroll Co., MO as "R. P. H. Tallent." Also: 1870 U.S. Census (Saline Co., MO), which notes Rider.

Hugh Mottram Brooks, alias "Walter Maxwell" (white, age 23). *Murder.* The crime was committed on

4/25/1885 in St. Louis County. Chloroform killing of 32-year-old Charles Arthur Preller, whose body was then stuffed into a storage trunk and left abandoned in a hotel room. Motive: robbery and gross perfidy. The culprit was hanged at St. Louis on August 10, 1888. Source: *St. Louis Post-Dispatch*, 8/10/88 (1:2). See also: *City of St. Louis Deaths Register*, 1885, 34, and 1888, 348. *Front Page Detective*, 12/43.

Henry Landgraff (white, age 27). *Murder.* The crime was committed on 3/5/1885 in St. Louis County. Handgun slaying of 22-year-old Annie Fisch (white). Motive: brutish male jealousy. It was enough to get him legally hanged at St. Louis on August 10, 1888. Source: *St. Louis Post-Dispatch*, 8/10/88 (1:2) & (3:7). See also: *City of St. Louis Deaths Register*, 1885, 895, and 1888, 347.

1889

John Matthews (white, age 38), **David Walker**, alias "Bull Creek Dave" (white, age 39) and **William Walker** (white, age 17). *Murder.* Their crime was committed on 3/11/1887 in Christian County. Shotgun slayings of about 27-year-old William Edmens and about 42-year-old Charles Green (whites). Motive: feuding and home invasion. All three legally met their fates at the end of a rope at Ozark, MO on May 10, 1889. Source: *St. Louis Post-Dispatch*, 5/10/89 (1:6). *Indian Journal* (Muscogee, OK), 3/16/87 (2:5). *Union Pilot* (Cuba, KS), 5/17/89 (2:4). See also: 1900 U.S. Census (Greene Co., MO), which notes survivors of the two murdered men.

1891

John Oscar Turlington (white, age 25). *Murder.* The crime was committed on 6/14/1890 in Cooper County. Police killer. Handgun slaying of 54-year-old Thomas C. Cranmer (white). Motive: escape from custody. Turlington took his last step from the gallows platform at Boonville, MO on March 6, 1891. Source: *St. Louis Post-Dispatch*, 3/6/91 (1:7). See also: 1880 U.S. Census (Cooper Co., MO), which notes Cranmer.

Webster Jackson (white, age 23). *Murder.* The crime was committed on 10/20/1886 in Franklin County. Executed for the murder of 50-year-old Alexander McVicker (white), who was shot twice in the head with a handgun and had his throat cut from ear to ear. Jackson was executed at Hermann, MO, on April 25, 1891. Motive: robbery. Venue changed from Franklin County to Gasconade County. Source: *Daily Kennebec (ME) Journal*, 10/25/86 (1:6). *Decatur (IL) Daily Republican*, 12/22/86 (2:4). *St. Louis Post-Dispatch*, 4/25/91 (3:3).

William Price (black, age 24). *Rape.* The crime was committed on 11/7/1890 in Saline County. Indecent assault on the person of 19-year-old Alice Ninas (white), she later having committed suicide rather than testify in court. Her attacker was legally hanged at Marshall, MO on May 8, 1891. Source: *Republic County Freeman* (Belleville, KS), 3/26/91 (3:2). *St. Louis Post-Dispatch*, 5/8/91 (1:7). See also: 1880 U.S. Census (Saline Co., MO), which notes Miss Ninas.

Henry Henson (white, age 34). *Murder.* The crime was committed on 2/4/1889 in St. Louis County. Uxoricide. Handgun slaying of 35-year-old Ida Kreitling Henson (white), she having been shot from behind. Motive: stupid male jealousy. This wife-killer was hanged at St. Louis on August 13, 1891. Source: *St. Louis Post-Dispatch,* 8/13/91 (5:1). See also: *City of St. Louis Deaths Register,* 1889, 552, and 1891, 384.

Christopher Young (white, age 26). *Murder.* The crime was committed on 12/11/1887 in Lafayette County. Fatal stabbing of about 30-year-old Stephen Ferguson (white). Motive: brawling. The killer was hanged at Lexington, MO on August 13, 1891. Source: *St. Louis Post-Dispatch,* 8/13/91 (5:2). *Wichita (KS) Daily Eagle,* 8/14/91 (1:2). *Sedalia (MO) Weekly Bazoo,* 8/18/91 (2:1).

Louis Bulling (white, age 23). *Murder.* The crime was committed on 1/29/1888 in Buchanan County. Uxoricide. Handgun slaying of 19-year-old Flora Brown Bulling (white), she having been shot three times. Motive: marital estrangement. Venue changed from Buchanan County to Andrew County. Young master Bulling was hanged at Savannah, MO on September 4, 1891. Source: *Wichita (KS) Daily Eagle,* 9/5/91 (1:3). *St. Louis Post-Dispatch,* 3/6/91 (2:1) & 9/4/91 (4:5), which says that it was an ax murder. See also: 1880 U.S. Census (Buchanan Co., MO), which notes the killer.

Thomas Andrew Williamson (white, age 54). *Murder.* The crime was committed on 5/29/1890 in Pettis County. Executed for the ax murders of 58-year-old Jefferson Moore and 29-year-old Charles Moore (whites), a father and son whom he then buried face down in shallow graves. Motive: to gain possession of their farm. Williamson is confirmed to have also murdered his wife by the same means on or about 10/1/1889 and to have secretly buried her on another Pettis County farm. Her maiden name was Susan Reed. She was aged 60 at the time of her death. Williamson insisted that she had died of natural causes although a gory ax was found near her grave. It was further determined that Williamson was a recidivist killer who had been spared from a previous death sentence. This had involved the murder of an unnamed German in Tazewell Co., IL circa 1868. The victim had been gambling with Williamson and two other men. He wound up robbed and buried beneath a house. Williamson was reportedly sentenced to death for this crime but reprieved by the governor of Illinois on condition that he serve a 22-year prison term. He was set loose on society after 17 years at the additional cost of three more lives. The hangman finally caught up with this character at Sedalia, MO on October 31, 1891. Source: *Sedalia (MO) Weekly Bazoo,* 6/3/90 (6:1), 6/10/90 (1:2), 6/17/90 (6:1) & 11/3/91 (1:1).

Charles Melville Seaton (white, age 16). *Murder.* The crime was committed on 6/5/1889 in Jasper County. Handgun slaying of 17-year-old Lewis Channell (white), who was shot in the back. Motive: to gain possession of the dead boy's heirloom watch. Venue changed from Jasper County to Lawrence County. This juvenile killer learned the price of folly when he was hanged at Mt. Vernon, MO on December 4, 1891. Source: *St. Louis Post-Dispatch,* 12/4/91 (1:7). *Joplin (MO) Herald,* 6/25/89 (1:5) & 12/6/91 (1:1). *Jefferson City (MO) Daily Tribune,* 12/6/91 (2:4).

1892

John William Harbin (white, age 40). *Murder.* The crime was committed on 7/4/1888 in Butler County.

Handgun slaying of A. L. Smith (white, age and full name not recorded), who was shot twice in the back; his body was then dumped in a river. Motive: to avoid payment of a $90 debt. The killer was hanged at Poplar Bluff on January 15, 1892. Source: *St. Louis Post-Dispatch,* 1/15/92 (1:7). *St. Louis Republic,* 11/13/89 (9:4) & 9/30/91 (1:6). See also: 1880 U.S. Census (Stoddard Co., MO), which notes Harbin. The Butler County courthouse was obliterated by a tornado in 1927, hence the loss of the original file for this case.

1893

William McCoy (black, age 33). *Murder.* The crime was committed on 4/6/1891 in Jackson County. Executed for the killing of 38-year-old Mollie Magruder (black), she having been clubbed at first but then finished off with a rock, her head being "beaten almost flat." Motive: lovers' quarrel. Venue changed from Jackson County to Lafayette County. This miscreant was hanged at Lexington, MO on February 16, 1893. Source: *St. Louis Post-Dispatch,* 2/16/93 (1:7). *Kansas City Times,* 4/8/91 (8:5). *Lexington (MO) News,* 2/23/93 (1:4).

Amos Avery (white, age 18). *Murder.* The crime was committed on 9/23/1891 in Barton County. Handgun slaying of 20-year-old James A. Miles (white), the victim having been shot in his sleep. Motive: highway robbery. Avery ended his own short life on the gallows at Lamar, MO on May 24, 1893. Source: *St. Louis Post-Dispatch,* 5/24/93 (1:5). *Wichita (KS) Daily Eagle,* 10/4/91 (2:7). *Lamar (MO) Democrat,* 5/25/93 (2:2). See also: 1880 U.S. Census (Prairie Co., AR), which notes Miles.

Joseph A. Howell (white, age 20). *Murder.* The crime was committed on 1/19/1889 in Linn County. Mass killer and child killer. Executed for the ax and hatchet massacre of pregnant 31-year-old Minnie Hall (white) and her four children: William Hall (age 9), May Hall (age 7), Nettie Hall (age 5) and Roy Hall (age 2), their house having also been fired with their bodies inside. Motive: ramifications of incest. Howell and Minnie Hall were first cousins. She was 5 months up-and-away by him. Dreading the consequences thereof, Howell had attempted to perform an abortion on the widowed Mrs. Hall. He botched the operation and then resorted to mass murder in a futile attempt to conceal the matter. Venue changed from Linn County to Grundy County. Howell was hanged at Trenton, MO on August 4, 1893. Source: *Kansas City Journal,* 1/21/89 (1:3). *St. Louis Post-Dispatch,* 8/4/93 (1:4). See also: 1880 U.S. Census (Linn Co., MO), which notes Minnie Hall.

Richard Robinson (black, age 25). *Murder.* The crime was committed on 10/23/1892 in Pettis County. Fatal stabbing of pregnant 24-year-old Johanna Schollman (white). Motive: sexual assault. This killer found himself subjected to capital punishment at Sedalia, MO on December 15, 1893. Source: *St. Louis Post-Dispatch,* 12/15/93 (1:5). *Sedalia (MO) Weekly Bazoo,* 11/1/92 (2:2) & 12/19/93 (1:1), which describes the murdered woman as a common trollop.

Charles Banks (black, age 33). *Murder.* The crime was committed on 8/29/1892 in Pettis County. Handgun slaying of 22-year-old Isaac Palmer (black). Motive: gambling dispute. Venue changed from Pettis County to

Johnson County. Black-on-black killer Charles Banks was hanged at Warrensburg, MO on December 29, 1893. Source: *Sedalia (MO) Weekly Bazoo*, 9/13/92 (8:6) & 4/11/93 (6:2). *St. Louis Post-Dispatch*, 12/29/93 (6:7). See also: 1880 U.S. Census (Pettis Co., MO), which notes Palmer as a minor.

1894

Martin Reed (black, age 55). *Murder.* The crime was committed on 9/16/1890 in Jackson County. Uxoricide. Handgun slaying of 50-year-old Hester Reed (black), she having been shot three times. Motive: marital estrangement. This prosaic black-on-black killer was hanged at Kansas City on January 5, 1894. Source: *Kansas City Star*, 9/16/90 (1:3). *Kansas City Times*, 1/6/94 (8:1). See also: 1880 U.S. Census (Jackson Co., MO), which notes both parties.

Samuel Welsor (white, age 42). *Murder.* The crime was committed on 8/4/1890 in St. Louis County. Handgun slaying of 33-year-old Clementina Manning (white), she having been shot four times. Motive: unsuccessful mooching. The victim of this homicide had been a prostitute. Welsor had bought her way out of a brothel and taken her as his own. The couple became estranged when Welsor ran out of money. He then left town for a while. However, during his absence Clementina won $5,000 in a lottery. This was close to a fortune in those days. Welsor heard of the woman's luck and hastened back to her, hoping to chisel a part of the prize. An argument erupted, with fatal results for both parties. Welsor died kicking at the end of a rope at St. Louis on January 12, 1894. Source: *St. Louis Post-Dispatch*, 1/12/94 (3:1). See also: *City of St. Louis Deaths Register*, 1890, 550, and 1894, 357.

Wilson Howard (white, age 26). *Murder.* The crime was committed on 4/27/1889 in Maries County. Feudist and multiple killer. Executed for the handgun slaying of Thomas McMichaels (white, a deaf-mute, age not recorded), who was abducted from his home and found dead in a ditch the next day shot through the head and the heart. Motive: because the murdered man had finked on Howard for using illegal means to expose him as a thief. Venue changed from Maries County to Laclede County. Wilson Howard was a ringleader of the notorious *Howard-Turner Feud*, which had devastated Harlan Co., KY for seven years up to that point at a cost of more than a dozen lives. Howard admitted to being personally responsible for five of those Kentucky killings, although the true extent of his homicides is uncertain. His confession may have been (at least in part) a ploy to exonerate imprisoned kinsmen by taking the blame for their misdeeds. One such assassination that can definitely be attributed to Howard was that of George Turner (white, age 28) in Harlan County by means of a rifle on 8/4/1889. The hangman finally caught up with Howard at Lebanon, MO on January 19, 1894. Source: *St. Louis Post-Dispatch*, 1/19/94 (1:1). *The Sun* (New York) 11/3/89 (1:5). *Semi-Weekly Interior Journal* (Stanford, KY), 8/13/89 (2:2). *Decatur (IL) Weekly Republican*, 5/9/89 (8:1). See also: 1880 U.S. Census (Harlan Co., KY), which notes both Howard and George Turner.

Charles Wisdom (black, age 23). *Murder.* The crime was committed on 4/24/1892 in St. Louis County. Executed for the killing of 45-year-old Edward A. Drexler (white), who was battered to death with an iron bar. Motive: burglary. "He Died a Craven!" said the *St. Louis Post-Dispatch* when this offender was swung from the gallows in that city on April 13, 1894. Source: *St. Louis Post-Dispatch*, 4/13/94 (1:6). Also: *City of St. Louis Deaths Register*, 1892, 106, and 1894, 462.

Jacob Brown, alias "John Coleman" (black, age abt. 38). *Murder.* The crime was committed on 8/3/1892 in Cole County. Executed for the killing of Frank Macklin (white, age not recorded), a civilian foreman at the Missouri State Prison shoemaker shop who was slashed to death with a cobbler's knife. Motive: because the murdered man had reported this prisoner for a disciplinary infraction. As a result, Brown-alias-Coleman took a one-way trip through the gallows trap at Jefferson City on May 4, 1894. Source: *Kansas City Times*, 8/4/92 (1:4). *Jefferson City (MO) Daily Tribune*, 8/4/92 (4:3). *St. Louis Post-Dispatch*, 5/4/94 (6:1).

Harry Jones (white, age 29) and **William Kicksher**, alias "John Clark" (white, age 36). *Murder.* Their crime was committed on 9/9/1893 in Jackson County. Both executed for the killing of 56-year-old Jane Wright (white, a law-abiding Kansas City business woman) who was found tied up in her office beaten and choked to death. Motive: robbery. The culprits were hanged at Independence, MO on June 29, 1894. Source: *Kansas City Journal*, 6/29/94 (3:1) & 6/30/94 (3:1).

Charles Wilson (black, age 27). *Murder.* The crime was committed on 11/8/1892 in St. Louis County. Handgun slaying of 21-year-old Moses Hodges (black), who succumbed to his wound 71 days later. Motive: rivalry for a female. Count another one for the hangman at St. Louis on July 26, 1894. Source: *St. Louis Post-Dispatch*, 7/26/94 (3:1). Appeal: 26 SW 357–360. See also: *City of St. Louis Deaths Register*, 1893, 457, and 1894, burial permit no. 5119.

William Henry Harrison Duncan (black, age 27). *Murder.* The crime was committed on 10–6-1890 in St. Louis County. Police killer. Handgun slaying of 31-year-old James Brady (white). Motive: fracas in a low resort. The subsequent sentence of death by hanging was inflicted on this offender at Clayton, MO on July 27, 1894. Source: *St. Louis Post-Dispatch*, 7/27/94 (1:1).

1895

Philip Martin (black, age 17). *Murder.* The crime was committed on 7/4/1893 in Jackson County. Fatal stabbing of 34-year-old Eli Stillwell (white). Motive: big attitude. The murdered man (while in an intoxicated state) had bumped into young Martin as they passed each other on a sidewalk. Martin then made the fatal mistake of letting his temper get the better of his judgment. He was hanged for capital felony at Kansas City on February 15, 1895. Source: *Kansas City Star*, 2/15/95 (1:1). *Kansas City Times*, 7/6/93 (5:4) & 2/15/95 (1:4).

Joseph Burries (black, age 19). *Attempted rape.* The crime was committed on 7/30/1894 in Buchanan County. Felonious assault on the person of 7-year-old Bertha Potter (white) with intent to commit a penetrative act of carnal knowledge on a minor. Although attempted rape was not in itself a capital offense in Missouri at this time, the trial court condemned Burries anyway because the victim had been badly injured in a female way to the extent that an actual rape consisting of complete involuntary coitus (which *was* punishable by death) might just as well have occurred. A noose and a beam ensured that Burries would nevermore do such a thing at St. Joseph, MO on May 11, 1895. Source: *St. Joseph (MO) Herald*, 5/11/95 (3:4) & 5/12/95 (3:1).

Edward Murray (black, age abt. 22). *Murder.* The crime was committed on 9/23/1893 in St. Louis County. Accomplice in the handgun slaying of 18-year-old Edgar Fitzwilliams (white). Motive: rowdiness on a trolley car. Venue changed from St. Louis County to Gasconade County. This offender suffered death by hanging at Hermann, MO on May 11, 1895. Source: *St. Louis Dispatch*, 5/11/95 (1:6). See also: *City of St. Louis Deaths Register*, 1895, which belatedly notes the homicide victim on 7/4/95 with a burial date of 9/23/93.

James Murray, alias "Peter Jackson" (black, age 24). *Murder.* The crime was committed on 9/23/1893 in St. Louis County. Handgun slaying of 18-year-old Edgar Fitzwilliams (white). Motive: obnoxious behavior on a trolley car. Such imprudent conduct cost Murray his life when he was hanged at Clayton, MO on May 11, 1895. Source: *St. Louis Post-Dispatch*, 5/11/95 (1:6). See also: *City of St. Louis Deaths Register*, 1895, 120, for details on the homicide victim. See also same source, 1895, 285, which notes James Murray.

1896

Emile David (white, age 34). *Murder.* The crime was committed on 1/8/1894 in Osage County. Fatal and deliberate poisoning of 24-year-old Frank Henderson (white), he having been served a glass of whiskey that was laced with strychnine. Motive: none apparent; possibly deranged. The killer was hanged at Linn, MO on February 15, 1896. Source: *St. Louis Post-Dispatch*, 2/15/96 (2:5). *Morning Times* (Wash., DC), 2/16/96 (1:4). *Kansas City Journal*, 2/16/96 (4:7). See also: 1880 U.S. Census (Osage Co., MO), which notes Henderson.

James Fitzgerald (white, age 27). *Murder.* The crime was committed on 11/24/1893 at St. Louis. Handgun slaying of 18-year-old Annie Naessens (white). Motive: lovers' quarrel. The public hangman for that fair city found another customer in the person of James Fitzgerald on February 20, 1896. Source: *St. Louis Post-Dispatch*, 2/20/96 (1:1). See also: *City of St. Louis Deaths Register*, 1893, 293, and 1896, 67.

John W. Nelson (white, age not recorded). *Murder.* The crime was committed on 8/5/1893 in Ralls County. Handgun slayings of about 35-year-old John Stull and 56-year-old Mary Stull Hughes (whites), a mother and her son. Motive: wrathful conduct and gross ingratitude. The homicide victims had tenderly nursed the killer's ailing mother so that she recovered her health. Nelson had ignored his sick mother during that time, perhaps hoping that she would succumb. Stull supposedly made a remark about this to a third party. Nelson found out about it and went on the warpath together with his reputedly wicked wife, Lavinia Nelson. She was acquitted at trial despite the fact that she had joined in the attack on John Stull and had even bludgeoned him with a chunk of iron. Venue changed from Ralls County to Marion County. The male half of this murderous pair was hanged at Palmyra, MO on February 28, 1896. Source: *St. Louis Republic*, 2/29/96 (3:6). *Morning Times* (Wash., DC), 2/29/96 (3:5). Appeal: 33 SW 809–812. See also: Marion Co. marriage cert. dated 10/2/68, which notes Mrs. Hughes.

William P. Taylor (white, age 32). *Murder.* The crime was committed on 5/10/1894 in Sullivan County. Mass killer, child killer, baby killer. Executed for the premeditated massacre of 31-year-old Gus Meeks and 27-year-old (pregnant) Delora Page Meeks (whites, a married couple) and their two young daughters: Hattie Meeks (age 4) and Mamie Meeks (age 1). The adult victims were initially shot with handguns. Then both they and their little children had their heads smashed with stones. Their bodies were found hidden under a haystack. Motive: vengeance that was cleverly disguised. Taylor and his equally guilty brother (George E. Taylor) had been indicted for cattle rustling. Gus Meeks had been in on it with them but obtained a pardon on condition that he testify against the Taylors. Slyly, the Taylors bribed Meeks to pack up and move out of Missouri with his family before the case came to trial. Meeks accepted this (the bribe money being substantial), perhaps suspecting that it would be unhealthy for him to refuse. Meeks and family made it only as far as Sullivan County where they were ambushed by the Taylors. In this way the Taylors eliminated a hostile witness and also got back their money. Their murder trial was held in Carroll County on a change of venue. Both of the Taylors were sentenced to death. George Taylor escaped before the time set for his execution and was never recaptured. His brother dangled solo at Carrollton, MO on April 30, 1896. Source: *Wichita (KS) Daily Eagle*, 5/12/94 (1:4). *St. Louis Post-Dispatch*, 4/30/96 (1:1). See also: Sullivan Co. marriages licenses, December 1886, 4, which notes Mr. & Mrs. Meeks. *Headline Detective*, 3/44. *Master Detective*, 7/37. *Real Detective*, 8/37.

William Wright (black, age abt. 40). *Murder.* The crime was committed on 6/29/1895 in Vernon County. Uxoricide. Ax murder of Betty Wright (black, age not recorded). Motive: a fit of pique, she having cooked his supper in a way that was not to his taste. This volatile wife-killer was hanged at Nevada, MO on August 10, 1896. Source: *St. Louis Post-Dispatch*, 8/10/96 (1:7). Appeal: 35 SW 1145–1148.

George W. Anderson (white, age 45). *Murder.* The crime was committed on 5/27/1896 in Macon County. Uxoricide. Executed for the killing of 27-year-old Cora Hutchinson Combs Anderson (white), she having had her throat cut with a pocket knife and her head battered with a hammer. Motive: domestic quarrel. This cranky wife-killer was hanged at Macon, MO on August 21, 1896. Source: *St. Louis Post-Dispatch*, 8/21/96 (1:3). See also: 1880 U.S. Census (Macon Co., MO), which notes Mrs. Anderson by her maiden name.

1897

James B. Inks (white, age 42). *Murder.* The crime was committed on 5/15/1895 in Holt County. Handgun slaying of 58-year-old John Patterson (white). Motive: landlord-tenant dispute. It was enough to secure a place on the gallows for Inks at Oregon, MO on January 30, 1897. Source: *Holt County (MO) Sentinel*, 5/17/95 (4:4), 11/8/95 (1:1) & 1/30/97 (1:1). See also: 1880 U.S. Census (Holt Co., MO), which notes Patterson.

Edward Perry (white, age 23). *Murder.* The crime was committed on 5/20/1896 in Douglas County. Hanged for the ax murders of 66-year-old Lafayette Sawyer, 66-year-old Sarah Sawyer (a married couple) and 27-year-old Ernest Sawyer, their son (whites). Motive: robbery. This gory triple killer was executed at Ava, MO on January 30, 1897. Source: *St. Louis Post-Dispatch*, 1/30/97 (2:2) & 1/31/97 (1:5). Appeal: 37 SW 804–805, which says that the murder weapon was a gas pipe. See also: 1875 Minnesota State Census, which notes the Sawyer family before its members came to Missouri.

Arthur Duestrow (white, age 24). *Murder.* The crime was committed on 2/13/1894 at St. Louis. Uxoricide and filicide. Handgun slayings of 29-year-old Albertine Duestrow and 2-year-old Louis Duestrow (whites), they being his wife and son. Motive: a complete and utter lack of ordinary decency. Duestrow was a besotted trust fund brat (and millionaire) who drank his way out of every advantage that life afforded him. The volume of his personal wealth would rank in the fabulous range by 21st century standards. He came home drunk and surly on the above date only to start shooting when something triggered his temper. His trial was held in Franklin County on a change of venue. The best legal representation that his money could buy proved unavailing against the weight of the evidence. Rich boy Duestrow was hanged for his crime at Union, MO on February 16, 1897, like any other common felon. It can be argued that this wastrel did serve one useful purpose with his otherwise misspent life: his case disproves the common myth that capital punishment as practiced in the United States falls entirely on the poor and disadvantaged. Source: *St. Louis Post-Dispatch*, 2/15/97 (1:1) & 2/16/97 (1:1). *St. Louis Republic*, 2/17/97 (1:1). See also: 1880 U.S. Census (St. Louis, MO), which notes this celebrated killer.

Peter Schmidt, alias "Cotton Head" (white, age 17) and **Samuel Foster** (black, age 22). *Murder.* Their crime was committed on 1/23/1896 in St. Louis County. Handgun slaying of 33-year-old Bertram Atwater (white). Motive: mugging. These young hoodlums were an unlikely pair, the one being an Aryan and the other an Afro. How they put in with each other is anyone's guess. There was a lot of speculation about it at the time. They were hanged at Clayton, MO on February 16, 1897. Source: *St. Louis Post-Dispatch*, 2/16/97 (2:1). See also: *County of St. Louis Deaths Register*, 1897, 132. See also: 1880 U.S. Census (Chicago, IL), which notes Mr. Atwater.

James Pollard (black, age 21). *Murder.* The crime was committed on 7/30/1895 in Buchanan County. Handgun slaying of 42-year-old Joseph Irvine (black). Motive: rivalry for a female. Actually, it was the homicide victim's younger brother against whom Pollard had a grudge. He shot at that man and his family as they ate their dinner, killing the wrong person. The price he paid was death by hanging at St. Joseph, MO on June 25, 1897. Source: *St. Joseph (MO) Weekly Herald,*

7/1/97 (1:1). *Kansas City Journal*, 6/25/97 (2:1). Appeal: 40 SW 949–951. See also: 1880 U.S. Census (Buchanan Co., MO), which notes both parties.

Thomas Johnson, alias "Henry Clay" (black, age 27). *Murder.* The crime was committed on 8/1/1896 at St. Louis. Handgun slaying of 21-year-old William Amend, alias "Chronicle Red," a white newspaper boy presumably so-called on account of his hair. Motive: gambling dispute. Johnson hobbled to the gallows (he having only one leg) at St. Louis on November 18, 1897. Source: *St. Louis Post-Dispatch*, 11/18/97 (1:1). See also: *City of St. Louis Deaths Register*, 1896, entry no. 6237, and 1897, entry no. 8388.

William Carr (white, age 37). *Murder.* The crime was committed on 10/10/1897 in Clay County. Filicide. Executed for the deliberate drowning of 3-year-old Belle Carr (white), she having been lashed to a heavy rock and thrown alive into the Missouri river. Motive: unwanted child and the alleged behest of a cruel stepmother. The brutality of this crime outraged people of all classes. The toddling girl was wide awake and screaming with terror when she hit the water. Her father (if he can be called such) was hanged without the benefit of appeal at Liberty, MO on December 17, 1897. Source: *St. Louis Post-Dispatch*, 12/17/97 (5:1). *Kansas City Journal*, 12/17/97 (1:5) & 12/18/97 (1:7).

1898

Toby Lanahan (black, age 26). *Murder.* The crime was committed on 12/25/1896 in Cole County. Child killer. Executed for the murder of 12-year-old Millie Gaines (black), she having been "beaten insensible" with a wooden bed slat, raped and then "horribly mutilated" with a knife. Motive: sexual assault. That was how Toby Lanahan observed Christmas Day in the year 1896. He was hanged at Jefferson City on June 22, 1898. Source: *St. Louis Post-Dispatch*, 6/22/98 (8:2). Appeal: 45 SW 1090–1092. See also: 1880 U.S. Census (Callaway Co., MO), which notes this culprit as "Tobe Launahan."

Edward McKenzie (black, age abt. 28). *Murder.* The crime was committed on 4/30/1896 in Cole County. Executed for the killing of 49-year-old Nicholas Linhardt (white), who was clubbed to death with no quarter given. Motive: highway robbery. The hangman sent McKenzie on his way at Jefferson City on June 22, 1898. Source: *St. Louis Post-Dispatch*, 6/22/98 (8:2). *Kansas City Journal*, 6/23/98 (6:3). Appeal: 45 SW 1117–1119. See also: 1880 U.S. Census (Cole Co., MO), which notes the murdered man as "Nick Leanhart."

John Thomascheutz (white, age 26). *Murder.* The crime was committed on 4/6/1897 at St. Louis. Handgun slaying of 18-year-old Annie Rausch (white), she having been shot in the back. Motive: because she had declined to marry him. This lovelorn killer paid his debt to society with his life at St. Louis on June 22, 1898. Source: *St. Louis Post-Dispatch*, 6/22/98 (8:1). Appeal: 45 SW 1106–1108. See also: *City of St. Louis Deaths Register*, 1897, no. 3512, and 1898, no. 4234.

James Albright (white, age 21). *Murder.* The crime was committed on 1/12/1897 in Mississippi County. Executed for the handgun slaying of George S. Elliott (white, age not recorded), a local district attorney who was shot three times. Motive: resisting arrest. James Albright and his younger brother Joseph Albright (white, age 18) were being sought at that time for the 9/15/1896 shotgun slaying of their brother-in-law, Isaac Large by name. A further report that James Albright had murdered a schoolmate with a baseball bat when he was 8 years old lacks confirmation. Joseph Albright died of typhus in the St. Louis City Jail on 4–3-1897. James Albright was hanged at Charleston, MO on July 9, 1898. Source: *Logansport (IN) Daily Reporter*, 1/18/97 (1:5). *St. Louis Post-Dispatch*, 7/10/98 (8:1). Appeal: 46 SW 620–622. See also: 1880 U.S. Census (Mississippi Co., MO), which notes the Albrights as minors.

George Thompson (black, age 29). *Murder.* The crime was committed on 9/29/1894 at St. Louis. Fatal and deliberate poisoning of 32-year-old Joseph Cunningham (white), who had been lulled into eating a snack laced with strychnine. Motive: revenge. Thompson had been displaced from his job as a church janitor. Cunningham was his replacement. Thompson visited his former jobsite on the pretense of fetching some personal belongings. He had some cheese and bottled beer in his lunchbox, which he offered to share with the unsuspecting victim. Those victuals had been premeditatedly poisoned. Through the gallows trap at the St. Louis City Jail went George Thompson on August 1, 1898. Source: *St. Louis Post-Dispatch*, 8/1/98 (8:4). See also: City of St. Louis burial permit (1894) no. 6711 and (1898) no. 5429.

James Brown (black, age 29). *Murder.* The crime was committed on 4/1/1896 in Jackson County. Handgun slaying of 28-year-old Henry Prather (black). Motive: rivalry for a female. A gallows marked the end for James Brown at Independence, MO on December 28, 1898. Source: *Kansas City Journal*, 12/29/98 (10:1). *Kansas City Times*, 12/28/98 (5:1). Appeal: 47 SW 789–791.

Ira Sexton (white, age 22). *Murder.* The crime was committed on 10/28/1897 in Mercer County. Handgun slaying of 26-year-old Nathan W. Stark (white), the victim having been shot in the crotch. Motive: attempted highway robbery. This killer was hanged at Princeton, MO on December 28, 1898. Source: *Kansas City Journal*, 10/30/97 (2:5). Appeal: 48 SW 452–455. *Des Moines (IA) Daily News*, 11/19/97 (5:1). *Evening Times* (Wash., DC), 12/29/98 (5:3). See also: 1880 U.S. Census (Mercer Co., MO), which notes both parties.

1899

Oscar Baker (white, age abt. 50). *Murder.* The crime was committed on 3/22/1898 in Shannon County. Uxoricide. Executed for the killing of about 45-year-old Annie Baker (white), she having been beaten with a club and stabbed with a butcher knife. Motive: alcoholic brutality. Death by hanging was the fate of Oscar Baker at Eminence, MO on January 10, 1899. Source: *The Current Wave* (Eminence, MO), 1/12/99 (1:1). *New Castle (PA) News*, 1/18/99 (1:4). Appeal: 48 SW 475–478.

James Reed (black, age 17). *Murder.* The crime was committed on 12/28/1897 in Jackson County. Handgun slaying of 26-year-old Susie Blakely (black), she having been shot four times. Motive: jilted lover. A terrible price was exacted from this smitten teenager when he was hanged at Kansas City on March 30, 1899. Source: *Kansas City Journal*, 12/29/97 (10:3). *Kansas City Times*, 3/31/99 (8:1). See also: 1880 U.S. Census (Jackson Co., MO), which notes the killer's parents and elder siblings. His father (Martin Reed) had been hanged from the same gallows on 1–5-1894. James Reed must have been born shortly after the taking of the 1880 Census.

Edwin Bates Soper (white, age 35). *Murder.* The crime was committed on 4/21/1891 in Cass County. Uxoricide and filicide. Executed for the ax murders of pregnant 34-year-old Delia Hunt Soper, 5-year-old Maud Soper and 2-year-old Gillis Soper (whites). Motive: disillusionment; possibly deranged. Soper was subsequently confirmed to have also murdered his father, John Lewis Soper (age 50), who had been found shot to death at Kearney, MO on 1/30/1880. He was also determined to have made away with his 2-year-old son by another wife (whom he had married under an assumed name) at Portland, OR, by throwing the babe into the Willamette River on or about 4/15/1897. The public hangman rid the world of Edwin Soper at Harrisonville, MO on March 30, 1899. Source: *Kansas City Journal*, 6/10/97 (1:5) & 3/30/99 (1:7). *Liberty (MO) Tribune*, 2/6/80. See also: 1870 U.S. Census (Clay Co., MO), which notes the killer and his family. Most accounts (including Soper's own marriage license) give his name as either Edward B. Soper, Bates Soper or E. B. Soper.

Matthew Hancock (black, age 23). *Murder.* The crime was committed on 7/25/1897 at St. Louis. Handgun slaying of 31-year-old George Horton (white), who was shot five times. Motive: obnoxious drunk. This whiskey-driven killer found sobriety at the end of a rope when he was hanged at the St. Louis City Jail on April 8, 1899. Source: *Kansas City Journal*, 7/26/97 (2:6). *St. Louis Post-Dispatch*, 4/8/99 (8:3). See also: *City of St. Louis Deaths Register*, 1897, no. 6801, and 1899, no. 3387.

Frederick Bronstine (white, age 46). *Murder.* The crime was committed on 3/12/1898 in Clark County. Uxoricide. Handgun slaying of 33-year-old Amelia Jane Rowe Bronstine (white). Motive: marital estrangement. A perjurer (because he was broken his marriage vows in just about the worst way possible) as well as a killer, Frederick Bronstine found himself cast out of human society altogether when he was hanged at Kahoka, MO on May 8, 1899. Source: *Clark County (MO) Courier*, 5/12/99 (8:1). Appeal: 49 SW 512–514. See also: 1880 U.S. Census (Clark Co., MO), which notes the victim by her maiden name. Also: *Clark County Birth Register*, entry dated 10/23/84, which notes this couple's first child and the age of its father.

William Burns (black, age 25). *Murder.* The crime was committed on 7/24/1897 in Scott County. Uxoricide. Shotgun slaying of Maggie Gregory Burns (black, age not recorded). Motive: marital estrangement. Domestic violence cases such as this cut an even swath across all ethnic, racial and religious lines. Burns paid the penalty for his transgression when he was hanged at Benton, MO on May 29, 1899. Source: *Benton (MO) Record*, 6/2/99 (8:1). See also: *Scott County Marriage Licenses*, 1894, 129. Also: 1880 U.S. Census (Scott Co., MO), which notes Burns as a minor.

Freeman Cochran (white, age 37). *Murder.* The crime was committed on 8/17/1897 in Harrison County. Shotgun slaying of 30-year-old George Stanbrough (white), who was blasted from behind. Motive: sore loser. These two men had vied for the attentions of a certain female of the species and agreed to settle the matter by having a fistfight. Cochran got the worst of it. He then shook hands with his rival in accordance with the Marquess of Queensberry rules and pretended to make peace with him. A short time later Cochran further displayed his sense of fair play by shooting Stanbrough in the back. He was hanged at Bethany, MO on June 7, 1899. Source: *Kansas City Journal*, 8/19/97 (1:4). *St. Louis Post-Dispatch*, 6/7/99 (9:5). See also: 1880 U.S. Census (Harrison Co., MO), which notes Cochran, and 1880 U.S. Census (DeKalb Co., MO), which notes Stanbrough as "Stambroy" due to a transcription error.

Peter S. Kindred (white, age 22). *Murder.* The crime was committed on 2/5/1898 in Mercer County. Handgun slaying of 27-year-old Andrew A. Alley (white) and concomitant maiming of 23-year-old Joseph V. Alley (by the same means), they being two associated storekeepers. Motive: dispute over a bill. This contentious killer was hanged at Princeton, MO on June 7, 1899. Source: *Kansas City Journal*, 2/6/98 (1:5). *St. Louis Post-Dispatch*, 6/7/99 (9:5). See also: 1880 U.S. Census (Mercer Co., MO), which notes all parties.

John E. Headrick (white, age 19). *Murder.* The crime was committed on 7/1/1898 in Cape Girardeau County. Handgun slaying of 44-year-old James Madison Lail (white), who was shot five times. Motive: revenge. Headrick had worked for Mr. Lail. He persisted in wooing that man's daughter despite being warned not to do so. This disobedience caused Lail to terminate Headrick's employment. The latter then retaliated in a manner that cost him his own life as well when he was legally hanged at Jackson, MO on June 15, 1899. Source: *St. Louis Post-Dispatch*, 6/15/99 (9:1). See also: 1880 U.S. Census (Cape Girardeau Co., MO), which notes both parties.

Carroll Monroe Rice (white, age 33). *Murder.* The crime was committed on 6/27/1898 in Oregon County. Uxoricide. Rifle slaying of 20-year-old Mary C. Rice. Motive: marital estrangement. This brutish bridegroom was hanged at Alton, MO on June 15, 1899. Source: *Oregon County (MO) Tribune*, 6/16/99 (1:1). Appeal: 51 SW 78–80.

James McAfee (white, age not recorded). *Murder.* The crime was committed on 7/31/1897 in Jasper County. Handgun slaying of about 24-year-old Eben M. Brewer (white). Motive: armed robbery. McAfee faced the hangman at Carthage, MO on July 6, 1899. Source: *The Sun* (New York), 8/2/97 (1:2). *Carthage (MO) Press*, 7/6/99 (1:3). Appeal: 50 SW 82–84.

1900

James Nettles (black, age 27). *Murder.* The crime was committed on 7/4/1898 at St. Louis. Handgun slaying of 46-year-old Samuel W. Mann (white). Motive: argument on a trolley car. As usual, attitude, quick temper and a concealed weapon proved a deadly combination. It proved even deadlier for Nettles when he was hanged at the St. Louis City Jail on May 7, 1900. Source: *St. Louis Post-Dispatch*, 5/7/00 (1:1). Appeal: 55 SW 70–73. See also: *City of St. Louis Deaths Register*, 1898, no. 4695, and 1900, no. 3803.

Ernest R. Clevenger (white, age 28). *Murder.* The crime was committed on 12/8/1898 in Clay County. Handgun slayings of 29-year-old George Allen and 32-year-old Della Clevenger (whites), the latter being a third cousin to him. Motive: male jealousy. The killer was a drunk and a loser. He became romantically obsessed with Della's sister but was denied permission to court her for two reasons: concerns about incest and his well-known character flaws. The knowledge that Allen had supplanted him was more than Ernest Clevenger could bear. He wound up kicking at the end of a rope at Liberty, MO on June 15, 1900. Source: *Kansas City Journal*, 12/9/98 (1:7). *St. Louis Post-Dispatch*, 6/15/00 (7:2). See also: 1880 U.S. Census (Clay Co., MO), which notes Allen and E. R. Clevenger, plus 1880 U.S. Census (Phillips Co., KS), which notes the female homicide victim.

John A. Holloway (white, age 35). *Murder.* The crime was committed on 12/24/1898 in Osage County. Handgun slaying of 27-year-old Julius Boillot (white), who was shot five times in the back. Motive: resentment over a real estate transaction. Boillot had purchased land from the estate of Holloway's deceased father. Holloway became enraged by this because he felt that the disputed land should have come to him by right of inheritance. Why he chose to act on Christmas Eve is unknown. He was hanged at Linn, MO on June 15, 1900. Source: *Kansas City Journal*, 12/26/98 (2:4). *St. Louis Republic*, 6/16/00 (8:2). See also: 1880 U.S. Census (Osage Co., MO), which notes the murdered man.

Samuel Walters (black, age 39). *Murder.* The crime was committed on 4/14/1899 in New Madrid County. Shotgun slayings of a married couple named Frank and Millie Holmes (blacks, ages not recorded). Motive: boundary dispute. As a result, New Madrid had a "hanging day" on June 15, 1900, with Samuel Walters as its star attraction. Source: *Southeast Missourian* (New Madrid, MO), 6/21/00 (1:1). Appeal: 56 SW 734–737. See also: 1900 U.S. Census (New Madrid, MO), which notes the killer.

Noah McGinnis (white, age 27). *Murder.* The crime was committed on 4/16/1899 in Bates County. Sniper slaying of Frederick Borcherding (white, age not recorded). Motive: attempted robbery. This killer met his end via the rope route at Butler, MO on December 31, 1900. Source: *Iola (KS) Daily Register*, 12/31/00 (1:2). *St. Louis Republic*, 1/1/01 (3:2). Appeal: 59 SW 83–85. See also: 1900 U.S. Census (Bates Co., MO), which notes the killer.

1901

James H. Tettalon (white, age 29). *Murder.* The crime was committed on 4/25/1899 in Dunklin County. Mass killer and child killer. Executed for the murders of 43-year-old Melinda Smith Tettalon, a.k.a. "Mary Jane Tettalon" (white, his stepmother), and her four children: George, Ben, Ada and Ida (whites, ages 6 thru 12), they being his siblings of the half blood. All were shot with a handgun and left to be cremated in their burning house. Motive: rancor over the settlement of an estate. News accounts give five variations of the killer's surname: Tettalon, Tetterton, Tulton, Tetaton and Tettaton. The correct one is a matter of conjecture. James T. wound up dead just the same when he was hanged for this massacre at Kennett, MO on February 19, 1901. Source: *Moberly (MO) Weekly Monitor*, 5/4/99 (3:5). *Kansas City Times*, 2/20/01 (2:1). Appeal: 60 SW 743–745. See also: 1880 U.S. Census (Stoddard Co., MO), which notes the killer, and 1880 U.S. Census (Dunklin Co., MO), which notes the victim as "Mary Smith," then the wife of D. M. Smith.

Milo L. Gregory (white, age 23). *Murder.* The crime was committed on 2/20/1899 in Dunklin County. Rifle slaying of Joseph Covert (white, age not recorded). Motive: dispute over an 11-cent store credit. This one-dime-and-one-penny killer was hanged for what he did at Kennett, MO on March 21, 1901. Source: *Arkansas Gazette*, 3/22/01 (5:4), which incorrectly says that Gregory was a negro. See also: 1900 U.S. Census (Dunklin Co., MO), which notes his correct race. Appeal: 59 SW 89–92.

Ellsworth Evans (black, age 18). *Murder.* The crime was committed on 3/26/1900 in Cooper County. Police killer. Handgun slaying of 40+ year old William L. Hennicke (white). Motive: resisting arrest. Exit Ellsworth Evans at the hands of the law at Boonville, MO on April 12, 1901. Source: *Des Moines (IA) Daily Capital*, 4/12/01 (1:1). Appeal: 61 SW 590–593. See also: 1900 U.S. Census (Cooper Co., MO), which notes this offender.

Ernest Reed (black, age not recorded). *Murder.* The crime was committed on 6/19/1900 in Jasper County. Uxoricide. Handgun slaying of 27-year-old Amanda Gertrude Reed (black). Motive: marital estrangement. This homicidal husband was hanged pursuant to law at Carthage, MO on July 5, 1901. Source: *Carthage (MO) Press*, 7/5/01 (1:1). *St. Louis Republic*, 7/6/01 (12:3). Appeal: 62 SW 982–984. See also: 1900 U.S. Census (Jasper Co., MO), which notes the murdered woman three days before she died.

1902

Joshua L. Craft (white, age 25). *Murder.* The crime was committed on 12/9/1899 in Cole County. Police killer. Rifle slaying of about 25-year-old Henry Spieker (white). Motive: resisting arrest. Craft was a convicted train robber who had escaped from the Missouri State Prison. Spieker had been specially deputized to hunt him down. Craft was subsequently hanged at Jefferson City on January 21, 1902. Source: *St. Paul (MN) Globe*, 12/10/99 (1:2). *St. Louis Post-Dispatch*, 1/21/02 (2:5). *Kansas City Journal*, 1/22/02 (2:4). Appeal: 65 SW 280–285. See also: 1900 U.S. Census (Cole Co., MO), which notes Craft.

Albert Garth (black, age 29). *Murder.* The crime was committed on 12/22/1899 in Jackson County. Fatal beating and stabbing of Minnie Woods (black, age not recorded). Motive: adultery turned deadly. This black-on-black woman-killer was hanged at Kansas City on January 21, 1902. Source: *Kansas City Star*, 12/23/99 (2:7). *Kansas City Journal*, 1/22/02 (3:3). Appeal: 65 SW 275–278. See also: 1900 U.S. Census (Jackson Co., MO), which notes Garth.

Henry Flutcher (black, age 26). *Murder.* The crime was committed on

8/27/1900 at St. Louis. Handgun slaying of 24-year-old Louis Roth (white). Motive: racial animosity. The killer's reward for this was death on the gallows. He collected that reward at the St. Louis City Jail on April 11, 1902. Source: *St. Louis Post-Dispatch*, 4/11/02 (1:5). Appeal: 66 SW 429–435. See also: *City of St. Louis Deaths Register*, 1900, no. 6754, and 1902, no. 3248.

James Jackson (black, age 26). *Murder.* The crime was committed on 12/22/1900 in Jackson County. Handgun slaying of 24-year-old Prophet Everett (black), the victim having been shot in the back. Motive: gambling dispute. A trial court taking a dim view of this, the shooter was ordered for execution. The hangman tendered him his services at Independence, MO on April 11, 1902. Source: *Kansas City Star*, 4/11/02 (1:1). *St. Louis Post-Dispatch*, 4/11/02 (3:6). Appeal: 66 SW 938–940.

General Armstrong (black, age 16). *Rape.* The crime was committed on 7/12/1900 in Clinton County. Indecent assault on the person of 16-year-old Ivy Turney (white), she having been knocked unconscious during an act of highway robbery and found (upon awakening) to have been sexually violated as well. Venue changed from Clinton County to Platte County. The precocious culprit was legally hanged for this outrage at Platte City on April 25, 1902. Source: Harriet C. Frazier, *Death Sentences in Missouri, 1803–2005* (Jefferson, NC: McFarland, 2006), 126–128, for a well researched but subjectively written account of this case.

Charles Reeves (black, age 28). *Murder.* The crime was committed on 2/24/1902 in Cooper County. Uxoricide. Handgun slaying of 22-year-old Mamie Smith Reeves (black). Motive: marital estrangement. It was the same old story: spousal abuse leads to separation, whereupon the "lord and master" resorts to violence. The hangman paid Reeves for his act of husbandly hubris at Booneville, MO on May 23, 1902. Source: *Missouri Democrat* (Booneville, MO), 5/23/02 (1:1). See also: *Cooper County Marriage Licenses*, 1900, 291. Also: 1900 U.S. Census (Cooper Co., MO), which notes both parties, the homicide victim by her maiden name.

Samuel Brown (white, age 29). *Murder.* The crime was committed on 3/20/1900 in Wayne County. Rifle slaying of George T. Richardson, age 50+ (white), and destruction of his body by fire. Motive: robbery. This killer was hanged at Greenville, MO on June 27, 1902. Source: *St. Louis Republic*, 5/14/02 (7:4) & 6/28/02 (6:5).

Jesse Johnson (black, age 24). *Murder.* The crime was committed on 4/28/1902 in Ralls County. Executed for the murder of 71-year-old Marcus D. McRae (white), who had been bludgeoned with a wooden wagon standard. Motive: robbery. A predator by any description, Jesse Johnson was hanged at New London, MO on September 12, 1902. Source: *St. Louis Republic*, 5/2/02 (14:3) & 5/11/02 (7:1). *Ralls County Times*, 9/12/02 (1:1). See also: 1850 U.S. Census (Marion Co., MO), which notes McRae as a young man.

1903

Thomas Dunn (black, age 27). *Murder.* The crime was committed on

10/29/1900 at St. Louis. Handgun slaying of 45-year-old Peter Jackson (black). Motive: an argument about a petty debt. This killer paid a much higher debt (to society) when he was swung from the gallows at the St. Louis City Jail on January 2, 1903. Source: *St. Louis Post-Dispatch*, 1/2/03 (1:1). Appeal: 70 SW 118–121. See also: *City of St. Louis Deaths Register*, 1900, no. 8218, and 1903, no. 77.

Charles Gurley (black, age 26). *Murder.* The crime was committed on 4/29/1901 at St. Louis. Fatal stabbing of 20-year-old Rosa Higgins (black). Motive: lovers' quarrel. This stabber made his last stand on the gallows platform at the St. Louis City Jail on February 3, 1903. Source: *St. Louis Post-Dispatch*, 2/3/03 (8:2). See also: *City of St. Louis Deaths Register*, 1901, no. 3558, and 1903, no. 1053.

Steven Clark (white, age 36). *Murder.* The crime was committed on 6/25/1901 in Butler County. Fatal stabbing of 26-year-old "Pearl Clark" (white), a known prostitute who was purported to be his wife. Motive: angry pimp. Attainted as a man of surpassingly bad character, Steven Clark was hanged at Poplar Bluff on February 6, 1903. Source: *Daily Republic* (Poplar Bluff, MO), 2/6/03 (1:1). See also: 1900 U.S. Census (Poplar Bluff, MO), which notes the homicide victim by her pseudonym.

William Gatlin (black, age 24). *Murder.* The crime was committed on 9/19/1901 in Butler County. Handgun slaying of 39-year-old Thomas Graham (black), who was shot in his own doorway. Motive: rivalry for a female. An equally guilty co-defendant named Zebulon Crite (black, age 19) killed himself in his death row cell by eating lye soap. Crite's self-imposed end was far more agonizing than that suffered by William Gatlin, who was hanged at Poplar Bluff on February 6, 1903. Source: *Daily Republic* (Poplar Bluff, MO), 2/6/03 (1:1). See also: 1900 U.S. Census (Poplar Bluff, MO), which notes Thomas Graham.

James L. Gartrell (white, age 58). *Murder.* The crime was committed on 3/25/1901 in Bates County. Executed for the ax murder of a wayfaring black man known only as "D. B. Donegan" (age not recorded), the victim's mangled body having also been wrapped in oilcloth and dumped into a creek. Motive: robbery and chicanery. Several details of this case were consistently misstated by the news media. First, Gartrell was at least ten years younger than reported. Secondly, his credentials as a physician were dubious despite being called "Doctor" by almost every newspaper account. Third, the homicide victim's Irish surname led hasty reporters to assume that he was a white man. Fourth, the date of the crime was repeatedly confused with the date on which the two men met. Fine points such as these became moot to Gartrell when he was hanged at Butler, MO on April 17, 1903. Source: *Cedar Rapids (IA) Republican*, 5/1/01 (1:4) which calls Donegan "the colored miner" lately come from Victor, Colorado. Also: *Daily News* (Marshall, MI), 5/1/01 (1:1). *St. Louis Post-Dispatch*, 4/17/03 (3:2). See also: 1900 U.S. Census (Kansas City, MO), which notes Gartrell as a hospital patient. Also: 1880 U.S. Census (Victoria, TX), which notes "J. L. Gartrell" as a married farmer with seven kids including the son (William) who was arrested with him 21 years later. Gartrell is confirmed to have come from that place.

Charles May (white, age 25). *Murder.* The crime was committed on 12/27/1900 in Buchanan County. Executed for the handgun slaying of 31-year-old Robert Martin (white). Motive: fracas in a dance hall. Recidivist killer. This same Charles May had previously been sentenced to death for an unrelated homicide. It had occurred at Rushville (Buchanan Co., MO), on 2/9/1896 following a church service. May and his uncle (George May) had picked a fight with a churchgoer named William J. Burdette against whom they held a grudge. The latter wound up fatally bludgeoned by a fence rail. Both of the Mays were convicted at trial and sentenced to be hanged. The verdict was subsequently reduced on appeal. George May was re-sentenced to 10 years in prison and Charles May to 2 years. The latter served his reduced term and was then set loose to kill again. He did not wriggle free the second time. The hangman saw to that at St. Joseph, MO on April 17, 1903. Source: *Kansas City Daily Journal,* 11/24/96 (1:2) & 12/12/96 (1:4). *Kansas City Star,* 4/17/03 (7:1). *St. Louis Post-Dispatch,* 4/17/03 (3:2). *St. Louis Republic,* 12/29/00 (Sec. 2) (2:2). See also: 1880 U.S. Census (Buchanan Co., MO), which notes the Mays, and 1900 U.S. Census (Buchanan Co., MO), which notes Martin.

John Taylor (white, age 26). *Murder.* The crime was committed on 3/2/1901 in Jackson County. Sniper killing of 18-year-old Ruth Nollard (white). Motive: adultery-turned-deadly. Taylor paid the price for what he had gotten himself into when he was hanged at Kansas City on April 17, 1903. Source: *Kansas City Journal,* 4/18/03 (3:3). *St. Louis Post-Dispatch,* 4/17/03 (3:2). Appeal: 71 SW 1005–1007. See also: 1900 U.S. Census (Kansas City, MO), which notes the homicide victim and her correct surname.

Sampson Gray (black, age 21). *Murder.* The crime was committed on 6/9/1901 at St. Louis. Handgun slaying of 34-year-old George Jones (black). Motive: mugging. This black-on-black predator was made to undergo the penalty of death by hanging at the St. Louis City Jail on May 8, 1903. Source: *St. Louis Post-Dispatch,* 5/8/03 (2:3). Appeal: 72 SW 698–701. See also: *City of St. Louis Burial Permits,* 1901, no. 4681, and 1903, no. 4151.

Henry Wilson (black, age 20). *Murder.* The crime was committed on 6/23/1900 at St. Louis. Handgun slaying of 63-year-old Thomas Mooney (white). Motive: armed robbery. Wilson was a thuggish young hoodlum in every respect. His criminal career and his life were both cut short on May 8, 1903, when the hangman's rope pulled tight around his neck at the St. Louis City Jail. Source: *St. Louis Republic,* 5/8/03 (2:2). Appeal: 72 SW 696–698. See also: *City of St. Louis Deaths Register,* 1900, no. 4938, and 1903, no. 4150.

Frank Clark (black, age 22). *Rape.* The crime was committed on 7/25/1903 in Clark County. Indecent assault on the person of 16-year-old Olla Hess (white), she having been accosted on a public road and mistreated in the basest of ways. Her attacker was legally hanged at Kahoka, MO on November 25, 1903. Source: *Kahoka (MO) Weekly Review,* 7/29/03 (3:4), 10/7/03 (3:3), 10/14/03 (1:1), 10/21/03 (1:1) & 11/25/03 (3:3). See also: 1900 U.S. Census (Clark Co., MO), which notes Miss Hess.

1904

John H. Robinson (white, age 40). *Murder.* The crime was committed on 11/13/1902 in Adair County. Handgun slaying of 58-year-old George W. Conkle (white, his father-in-law), who was shot three times. Motive: because the older man had refused to co-sign for a loan. The killer was hanged at Kirksville, MO on January 15, 1904. Source: *St. Louis Republic,* 11/14/02 (4:2). *St. Louis Post-Dispatch,* 1/15/04 (1:1). See also: 1900 U.S. Census (Salt River, Adair Co., MO), which notes both parties, the gunman as "J. H. Robinson."

Mark Dunn (white, age 36). *Murder.* The crime was committed on 7/20/1902 in Buchanan County. Shotgun slaying of 25-year-old Alfred M. Fenton (white), the victim having had his guts blown out as he drove his buggy along a public street. Motive: personal grudge. Dunn died gurgling in a hangman's noose at St. Joseph, MO on March 11, 1904. Source: *Salt Lake Herald* (Utah), 7/22/02 (1:6). *St. Louis Post-Dispatch,* 3/11/04 (2:3). Appeal: 77 SW 848–850. See also: 1900 U.S. Census (Buchanan Co., MO), which notes both parties.

George Collins (white, age 23). *Murder.* The crime was committed on 1/24/1903 in Franklin County. Handgun slaying of 35-year-old Charles J. Schumacher (white, a Pinkerton detective), who was shot five times while on the trail of two bank robbers. Motive: resisting arrest. A *danse macabre* at the end of a hangman's rope was the last earthly act of George Collins at Union, MO on March 26, 1904. Source: *St. Louis Republic,* 1/25/03 (1:6), 1/26/03 (1:2), 3/27/04 (1:5). *St. Louis Post-Dispatch,* 3/26/04 (1:6). See also: City of St. Louis Burial Permit (1903) dated 1/26/03, which released Schumacher's corpse for shipment to Chicago. See also: William Randolph (executed 5/8/05).

1905

Elias Smith (white, age 40). *Murder.* The crime was committed on 11/7/1904 in Pulaski County. Executed for the murder of 25-year-old James H. Smith (white), the victim having been bludgeoned with a crowbar and his body dumped in a ravine where it was set ablaze with a flammable liquid. Motive: robbery and gross perfidy. Elias Smith was hanged by the neck until dead at Waynesville, MO on April 21, 1905. Source: *St. Louis Republic,* 11/11/04 (8:7). *St. Louis Post-Dispatch,* 4/21/05 (13:4). See also: 1900 U.S. Census (Pulaski Co., MO), which notes the killer, and 1900 U.S. Census (Atchison Co., MO), which notes the murdered man.

William Rudolph (white, age 20). *Murder.* The crime was committed on 1/24/1903 in Franklin County. Accomplice in the handgun slaying of 35-year-old Charles J. Schumacher (white, a Pinkerton detective), who was shot five times while on the trail of two bank robbers. Motive: resisting arrest. The gallows claimed this young offender at Union, MO on May 8, 1905. Source: *St. Louis Post-Dispatch,* 5/8/05 (1:6). See also: George Collins (executed 3/26/04). See also: City of St. Louis burial permit dated 5/9/05, which notes Calvary Cemetery as Rudolph's last abode.

Allen Henderson (black, age 17). *Murder.* The crime was committed on

4/12/1903 in St. Charles County. Executed for the murder of 58-year-old Joseph Buckner (black), who was blasted by a shotgun and had his house burned down around him. Two co-defendants (including the catalyst) died in prison before the case came to trial. Motive: vendetta. The person who had put Henderson up to the deed had blamed the victim for wrecking his marriage. Four black males died in this racially internecine squabble. The last to go was Allen Henderson when he walked to the gallows at St. Charles, MO on June 15, 1905. Source: *St. Louis Republic*, 6/16/05 (16:2). Appeal: 85 SW 576–584, See also: 1900 U.S. Census (St. Charles, MO), which notes both parties along with the fact that Henderson was born in May 1885.

Henry Heusack (white, age 55). *Murder.* The crime was committed on 3/16/1904 in St. Louis. Hatchet killing of 75-year-old August Raphael (white), his father-in-law. Motive: a drunkard's folly. Heusack had become enraged when his wife would not give him money to squander on liquor. He presumed that her authoritarian father had something to do with this and so re-focused his anger on that gentleman. Note: Heusack also bears responsibility (to at least some extent) for the subsequent death of his mother-in-law (Julia A. Raphael, white, age 83), who succumbed on 6/28/1904 because she was unable to bear the strain of what had happened. A long drop from the gallows put an end to Heusack's lament at the St. Louis City Jail on August 21, 1905. Source: *St. Louis Republic*, 3/17/04 (2:2), 8/21/05 (1:4) & 8/22/05 (5:2). Appeal: 88 SW 21–25. See also: 1904 City of St. Louis burial permit nos. 2703 and 6061, plus 1905 burial permit no. 5064.

1906

Curtis Jackson (black, age 16). *Rape.* The crime was committed on 2/2/1906 in Butler County. Indecent assault on the person of 28-year-old Annie Norman (white), she having been accosted at knifepoint and choked into unconsciousness next to a pool of putrid swill water. Jackson was a precocious pervert. No stretch of the imagination could substantiate a theoretical defense that he had been enticed by a manipulative older woman. He was executed without the benefit of appeal at Poplar Bluff on March 23, 1906. Source: *St. Louis Post-Dispatch*, 3/23/06 (1:3). *Poplar Bluff (MO) Citizen*, 2/8/06 (1:1), 2/22/06 (1:1) & 3/22/06 (1:1). *Alton (IL) Evening Telegraph*, 2/5/06 (3:3). *Kansas City Star*, 2/4/06 (13:5). See also: 1910 U.S. Census (Craighead Co., AR), which notes Annie Norman and her later whereabouts.

Edward Bateman (black, age 22). *Rape.* The crime was committed on 3/1/1905 in Lawrence County. Indecent assault on the person of 20-year-old Myrtle Digby (white). Further details about this case are elusive but they were deemed to be of such a nature as to make the act a capital felony. An appeals court concurred. As a result, this sex offender was legally hanged at Mt. Vernon, MO on August 7, 1906. Source: *Lawrence Chiefton* (Mt. Vernon, MO), 8/9/06 (8:1). Appeal: 94 SW 843–846.

Joda Hamilton (white, age 20). *Murder.* The crime was committed on 10/12/1906 in Texas County. Mass killer, child killer, and baby killer. Executed for the massacre of 31-year-old Carney L. Parsons and 22-year-old

Minnie Strange Parsons (whites, a married couple) along with their three small children: Jesse (age 6), Frank (age 3) and Edward (age 1). The man and woman were initially blasted by a shotgun. Then their heads were smashed with the butt of that weapon. The little ones all had their throats cut (from ear to ear) by means of a pocket knife before being similarly bludgeoned with the gun butt. Their bodies were thrown into a nearby river where fishermen later found them. Motive: because the killer suspected that Mr. Parsons had purloined a saddle. This aggrieved saddle owner who had so obstreperously overreacted to the loss of his property was hanged at Houston, MO on December 21, 1906. Source: *Licking (MO) News*, 10/18/06 (1:1). *St. Louis Post-Dispatch*, 12/21/06 (2:1). See also: *Miller County (MO) Marriage Licenses*, 1899, 534. Also: 1900 U.S. Census (Benton Co., MO), which notes Parsons and wife. *Front Page Detective*, 1/45. *Official Detective*, 9/46.

1907

William E. Church (white, age 21). *Murder.* The crime was committed on 8/31/1903 in Warren County. Executed for the simultaneous killings of 66-year-old Henry W. Yeater and 59-year-old Nettie Yeater (whites, his foster parents), they having been murdered in their beds, each slashed to death with a razor. Motive: speculative. Church said that the Yeaters had disinherited him. Other evidence suggests that the real reason was because they had caught him masturbating. Whatever the truth, this double murderer was hanged at Warrenton, MO on January 10, 1907. Source: *St. Louis Post-Dispatch*, 1/10/07 (13:4). Appeal: 98 SW 16–20. See also: 1900 U.S. Census (Warren Co., MO), which notes the Yeaters.

John King (black, age 19). *Murder.* The crime was committed on 11/28/1905 at St. Louis. Handgun slaying of 20-year-old Hallie Douglas (black), who was shot multiple times. Motive: lovers' quarrel. This passionate young fellow found that it was too late for recriminations when he was hanged at the St. Louis City Jail on June 27, 1907. Source: *St. Louis Post-Dispatch*, 6/27/07 (3:2). *St. Louis Globe-Democrat*, 6/27/07 (4:3). Appeal: 102 SW 315–318.

Edward Raymond (white, age 23), **George Ryan** (white, age 24) and **Harry S. Vaughn** (white, age 33). *Murder.* Their crime was committed on 11/24/1905 in Cole County. Prison-guard killers. Executed for the handgun slayings of 69-year-old Ephraim Allison and 46-year-old John A. Clay (whites). Motive: sensational jailbreak involving smuggled guns and nitro. All three members of this truculent trio were hanged at Jefferson City on June 27, 1907. Source: *St. Louis Republic*, 11/25/05 (1:3), 11/26/05 (1:3). *St. Louis Post-Dispatch*, 6/27/07 (1:1). See also: 1900 U.S. Census (Cole Co., MO), which notes Allison and "J. A. Clay."

1908

William Jeffries (white, age 25). *Murder.* The crime was committed on 3/3/1905 in St. Charles County. Handgun slaying of 32-year-old William Wussler (white), the victim having been shot in the back. Motive: attempted robbery. The killer was swung from the gallows at St. Charles, MO on June 4, 1908. Source: *St. Louis Republic*, 3/4/05 (3:6). *St. Louis Post-*

Dispatch, 6/5/08 (1:1). See also: 1900 U.S. Census (St. Louis, MO), which notes Wussler, and 1908 City of St. Louis burial permit no. 740, which notes Jeffries.

Albert Filley (white, age 32). *Murder.* The crime was committed on 12/21/1907 in Caldwell County. Uxoricide, fratricide, and filicide. Executed for the killings of 28-year-old Fanny Riley Filley (his wife), 7-year-old Dolly Filley (his daughter) and 37-year-old Henry Clay Filley (his brother), whites. The females were battered to death with a hammer. The male homicide victim was shot with a handgun. Filley was executed at Kingston, MO, on September 21, 1908. Motive: probably deranged. Source: *Chillicothe (MO) Constitution*, 12/24/07 (3:6) & 9/21/08 (1:5). *Postville (IA) Review*, 12/27/07 (3:6). See also: 1880 U.S. Census (Caldwell Co., MO), which notes the Filley brothers as youngsters, plus 1900 U.S. Census (Caldwell Co., MO), which notes the killer and his family.

1909

Claude Brooks (black, age 21). *Murder.* The crime was committed on 1/12/1908 in Jackson County. Executed for the killing of 46-year-old Sidney Herndon (white), who had been battered to death with a hammer. Motive: robbery and overt perfidy. Brooks paid the penalty of death by hanging at Kansas City on July 30, 1909. Source: *Emporia (KS) Gazette*, 1/16/08 (1:4). *Kansas City Times*, 7/30/09 (1:1).

1910

George Reynolds (black, age 22) and **John Williams** (black, age 23). *Rape.* Their crime was committed on 12/23/1909 in Jackson County. Indecent assault on the person of 27-year-old Matilda Taylor Jackson (white), the details being too obscene for repetition. Both of these sexual predators were hanged at Kansas City on February 8, 1910. Source: *Iola (KS) Daily Register*, 1/4/10 (1:5), 1/5/10 (1:7) & 2/8/10 (1:5). See also: 1905 Jackson County marriage license no. 33558, which notes the female party.

William Wilson (black, age 24). *Murder.* The crime was committed on 7/12/1908 in Jasper County. Hanged for the purposeful killing of 25-year-old Millie Plumb (white), who was struck on the head with an unknown blunt instrument, raped and then dragged to a place of concealment by means of a rope around her neck. Motive: sexual assault. Wilson died with a rope around his own neck at Carthage, MO on March 4, 1910. Source: *Evening Press* (Carthage, MO), 3/4/10 (1:1). *St. Louis Post-Dispatch*, 3/4/10 (6:4). Appeal: 122 SW 671–675.

Robert Davis (black, age 22). *Murder.* The crime was committed on 11/14/1908 in Jackson County. Executed for the killing of 17-year-old Harry Evans (black), who had been bludgeoned with a rock. Motive: robbery and treachery. The hangman added this black-on-black assassin to his list at Kansas City on June 10, 1910. Source: *Kansas City Star*, 6/10/10 (1:1). Appeal: 126 SW 470–474.

George Albert Jackson (black, age abt. 18). *Rape.* The crime was committed on 10/28/1909 in Mississippi County. Indecent assault on the person of 60-year-old Isophrenia Henderson (white), she having been chased down and brutally beaten (as well as raped) in the yard of her own home. Her teenage (although brawny) attacker was legally hanged for this act of violence at Charleston, MO on June 10, 1910. Source: *Charleston (MO) Republican*, 4/7/10 (1:3) & 6/16/10 (1:1). See also: 1910 U.S. Census (Mississippi Co., MO), which notes the culprit as aged 16, versus his death certificate (no. 17282), which says that he was "abt. 19."

1912

Hezekiah Rasco (white, age 30). *Murder.* The crime was committed on 11/20/1910 in Nodaway County. Mass killer and child killer. Executed for the massacre of 29-year-old Oda Hubbell and 29-year-old Clara E. Hubbell (whites, a married couple), and their two young children: Jessie O. Hubbell (female, age 6) and Welton O. Hubbell (male, age 4). All were shot multiple times with a handgun (the children in their beds) and badly charred when the culprit fired their house. Motive: sore loser. Rasco had lost what he considered to be a substantial sum of money to Oda Hubbell in a card game. Recidivist killer. On 10/10/1896 this same Hezekiah Rasco (then aged 16) had murdered a Nodaway County woman named Kate Baumley (white, age 36) by beating her on the head with a cast iron stove grate. Motive: sexual assault. He served 10 years in prison for that offense. Then he sweet-talked a parole board into giving him the chance to repeat his crime fourfold. The hangman ensured that there would be no further additions to Rasco's body count when he performed his official duty at Maryville, MO on March 26, 1912. Source: *St. Louis Post-Dispatch*, 11/21/10 (1:1), 11/22/10 (1:4), 3/26/12 (4:4). See also: 1910 U.S. Census (Nodaway Co., MO), which notes the Hubbells, and 1912 Nodaway Co. death cert. no. 10329, which notes Rasco. *Actual Detective*, 6/29/38.

1915

John Wesley Robinson (black, age 48). *Murder.* The crime was committed on 4/11/1913 and discovered on 5/17/1913 in Jackson County. Uxoricide and child killer. Executed for the manual strangulations and dismemberments of about 48-year-old Mary Felton Robinson and 11-year-old Alma Felton (blacks), they respectively being his wife and stepdaughter. The limbs of both victims were hacked off with a hatchet after death and burned in a stove. Their torsos and heads were buried separately. Recidivist killer. This same John Wesley Robinson had previously served 11 years in prison for strangling a young woman named Ella Jones (black, age abt. 25) at St. Louis, MO on 6/20/1896. Her putrefying corpse was found concealed beneath the floorboards of a den they shared at 1328 North 8th Street rear, St. Louis. Motive: in each case, brutish male jealousy. Onto the trap walked John Wesley Robinson at Kansas City on February 15, 1915. He was pronounced dead a few minutes later. Source: *St. Louis Republic*, 6/22/96 (3:3) & 6/24/96 (7:4). *Emporia (KS) Gazette*, 5/22/13 (1:1). *Kansas City Star*, 2/15/15 (3:2). Appeal: 172 SW 598–602. See also: 1910 U.S. Census (K.C., MO), which notes Robinson. Also see: *Jackson County Marriage Licenses*, 1911, 178, which notes his wedding on April 9 of that year. Also: 1913 Jackson Co. death cert. no. 16722.

William Sprouse (white, age abt. 40). *Murder.* The crime was committed on 10/31/1914 in St. Louis County.

Uxoricide. Executed for the killing of about 37-year-old Anna Sprouse (white), she having been lured from their home, beaten with leaden knuckles and then finished off with a hammer, her body left to rot in a farmer's field. Motive: adultery. Sprouse had left his six children at home that day, saying that their mother and he were going out for a while. He returned that evening with his paramour and had the nerve to tell his kids that they would thenceforth have a new mom. This did not go over very well with either the incredulous six or the law. Onto the gallows trap walked William Sprouse at Clayton, MO on July 16, 1915. Source: *Ogden (UT) Standard*, 3/6/15 (magazine section). *St. Louis Post-Dispatch*, 7/16/15 (1:4). See also: 1915 St. Louis Co. death cert. no. 22873.

1916

Andrew Black (black, age 23) and **Harry Black** (black, age 25). *Murder.* Their crime was committed on 12/6/1913 in St. Charles County. Police killers. Both hanged for the handgun slayings of 41-year-old John D. Blair and 41-year-old James David Lamb (whites). Motive: disorderly conduct and resisting arrest. A double execution brought this case to its finale at St. Charles, MO on August 18, 1916. Source: *St. Louis Post-Dispatch*, 12/7/13 (1:7) & 8/18/16 (1:6). See also: 1913 St. Chas. Co. death cert. nos. 40481 and 40482. Also: 1916 St. Chas. Co. death cert. nos. 28982 and 28983.

1920

Adam Jackson (black, age 39). *Rape.* The crime was committed on 2/9/1920 in Butler County. Indecent assault on the person of 45-year-old Emma Mann (white), a widowed woman. The details were tamped down by printed media as a means of forestalling civil unrest. The law took its course without further incident. Jackson was legally hanged for what he did at Poplar Bluff on March 26, 1920. Source: *Poplar Bluff (MO) Republican*, 4/1/20 (1:1). *St. Louis Post-Dispatch*, 3/27/20 (4:2). See also: 1920 U.S. Census (Butler Co., MO), which notes Mrs. Mann.

1921

Charles Jacoy (white, age 22). *Murder.* The crime was committed on 11/20/1920 in Franklin County. Handgun slaying of 24-year-old Benjamin Schobe (white), the victim having been shot in the back. Motive: dirty dealing. Schobe had responded to a distress call about a disabled automobile. Two of its tires were blown out. It was in fact a stolen vehicle bearing Jacoy and an accomplice. Schobe fixed the tires so that the car could resume its journey. However, when he asked payment for his services he got two bullets in the back instead of money. The gallows exacted its own kind of payment from Charles Jacoy at Union, MO on August 12, 1921. Source: *St. Louis Post-Dispatch*, 8/12/21 (1:3). See also: 1921 Franklin Co. death cert. no. 20306. See also: John W. Carroll (executed 9/12/21).

Walker Lee (black, age 37). *Rape.* The crime was committed on 6/28/1920 in Jackson County. Indecent assault on the person of 52-year-old Elizabeth Whete Dahmn (white), she having also been battered with a broken piece of fence rail. Sex offender Walker Lee was legally hanged for his obscene acts of violence at Kansas City on August 17, 1921. Source: *Independence (MO) Examiner,* 6/30/21 (1:4) & 8/17/21 (1:3). See also: 1920 U.S. Census (Jackson Co., MO), which notes Mrs. Dahmn, and 1921 Jackson Co. death cert. no. 20658, which notes the miscreant.

John W. Carroll (white, age 22). *Murder.* The crime was committed on 11/20/1920 in Franklin County. Accomplice in the handgun slaying of 24-year-old Benjamin Schobe (white), who was shot two times in the back. Motive: dirty dealing. Carroll met the same fate as his cohort at Union, MO on September 12, 1921. Source: *St. Louis Post-Dispatch,* 9/12/21 (1:4). Also: 1921 Franklin Co. death cert. no. 23086. See also: Charles Jacoy (executed 8/12/21).

1923

Sterling Jackson (black, age 21) and **Ralph Long**, alias "Casteel Stapleton" (black, age 19). *Murder.* Their crime was committed on 4/8/1922 in Jasper County. Both executed for the killing of 66-year-old George Babcock (white), the slain man having been assaulted in his place of business, held at knifepoint and then shot dead with a handgun. Motive: armed robbery. The perpetrators were hanged for this at Carthage, MO on August 3, 1923. Source: *St. Louis Post-Dispatch,* 8/3/23 (12:1). See also: 1922 Jasper Co. death cert. no. 12858 and 1923 Jasper Co. death cert. no. 24463 and 24465.

1924

Charles Merrell (white, age 21) and **Hugh Pinkley** (white, age 32). *Murder.* Their crime was committed on 4/22/1922 at St. Louis. Police killers. Handgun slayings of 44-year-old Michael O'Connor and 52-year-old Bernard C. Mengel (whites). Motive: armed robbery gone awry. Merrell and his accomplice also bear responsibility (at least in part) for the untimely death of police widow Lillie Linsenmann Mengel (white, age 49), who died of grief on 6/5/1923 because she was unable to bear the loss of her beloved husband. The gunmen were hanged by their necks until dead at the St. Louis City Jail on July 18, 1924. Source: *St. Louis Post-Dispatch,* 7/18/24 (1:1) & 7/19/24 (2:1). See also: 1922 City of St. Louis death cert. nos. 14311 and 14319. Also: 1923 cert. no. 19827 and 1924 death cert. nos. 21926 and 21927.

1925

James Crump (black, age abt. 25). *Murder.* The crime was committed on 2/10/1924 in Audrain County. Police killer. Handgun slaying of 54-year-old Chalmus Lee Blum (white). Motive: resisting arrest. Venue changed from Audrain County to Montgomery County. The culprit was hanged at Montgomery City, MO on July 17, 1925. Source: *Daily Constitution* (Chillicothe, MO), 2/12/24 (5:6). *Montgomery (MO) Standard,* 7/24/25 (1:1). See also: 1924 Audrain Co. death cert. no. 3480 and 1925 Montgomery Co. death cert. no. 21404.

Leon Williams (black, age abt. 25). *Murder.* The crime was committed on 12/30/1923 at St. Louis. Handgun slaying of 43-year-old Harry Leonard (white, a soda fountain proprietor), who was shot in the back. Motive: armed robbery. Leon Williams dropped to his own death from the gallows at the St. Louis City Jail on July 17, 1925. Source: *St. Louis Post-Dispatch*, 7/17/25 (1:1). See also: 1923 City of St. Louis death cert. no. 38448 and 1925 death cert. no. 22502.

1927

Robert Johnson (black, age 27). *Rape.* The crime was committed on 3/9/1926 in St. Louis County. Indecent assault on the person of 26-year-old Mabel L. Faenger (white), the details being reprehensible enough to sustain a capital verdict. The attacker was legally hanged at Clayton, MO on February 28, 1927. Source: *St. Louis Post-Dispatch*, 2/28/27 (1:1). See also: 1927 St. Louis Co. death cert. no. 5946. See also: *Social Security Death Index*, which notes that Mrs. Faenger was born on 12/24/1899 and died on 9/5/1992.

1929

Thomas E. Lowry (white, age 21). *Murder.* The crime was committed on 9/25/1926 at St. Louis. Police killer. Handgun slaying of 23-year-old Eugene N. Lovely (white). Motive: high-speed chase turned deadly. This young speedster-turned-murderer was hanged at the St. Louis City Jail on February 1, 1929. Source: *St. Louis Post-Dispatch*, 2/1/29 (1:8). See also: 1926 City of St. Louis death cert. no. 30339 and 1929 death cert. no. 7970. *Real Detective*, 1/53.

Leonard R. Yeager (white, age 29). *Murder.* The crime was committed on 11/17/1926 at St. Louis. Handgun slaying of 62-year-old Gunerius Schou (white). Motive: armed robbery gone awry. This condemned prisoner shared the same stage with the previous one at the St. Louis City Jail on February 1, 1929. Cause of death: legal hanging. Source: *St. Louis Post-Dispatch*, 2/1/29 (1:8). See also: 1926 City of St. Louis death cert. no. 36643 and 1929 death cert. no. 4841. *Crime Detective*, 6/47.

1930

Lawrence Mabry (white, age 17). *Murder.* The crime was committed on 2/4/1928 in Pettis County. Handgun slaying of 23-year-old William Busch (white). Motive: armed robbery. Venue changed from Pettis County to Cooper County. The young culprit was hanged at Boonville, MO on January 31, 1930. Source: *St. Louis Post-Dispatch*, 1/31/30 (3:4). See also: 1928 Pettis Co. death cert. no. 5894 and 1930 Cooper Co. death cert. no. 610, which notes that Mabry was four days shy of his 18th birthday when he gunned down Mr. Busch.

William Mosley (black, age abt. 52). *Murder.* The crime was committed on 9/10/1927 at St. Louis. Executed for the murders of about 32-year-old Mildred White (a black woman who was the mother of his four bastard children) and a married caucasian couple named Marcus Bass (age abt. 53) and Beckey Bass (age 44), who owned a neighborhood grocery store. Mildred White (who was holding a baby in her arms at the time) was shot with a handgun and stabbed 13 times with a butcher knife. The grocers (Mr. & Mrs. Bass) were shot dead when they tried to dissuade Mosley from attacking Mildred White. Motive: irrational male jealousy. The fact that Mildred White had dallied too long at the Bass grocery store filled Mosley's mind with morbid suspicions. So he hunted the woman down and killed her. Likewise the store owners, when they tried to reason with him. This brutish man was hanged at the St. Louis City Jail on January 31, 1930. Source: *St. Louis Post-Dispatch*, 1/31/30 (1:3). See also: City of St. Louis death cert. 1927 nos. 28650, 28657 and 28535, plus 1930 cert. no. 3537.

John Messino (white, age 27), **Antonio Mangiaracina** (white, age 28) and **Carlo Nasello** (white, age 20). *Murder.* Their crime was committed on 6/14/1928 in Jackson County. Police killers and urban terrorists. All three executed for the shotgun slaying of 38-year-old James Horace Smith (white). Motive: spectacular bank robbery. These offenders belonged to a six-man gang that brazenly attacked a downtown Kansas City financial institution while the Republican National Convention was in session close by. They sprayed the interior of the bank with machine-gun fire and also shot up the street outside to more effectively terrify would-be onlookers. The police officer was cut down by buckshot when he ran to the scene of the commotion. Three nooses awaited the three gang members, who were subsequently apprehended. They were hanged side by side at Kansas City on July 25, 1930. Source: *Kansas City Star*, 7/25/30 (12:1). *St. Louis Post-Dispatch*, 7/25/30 (1:4). See also: 1928 Jackson Co. death cert. no. 20749 plus 1930 death cert. nos. 23092, 23095 and 23104. *Detective Tabloid*, 2/35 & 3/35. *Master Detective*, 11/29 & 2/31.

1932

Joseph Hershon (white, age 24). *Murder.* The crime was committed on 12/2/1929 in Jackson County. Police killer. Handgun slaying of 28-year-old Charles H. Dingman Jr. (white). Motive: armed robbery gone awry. Hershon was hanged at Kansas City on January 15, 1932. Source: *Kansas City Star*, 1/15/32 (1:8). *St. Louis Post-Dispatch*, 1/15/32 (Section C), (4:5). See also: 1929 Jackson Co. death cert. no. 40565. *Master Detective*, 12/34.

Lew Edward Worden (white, age 33). *Rape.* The crime was committed on 11/15/1931 in Jasper County. Executed for robbing and sexually forcing himself on a 16-year-old white female (name withheld) during the course of a crime spree. Worden and two accomplices specifically targeted teenage couples whom they found parked in secluded areas. Six such pairs are known to have been attacked by these hooligans all on the same evening. Three of the female victims were sexually assaulted, picked clean of valuables, beaten up and otherwise mistreated. Their boyfriends were also beaten and robbed. The names of the male victims were: Norman Parks, George Mimms, Don Davis, Paul Gudgen, Arthur Poundstone, Henry Black and Thomas Wills. The names of the female victims were never made public, although two of them were reportedly aged 15. Marauder number one (Lew Worden) was hanged at Carthage, MO on March 3, 1932. Source: *Joplin (MO) Globe*, 11/28/31 (2:1), 12/8/31 (3:2), 12/9/31 (7:1), 1/27/32 (1:8), 3/3/32 (1:7) & 3/4/32 (1:1). *Front Page Detective*, 6/41. See also: Harry E. Worden (executed 2/10/33).

Emerson White (black, age 29). *Murder.* The crime was committed on 1/1/1930 at St. Louis. Hatchet killing of about 55-year-old Pinckney Hollis (black). Motive: robbery. The killer made off with the decedent's clothes (which he was caught wearing) and a cheap watch that he pawned for a dollar. This hatchet man who had literally stripped the bloodstained garments from the corpse of his victim and then donned them himself was hanged at the St. Louis City Jail on August 12, 1932. Source: *St. Louis Post-Dispatch*, 8/12/32 (3:5). See also: 1930 City of St. Louis death cert. no. 2980 and (1932) death cert. no. 27631.

1933

James W. Kellar, alias "Charles Campbell" (white, age 29). *Murder*. The crime was committed on 1/4/1932 in St. Louis County. Executed for the killing of 44-year-old Etta Wayman Sauer (white), she having been battered to death in her own home by means of an iron pipe. Motive: disgruntled employee and robbery. Kellar had worked for the woman's husband. He either quit or was fired from his job four days prior to the crime. The times being desperate, he showed up at the Sauer home on the above date demanding severance pay. Displeased with the answer he received, Kellar then murdered the lady of the house and stole money from her pocketbook. He was hanged at Clayton, MO on January 20, 1933. Source: *St. Louis Post-Dispatch*, 1/20/33 (1:1). See also: 1932 St. Louis Co. death cert. no. 2245 and (1933) cert. no. 3073. *Master Detective*, 9/33. *Dynamic Detective*, 6/40. *Crime Detective*, 1/49.

David Andrew Miller (white, age 44). *Murder.* The crime was committed on 8/22/1929 in St. Charles County. Handgun slaying of 47-year-old Paulina Duebbert (white), a maiden woman. Motive: robbery and home invasion. Miller was marched to the gallows for this at St. Charles, MO on February 10, 1933. He did not survive the ordeal. Source: *Joplin (MO) Globe*, 8/24/29 (9:6). *St. Louis Post-Dispatch*, 2/10/33 (1:4). See also: 1929 St. Chas. Co. death cert. no. 28686 and 1933 death cert. no. 6963. *Daring Detective*, 8/38. *Crime Detective*, 4/47.

Harry E. Worden (white, age 26). *Rape.* The crime was committed on 1/15/1931 in Jasper County. Executed for indecently assaulting a 15-year-old white female (name withheld) during the course of a crime spree in which seven young men were robbed and at least three of their female companions raped. He was hanged at Carthage, MO on February 10, 1933. Source: *St. Louis Post-Dispatch*, 2/10/33 (sec. 3) (1:4). See also: Lew Edward Worden (executed 3/3/32).

John Winston Boyd (black, age 32). *Rape.* The crime was committed on 8/11/1933 in St. Louis County. Serial Rapist. Specifically executed for the rape and robbery of a "young" white female who was attacked in her home on the aforesaid date. He also confessed to having forced himself on no less than 18 other women throughout the suburban St. Louis area from May to August 1933. Four of these were of his own color. The others were white. It all added up to a death sentence for John Winston Boyd. The public hangman did his duty in this case at Clayton, MO on November 2, 1933. Source: *St. Louis Post Dispatch*, 11/2/33 (1:1).

Samuel Gordon (black, age 21) and **March Jefferson** (black, age 27). *Murder.* Their crime was committed on 6/26/1931 in Jackson County. Both executed for the killing of 59-year-old Morris Kross (white, a grocer), who was beaten on the head with a heavy gas pipe. Motive: robbery. These men also bore responsibility for the untimely death of Mrs. Celia Kross (white, age 60), who reportedly succumbed to the deleterious effects of a nervous breakdown later that summer, she having been the slain man's devoted spouse. Thugs by any description, the above-named duo suffered death by hanging at Kansas City on December 15, 1933. Source: *Kansas City Star*, 12/15/33 (1:3). Appeal: 64 SW (2nd) 929–932. See also: 1931 Jackson Co. death cert. no. 24923.

1934

Eugene Copeland (black, age 32). *Murder.* The crime was committed on 6/1/1931 at St. Louis. Handgun slaying of 45-year-old Jacob P. Davis (white). Motive: armed robbery gone awry. The end for this killer came at the St. Louis City Jail on June 29, 1934, when he was hanged by the neck until dead. Source: *St. Louis Post-Dispatch*, 6/29/34 (1:1). *Kansas City Star*, 6/29/34 (2:1). Appeal: 71 SW (2nd) 746–750. See also: 1931 City of St. Louis death cert. no. 22786.

Paul H. Kauffman (white, age 32). *Murder.* The crime was committed on 8/17/1930 in Jackson County. Executed for the killing of 17-year-old Avis Woolery (white), she having been lured to a rendezvous under false pretenses, strangled, stripped and buried in a shallow grave. Motive: sexual assault. An extensive investigation finally led to Kauffman. He was hanged at Kansas City on June 29, 1934. Source: *Kansas City Star*, 10/15/30 (1:6) & 6/29/34 (1:7). *Intimate Detective*, 1/42. *Official Detective*, 5/35. *Front Page Detective*, 9/53. *Dynamic Detective*, 3/37. *Master Detective*, 6/31 & 12/54. *Real Detective*, 11/34 & 11/38.

1935

Frank McDaniel (black, age 28). *Murder.* The crime was committed on 3/28/1933 in Greene County. Handgun slaying of 25-year-old Savilla Scott (black), she having been shot five times. Motive: love affair gone bad. McDaniel paid the death penalty for this when he was hanged at Springfield, MO on April 12, 1935. Source: *Springfield (MO) Leader & Press*, 4/12/35 (1:8). *St. Louis Post-Dispatch*, 4/12/35 (1:7). Appeal: 80 SW (2nd) 185–189. See also: 1930 U.S. Census (Greene Co., MO), which notes both parties.

William A. Roland (black, age 42). *Murder.* The crime was committed on 4/17/1934 in Gasconade County. Police killer. Handgun slayings of 28-year-old Edwin C. Shane and 42-year-old John W. Whitted (whites), two railroad detectives. Motive: boxcar break in gone awry. Recidivist killer. Roland had formerly been a cavalryman in a black military unit (they then being racially segregated) along the Mexican border. He faced a court-martial for murdering two Mexicans with malice aforethought at Columbus, NM, circa 1922 and was sentenced to a term of life imprisonment. Paroled from Leavenworth after only 10 years, Roland made use of his newly gained freedom to murder two more people. This four-time killer found a Missouri court to be less mushy than the military court. He was ordered for execution and hanged at Hermann, MO, on April 12, 1935. Source: *Daily Capitol News* (Jefferson City, MO), 5/16/34 (1:2). *St. Louis Post-Dispatch*, 4/12/35 (Sec. C), (6:4). See also: 1930 U.S. Census (Fort Leavenworth, KS), which notes Roland, and 1930 U.S. Census (Jackson Co., MO), which notes Shane.

C. D. Ward (black, age 21). *Rape.* The crime was committed on 5/28/1933 in Dunklin County. Executed for terrorizing and indecently assaulting two white females (sisters, aged about 25 and 27) as they walked home from church, names withheld. The public hangman rid society of this menace at Kennett, MO on August 16, 1935. Source: *St. Louis Post-Dispatch,* 8/16/35 (4:1). Appeal: 85 SW (2nd) 1–8. See also: 1920 U.S. Census (Phillips Co., AR), which notes the culprit as a child but without specifying his first name, assuming that he ever had one in the first place.

Edward Gayman, alias "Dave Eddy" (white, age 42) and **Roy Eldon Hamilton** (white, age 24). *Murder.* Their crime was committed on 12/24/1933 in New Madrid County. Handgun slaying of 28-year-old Arthur Cashion (white). Motive: armed robbery. These Christmas Eve killers were hanged at New Madrid on August 30, 1935. Source: *Jefferson City (MO) Post-Tribune,* 1/5/34 (7:6) & 1/16/34 (6:1). *St. Louis Post-Dispatch,* 8/30/35 (1:4). See also: 1930 U.S. Census (New Madrid Co., MO), which notes Mr. Cashion. *Official Detective,* 1/40. *Master Detective,* 11/43.

1936

George McKeever (white, age 31). *Murder.* The crime was committed on 6/14/1933 in Boone County. Police killer. Handgun slayings of 35-year-old Ben B. Booth and 42-year-old Roger I. Wilson (whites). Motive: traffic stop turned deadly. Venue changed from Boone County to Callaway County. Note another job for the hangman at Fulton, MO on December 18, 1936. Source: *Jefferson City (MO) Post-Tribune,* 6/14/33 (1:8) & 6/15/33 (1:8). *St. Louis Post-Dispatch,* 12/18/36 (1:4). See also: 1920 U.S. Census (Lee Co., IA), which notes McKeever, and 1930 U.S. Census (Boone Co., MO), which notes the slain men. *Master Detective,* 5/39. *Dynamic Detective,* 10/39.

1937

Hurt Hardy Jr. (white, age 26). *Murder.* The crime was committed on 9/28/1935 in Ste. Genevieve County. Handgun slaying of 19-year-old Ethel Fahnestock (white), who was shot three times in the back. Motive: unreciprocated love. This smitten young man who could not take "no" for an answer was hanged for his transgression at Ste. Genevieve on February 26, 1937. Source: *Joplin (MO) Globe,* 9/29/35 (1:7). *St. Louis Post-Dispatch,* 2/26/37 (2:8). Appeal: 98 SW (2nd) 593–597. See also: 1930 U.S. Census (Ste. Genevieve Co., MO), which notes the homicide victim. *Daring Detective,* 3/36.

Fred Adams (white, age 19). *Murder.* The crime was committed on 3/28/1934 in Dunklin County. Police killer. Shotgun slaying of 25-year-old Clarence Andrew Green. Motive: armed robbery gone awry. Adams was accordingly sent through the gallows trap at Kennett, MO on April 2, 1937. Source: *Jefferson City (MO) Post-Tribune,* 3/29/34 (1:4). *St. Louis Post-Dispatch,* 4/2/37 (3:1). See also: 1920 U.S. Census (Dunklin Co., MO), which notes the homicide victim.

Dudley Barr, alias "Hard Face" (black, age 35). *Murder.* The crime was committed on 12/14/1932 in Jackson County. Handgun slaying of 40-year-old Walter Milton (black). Motive: armed robbery. The perpetrator was hanged at Kansas City on May 21, 1937. Source: *Kansas City Star*, 5/21/37 (1:3). Appeal: 102 SW (2nd) 629–632. See also: 1932 Jackson Co. death cert. no. 39926 and 1930 U.S. Census (K.C., MO), which notes the killer.

Roscoe Jackson (white, age 33). *Murder.* The crime was committed on 8/2/1934 in Taney County. Handgun slaying of 55-year-old Pearl L. Bozarth (white male). Motive: carjacking. Venue changed from Taney County to Stone County. Roscoe Jackson is also confirmed to have murdered another man named Albert Ocy Garrison (white, age 41) at Paul's Valley, OK, on 7/26/1934. He was hanged at Galena, MO, on May 21, 1937. Source: *Joplin (MO) Globe*, 8/9/34 (1:6). *St. Louis Post-Dispatch*, 5/21/37 (1:6). See also: 1930 U.S. Census (Evansville, IN), which notes Mr. Bozarth. *Dynamic Detective*, 8/38.

1938

John Brown (black, age 33). *Murder.* The crime was committed on 4/7/1936 in Jackson County. Police killer. Handgun slaying of 31-year-old William Cavanaugh (white). Motive: armed robbery gone awry. The penitentiary at Jefferson City having been by this year designated as the official place of execution for all condemned Missouri criminals, John Brown became one of the first to meet his end there at the hands of the State rather than the individual County. The gallows had also been replaced by what was then believed to be a more humane alternative: death by cyanide gas. The date was March 4, 1938. Source: *Moberly (MO) Monitor-Index*, 3/3/38 (7:1). *Jefferson City Post-Tribune*, 3/4/38 (1:6). Appeal: 112 SW (2nd) 568–571. See also: 1930 U.S. Census (K.C., MO), which notes Wm. Cavanaugh.

William Wright (black, age 27). *Murder.* The crime was committed on 3/15/1933 in Jackson County. Handgun slaying of 52-year-old John Thomas McCampbell (black), the proprietor of a pharmacy that served a predominantly non-white clientele. Motive: attempted armed robbery. The Missouri gas chamber became this killer's last port of call on March 4, 1938. Source: *Jefferson City Post-Tribune*, 3/4/38 (1:6). Appeals: 85 SW (2nd) 7–10 and 112 SW (2nd) 571–574. See also: 1930 U.S. Census (K.C., MO), which notes McCampbell.

Raymond Boyer (white, age 32). *Murder.* The crime was committed on 4/9/1936 in Jackson County. Handgun slaying of 29-year-old Walter Dale Sandford (white), who was shot three times in the head. Motive: carjacking and identity theft. Boyer was gassed on March 5, 1938. Source: *Moberly (MO) Monitor-Index*, 3/5/38 (1:7). *Iola (KS) Daily Register*, 4/11/36 (3:4). *Emporia (KS) Daily Gazette*, 6/4/36 (4:7). See also: 1920 U.S. Census (Wyandotte Co., KS), which notes Sandford.

Raymond Batson (black, age 33). *Murder.* The crime was committed on 12/28/1934 in St. Louis County. Handgun slayings of 43-year-old Philip Rabenau and 47-year-old William E. Poole (whites), the former having been shot four times in the back. Motive: irate litigant. The gas got Raymond Batson on June 30, 1938, in the manner prescribed by law. Source: *Joplin (MO) Globe*, 12/29/34 (2:1). *Jefferson City Post-Tribune*, 6/30/38 (1:4). See also: 1930 U.S. Census (St. Louis Co., MO), which notes Batson and Poole. Also:

1920 U.S. Census (St. Louis Co., MO), which notes Rabenau.

Johnny Jones (black, age 34). *Rape.* The crime was committed on 2/5/1938 in New Madrid County. Indecent assault on the person of a 45-year-old white female (name withheld) during the course of a home invasion. The victim's husband was overpowered and tied up by the armed intruder. Then he was made to watch his wife being ravished. The perpetrator of this outrage was gassed on July 15, 1938. Source: *New Madrid Weekly Record*, 2/11/38 (1:6). *Joplin (MO) News-Herald*, 7/15/38 (6:4).

Adam Richetti (white, age 32). *Murder.* The crime was committed on 6/17/1933 in Jackson County. Alleged police killer. Specifically executed for the machine-gun slaughter of 46-year-old Frank Hermanson (white) during the course of what was dubbed the *Kansas City Massacre*, one of the most notorious incidents of America in the 1930s. Five men were slain on that occasion when an underworld hit team opened fire on them in a public place in broad daylight. The other fatalities in addition to that of Frank Hermanson were those of: Raymond Caffrey (white, age 31), an FBI agent then on assignment; Otto H. Reed (white, age 49), the police chief of McAlester, OK; William J. Grooms (white, age 29), a Kansas City police officer as was his colleague Hermanson; and Frank Nash (white, age 46), a serial bank robber and prison escapee who was then being transported under guard. Motive: highly debatable. The most popular version of events holds that it was an attempted rescue of Nash from custody that went terribly awry. Another tempting possibility is that Nash was the intended target of assassins who feared that he might turn informer. The true extent (if any) of Richetti's involvement is speculative at best. The FBI claimed to have matched a shell casing found at the scene to a gun in the possession of big-name outlaw Charles Arthur "Pretty Boy" Floyd, a known associate of Richetti. This in turn caused lawmen to surmise that Floyd's entire gang (including Richetti) bore guilt for the Kansas City Massacre. The evidence against Richetti was flimsy—to say the least—but law enforcement authorities may or may not have been over-eager to assign blame. Richetti was chosen to bear the brunt of this because other members of the Floyd gang (including Floyd himself) had been hunted down and killed in the aftermath of the massacre. The entire case remains controversial to this day. The official FBI version of events (even after eight decades) is uncompromising in assigning blame to Floyd, Richetti and a third member of their clique named Verne Miller. Posthumous attempts to exonerate Richetti (and thereby discredit both the State of Missouri and the practice of capital punishment in general) have been suggestive but inconclusive. As for Adam Richetti himself, he was gassed on October 7, 1938. Source: *The Union Station Massacre: The Original Sin of J. Edgar Hoover's FBI*, by Robert Unger (K.C., MO: Andrews McMeel, 1997). Also: *Triple Crossfire! J. Edgar Hoover and the Kansas City Union Station Massacre*, by Larry R. Kirchner (K.C., MO: Janlar, 1993).

Granville Allen (black, age 24). *Murder.* The crime was committed on 10/20/1936 in Jackson County. Handgun slaying of 47-year-old Howard Preston (white). Motive: burglary gone awry. The Missouri gas chamber eradicated Granville Allen on October 28,

1938. Source: *Jefferson City Post-Tribune*, 10/20/36 (8:6). *Joplin (MO) News-Herald*, 10/28/38 (3:1).

Byron King (white, age 25). *Murder.* The crime was committed on 1/17/1936 at St. Louis. Handgun slaying of 68-year-old George Speer (white), a cabbie. Motive: armed robbery. Lethal fumes put an end to this killer's worldly existence on November 4, 1938. Source: *Sunday News & Tribune* (Jefferson City, MO), 1/19/36 (11:1). *St. Louis Post-Dispatch*, 11/4/38 (1:4). *Real Detective*, 7/48.

1939

John Flannery Williamson (white, age 48). *Murder.* The crime was committed on 8/10/1935 in Ste. Genevieve County. Shotgun slaying of 64-year-old George Williams (white), who was blasted from behind. Motive: robbery and despoilment. Recidivist killer. This same offender had previously served 22 years of a life sentence for an equally aggravated murder in Illinois. It happened that on 2/18/1913 he assassinated a Marion County farmer named Andrew J. Smothers (white, age 55) by shooting him in the back of the head. Then he assumed ownership of the slain man's property through means of forged papers purporting to show that he had bought the Smothers farm. Williamson dodged the gallows on that occasion by pleading guilty to an indictment for capital murder. He was then sent to the maximum security prison at Menard to serve what was supposed to be a life sentence. He got out after 22 years only to do the same thing all over again. The Missouri gas chamber ensured that there would be no third time on February 15, 1939. Source: *Joplin (MO) Globe*, 8/15/35 (10:1), 10/27/35 (1:4) & 2/15/39 (1:6). See also: 1930 U.S. Census (Randolph Co., IL), which notes Williamson as a convict. Also see the well-preserved gravestone of Andrew J. Smothers in Bell Cemetery, Iuka, IL.

Robert Kenyon (white, age 21). *Murder.* The crime was committed on 1/26/1937 in Howell County. Handgun slaying of 66-year-old James Clinton Davis (white), who was shot five times execution-style. Motive: kidnapping for ransom. Venue changed from Howell County to Oregon County. The killer was gassed on April 28, 1939. Source: *Joplin (MO) Globe*, 2/4/37 (1:8) & 4/28/39 (1:4). See also: 1910, 1920 and 1930 U.S. Censuses (Howell Co., MO), which note Davis. *Master Detective*, 2/38. *Official Detective*, 4/15/37.

1940

Chester Jackson (black, age 29). *Murder.* The crime was committed on 8/3/1938 in Jasper County. Handgun slaying of 32-year-old Daisy Esmond (black), she having been shot in the back. Motive: estranged lover. This misdeed earned Chester Jackson a seat in the Missouri gas chamber on September 20, 1940. Source: *Joplin (MO) Globe*, 8/4/38 (7:6) & 9/28/38 (2:6). *Joplin (MO) News-Herald*, 9/20/40 (2:1).

Robert West (white, age 22). *Murder.* The crime was committed on 6/8/1938 in St. Louis County. Shotgun slaying of 20-year-old Vivian Brewer Davidson (white). Motive: because she had jilted him for being a jailbird. The anti-death-penalty propaganda machine seized on this example of thwarted love to circulate a tale to the effect that West was a despondent suitor who acted out of a death wish that would propel him into the gas chamber, thereby making his execution tantamount to state-assisted suicide. The truth was much more earthy. West met his end on September 20, 1940. Source: *Jefferson City Post-Tribune*, 6/9/38 (1:3). *Moberly (MO) Monitor-Index*, 6/9/38 (1:6). *Joplin (MO) News-Herald*, 9/20/40 (2:1).

1941

Wilburn Johnson (black, age 39). *Murder.* The crime was committed on 9/27/1940 in Butler County. Child killer. Shotgun slayings of 15-year-old Willis Mitchell and 13-year-old Sarah Mitchell (blacks, cousins). Motive: because somebody (apparently the girl) had swiped five dollars from him. The State of Missouri made that five dollars even dearer to Johnson when it sealed him in the gas chamber on January 3, 1941. Source: *Sikeston (MO) Herald*, 10/3/40 (7:1). *Joplin (MO) Globe*, 1/3/41 (2:6).

1942

Ernest Tyler (black, age 34). *Murder.* The crime was committed on 8/16/1940 in Jackson County. Handgun slaying of 40-year-old Erwin Schwarenholz (white). Motive: burglary. Tyler sniffed the fumes of death on April 24, 1942. Source: *Kansas City Times*, 8/17/40 (1:2) & 4/24/42 (12:2). Appeal: 159 SW (2nd) 777–781. See also: 1940 Jackson Co. death cert. no. 27624.

1944

Allen Lambus (black, age 71). *Murder.* The crime was committed on 7/16/1943 in Mississippi County. Child killer. Executed for the slaying of 14-year-old Juanita Harris (black), who was gaffed in the gullet with a hay hook. Motive: attempted sexual assault. Recidivist killer. Lambus had reportedly served time at Parchman Prison for a 1910 manslaughter conviction in Monroe Co., MS. It was the State of Missouri that finally extirpated him on June 16, 1944. Source: *Joplin (MO) Globe*, 8/13/43 (2B:1) & 6/16/44 (8B:8). See also: 1944 Cole Co. death cert. no. 21416.

James Thomas (black, age 20). *Rape.* The crime was committed on 1/10/1943 in St. Louis County. Indecent assault on the person of a 23-year-old white female (name withheld), she having been terrorized in her own home by a knife-wielding intruder who slashed her in two places and threatened to kill her 4-month-old baby unless she acquiesced. This violent sex offender was gassed on October 20, 1944. Source: *Jefferson City Post-Tribune*, 2/11/43 (1:3). *Joplin (MO) News-Herald*, 10/20/44 (B3:2).

1945

Leo Lyles (black, age 18). *Murder.* The crime was committed on 9/30/1941 in St. Louis County. Firearm slaying of 23-year-old Martin Twillman (white) and severe wounding of that man's mother, they both having been shot in their backs by a fusillade from multiple weapons. Motive: attempted carjacking. This trigger-happy teenage killer was gassed on May 25, 1945. Source: *St. Louis Post-Dispatch*, 10/1/41 (1:1). *Joplin (MO) Globe*, 5/25/45 (8:7). Appeal: 175 SW (2nd) 587–594. See also: 1945 Cole Co. death cert. no. 16675. See also: William Edward Talbert (executed 11/16/45).

William Edward Talbert (black, age 20). *Murder.* The crime was committed on 9/30/1941 in St. Louis County. Accomplice in the firearm slaying of 23-year-old Martin Twillman and severe wounding of that man's mother, both of whom were shot in the back. Motive: attempted carjacking. The Missouri gas chamber did for Talbert as it had for his partner on November 16, 1945. Source: *Moberly (MO) Monitor-Index*, 11/16/45 (4:3). See also: Leo Lyles (executed 5/25/45).

1946

Fred Ellis (black, age 20) and **Jesse Sanford** (black, age 34). *Murder.* Their crime was committed on 12/12/1943 in Franklin County. Both executed for the fatal beating of 56-year-old Mary Santo (white), who was attacked in her own home. Four bottles were literally smashed over the woman's head. Other traumatic injuries were inflicted by means of a meat cleaver and brass knuckles. Then the killers set the house on fire. Motive: robbery and home invasion. The needless ferocity of this murder had few equals. It landed Ellis and Sanford in the Missouri gas chamber on August 16, 1946. Source: *Joplin (MO) Globe*, 12/14/43 (8:8) & 8/16/46 (9:3). *Moberly (MO) Monitor-Index*, 8/15/46 (4:1). *Official Detective*, 1/45.

1947

Van Lee Ramsey (black, age 35). *Murder.* The crime was committed on 5/1/1945 at St. Louis. Executed for the killing of 19-year-old Lena Davidson (white), she having been fatally slashed when she tried to fight off a purse snatcher later identified as Van Lee Ramsey. The culprit was gassed on January 10, 1947. Source: *Daily Capitol News* (Jefferson City, MO), 1/10/47 (1:3). See also: 1947 Cole Co. death cert. no. 604.

Marshall Perkins (black, age 57). *Rape.* The crime was committed on 6/2/1945 in Jackson County. Indecent assault on the person of 13-year-old Gladys Jeffries (white), who was attacked as she walked home from a movie. This sexual predator was gassed on January 24, 1947. Source: *Moberly (MO) Monitor-Index*, 1/24/47 (2:4).

Floyd Cochran (black, age 34). *Murder.* The crime was committed on 2/5/1946 in Boone County. Executed for the fatal strangulation of 20-year-old Mary Lou Jenkins (white), she having been attacked in her own home. Motive: sexual assault. Cochran is confirmed to have also murdered his wife. This happened on 2/23/1946. He shot the woman–Mae Anna Cochran (black, age 37)–multiple times and unsuccessfully tried to end his own life in the same manner, claiming despondency over what he had done to the white girl 18 days earlier. The State of Missouri succeeded where Cochran had failed (in the matter of taking his life) on September 26, 1947. The method employed was cyanide gas. Source: *Chillicothe (MO) Constitution-Tribune*, 2/26/46 (2:3) & 3/1/46 (8:1). *Moberly (MO) Monitor-Index*, 9/26/47 (2:1). See also: 1946 Boone Co. death cert. no. 8493. *Official Detective*, 10/46.

1949

Ernest Afton Scott (white, age 48). *Murder.* The crime was committed on 3/29/1948 in Douglas County. Uxoricide, etc. Executed for the rifle slaying of 40-year-old Verla Marie Raney Scott (white). Motive: acrimonious divorce. Confirmed to have also murdered 54-year-old Charles Hairston Jackson (a circuit court judge) by the same means earlier that day for the same reason. Venue changed from Douglas County to Wright County. This wrathful husband—who feared no one from the divorce court judge on down—went to his death in the Missouri gas chamber on November 4, 1949. Source: *Moberly (MO) Monitor-Index*, 3/31/48 (2:1) & 11/4/49 (5:1). See also: 1948 Douglas Co. death cert. no. 12026. Also: 1948 Wright Co. death cert. no. 18529 and 1949 Cole Co. death cert. no. 36703.

George U. Bell (black, age 36). *Murder.* The crime was committed on 9/20/1948 in Jackson County. Police killer. Specifically executed for the gunshot slaying of 30-year-old Charles William Neaves (black) during the course of a larger shootout that left a total of six men dead, four of them police officers. Handguns and a shotgun were used during the melee. It all stemmed from a complaint about a loud party. The other fatalities were Charles H. Perrine (white, age 45, a policeman), Sandy Washington (black, age 27, a policeman), William S. Wells (white, age 36, a policeman who was shot five times), William Bell (black, age 33, one of the gunmen) and Burton Edwin Warren (black, age 27), who was cut down by police bullets when he bolted from a paddy wagon. The deaths of the other three police officers were attributed to William Bell although George U. Bell was an accomplice and accessory thereto. The latter was gassed for his part in this deadly fracas on December 2, 1949. Source: *Moberly (MO) Monitor-Index*, 9/21/48 (1:6), 9/22/48 (2:3). *Daily Capitol News* (Jefferson City, MO), 12/2/49 (1:3). See also: 1948 Jackson Co. death cert. nos. 30013, 29915, 33153, 30010 and 29891. Also: 1949 Cole Co. death cert. no. 40600.

1950

Charles Tiedt (white, age 51). *Murder.* The crime was committed on 11/25/1945 in Buchanan County. Shotgun slayings of 44-year-old Delbert Matchett, 37-year-old Edna Matchett (whites, a married couple) and 29-year-old Frederick Matchett (white). Motive: feud between neighbors. The killer was gassed on May 19, 1950. Source: *Chillicothe (MO) Constitution-Tribune*, 11/26/45 (1:4). *Sedalia (MO) Democrat*, 5/19/50 (1:3).

1951

Claude McGee (white, age 35). *Murder.* The crime was committed on 1/10/1948 in Cole County. Executed for the murder of 47-year-old John B. Manor (white, his fellow penitentiary inmate and erstwhile crime partner), who was struck down from behind with a contraband claw hammer that had had its prongs sharpened into points. Motive: quarrel over a petty debt. Recidivist killer. McGee and Manor had been part of a four-man gang that on 5/8/1935 invaded the home of a Scott County gentleman named William Thomas Carlton (white, age 50) and terrorized his family. Mr. Carlton was shot dead with a handgun when he unsuspectingly walked in on the home invasion while it was in progress. All of the culprits were caught. McGee was tried in Mississippi County on a change of venue. He was sentenced to death when it was proven that he had fired the fatal shot. His accomplices got prison terms of varying lengths. The governor of Missouri commuted McGee's death sentence to a term of life imprisonment. The efficacy of that decision to grant clemency was shown 12 years later when lifer Claude McGee committed murder a second time. The Missouri gas chamber ensured that there would be no third time on January 5, 1951. Source: *News and Tribune* (Jefferson City, MO), 1/11/48 (1:8). *Jefferson City (MO) Post-Tribune*, 5/10/35 (2:5) & 1/5/51 (1:4).

1952

Willie Porter (black, age 29). *Rape.* The crime was committed on 8/9/1952 in Cole County. Indecent assault on the person of 70-year-old Belle Agee (white), she having been attacked by a drunken prison "trusty" (Porter) one block away from the walls of the Missouri State Penitentiary. So flagrant was the crime that its perpetrator was gassed without the benefit of appeal on October 28, 1952. Source: *Jefferson City (MO) Post-Tribune*, 8/11/52 (1:8). *Daily Capitol News* (Jefferson City), 10/28/52 (1:2). See also: 1930 U.S. Census (Cole Co., MO), which notes the injured woman.

1953

Ulas Quilling (black, age 50). *Murder.* The crime was committed on 5/19/1951 in Jackson County. Handgun slayings of 42-year-old Lauvinia Julia Wright Webb, 36-year-old Irene Bragg and 55-year-old Carl Dodd (blacks). Motive: estranged lover gone loco. Quilling atoned for this triple homicide in the Missouri gas chamber on May 29, 1953. Source: *Joplin (MO) Globe*, 5/29/53 (1:7). Appeal: 256 SW (2nd) 751–754. See also: 1951 Jackson Co. death cert. nos. 16875, 16436 and 23003.

Kenneth Boyd (black, age 21). *Murder.* The crime was committed on 1/13/1951 at St. Louis. Handgun slaying of 54-year-old Samuel Barrenfeld (white), a grocer. Motive: armed robbery. The young gunman realized all too late that he had made a fatal mistake when he took his last breaths in the gas chamber on July 10, 1953. Source: *St. Louis Post-Dispatch*, 7/10/53 (5:3). Appeal: 256 SW (2nd) 765–768.

Carl Austin Hall (white, age 34) and **Bonnie Brown Heady** (white, age 41). *Murder.* Their crime was committed on 9/28/1953 in Jackson County. Child killers. Both executed under federal authority for the abduction, handgun slaying and illegal burial of 6-year-old Robert Cosgrove Greenlease, Jr. (white). Motive: kidnapping for ransom. The perpetrators of this atrocity were both lovers and hardcore alcoholics. Their lives had been on a steadily downhill slide for a considerable number of years. They had hit rock bottom by the time of their chance meeting in a tavern and plotted a nefarious means of sustaining themselves in a monetary sense. The male member of this symbiosis was without a single redemptive characteristic. He was the wastrel son of a well-to-do attorney who had died in 1932. He had also had the advantage of a private school (military academy) education. His widowed mother had died in 1944, leaving him an inheritance in the amount of $200,000—the equivalent of more than a million dollars in today's money. Within the space of two years, however, Carl Austin Hall had squandered every single penny of this. He descended to the level of a common drunk who tottered his way from bar room to bar room drinking whatever quarters and 50-cent pieces he happened to have in his pockets. This was how he met the equally sodden female who became his partner in crime. In fact, Hall was so down on his luck by then that he had to accept *her* hospitality.

The victim's grave was dug in advance. This fact was proof positive that the culprits never had any intention of releasing the little boy after collecting his ransom. Bonnie Brown Heady went to the child's school (a Roman Catholic institution), where she tricked a sympathetic nun with a contrived story about the child being called for by its ailing mother. So convincingly did Heady play this ruse that she even went to chapel there and prayed on the matter at the nun's benevolent suggestion. She then drove off with the spiffy little lad to a pre-arranged rendezvous where Carl Austin Hall awaited them. He at first tried to strangle the child but wound up shooting him through the head. Then the guilty pair drove to where they had prepared the grave (a flower garden) and buried the slaughtered victim. Next, they demanded and received a ransom of $600,000 in cash, which they immediately began to fritter away in a manner that drew attention. It is impossible to overstate the degree of public revulsion that followed. The gratuitous brutality of what these killers did was especially galling to human sensitivity. Hall and Heady went to their court-ordered demise without the benefit of appeal on December 18, 1953. The price they paid was death by cyanide gas. Source: *Official Detective*, 12/53. *Front Page Detective*, 1/54. *Master Detective*, 3/54 & 1/74.

1955

Dock Booker (black, age abt. 43). *Murder.* The crime was committed on 8/15/1953 at St. Louis. Handgun slaying of about 43-year-old Earl Harrison (black). Motive: an argument over who was a better baseball player. Booker's trigger finger earned him a seat in the Missouri gas chamber on April 1, 1955. Source: *St. Louis Post-Dispatch*, 4/1/55 (7:3). Appeal: 276 SW (2nd) 104–107.

1956

Arthur Ross Brown (white, age 30). *Murder.* The crime was committed on 8/4/1955 at Kansas City. Executed under federal authority for the abduction and killing of 34-year-old Wilma Frances Allen (white), she having been carjacked, raped, and robbed; her wrists were bound with her own scarf and she was then left naked in a field, the top of her head blown off by two shots from a .45 automatic. Motive: robbery and sexual assault. The Missouri gas chamber closed this customer's account on February 24, 1956. Source: *Official Detective*, 2/56. *Master Detective*, 10/59 & 1/75. *Crime Detective*, 1/57 & 5/60. *Real Detective*, 4/56, 3/70 & 9/74.

1957

Thomas Moore (black, age 40). *Murder.* The crime was committed on 5/5/1955 in Jackson County. Uxoricide. Shotgun slaying of 36-year-old Opal Irene Moore (black). Motive: marital estrangement. This wife-killer was gassed on September 13, 1957. Source: *Kansas City Star*, 5/5/55 (1:4). *Kansas City Times*, 9/13/57 (19:1). Appeal: 303 SW (2nd) 60–64.

1963

Sammy Aire Tucker (white, age 24). *Murder.* The crime was committed on 3/10/1961 in Cape Girardeau County. Police killer. Executed for the rifle and handgun slayings of 67-year-old Herbert L. Goss and 27-year-old Donald Crittendon (whites). Motive: deadly pursuit and resisting arrest. Tucker was specifically condemned for killing Officer Crittendon. He was an accessory in the matter of Herbert Goss. The actual killer of Goss was a second felon named Douglas Wayne Thompson. He too was sentenced to death but managed to euchre a reprieve. Tucker went to the gas chamber alone on July 26, 1963. Source: *Southeast Missourian* (Cape Girardeau, MO), 3/11/61 (1:1) & 7/26/63 (1:8). *Official Detective*, 6/61. *Master Detective*, 10/66.

1964

Charles Harvey Odom (white, age 29). *Rape.* The crime was committed on 7/23/1961 in Jasper County. Executed for an aggravated sexual assault upon the person of 13-year-old Lisa Schuh (white), she having been abducted at gunpoint and battered with rocks so that she remained physically disabled for life. Odom had been a habitual criminal since the age of 14. He had absolutely no regard for the rights and property of others. His specialty was residential burglaries that he carried out on a serial basis. A jailbird with multiple sentences to his discredit, Odom had sweet-talked his way through one parole hearing after another. His arms (and several other body parts) were loaded with prison tattoos by the time he made the transition from thief to sexual predator. By outward appearance he was a tousle-haired blond of unassuming physique. The Missouri gas chamber put an end to Odom's misadventures on March 6, 1964. Source: *Master Detective*, 8/64, 11/70 & 9/82. Appeal: 369 SW (2nd) 173–177.

Ronald Lee Wolfe (white, age 29). *Rape.* The crime was committed on 10/18/1959 in Lawrence County. Indecent assault on the person of an 8-year-old white female (name withheld), she having been lured into the culprit's car by means of a proffered candy bar. Venue changed from Lawrence County to Pike County. The severity of the physical injuries that Wolfe inflicted on the little girl were in themselves deemed sufficient to warrant his death. He was gassed on May 8, 1964, in what has been to date the USA's last legal execution for rape. Source: *Jefferson City (MO) Post-Tribune*, 5/8/64 (2:6). Appeal: 343 SW (2nd) 10–15.

1965

Lloyd Leo Anderson (black, age 18). *Murder.* The crime was committed on 5/18/1961 at St. Louis. Child killer, etc. Executed for the handgun slaying of 15-year-old Thomas E. Grupe (white), a pharmacy delivery boy. Motive: armed robbery. Anderson is confirmed to have also murdered a St. Louis storekeeper named William W. Schulze (white, age 59) on 3/25/1961 by the same means and for the same reason. He was furthermore an accessory or accomplice in the fatal shooting of a St. Louis deli owner named Emerson Wright (white, age 47) on 5/24/1961. This incipient urban terrorist was gassed on February 26, 1965.

Source: *St. Louis Post-Dispatch*, 5/19/61 (1:3) & 2/26/65 (1:3). *Morning Advocate* (Baton Rouge, LA), 5/31/61 (6:7). *Official Detective*, 10/61.

Appendix: List of Executions Before 1866

These lists are subject to revision and are probably incomplete.

Illinois

Date	Name	Location	Offense
06/15/1779	Negro Manuel	Kankaskia	Murder
06/15/1779	Negro Moreau	Cahokia	Murder
08/25/1807	Emsley Jones	Kankaskia	Murder
09/23/1809	James McGlaughlin	Kankaskia	Murder
07/14/1819	John Killduck	Palestine	Murder
08/14/1821	Whorahjinkah	St. Clair	Murder
09/03/1821	Timothy Bennett	Belleville	Murder
02/12/1824	Eliphalet Green	Edwardsville	Murder
05/10/1824	Martin Frazier	Shawneetown	Murder
11/26/1826	Nathaniel van Noy	Springfield	Murder
04/25/1832	Patrick Cavanaugh	Carrollton	Murder
04/30/1834	William Ledbetter	Carmi	Murder
06/09/1834	Henry Shouse	Golconda	Murder
12/22/1834	Thomas Bennett	Quincy	Murder
06/29/1835	Elias McFadden	Rushville	Murder
06/29/1835	David McFadden	Rushville	Murder
06/10/1836	Joseph Thomason	Watseka	Murder
11/06/1837	Cornelius McGuire	Jonesboro	Murder
05/18/1839	William Fraime	Carthage	Murder
06/02/1840	Aaron Todd	Carlinville	Murder
07/10/1840	John Stone	Chicago	Murder
11/18/1842	George Ogle	Vandalia	Murder
05/23/1845	Elizabeth Reed	Lawrenceville	Murder
10/19/1845	Aaron Long	Rock Island	Murder
10/19/1845	John Long	Rock Island	Murder
10/19/1845	Granville Young	Rock Island	Murder
10/11/1850	Milton Jones	Mt. Carmel	Murder
01/15/1851	Thomas Brown	Peoria	Murder
01/15/1851	George Williams	Peoria	Murder
05/24/1853	Henry Voltz	Fairfield	Murder
06/28/1853	George Gates	Ottawa	Murder
04/21/1854	John Collins	Geneva	Murder
05/12/1854	Patrick Doyle	Naperville	Murder
09/04/1854	Joseph Urban	Belleville	Murder

Date	Name	Location	Offense
10/24/1854	John Brown	Jonesboro	Murder
01/19/1855	John Taylor	Galena	Murder
07/13/1855	David Stoddard	Rock Island	Murder
03/27/1857	Alfred Countryman	Rockford	Murder
06/19/1857	William Jackson	Chicago	Murder
06/19/1857	John Johnson	Edwardsville	Murder
06/19/1857	George Sharpe	Edwardsville	Murder
07/03/1857	Andrew Ingram	Rock Island	Murder
04/20/1858	Albert Staub	Chicago	Murder
09/28/1858	James Gaffney	Carrollton	Murder
09/28/1858	Vincent Hall	Carrollton	Murder
05/06/1859	Michael McNamee	Chicago	Murder
12/28/1860	Henry Alter	Waterloo	Murder
03/01/1861	John Ott	Pekin	Murder
05/17/1861	Wiley Morris	Kankakee	Murder
08/15/1861	James White	Salem	Murder
10/02/1861	Robert Dickman	Mound City	Murder
11/29/1861	Addison Cunningham	Quincy	Murder
02/07/1862	John McDonnell	Watseka	Murder
06/13/1865	William Bell	Waukegan	Murder
09/01/1865	Thomas Moss	Jerseyville	Murder
12/15/1865	Jerry Corbett	Chicago	Murder
12/15/1865	Matthew Fleming	Chicago	Murder
12/22/1865	Francis Harper	Watseka	Murder

Indiana

Date	Name	Location	Offense
1805	Robert Slaughter	Vincennes	Murder
04/01/1817	Henry Chryst	Richmond	Murder
10/01/1818	James Ouley	English	Murder
08/14/1820	Amasa Fuller	Lawrenceburg	Murder
07/26/1821	John Dahmen	New Albany	Murder
10/22/1822	Thomas McKinney	Vincennes	Murder
12/06/1822	Hampshire Pitts	Richmond	Murder
06/27/1823	John Harvey	Evansville	Murder
04/09/1824	William Cox	Vincennes	Murder
01/12/1825	James Hudson	Anderson	Murder
06/03/1825	John Bridge	Anderson	Murder
06/03/1825	Stephen Sawyer	Anderson	Murder
05/11/1829	Edward Swanson	Rushville	Murder
06/30/1829	Jacob Lamb	New Albany	Murder
11/12/1830	John Richardson	Covington	Murder
06/11/1833	Kader Herring	Columbus	Murder
06/11/1833	John Jones	Columbus	Murder
04/25/1836	Isaac Heller	Liberty	Murder
06/15/1838	David Scott	La Porte	Murder
06/29/1838	Francis Staves	Valparaiso	Murder
11/13/1840	John Lechner A	lbion	Murder
02/12/1841	William Thompson	Greencastle	Murder
10/07/1841	James Sumner	Brownstown	Murder

Date	Name	Location	Offense
12/30/1842	Noah Beauchamp	Rockville	Murder
07/05/1844	Henry Dyas	Terre Haute	Murder
12/18/1846	James Fields	English	Murder
12/13/1850	Ernest Gross	New Albany	Murder
07/25/1851	Hiram Bland	Bloomington	Murder
12/05/1851	John Bennett	Versailles	Murder
04/27/1855	George Keefer	Ft. Wayne	Murder
04/27/1855	Benjamin Madden	Ft. Wayne	Murder
12/13/1855	John Hubbard	Wabash	Murder
01/11/1856	Timothy Driscoll	Lafayette	Murder
01/11/1856	Abram Rice	Lafayette	Murder
01/11/1856	David Stocking	Lafayette	Murder
12/18/1857	Greenbury Mullinix	Greencastle	Murder
04/02/1858	Henry Todd	Sullivan	Murder
01/04/1861	Louis Bradford	Terre Haute	Murder
03/27/1863	Robert Gay	(U.S. Army), Indianapolis	Desertion
06/17/1864	Henry Harden	Jeffersonville	Murder
12/23/1864	Charles Billingsby	(U.S. Army), Indianapolis	Desertion
12/23/1864	John Murray	(U.S. Army), Indianapolis	Desertion
12/23/1864	Thomas Ryan	(U.S. Army), Indianapolis	Desertion
12/29/1865	John Hendley	Indianapolis	Murder

Iowa

Date	Name	Location	Offense
06/20/1834	Patrick O'Connor	Dubuque	Murder
07/15/1842	Joseph Jackson	Andrew	Murder
07/15/1845	Stephen Hodge	Ft. Madison	Murder
07/15/1845	William Hodge	Ft. Madison	Murder
04/04/1846	William McCauley	Keosauqua	Murder
08/13/1858	William Hinkle	Dubuque	Murder
04/27/1860	Francis Gillick	Dubuque	Murder
05/18/1860	Nies Johnson	Manchester	Murder
10/19/1860	Daniel Clifford	Dubuque	Murder
09/09/1864	William Dowdy	(U.S. Army), Florence	Desertion
02/17/1865	Benjamin McComb	Ottumwa	Murder

Kentucky

There are, without any doubt, numerous pre–1866 Kentucky executions that still await discovery. A great deal of research still remains to be done in this area.

Date	Name	Location	Offense
09/28/1787	Negro Daniel	Greenville	Arson
07/30/1791	Negro Bill	Versailles	Murder

Date	Name	Location	Offense
05/29/1795	David Boyd	Lexington	Murder
04/02/1796	Negro Jacob	Elizabethtown	Murder
05/10/1798	Catherine London	Frankfurt	Murder
04/29/1799	Augustine Adams	Frankfurt	Murder
08/03/1799	Negress Fanny	Versailles	Murder
09/19/1799	Henry Fields	Frankfurt	Murder
11/[?]/1801	Christopher Walbeck	Bardstown	Murder
01/27/1802	Yellow John	Smithland	Murder
08/04/1809	Negress Nancy	Columbia	Murder
08/04/1809	Negro Peter	Columbia	Murder
06/08/1810	William Clutter	Burlington	Murder
10/18/1811	Negro Isaac	Bardstown	Murder
08/08/1814	Negress Isbel	Paris	Murder
10/27/1815	Negro George	Vanceburg	Attempted Rape
01/10/1816	Negro Bill	Bardstown	Rape
08/24/1816	Negro Tim	Greenville	Murder
03/[?]/1817	Negro Major	Louisville	Burglary
05/17/1817	Thomas Begley, Jr.	Barbourville	Murder
05/17/1817	Isaac Callahan B	arbourville	Murder
07/26/1817	Eleanor Gillespie	Owingsville	Murder
11/21/1817	Negro Ben	Maysville	Murder
05/07/1818	John Hamilton	Glasgow	Murder
08/25/1818	John Moore	Mt. Sterling	Murder
08/30/1818	Wharton Ransdale	Frankfurt	Murder
07/26/1819	Charles Carr	Henderson	Murder
03/04/1820	Negro Will	Maysville	Burglary
03/26/1821	Negro Pompey	Lancaster	Murder
03/26/1821	Negro Tom	Lancaster	Murder
11/10/1821	Negro Jacob	Vanceburg	Uncertain
05/28/1823	Daniel Walker	Louisa	Murder
10/01/1823	Jeff King	Shelbyville	Murder
07/23/1825	Simon Landry	Elizabethtown	Murder
05/04/1826	Samuel Calvin Sugg	Henderson	Murder
05/13/1826	Francis Irvin	Hartford	Murder
07/07/1826	Jeroboam Beauchamp	Frankfurt	Murder
08/25/1826	Thomas Bradley	Lexington	Murder
11/29/1826	Negro Dick	Hardinsburg	Murder
11/29/1826	Negro Joe	Hardinsburg	Murder
11/29/1826	Negro Raisin	Hardinsburg	Murder
11/29/1826	Negro Stephen	Hardinsburg	Murder
05/12/1827	James Watson	Bardstown	Murder
08/20/1827	Willis Beasley	Stanford	Murder
12/23/1828	Negro Manuel	Bowling Green	Attempted Rape
06/25/1829	Negro James	Paris	Murder
11/20/1829	Negro Fisher	Greenup	Murder
11/20/1829	Negro Hooper	Greenup	Murder
11/20/1829	Negro Jesse	Greenup	Murder
11/20/1829	Negro John	Greenup	Murder
11/20/1829	Negro Levin	Greenup	Murder
12/11/1829	Daniel McLaughlin	Flemingsburg	Murder
04/03/1830	Negro Briscoe	Bardstown	Rape
09/04/1830	Negress Mary	Nicholasville	Murder

Date	Name	Location	Offense
09/04/1830	Negro Stephen	Nicholasville	Murder
08/13/1831	Negro Harry	Lexington	Poisoning
08/13/1831	Negro Bill	Lexington	Arson
08/13/1831	Negro Bill	Lexington	Attempted Rape
08/13/1831	Negro Moses	Lexington	Attempted Rape
10/07/1831	Negro Dick	Maysville	Uncertain
12/30/1831	William Stovall	Scottsville	Murder
10/19/1832	Negress Catherine	Flemingsburg	Murder
10/27/1832	Negro Randolph	Lancaster	Murder
11/16/1832	Negro Jack	Harrodsburg	Murder
11/16/1832	Negro Nat	Harrodsburg	Murder
11/23/1832	Negro Ben	Lexington	Attempted Rape
07/05/1833	Negro Lewis	Columbia	Murder
10/02/1833	Negress Cassy	Hopkinsville	Murder
10/02/1833	Negro Squire	Hopkinsville	Murder
12/02/1833	Negro Joe	Lexington	Murder
04/30/1834	Hannah Hazelwood	Henderson	Murder
08/01/1834	Michael Jones	Louisville	Murder
08/01/1834	George Lovett	Louisville	Murder
05/16/1836	Negro Amos	Elizabethtown	Murder
05/31/1836	Negress Caroline	Russellville	Murder
08/05/1836	Negro Fielding	Owensboro	Attempted Rape
06/24/1837	Negress Sarah	Maysville	Murder
09/01/1837	Adam Jones	Louisville	Murder
09/01/1837	John Thompson	Louisville	Murder
11/16/1837	Michael Schieslan	Louisville	Murder
04/28/1838	Henry McAllister	Henderson	Murder
04/28/1838	Joseph Wurnell	Henderson	Murder
06/01/1838	Patrick Burns	Newport	Murder
07/06/1838	Negro Isaac	Greenville	Murder
06/07/1839	Negro Sam	Hopkinsville	Rape
06/28/1839	James Cosgrove	Louisville	Murder
06/28/1839	John Miller	Louisville	Murder
06/28/1839	David Scott	Louisville	Murder
07/31/1839	David Bailey	Russellville	Murder
07/31/1839	Eden Good	Williamsburg	Murder
10/04/1839	Negro Burrell	Georgetown	Rape
10/04/1839	Negress Martha	Georgetown	Attempted Murder
11/15/1839	Negro Bartlett	Carrollton	Murder
11/25/1840	Gilbert Richey	Carlisle	Murder
04/08/1841	John White	Louisville	Murder
07/30/1841	Negro Jerry	Cadiz	Uncertain
09/21/1841	Carrington Simpson	Greensburg	Murder
10/15/1841	Negro Bob	Stanford	Murder
12/31/1841	Moses Kean	Maysville	Murder
07/23/1842	Negro Willis	Versailles	Murder
09/02/1842	Negro Jesse	Hopkinsville	Murder
10/07/1842	James Wilcox	Princeton	Murder
10/28/1842	Negro Paris	Stanford	Murder
04/14/1843	Negro Neat	Nicholasville	Aggravated Burglary

Date	Name	Location	Offense
05/13/1843	John Spencer	Elizabethtown	Murder
07/14/1843	Negro Sam	Williamstown	Murder
08/[?]/1843	Negro Addison	Henderson	Attempted Rape
04/11/1844	Negress Hannah	Richmond	Murder
10/19/1844	Negro Isaac	Versailles	Uncertain
11/19/1844	Negro Richard	Lexington	Murder
11/30/1844	Negress Amy	Shepardsville	Murder
05/20/1845	Negro Tom	Paris	Murder
05/30/1845	Negro Tom	Lexington	Murder
10/03/1845	Abner Baker, Jr.	Manchester	Murder
11/06/1845	Negro Preston	Bowling Green	Arson
01/02/1846	John W. Parker	Danville	Murder
04/05/1846	Negro Skelt	Paris	Murder
05/01/1846	Edward Pennington	Hopkinsville	Murder
07/04/1846	Negro Caudill	Booneville	Rape
10/02/1846	Negro David	Lancaster	Murder
11/27/1846	Negro Edmund	Pikeville	Murder
04/20/1847	Charles Smith	Hickman	Murder
04/23/1847	Negro George	Bowling Green	Rape
05/01/1847	Negro John	Stanford	Murder
05/25/1847	Joe Coleman	Burkesville	Murder
06/05/1847	Wm. Henry Stepter	Greenup	Murder
07/21/1847	Negro Jack	Mt. Sterling	Rape
09/06/1847	Negro Spencer	Flemingsburg	Murder
11/19/1847	David Sheely	Cynthiana	Murder
03/17/1848	Negro John	Louisville	Murder
06/01/1848	Negress Lucy	Brandenburg	Murder
10/28/1848	Negro Harry	Brookville	Rebellion
10/28/1848	Negro Prestley	Brookville	Rebellion
10/28/1848	Negro Shadrach	Brookville	Rebellion
04/27/1849	Negress Sally	Madisonville	Murder
06/01/1849	Negro Aaron	Lexington	Murder
06/01/1849	Negro Henry	Lexington	Murder
07/12/1849	Negro Lewis	Mt. Sterling	Murder
07/16/1849	Negro George	Mt. Sterling	Murder
10/30/1849	Negro Jesse	Bowling Green	Arson
11/02/1849	Negro Philip	Henderson	Murder
11/22/1849	Negro Warren	Lexington	Murder
01/15/1850	William Baker	Manchester	Murder
04/26/1850	Mitchell Martin	Greenville	Rape
12/27/1850	Negro Tom	Winchester	Murder
07/19/1851	Negro Martin	Lexington	Murder
07/26/1851	Negro Dudley	Lexington	Murder
08/07/1851	Negro Henry	Lexington	Murder
08/16/1851	Negro Anthony	Lexington	Murder
08/16/1851	Negro Gabriel	Lexington	Murder
09/05/1851	Negro Abner	Carrollton	Uncertain
10/10/1851	Philip Murphy	Campbellsville	Murder
11/29/1851	Negro Anthony	Elizabethtown	Uncertain
06/28/1852	Turner Clark	Greenup	Murder
08/30/1852	Reuben Clark	Greenup	Murder
09/03/1852	Negro Marion	Harrodsburg	Murder

Date	Name	Location	Offense
09/03/1852	Thomas Sheldon	Cynthiana	Murder
09/17/1852	William Wallingford	Marion	Murder
[?]/1853	Negro Pitman	Danville	Uncertain
06/17/1853	Negro Edmund	Greenville	Rape
09/03/1853	Robert Robertson	Newport	Murder
10/28/1853	Moses Kelly	Hawesville	Murder
10/28/1853	Robert Kelly	Hawesville	Murder
11/18/1853	Negro John	Hopkinsville	Murder
12/09/1853	William Brown	West Liberty	Murder
03/31/1854	Negro Isaac	Elkton	Murder
04/[?]/1854	Negro Henry	Princeton	Murder
04/[?]/1854	Negro Perry	Princeton	Murder
06/16/1854	Negro Achilles	Benton	Murder
06/17/1854	Negro Alfred	Versailles	Murder
06/17/1854	Negro Archie	Versailles	Murder
06/17/1854	Negro Warner	Versailles	Murder
06/17/1854	William Wilson	Versailles	Murder
08/11/1854	Henry Simpson	Louisville	Murder
08/12/1854	William Weigart	Lexington	Murder
10/13/1854	Negro John	Danville	Rape
11/01/1854	Curtis Richardson	Owensboro	Murder
11/24/1854	Negro Levi	Paris	Rape
11/24/1854	Negro Ned	Blandville	Murder
12/15/1854	John Hastings	Paris	Murder
[?]/1855	Negro George	Cadiz	Uncertain
[?]/1855	Negress Martha	Cadiz	Uncertain
01/19/1855	William Hanning	Greenup	Murder
01/19/1855	Stephen Short	Greenup	Murder
12/14/1855	Solomon Smith	Paris	Murder
02/01/1856	George Huffner	Louisville	Murder
02/09/1856	Negress Minerva	Cadiz	Arson
03/21/1856	John Graham	Paducah	Murder
05/16/1856	Daniel Hagan	Hickman	Murder
06/06/1856	Negro Warwick	Williamstown	Murder
08/15/1856	John Adwell	Glasgow	Murder
09/05/1856	Larkin Ray	Greenup	Murder
10/10/1856	Thomas Jenkins	Paducah	Murder
12/05/1856	Negro Nat	Harrodsburg	Uncertain
12/12/1856	Negro Jacob	Hopkinsville	Murder
12/19/1856	John Comely	Lancaster	Murder
12/19/1856	Solomon Young	Cadiz	Murder
02/06/1857	Negro Anthony	Cadiz	Rebellion
05/13/1857	Negro Albert	Flemingsburg	Murder
05/29/1857	Edward Hawkins	Irvine	Murder
10/23/1857	Pleasant Coleman	Russellville	Murder
11/20/1857	Milton Tackett	Owingsville	Murder
[?]/1858	Negro Nick	Lebanon	Uncertain
05/07/1858	Negro Ben	Bardstown	Murder
05/07/1858	Negro Cyrus	Bardstown	Murder
05/07/1858	Negro Jake	Bardstown	Murder
05/19/1858	Negro Joe	Burlington	Uncertain
06/11/1858	Little Jack	Scottsville	Murder

Date	Name	Location	Offense
07/24/1858	Joshua Arnold	Nicholasville	Murder
11/19/1858	Negro Horace	Hardinsburg	Uncertain
06/[?]/1859	James Jaggers	Munfordville	Murder
06/17/1859	Negro John	Hodgenville	Murder
06/24/1859	Negro Carey	Maysville	Murder
08/[?]/1859	John Murphy	Henderson	Murder
11/[?]/1859	Negro Horace	Morganfield	Uncertain
11/25/1859	George Hunter	Greensburg	Murder
12/23/1859	Negro Jackson	Elkton	Rape
01/20/1860	Hiram Bird	Eddyville	Murder
04/12/1860	Andrew Jackson	Cadiz	Murder
06/01/1860	Jack Santafer	Harrodsburg	Uncertain
08/31/1860	Hezekiah Clemons	Harlan	Murder
08/31/1860	Negro Milton	Glasgow	Murder
09/07/1860	Negress Frances	Frankfurt	Poisoning
12/14/1860	Negress Jane	Owenton	Murder
[?]/1861	Negro Bill	Lebanon	Uncertain
01/25/1861	David Caution	Louisville	Rape
09/20/1861	Charles Collins	Maysville	Murder
02/05/1862	Samuel Calhoun	Bardstown	Murder
05/09/1862	Negro Henry	Stanford	Aggravated Assault
05/16/1862	Negro Ned	Hopkinsville	Murder
06/14/1862	Negro Preston	Paris	Attempted Murder
09/21/1862	Lewis Stivers	Louisville	Murder
11/[?]/1862	Negro Nelson	Russellville	Uncertain
11/28/1862	Negro Jerry	Maysville	Murder
02/06/1863	Negro Daniel	Henderson	Uncertain
04/[?]/1863	Negro Gip	Mt. Sterling	Aggravated Assault
05/15/1863	Negro Elijah	Clinton	Arson
05/15/1863	Negro James	Clinton	Arson
05/15/1863	Jefferson McGraw	Lexington	Uncertain
08/01/1863	Negro Claiborne	Richmond	Murder
08/14/1863	Negress Caroline	Louisville	Murder
09/04/1863	John Anderson	(U.S. Army) Munfordville	Desertion
09/04/1863	Frazier Carmen	(U.S. Army) Munfordville	Desertion
09/04/1863	Christopher Coffey	(U.S. Army) Munfordville	Desertion
09/04/1863	John Coffey	(U.S. Army) Munfordville	Desertion
09/04/1863	James Pointer	(U.S. Army) Munfordville	Desertion
09/04/1863	William Ray	Columbus	Murder
09/04/1863	Lewis Stevenson	Columbus	Murder
09/04/1863	Jim Webb	Columbus	Murder
10/30/1863	Negro William	Dixon	Murder
11/06/1863	Negro Henry	Calhoun	Rape
11/27/1863	Negro Alfred	Flemingsburg	Rape

Date	Name	Location	Offense
12/[?]/1863	Negro Finis	Madisonville	Aggravated Assault
12/[?]/1863	Negro Henry	Madisonville	Aggravated Assault
12/11/1863	Negro Bob	Morganfield	Aggravated Assault
01/24/1864	James Love	Columbus	Uncertain
05/27/1864	Negro George	Sherpardsville	Murder
07/22/1864	John P. Powell	Henderson	Marauding
07/22/1864	William Thompson	Henderson	Marauding
07/28/1864	Two CSA Guerrillas	Georgetown	Marauding
07/29/1864	Thomas (CSA)	Russellville	Marauding
08/15/1864	Richmond Berry	Bloomfield	Marauding
08/15/1864	May Hamilton	Bloomfield	Marauding
08/15/1864	John Lingenfelter	Williamstown	Marauding
08/15/1864	William Lingenfelter	Williamstown	Marauding
08/15/1864	George Wainscott	Williamstown	Marauding
08/20/1864	J. Bloom	Franklin	Marauding
08/20/1864	N. B. McGlasson	Franklin	Marauding
08/23/1864	Joe Bethany	Paducah	Uncertain
08/23/1864	William Taylor	Paducah	Uncertain
08/26/1864	Joe Finnell	Irvine	Attempted Rape
09/04/1864	Frank M. Holmes	Brandenburg	Marauding
09/04/1864	Three CSA Guerrillas	Brandenburg	Marauding
09/15/1864	(?) Cheney (CSA)	Munfordville	Marauding
09/15/1864	(?) Jones (CSA)	Munfordville	Marauding
10/01/1864	(?) Six Men (CSA)	Osceola	Marauding
10/15/1864	(?) James Hopkins	Bloomfield	Marauding
10/15/1864	(?) J. W. Sipple	Bloomfield	Marauding
10/15/1864	(?) Samuel Stagdale	Bloomfield	Marauding
10/24/1864	M. Blincoe	Jeffersontown	Marauding
10/24/1864	L. P. Buckner	Jeffersontown	Marauding
10/24/1864	Sherwood Hatley	Jeffersontown	Marauding
10/24/1864	Wilson Lilly	Jeffersontown	Marauding
10/25/1864	Two CSA Guerrillas	Hopkinsville	Marauding
11/02/1864	Elijah Horton	Frankfurt	Marauding
11/02/1864	Thomas Hunt	Frankfurt	Marauding
11/02/1864	Thornton Lafferty	Frankfurt	Marauding
11/02/1864	John Long	Frankfurt	Marauding
11/03/1864	William Darbrough	Christiansburg	Marauding
11/03/1864	William Jones	Christiansburg	Marauding
11/03/1864	William Tigher	Christiansburg	Marauding
11/03/1864	G. W. Yates	Christiansburg	Marauding
11/05/1864	N. Adams	Midway	Marauding
11/05/1864	J. Jackson	Midway	Marauding
11/05/1864	M. Jackson	Midway	Marauding
11/05/1864	C. Risinger	Midway	Marauding
11/07/1864	Three CSA Guerrillas	Nelson Co.	Marauding
11/08/1864	Two CSA Guerrillas	Lynn's Camp	Marauding
11/13/1864	Forrest (CSA)	Henderson	Marauding
11/13/1864	John Frye	Henderson	Marauding
11/13/1864	Horton (CSA)	Henderson	Marauding

DATE	NAME	LOCATION	OFFENSE
11/13/1864	Horton (CSA)	Henderson	Marauding
11/13/1864	Horton (CSA)	Henderson	Marauding
11/15/1864	Walter Ferguson	Lexington	Marauding
11/15/1864	McGee (CSA)	Lexington	Marauding
11/19/1864	Jacob Baker	Munfordville	Marauding
11/19/1864	W. B. Dunn	Munfordville	Marauding
11/19/1864	John Henn	Munfordville	Marauding
11/19/1864	Lycurgus Morgan	Munfordville	Marauding
11/19/1864	W. T. Thornton	Munfordville	Marauding
11/19/1864	A. B. Tudor	Munfordville	Marauding
01/10/1865	One CSA Guerrilla	Christian Co.	Marauding
01/20/1865	Nathaniel Marks	Louisville	Marauding
01/26/1865	One CSA Guerrilla	La Grange	Marauding
02/03/1865	Richard Smith	Columbia	Murder
03/15/1865	Marcellus Jerome Clark	Louisville	Marauding
03/31/1865	Thomas Payne	Lexington	Marauding
04/06/1865	Enoch Downs	Louisville	Marauding
04/06/1865	John Hedges	Louisville	Marauding
04/27/1865	J. J. Straney	Louisville	Marauding
05/31/1865	Samuel Robertson	Lexington	Marauding
06/13/1865	John Lewis	Louisville	Murder
08/18/1865	John Bishop	Lexington	Marauding
08/18/1865	Aaron Collins	Lexington	Murder
08/21/1865	Dow Nailen	Paducah	Rape
08/21/1865	George Naiven	Paducah	Rape
08/25/1865	Green Johnson	Burkesville	Murder
10/20/1865	Henry Magruder	Louisville	Marauding

Missouri

DATE	NAME	LOCATION	OFFENSE
01/03/1803	Tewanye (Indian)	New Madrid	Murder
06/10/1806	Quabesca (Indian)	St. Louis	Murder
06/10/1806	Ouifumcaka (Indian)	St. Louis	Murder
09/16/1809	John Long	St. Louis	Murder
08/03/1810	Peter Johnston	Ste. Genevieve	Murder
03/09/1812	Charles Heath	Ste. Genevieve	Murder
04/05/1821	John Duncan	Fredericktown	Murder
04/17/1824	William Short	Fayette	Murder
09/02/1826	Negro Luke	Boonville	Murder
05/19/1827	Hugh King	St. Louis	Murder
05/26/1828	Presley Morris	Jackson	Murder
08/23/1828	Negress Annice	Liberty	Murder
05/[?]/1829	Negro Moses	Mont. City	Murder
09/26/1829	Michael Cogland	St. Louis	Murder
04/13/1830	Jacob Stewart	Fayette	Murder
09/29/1830	James Jenkins	St. Louis	Murder
12/13/1831	Samuel Earles	Columbia	Murder
03/23/1832	Negro Hampton	Fayette	Murder
01/30/1833	Isaac Whitson	Jackson	Murder
01/31/1834	James Hubbard	St. Louis	Murder

Date	Name	Location	Offense
04/04/1834	Leland Trumley	Lexington	Murder
04/30/1834	Mary Andrews	Lexington	Murder
04/08/1836	Negro Conway	Fulton	Murder
06/20/1836	Negro Jake	Fulton	Murder
08/[?]/1837	Negro David	Fayette	Murder
08/[?]/1837	Negro Washington	Fayette	Murder
08/11/1837	Negro Henry	Richmond	Murder
08/11/1837	Negro Ish	Richmond	Murder
09/30/1838	Negress Mary	Steelville	Murder
05/10/1839	George Goster	Independence	Murder
10/14/1839	Henry Lane	Jeff. City	Murder
01/03/1840	James Buchanan	St. Louis	Murder
07/09/1841	Negro Charles	St. Louis	Murder
07/09/1841	Negro James	St. Louis	Murder
07/09/1841	Negro Amos	St. Louis	Murder
07/09/1841	Negro Madison	St. Louis	Murder
08/07/1841	Negro Lewis	Bowling Green	Murder
08/13/1841	Howard	Boonville	Murder
08/13/1841	Ben White	Richmond	Murder
01/28/1842	Joseph Savilia	Lexington	Murder
02/10/1842	William Berry	Jeff. City	Murder
07/08/1842	Dedimus Burr	Jeff. City	Murder
03/03/1843	Henry Johnson	St. Louis	Murder
06/10/1843	Negress America	Columbia	Murder
06/10/1843	Negro Henry	Columbia	Murder
05/24/1844	Conrad Myers	Steelville	Murder
08/16/1844	Joseph Brown	St. Louis	Murder
08/16/1844	John McDaniel	St. Louis	Murder
07/31/1846	John Lester	Clinton	Murder
02/20/1847	Negro Nathan	Jackson	Murder
01/11/1850	Negro Ben	Palmyra	Murder
12/13/1850	Hugh Gallagher	St. Louis	Murder
02/14/1851	John Thomas	St. Louis	Murder
11/14/1851	Negro Isaac	Warrenton	Murder
09/10/1852	Joel Elliott	Lexington	Murder
06/24/1853	Negro Abe	Platte City	Murder
07/22/1853	John Schoen	St. Louis	Murder
07/22/1853	Joseph V. Dodge	St. Louis	Murder
09/02/1853	Augustus Jennings	St. Joseph	Murder
08/25/1854	Willis Washam	Springfield	Murder
08/31/1855	John Hutting	Mont. City	Murder
11/23/1855	William Nottingham	Butler	Murder
12/21/1855	Negress Celia	Fulton	Murder
07/11/1856	Negro Henry	Lexington	Murder
06/05/1857	James Nichols	Warrensburg	Murder
06/19/1857	Jacob Neuslein	St. Louis	Murder
06/19/1857	John La Pointe	St. Louis	Murder
06/19/1857	Israel Shultz	St. Louis	Murder
06/27/1857	Edward Worrell	Union	Murder
11/13/1857	Negro Joe	Columbia	Murder
07/16/1858	John Chapman	Fayette	Murder
08/07/1858	Robert Shehane	Alton	Murder

Date	Name	Location	Offense
12/31/1858	Negro Farrel	Lexington	Murder
12/31/1858	Negro John	Lexington	Murder
01/07/1859	Negro George	Huntsville	Murder
06/17/1859	George Lamb	St. Louis	Murder
11/11/1859	Joseph W. Thornton	St. Louis	Murder
12/02/1859	Negro Green	St. Joseph	Murder
08/31/1860	Samuel Brust	St. Louis	Murder
05/10/1861	Joseph Baird	Monticello	Murder
07/25/1861	John Cole	Springfield	Murder
06/08/1862	John Cole	Monroe Co.	Marauding
06/08/1862	Eight CSA Guerrillas	Monroe Co.	Marauding
06/27/1862	William Wilson	St. Louis	Murder
08/07/1862	William Ballee	Adair Co.	Parole Breaking
08/07/1862	William Bates	Adair Co.	Parole Breaking
08/07/1862	Hamilton Brannon	Adair Co.	Parole Breaking
08/07/1862	James Christian	Adair Co.	Parole Breaking
08/07/1862	R. M. Galbreath	Adair Co.	Parole Breaking
08/07/1862	Reuben Green	Adair Co.	Parole Breaking
08/07/1862	Columbus Harris	Adair Co.	Parole Breaking
08/07/1862	Bennett Hayden	Adair Co.	Parole Breaking
08/07/1862	John Kent	Adair Co.	Parole Breaking
08/07/1862	Lewis Rollins	Adair Co.	Parole Breaking
08/07/1862	Reuben Thomas	Adair Co.	Parole Breaking
08/07/1862	Thomas Webb	Adair Co.	Parole Breaking
08/07/1862	William Wilson	Adair Co.	Parole Breaking
08/07/1862	David Wood	Adair Co.	Parole Breaking
08/07/1862	Jesse Wood	Adair Co.	Parole Breaking
08/08/1862	Frisbie McCullough	Adair Co.	Parole Breaking
08/15/1862	Calvin Sartain	Linn Co.	Murder
09/06/1862	Male Slave	Richmond	Attempted Rape
09/26/1862	David Bell	Macon	Marauding
09/26/1862	Frank Drake	Macon	Marauding
09/26/1862	J. H. Fox	Macon	Marauding
09/26/1862	James Hall	Macon	Marauding
09/26/1862	Elbert Hamilton	Macon	Marauding
09/26/1862	John Oldham	Macon	Marauding
09/26/1862	Edward Riggs	Macon	Marauding
09/26/1862	A. C. Rowe	Macon	Marauding
09/26/1862	William Searcy	Macon	Marauding
09/26/1862	J. A. Wysong	Macon	Marauding
09/26/1862	D. S. Washburne	Macon	Marauding
10/18/1862	Willis Baker	Marion Co.	Marauding
10/18/1862	Morgan Bixler	Marion Co.	Marauding
10/18/1862	Herbert Hudson	Marion Co.	Marauding
10/18/1862	Thomas Humston	Marion Co.	Marauding
10/18/1862	Francis Lair	Marion Co.	Marauding
10/18/1862	Eleazer Lear	Marion Co.	Marauding
10/18/1862	John McPheeters	Marion Co.	Marauding
10/18/1862	Hiram Smith	Marion Co.	Marauding
10/18/1862	Thomas Sidenor	Marion Co.	Marauding
10/18/1862	John Wade	Marion Co.	Marauding
01/23/1863	Michael Kearns	St. Louis	Murder

Date	Name	Location	Offense
03/06/1863	James Edmonds	Hillsboro	Murder
05/08/1863	Joseph Burns	St. Louis	Murder
05/26/1863	Samuel Dale	Clark Co.	Marauding
05/26/1863	Aquilla Standiford	Clark Co.	Marauding
08/15/1863	Benjamin Snelling	Henry Co.	Marauding
08/28/1863	Negro Henry	California	Murder
09/09/1863	Carlyle	Lafayette Co.	Marauding
09/25/1863	Frederick Hamilton	California	Marauding
09/25/1863	M. D. Zimmerman	California	Marauding
10/30/1863	John Nichols	Cole Co.	Marauding
11/06/1863	William Linville	St. Joseph	Murder
11/27/1863	Paul Kingston	(U.S. Army) Cape Girardeau	Desertion
04/16/1864	Valentine Hansen	St. Louis	Murder
04/23/1864	Patrick Mullins	Moniteau Co.	Marauding
04/29/1864	John Reilly	Warrensburg	Murder
05/06/1864	Andrew Snyder	Macon	Marauding
05/20/1864	Willard Hadley	Warrensburg	Marauding
06/10/1864	Joseph Lanier	Savannah	Sedition
06/12/1864	Fielding	Platte City	Marauding
06/12/1864	Oldham	Platte City	Marauding
08/12/1864	Barney Gibbons	(U.S. Army) St. Louis	Murder
08/12/1864	John Wilcox	Cole Co.	Marauding
08/19/1864	William Livingston	St. Louis	Espionage
09/09/1864	A. J. Bowzer	St. Joseph	Marauding
09/09/1864	Stephen Smith	St. Louis	Espionage
09/09/1864	William Moore	St. Louis	Espionage
09/23/1864	Henry Griffith	St. Joseph	Marauding
10/07/1864	Peter Keiffe	Springfield	Murder
10/10/1864	William Gallup	Lewis Co.	Marauding
10/17/1864	John Abshire	St. Louis	Murder
10/28/1864	Jefferson Jackson	St. Joseph	Murder
10/29/1864	Harvey Blackburn	St. Louis	Wartime Reprisal
10/29/1864	George Bunch	St. Louis	Wartime Reprisal
10/29/1864	James Gates	St. Louis	Wartime Reprisal
10/29/1864	Asa Ladd	St. Louis	Wartime Reprisal
10/29/1864	Charles Minniken	St. Louis	Wartime Reprisal
10/29/1864	John Nichols	St. Louis	Wartime Reprisal
11/25/1864	Edward Eastman	Rolla	Pillaging
12/26/1864	James Utz	St. Louis	Espionage
01/13/1865	Abraham Purvis	St. Louis	Murder
01/13/1865	Ephraim Richardson	St. Louis	Murder
03/03/1865	James Hamilton	Macon	Marauding
03/24/1865	William Harris	St. Louis	Marauding
05/01/1865	Thomas Thorpe	St. Louis	Marauding
06/02/1865	G. P. Wright	Warrensburg	Marauding

Index

www.ingramcontent.com/pod-product-compliance
Ingram Content Group UK Ltd.
Pitfield, Milton Keynes, MK11 3LW, UK
UKHW041835100926
8556IPUK00018B/968

9 780786 498703